FINE CERAMICS

Editor

Shinroku Saito   738 134

President, The Technological University of Nagaoka and
Emeritus Professor, Tokyo Institute of Technology

Editorial Board
Noboru Ichinose
Osami Kamigaito
Shigeharu Naka
Shin-ichi Shirasaki
Hiroaki Yanagida

Elsevier
New York • Amsterdam • London

Ohmsha, Ltd.
Tokyo

English language edition copublished in 1988 by Ohmsha, Ltd., 3–1 Kanda Nishiki-cho, Chiyoda-ku, Tokyo 101, Japan, and by Elsevier Science Publishing Co., Inc., 52 Vanderbilt Avenue, New York, New York 10017.

Sole distributors of the English language edition outside the United States and Canada:

Elsevier Applied Science Publishers Ltd.
Crown House, Linton Road, Barking, Essex IG11 8JU, England

Library of Congress Cataloging-in-Publication Data

Fine Ceramics

    Includes index.
    1. Ceramics.   I. Saito, Shinroku, 1919–
TP807.F48   1988   666   87–27154

ISBN 0–444–01193–5

Current printing (last digit):
10 9 8 7 6 5 4 3 2 1

Manufactured in the United States of America

CONTENTS

v

CONTRIBUTORS

Tsuneo Akashi, Ph.D.
President, Japan Yttrium Co., Ltd.

Toshiyasu Asano
NGK Spark Plug Co., Ltd.

Yoshichika Bando, Ph.D.
Professor, Institute for Chemical Research, Kyoto University

Isamu Fukuura
Executive Director, NGK Spark Plug Co., Ltd.

Takao Fujikawa
Mechanical Engineering Research Laboratory, Kobe Steel, Ltd.

Yoshio Furuhata
Central Research Laboratory, Hitachi, Ltd.

Teizo Hase, Ph.D.
Research Associate, Tokyo Institute of Technology; and Toyota Motor Corporation

Shin-ichi Hirano, Ph.D.
Professor, Department of Applied Chemistry, Faculty of Engineering, Nagoya University

Shigeo Horiuchi, Ph.D.
National Research Institute of Inorganic Materials

Noboru Ichinose, Ph.D.
Professor, School of Science and Engineering, Waseda University

ix

Takayoshi Iseki, Ph.D.
Professor, Research Laboratory for Nuclear Reactors, Tokyo Institute of Technology

Shoji Ito
Production Engineering Division, Government Industrial Research Institute, Nagoya

Kazuyuki Kakegawa, Ph.D.
Research Associate, Department of Chemical Engineering, Faculty of Engineering, Chiba University

Osami Kamigaito, Ph.D.
Director, Toyota Central Research and Development Laboratories, Inc.

Kanichi Kamiya, Ph.D.
Professor, Department of Industrial Chemistry, Faculty of Engineering, Mie University

Shinichi Kikkawa, Ph.D.
Research Associate, Institute of Scientific and Industrial Research, Osaka University

Shiushichi Kimura, Ph.D.
Professor, Faculty of Engineering, Tokyo Institute of Technology

Yoshiyasu Koike, Ph.D.
Toshiba Research and Development Center, Toshiba Corporation

Mitsue Koizumi, Ph.D.
Professor of Ceramic Science, Director of Research Center of High Pressure Synthesis, Institute of Scientific and Industrial Research, Osaka University

Katsutoshi Komeya, Ph.D.
Toshiba Research and Development Center, Toshiba Corporation

Kunihito Koumoto, Ph.D.
Lecturer, Industrial Chemistry, Faculty of Engineering, The University of Tokyo

Makoto Kuwabara, Ph.D.
Associate Professor, Faculty of Engineering, Kyushu Institute of Technology

Akio Makishima, Ph.D.
National Research Institute of Inorganic Materials

Soichiro Matsuzawa, Ph.D.
Electronic Materials Laboratory, NGK Insulators, Ltd.

Mamoru Mitomo, Ph.D.
National Research Institute of Inorganic Materials

Masaru Miyayama
Department of Industrial Chemistry, Faculty of Engineering, The University of Tokyo

Eizo Miyazaki, Ph.D.
Associate Professor, Department of Chemistry, Tokyo Institute of Technology

Yuusuke Moriyoshi, Ph.D.
National Research Institute of Inorganic Materials

Masayuki Nagai, Ph.D.
Associate Professor, Laboratory of Inorganic Chemistry, Faculty of Engineering, Musashi Institute of Technology

Shigeharu Naka, Ph.D.
Professor, Synthetic Crystal Research Laboratory, Faculty of Engineering, Nagoya University

Hiroshi Okuda, Ph.D.
Ceramic Engineering Division, Government Industrial Research Institute, Nagoya

Shinroku Saito, Ph.D.
President, The Technological University of Nagaoka; and Emeritus Professor, Former President, Tokyo Institute of Technology

Shigeki Sakaguchi, Ph.D.
Optical Fiber Section, Ibaraki Electrical Communication Laboratory, Nippon Telegraph and Telephone Corporation

Shin-ichi Shirasaki, Ph.D.
Group Leader, First Research Group, National Research Institute of Inorganic Materials

Naohiro Soga, Ph.D.
Professor, Department of Industrial Chemistry, Faculty of Engineering, Kyoto University

Kohzo Sugiyama, Ph.D.
Professor, Department of Applied Chemistry, Faculty of Engineering, Nagoya University

Toshio Takada, Ph.D.
Professor, Institute for Chemical Research, Kyoto University

Shiro Takahashi, Ph.D.
Inorganic Materials Section, Ibaraki Electrical Communication Laboratory, Nippon Telegraph and Telephone Corporation

Gyozo Toda
Production Engineering Research Laboratory, Hitachi, Ltd.

Mitsuru Ura
Hitachi Research Laboratory, Hitachi, Ltd.

Kikuo Wakino, Ph.D.
Executive Director, Murata Manufacturing Co., Ltd.

Noboru Yamamoto
Executive Managing Director, Corporate Research and Development, NGK Insulators, Ltd.

Hiroaki Yanagida, Ph.D.
Professor, Department of Industrial Chemistry, Faculty of Engineering, The University of Tokyo

Eiichi Yasuda, Ph.D.
Associate Professor, Research Laboratory of Engineering Materials,
Tokyo Institute of Technology

Itaru Yasui, Ph.D.
Associate Professor, Institute of Industrial Science, The University of Tokyo

PREFACE

There were two so-called new material booms after World War II, in the mid-1950s and mid-1960s. We are now in a third boom which began slowly but is now gaining momentum. The significant difference in this boom is the development of tertiary industrial infrastructure.

Functional ceramics for electronics, opto-electronics, and related devices have been developed with considerable success. However, structural ceramics development has been slower despite the demand by the military and other sources for high temperature material capable of withstanding high mechanical stress, such as in ceramic turbines.

This book on ceramics development consists of four chapters. The first chapter concerns ceramic fabrication, including recent developments in powder synthesis through hot press and hot isostatic press. The second chapter discusses the relationship between properties and structures, involving observation methods. The third chapter covers structural ceramics made from oxides and nonoxides, through composites and their evaluation. The last chapter describes various recently developed ceramics for electronics.

The authors would be very pleased if this book were accepted abroad as a greeting from Japan to colleagues in the ceramics industry worldwide, a step toward future communication and deeper understanding.

Shinroku Saito

INTRODUCTION

Shinroku Saito

Japanese skills in porcelain have been well known internationally since before World War II. After the war, Japanese technology in fire brick supported the development of its famous steel industry. However, these achievements belong to the field of "old" ceramics, now made obsolete by research and development in the field of advanced ceramics.

The terms "fine ceramics" and "new ceramics" are often used interchangeably in Japan to denote the products of this R&D work. The former term is an official technological designation established by Japan's Ministry of International Trade and Industry (MITI) to characterize ceramics of a texture much finer than that of traditional types of ceramics such as bricks, sanitary ware, and household porcelain. (Additionally, there are many names for ceramics recently developed by high technologies, including advanced ceramics, high-tech ceramics, high-performance ceramics, engineering ceramics, super-ceramics, ultra-ceramics, and hyper-ceramics.) Some functions and applications of fine ceramics, including thermal, mechanical, biological, magnetic, optical, and nuclear applications, are shown in Figure 1.

Fine ceramics can be roughly classified in two categories: functional and structural. The former term is used for ceramics that perform electronic, electromechanical, optical, opto-electronic, or magnetic functions. Defining the latter category is more complicated, as

Functions and applications of fine ceramics (examples)

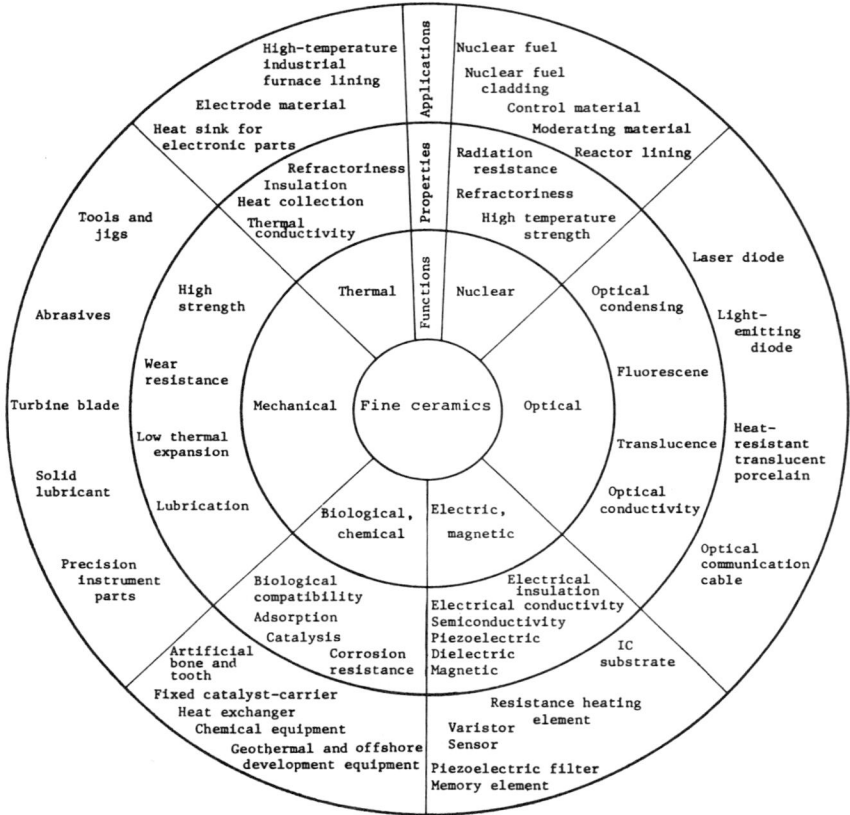

Figure 1 Some functions and applications of fine ceramics (from Japan Fine Ceramics Assoc., "Survey of Trends in Development of Fine Ceramics Technologies and Situation of Development of Related Equipment," April 1983).

the term "structural ceramics" does not denote the customary use of ceramic products for structural materials such as bricks, roofing tiles, and cement. Thus, "fine" must be emphasized to underscore the revolutionary applications of new ceramics for structural materials in machinery, especially for high-temperature machinery parts. Although ceramics have been well known as excellent refractory materials for products such as fire brick, they could not be successfully utilized under high thermal and mechanical loading until fine ceramics were developed using pure, ultra-minute particles whose green compacts are sintered, machined, and finished under highly controlled conditions and strict quality control.

The production values of fine ceramic materials for various purposes are given in Figure 2. More than 60% of fine ceramics are used for electromagnetic parts; 25–26% are used for machine parts and 6–7% for biochemical purposes. These percentages have not fluctuated much over the years. Although thermal uses and optical parts constituted only 4% and 0.7%, respectively, of fine ceramic usage in 1981, both increased to 4.5% and 1.5% in 1983. If we use 1981 production as the base (i.e., 1981 = 100), we see that the increase in thermal uses up to 1983 is 118, and that of optical parts is 250.

Analysis of these data reveals that the market for structural fine ceramics is still immature. Although large investments have been made in structural ceramics for the purpose of creating a sizable market, the main products are still cutting tools, abrasives, grinding balls and mills, mechanical seals, small chemical pumps, and the like. However, investment in the electromagnetic ceramics field is increasing because of a widening market, severe competition, and the emergence of unexpected new materials and inventions. Such investment accounts for more than 10% of all national research expenditures, although business sales are still only about 1% of total earnings.

Recently, the popularity of fine ceramics in Japan has grown so much that one could say that a "ceramics fever" has broken out among Japanese ceramics manufacturers and other industries, although foreign manufacturers view this trend suspiciously. Will fine ceramics be the star industry of the 1990s? Will fine ceramics be at the forefront of a new "Materials Revolution"? Only the future will tell.

The Materials Revolution can be traced back to the Industrial Revolution, which began with many mechanical inventions such as the power loom and the steam engine. Steelmaking during the Industrial Revolution first encountered problems in using charcoal for fuel. Charcoal steel required tremendous amounts of wood and afforded only a limited scale of manufacture. The need for wood raised ecological problems, while the problems of scale affected the quality of the steel. If the coke furnace had not been invented, one could easily surmise that the Industrial Revolution would have been halted or significantly slowed by limits in available wood resources. But new technologies in steelmaking facilitated large-scale production, resulting in fairly good quality control. Thus, the invention of new steel-manufacturing methods helped to promote the Industrial Rev-

Unit: 100 million lb.

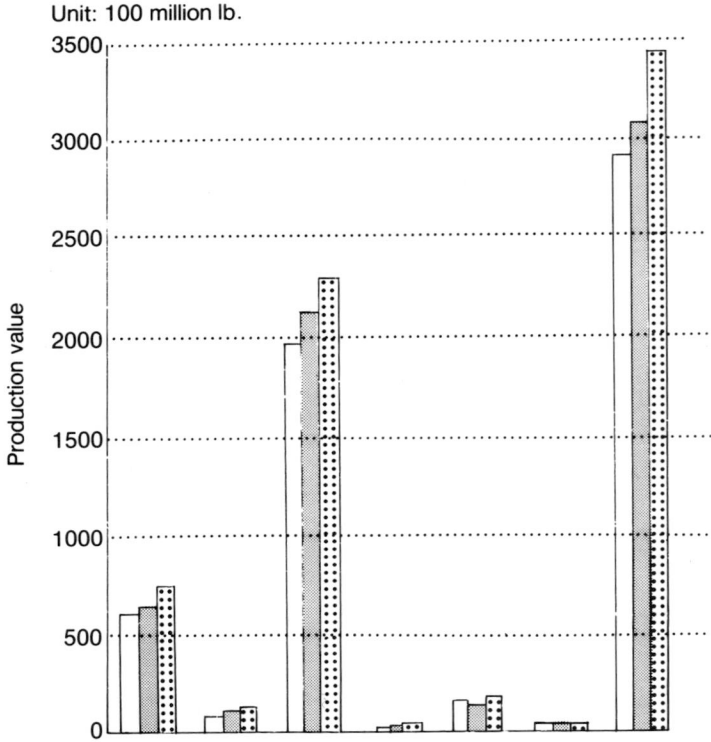

Year	Mechanical	Heat-resistant	Electro-magnetic	Optical	Chemico/biological	Others	Total
1981	614	94.9	1,970	17.2	162	43.9	2,902
1982	624	112	2,119	29.4	156	45.7	3,086
1983	740	135	2,304	42.3	186	51.2	3,458

Mechanical members: Cutting tools, mechanical seals, pumps, pump parts, crushing/pulverization members, valves

Heat resistant members: Adiabatic/heat insulation members, heat transmission/radiation members, heating elements, high-temperature corrosion-resistant members, crucibles

Electromagnetic materials: Magnetic members, capacitors, IC circuit substrate, IC baseplate packages, electrical insulation members, varistors, gas sensors

Optical materials: Light permissive members, optical fibers

Chemico/biological materials: Catalyst carriers, catalysts, prosthetic teeth and bones

Others: Artificial gems, filtration materials

Figure 2 Production values of fine ceramic materials.

olution; and, in short, a Materials Revolution occurred simultaneously with the Industrial Revolution.

Arguably the most important aspect of the Industrial Revolution is the drastic change in human thinking that it engendered, especially with regard to materials. In the past, every kind of material, even if artificial, was regarded as a result of natural forces; the human element was given only marginal credit. Confidence in human capabilities has risen greatly since then, resulting in the emergence of the material design concept. This conceptual change has given birth to a number of new processes.

Functional ceramics are fascinating materials from the perspective of both design and processing. Much of the basic research in ceramics is concentrated in this area. Several years ago, Japan's National Research Institute of Inorganic Materials (NRIIM) reported success in achieving single-crystal growth of LaB_6 and announced the commercial applicability of the new material as a strong new optical beam source for LSI processing. NRIIM is now carrying out research on rare-metal doped perovskite such as $Ba_{0.9}^{2+}La_x^{3+}Ti^{4+}O_3$ for use as semiconductors.

PZT, PLZT, and $(Pb_{1-x}Na_yO_{x-y})(Zr\cdot Ti)O_3$-type dielectric ceramics and the like are also attracting wide interest from researchers. Although ZnO has already achieved a high commercial reputation as a result of the work of Matsushita Electric Company, there is still a strong research interest in developing various other applications, including varistors, surface elastic-wave filters, electronic photograph sensitizers, synthesizing menthanol catalyzers, and gas sensors. ZnO and TiO_2 have in the past been used only for pigments and fillers; however, they and their derivatives have now become very important electronic materials. Recent research on TiO_2 shows a promising potential for its application as a catalyzer for separating oxygen and hydrogen from water using energy from the sun, thereby opening up new possibilities for various semiconductors such as CdS and $SrTiO_3$.

Moreover, new technologies such as rapid quenching of molten states and shock-wave treatment on powder and microbeam techniques are opening the way for beneficial uses for functional ceramics. Rapidly quenched $LiNbO_3$ and $PbTiO_3$, for instance, have shown very high dielectric constants. Solid electrolytes can be used in gas sensors, ion sensors, electronic memory elements, batteries, and ion pumps. These are usually made of polycrystalline ceramics. Beta-aluminum is presently the most promising candidate for use in sodium-sulfur batteries. Partially stabilized zirconia is now used as an excellent oxygen sensor in steelmaking and as an oxygen pump to adjust biological oxygen environments. Development of amorphous-state electrolytes by rapid quenching is expected to provide various other future applications. (The oxide magnet was invented by Professors Y. Kato and T. Takei long before World War II.)

Much research has been carried out on $Zn_{1-x}Mn_xFe_2O_4$ (soft), $\propto$-Fe_2O_3 (soft), and $SrO \cdot 6Fe_2O_3$ (hard). Transparent and translucent ceramics are also very important products. Transparent alumina tubes are already being used for sodium lamps. However, the transparent sialon produced by NRIIM is presently regarded as the most attractive material for high-temperature windows through which elevated temperature states of materials and processes can be directly observed. Additionally, many kinds of thermistors, varistors, gas sensors, electric resistance heaters, and nonlinear semiconductors such as the CdS-Cu_2S junction have already been or are being developed in Japan. Because of their applicability as semiconductors, electronic elements, integrated circuits (ICs), large-scale integrated (LSI) circuits, and ceramic substrates and packages, transparent and translucent ceramics promise to foster lucrative and prosperous industries. Production trends for products made from electronic, magnetic, and optical ceramics from 1981 through 1983 are shown in Figure 3.

The costs of R&D for structural fine ceramics cannot yet be recovered. However, R&D has been greatly stimulated by government support through the Project for Future Fundamental Industrial Technology. This project was started by MITI three years ago to promote basic industrial technologies ranging from fine ceramics to biotechnology. The reason such a project was implemented lies in the fact that various government projects such as the Sunshine Project, the Moonlight Project, and the Large-Scale Project have been hampered by the lack of practical basic technologies, including a lack of knowledge about new materials. The project was also intended to counter criticisms from abroad that Japan has always received a "free ride" on foreign technology. In this context, MITI chose to implement a project with a definite selection standard; its support would be limited to fields too risky for private companies to carry out R&D, and to immature markets. Consequently, only structural ceramics was adopted under the project, and the development of functional ceramics was left to market forces.

A research association was recently established to carry out a cooperative study among the 15 member companies constituting the leading users and manufacturers of fine ceramics. The study emphasized the development of silicon carbide and silicon nitride as well as the following three subjects: refractory ceramics for elevated-

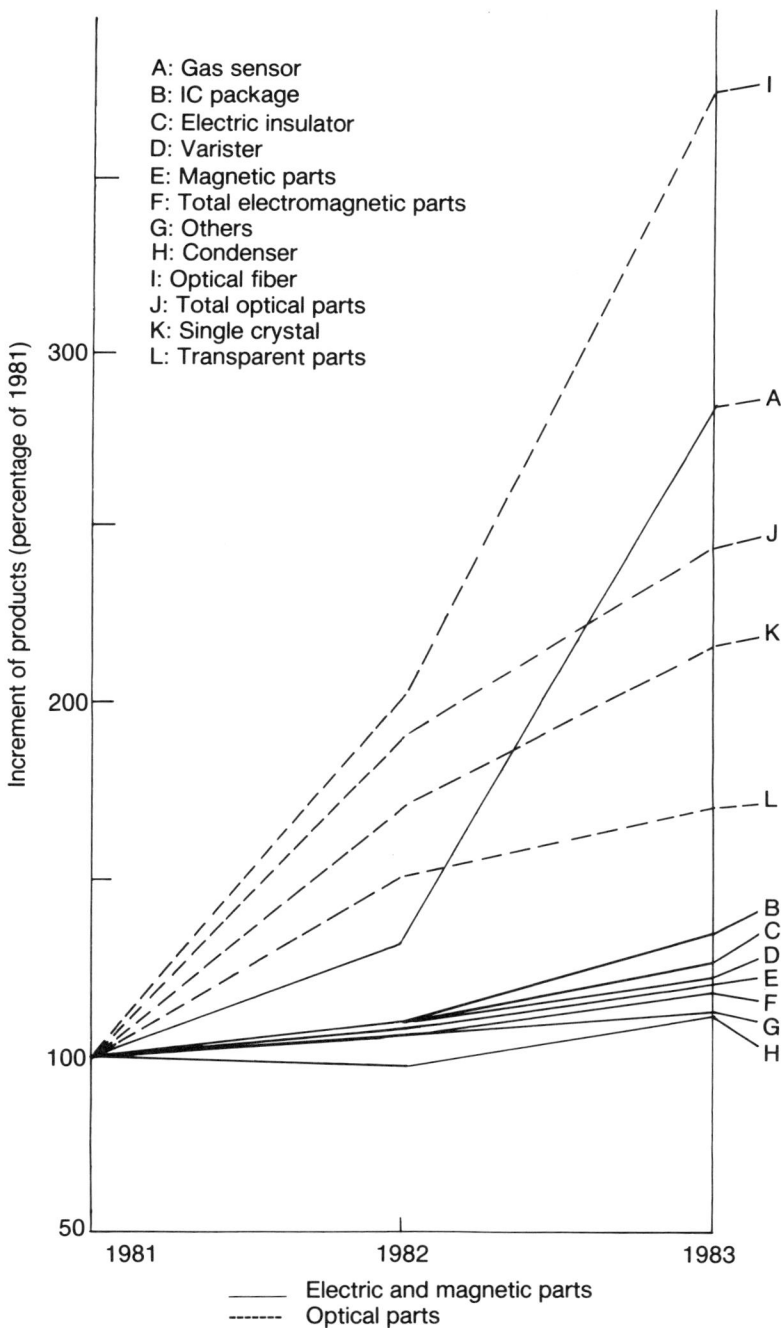

A: Gas sensor
B: IC package
C: Electric insulator
D: Varister
E: Magnetic parts
F: Total electromagnetic parts
G: Others
H: Condenser
I: Optical fiber
J: Total optical parts
K: Single crystal
L: Transparent parts

Increment of products (percentage of 1981)

300

200

100

50

1981   1982   1983

——— Electric and magnetic parts
------- Optical parts

Figure 3 Functional ceramics production trends for 1981 through 1983.

temperature machines, ceramics for precision machinery, and wear-proof and chemical-resistant ceramics. This study is expected to last as long as ten years, during which time three inspections will be carried out.

One of the most attractive areas in structural ceramics being researched in the MITI project is the development of a ceramic engine. There are already many approaches to developing ceramic engines, including the American auto gas turbine (AGT) series and several Japanese types of reciprocating engines and turbines. For reciprocating ceramic engines, the calculated thermal efficiencies from mere adiabatic effects are 32.53% and 40.41% for gasoline and diesel engines, respectively, as against 29.90% and 38.31% for metal engines. These energy gains themselves are not so large, but the ceramic engine has many additional advantages, including high refractoriness and light weight. Further, its total efficiency can be expected to be increased by combining such systems as adiabatic engines and turbochargers. Also, in other fields such as very high-temperature furnaces, high-temperature heat exchangers (made of SiC, for instance) will be greatly beneficial not only in reducing energy consumption but also in producing an extremely elevated temperature source by fuel combustion. These traits will be particularly advantageous in producing high-temperature gas turbines that can be operated without voluminous cooling systems.

Zirconia and alumina are regarded as important for high-temperature as well as high-strength ceramics. It is interesting that household merchandise such as knives and scissors have begun to be made of zirconia and alumina in Japan, while no foreign ceramists have yet thought of such applications. However, these are not just casual Japanese ideas. The world's nations, especially the advanced countries, have begun a significant shift to so-called tertiary industries—that is, the very soft industries. Therefore, the new Japanese fine ceramics industries must reorient toward secondary production.

1

CERAMIC PROCESSING

1.1 Overview

Shigeharu Naka

Remarkable progress in synthetic chemistry and related fields has led to epochal advances in material science, making possible the synthesis of various substances and materials. Highly homogeneous and stable industrial materials not existing in nature have been commercially produced by use of artificially synthesized starting materials. The creation of these artificial starting materials required the development of ceramic processing from a technology to a science. This development has supported the basis of so-called fine (advanced) ceramics.

Fine ceramics includes inorganic and nonmetallic solid materials of polycrystalline sintered bodies; fine powders; single crystals; noncrystalline materials; thick or thin films; and fibers with various morphologies. The functions of these materials depend on their morphology, over which control has been gained through advances in production processes.

Innovation in technology has always resulted from improvement in materials. For ceramics to be the key to such innovation, new materials must be developed and processes established for their production. The development of processes for new functional ceramics will lead to the further discovery of new materials and functions. However, certain difficulties are involved in establishing the neces-

1

sary processes. The proper preparation of synthesized raw materials is an especially important factor in the ability of ceramics technology to meet the demand for materials.

The raw material properties to be controlled are chemical composition, particle morphology, crystal structure, lattice defects, and surface features, among others. These properties are of great importance to producing the desired ceramic materials. Although the relations between the properties of raw materials and those of formed ceramics are not yet clearly understood, the dependence of ceramic properties on the microstructure is under study. The preparation of powders of the desired material enforces the technology for the design of raw materials. The solution method and chemical vapor method as chemical processes have attracted special attention in the processing of highly pure powders.

As the functions and accuracy demanded of ceramics have increased, the variety of ceramics and their composition has also increased, giving rise to new requirements in quality control and reliability. The demand for the production of sintered bodies of composites, highly dense and transparent sintered bodies, and non-oxide sintered bodies is stimulating the development and improvement of ceramic processing.

Advances in Japanese ceramic processing have been promoted in part by the Japanese government. Areas under governmental development are a technology for pulverizing into fine powders, forming technology, sintering technology, and machining and joining technology. The main objectives are the preparation of ultra-fine powders, the forming of ceramics with complex matrices, the creation of homogeneous sintered bodies through development of high-pressure sintering or continuous sintering techniques, and the development of precise high-strength joints.

Ceramic processing related to industrial production has been extensively studied in Japan. Various aspects are highlighted in this chapter.

1.2 High-Pressure Synthesis: Diamond and Cubic Boron Nitride

Shin-ichi Hirano and Shigeharu Naka

1.2.1 Introduction

Diamond is the hardest and the most thermally conductive of all known substances. Cubic boron nitride (BN), which is somewhat softer and has a lower thermal conductivity than diamond, is used in machining hard iron- or nickel-containing metals because of its less reactive character. Extensive studies have been made on the syntheses of diamond and cubic BN since researchers in the General Electric Company discovered the method and developed the high-pressure apparatus needed to synthesize diamond and cubic BN under high pressure and temperature conditions.

This section focuses mainly on recent progress in the synthesis of grains of these superhard crystalline materials.

1.2.2 Diamond Synthesis

The transformation of graphite into diamond had been an aim of chemists for many years. There have been many hypotheses on the synthesis of diamond since Tennant (1879) discovered by his combustion experiments that diamond is a crystalline form of elementary carbon.

In 1894 Moissan[1] reported his clever idea that diamond would form as the precipitating carbon from quenched liquid iron droplets saturated with carbon. He believed that high internal pressures could be developed in a liquid core when quenched. Moisson claimed that tiny refractory crystals with diamondlike properties were obtained. After his announcement, many experimenters tried to reproduce this process precisely but finally decided that it did not yield diamond, at least reproducibly.

The first reproducible, publicly announced success in diamond synthesis came in 1955 when a research group at the General Electric Company discovered a high-pressure, high-temperature process for transforming graphite to diamond.[2] This successful process was carried out at very high pressures and temperatures obtained through use of molten-metal solvent catalysts, which was the basis of Moisson's original idea.

Because diamond is 64% more dense than graphite, the application of high pressure would favor diamond formation. High temperature would also be required to disrupt carbon-carbon bonds in graphite and allow a rearrangement of carbon atoms, as indicated by the fact that graphite has a very high melting point. Figure 1.2.1 is a phase and reaction diagram for carbon[3] wherein the various thermodynamic phase boundaries are sketched and the pressure-temperature regions in which the various reactions take place are marked.

After diamond was synthesized in the laboratory, it became possible to confirm the location of the graphite-diamond equilibrium line within the limits of accuracy of calibration of pressures and

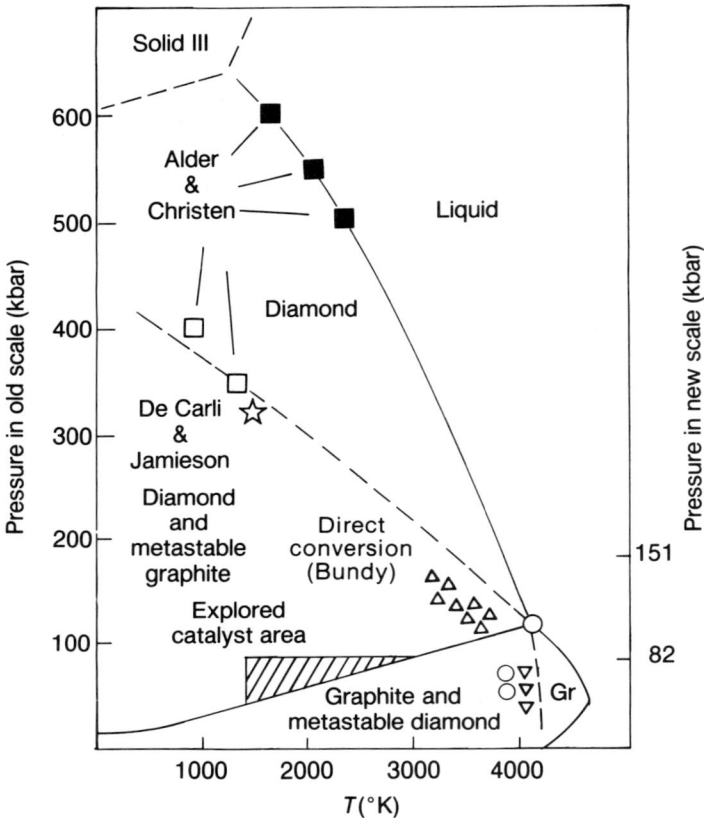

Figure 1.2.1 Phase diagram of carbon [from F. P. Bundy, *Science* 137:1057 (1962)]. Note that the dashed line in the figure indicates metastable phase relation.

temperatures. Bundy and co-workers[4] indicated that the Berman–Simon equilibrium line,[5] which was calculated on the basis of thermodynamic data, could be extrapolated to the graphite-diamond-liquid triple point. Recently, Kennedy and co-workers[6] examined the location of the equilibrium line, taking precise measurements of pressure and the effects of pressure on the electromotive force (EMF) of thermocouples into consideration. Their newly determined slope of the graphite-diamond equilibrium line of 0.025 kbar/°K is very consistent with that of the 0.027 kbar/°K determined by Berman–Simon.

It was thought that diamond crystals could be formed satisfactorily by cooling liquid carbon to the diamond stable region at pressures above the triple point, but this process yielded only a small amount of very finely grained diamond embedded in flaky graphite crystals. DeCarli and Jamieson[7] first reported a proven instance of direct transformation of polycrystalline graphite into diamond by shock-wave compression (marked by ※ in Fig. 1.2.1) with a yield of a small percentage of very fine diamond within microseconds. The transformation zone is located near the melting line of metastable graphite (pseudomelting). If pseudomelting takes place, the intermediate would behave like a fluid, and the carbon atoms could be rearranged in a stable cubic diamond form for a very short duration. Soon after, Bundy[8] succeeded in synthesizing diamond by statically compressing graphite specimens under a pressure of about 130 kbar (13 GPa) and flash-heating them to temperatures above 3300°K with a belt-type high-pressure apparatus (marked by Δ in Figure 1.2.1). The diamond formed by these processes is cubic-type, randomly oriented crystallites with crystallite sizes of less than 100 Å for shock-wave compression and 200–500 Å for flash-heating at a high static pressure. Hexagonal diamond was produced by flash-heating a single crystal of graphite compressed in the c-axis direction at pressures exceeding 130 kbar at a relatively low temperature below 2000°K.[9]

The direct conversion of graphite into diamond does not result in an appreciable rate of diamond formation except at very high pressures and temperatures (e.g., above 100 kbar, 3000°K) or with longer exposure to pressures and temperatures. This behavior is consistent with the concept that the tightly bound carbon atoms of the graphite crystal must be subjected to thermal agitation vigorous enough to disrupt the lattice and allow it to rearrange in a thermodynamically stable diamond form.

Some technological problems remain unsolved for the development of a high-pressure and high-temperature apparatus that would enable the generation of pressures above 100 kbar in large volumes for practical use. At some intermediate pressures and temperatures, Bovenkerk and co-workers[10] found catalysts that greatly accelerated the formation of diamond as a thermodynamically stable phase, which made possible the commercial production of industrial diamond without the prohibitively high cost for manufacturing a high-pressure apparatus. The catalysts that have been found to be effective are essentially the group VIII metals of the periodic table, such as iron, nickel, cobalt, platinum, and palladium, as well as manganese, chromium, and, to a lesser degree, tantalum (and also alloys of these metals).[11]

A convenient procedure for synthesizing diamond from graphite is to set the mixture of graphite and, for example, nickel into a pressure cell and heat it above the nickel-graphite eutectic temperature at some satisfactory pressure, such as 54 to 60 kbar. The nickel becomes saturated with carbon relative to graphite of the metastable phase and supersaturated relative to diamond, as shown in Figure 1.2.2. Thus, diamond begins to crystallize as a stable solid phase at the expense of graphite. Gem-quality diamond crystal up to 6 mm was grown on diamond seed by careful application of this method.[12-14] Single crystals of diamond can be grown in the presence of solvent catalysts by the temperature gradient method under pressure. Carbon species supersaturated in solvents precipitate epitaxially on the diamond seed set at a lower temperature zone. In Japan, extensive studies on the growth of large diamonds have been undertaken recently.[15,16]

The progress made of greatest scientific importance in this field is the growth of diamond under metastable conditions. The methods that have been reported to be successful make use of diamond seed beds as substrates, and the low flux of carbon is delivered over diamond seeds at about 1300°K and pressures less than atmospheric by cracking of hydrocarbon (e.g., methane) gas or by molecular or ion

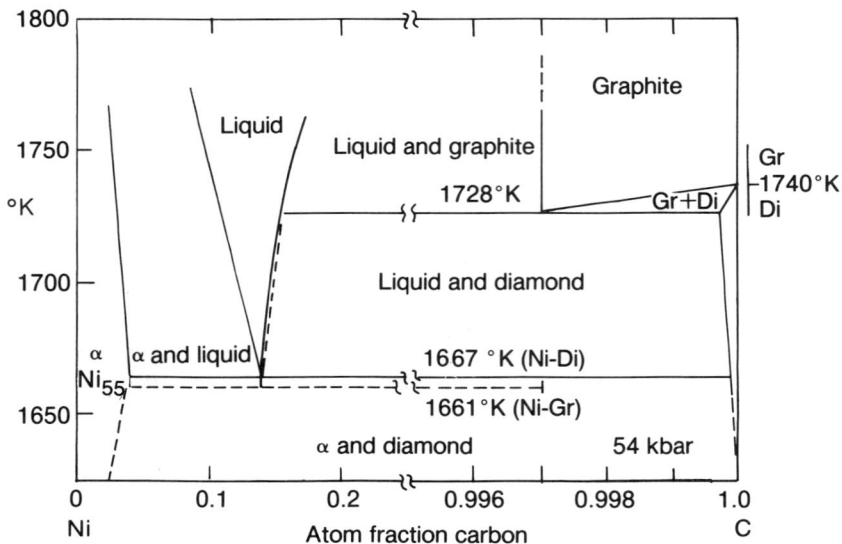

Figure 1.2.2 Phase diagram of nickel and carbon at 54 kbar [from H. M. Strong and R. E. Hanneman, *J. Chem. Phys.* 75:1838 (1971)].

beams of carbon.[17-22] The diamond growth is thought to be epitaxial for the thin film formation and to be through the vapor-liquid-solid (VLS) process for the formation of whiskers. Eversole first reported the results of forming diamond on diamond substrates by the pyrolysis of methane at 1320°K under reduced pressure.[17,18] The growth of diamond was tremendously slow and associated with the co-deposition of graphite. The details of this metastable diamond formation through the pyrolysis of hydrocarbons were examined by Angus and co-workers.[19] Sophisticated techniques needed to synthesize diamond metastably under reduced pressure were also developed by use of carbon ion beams,[20] the plasma chemical vapor deposition (CVD),[21] and the sputtering method.[22] In Japan a similar metastable formation of diamond under reduced pressure has been also extensively carried out.[23,24] The development of a suitable technique to increase the thickness of diamond layers is eventually expected for industrial application.

Bundy first reported the direct conversion of graphite to diamond under static pressure, using an electric flash-heating technique.[25] At pressures above about 125 kbar (old pressure; about 110 kbar on the new pressure scale), he found that graphite spontaneously collapsed to nonconducting polycrystalline diamond of the cubic type with a crystallite size of 200–500 Å in times of a few milliseconds or less. Naka and co-workers revealed that the conversion of graphite to diamond could be detected by the drastic change in the electrical resistance of a graphite bar specimen during passage of 60-cycle a.c. electricity directly through the specimen itself at 140 kbar.[26] The direct conversion without the solvent catalyst may provide an important concept for synthesis of a carbonado-type diamond.

1.2.3 Effect of Starting Carbons on Diamond Synthesis

Wentorf found that the amount and character of diamond converted depended strongly on the kind of starting carbonaceous materials used.[27] He heated various kinds of carbons to temperatures of about 1300 to 3000°C at pressures of 95 to 150 kbar (80 to 125 kbar on the new pressure scale). He then suggested that apparently structural factors of carbonaceous materials were involved and that the actual transformations to diamond may have followed a number of complex reaction paths.

Kosatochkin and co-workers reported that well-crystallized graphite transformed to diamond directly in the presence of a solvent catalyst under 80 kbar at temperatures of 1700°C, while a partially

graphitized carbon was crystallized into graphite at first and then converted to diamond under the same conditions.[28] These researchers also mentioned that the amount of diamond formed was larger by use of the graphitizable carbon rather than the nongraphitizable carbon. Gankevich and co-workers also found that the formation of diamond depended on the crystallinity of the starting carbon before the high temperature and pressure treatment.[29] Hirano and co-workers recently revealed that glassy carbon with its characteristic bond nature could not be transformed directly to diamond by heat treatment under static pressure in the diamond stable region, but rather to metastable graphite, according to Ostwald's step rule as shown in Figure 1.2.3.[30]

It is worthwhile from both scientific and industrial points of view to study the behavior of the starting carbon specimen under high pressure and temperature conditions, which leads to establishing the criteria for the selection of a carbon specimen suitable for industrial diamond production.[31-33] It has been known for some time that the greater the free-energy difference between the starting carbon source and diamond, the greater the rate of diamond nucleation and growth.

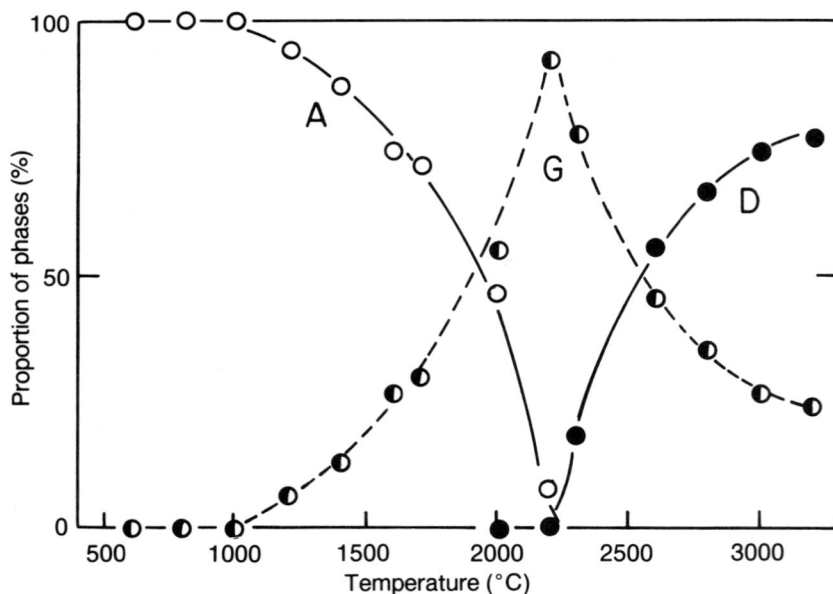

Figure 1.2.3 Changes in amounts of graphitic component and diamond formed from glassy carbon at 90 kbar [from S. Hirano et al., *J. Mat. Sci.* 17:1856 (1982)]. (A: amorphous glassy carbon; G: graphite; D: diamond).

Tsuzuki and co-workers found that diamond could form easily from graphitized pitch cokes and partially in smaller amounts by heat treatment at 3000°C of glassy carbon composed partially of graphitic structure. Carbons composed only of turbostratic structure were crystallized only to metastable graphite but not to diamond in the diamond stable region, even in the presence of nickel as the solvent catalyst.[34] The solubility of carbon in nickel under high temperature and pressure conditions was found to be higher with less-graphitized carbon than with well-graphitized carbon. This result shows that the difference in carbon solubility between diamond and the starting carbon in the solvent catalyst is not the only factor for diamond formation, as had been believed. Other influencing factors for the conversion of carbon to diamond have yet to be determined. The most important inhibitor to diamond formation was found to be an adsorbant on starting carbons of hydrogen gas and compound, especially water and organic compounds that leave hydrogen gas by pyrolysis during the heat treatment under pressure.[35] Diamond can be efficiently produced using well-crystallized graphite without any hydrogen gas absorbant.

1.2.4 Synthesis of Cubic Boron Nitride

Cubic BN was first discovered by Wentorf.[36] Like diamond, the substance is extremely hard (≈ 7500 kg/cm^2 as Vickers microhardness) and thermally highly conductive (13 W/cm°K theoretical value at room temperature). The less-reactive character of cubic BN with iron makes it somewhat more applicable for engineering materials than is diamond. Because of its applicability, extensive studies have been made on developing a practical method to synthesize cubic BN from the hexagonal modification under moderate pressure and temperature conditions.

The direct conversion of hexagonal BN (hBN) into cubic BN was first performed by Bundy and co-workers.[37] They found that the wurtzite-type BN (wBN) was formed from hBN at room temperature under compression above 100 kbar (10 GPa), and the cubic BN could be synthesized by heating above 2000°K under pressure. Wakatsuki and co-workers prepared cubic BN from less-crystallized hBN at 55 kbar and 1100°C without any substantial catalyst addition.[38] Ichinose and co-workers determined the suitable crystallinity of the starting BN powder to be $L_a < 500$ Å and $L_c < 200$ Å for this kind of direct conversion.[39] In contrast, well-crystallized BN transformed into wBN only under a very high pressure of 100 kbar.[40] Water is the most effective catalyst for the synthesis of cubic BN. The report of the direct formation of cubic BN should be reexamined, especially with respect to the adsorbed water of the less-crystallized BN powder.

The wBN powders were synthesized by shock compression.[41,42] The wBN is the metastable phase and is transformed into cubic BN under high pressure and temperature conditions.

In order to make the synthesis condition more moderate, many studies have been performed that are aimed toward the discovery of new effective catalyst. Wentorf found the presence of the cubic form of BN by use of a catalyst. Alkali and alkaline earth metals or their nitrides have been known to act as suitable solvents for hBN.[43-47] The pressure and the temperature necessary for the synthesis of cubic BN were lowered to 65-90 kbar and 1500-2000°C as compared with those for direct conversion. DeVries and Fleischer indicated that the intermediate compound Li_3BN_2 between Li or Li_3N and hBN acts as a solvent that dissolves the hBN to precipitate cubic BN under the thermodynamic stable conditions of cubic BN.[45]

Saito and co-workers reported that alloys of Fe-Al, Ag-Cd, Cu-Sn, and Mg-Sn were also catalysts for the synthesis of cubic BN.[48,49] The amount of the conversion to cubic BN was low with these catalysts, and it has been pointed out that the reproducibility is required.

Susa and co-workers found the solvent effect of water for conversion of hBN into cubic BN.[50] Cubic BN was formed by the addition of 40 wt% water even at the lower pressure and temperature of 50 kbar and 600°C. The grain size, however, was only 0.01-0.2 μm. In this case, ammonium borate coexisted as the reaction product of hBN and water at high pressures and temperatures.

A melt of ammonium borate was thought to act as a flux for hBN to precipitate cubic BN. This assumption led to the discovery of other new solvents such as ammonium borate, urea, ammonium nitrate, ammonium halides, galium fluoride, and bismuth fluoride.[51-53]

Aluminum nitride (AlN) has high thermal conductivity (3.2 W/cm°K at 25°C) and like cubic BN is an electrical insulator. Fischer reported that cubic BN was formed from supersaturation in AlN-BN complex under pressure.[54]

Kabayama also proposed the catalytic effect of the system Si-AlN on the formation of cubic BN and postulated that hBN or boron compounds and catalyst metals interact at high pressures and temperatures to form a complex of hBN and catalyst metal nitride, including silicon.[55]

Hirano and co-workers found that AlN acts as the catalyst for the synthesis of cubic BN by sealing the mixture of hBN and AlN in a

Table 1.2.1 Effect of Atmosphere in High-Pressure Cell on Yield of Cubic BN (from S. Hirano et al., *J. Am. Ceram. Soc.* 64:734 (1981).

Atmosphere	Yield (%)[a]	Atmosphere	Yield
O_2	0	Ar + toluene	100
Air	0	N_2	66
Ar	35	N_2 + toluene	100
Ar + ethanol	85		

NOTE: The sample was 80 mol% hexagonal BN-20 AlN; cubic BN was synthesized at 6.5 GPa and 1600°C for 15 min. Conversion to cubic BN was not detected when no AlN was added.
[a] ±5%.

pressure cell under an inert or reduced atmosphere.[56] To enhance the catalytic effect of AlN, the atmosphere in the high-pressure cell should be reduced as shown in Table 1.2.1. The effect of AlN addition and the atmosphere on the yield of cubic BN is shown in Figure 1.2.4. No conversion of hBN to cubic BN was observed under pressures below 70 kbar without AlN addition. All hBN could be completely converted to cubic BN under 65 kbar at 1600°C by the addition of 20

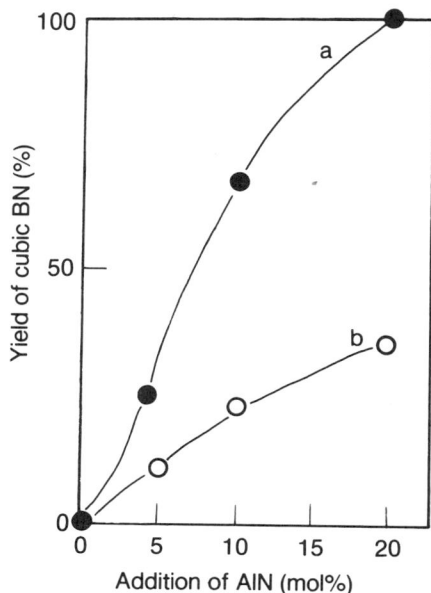

Figure 1.2.4 Effects of AlN addition and atmosphere on yield of cubic BN at 65 kbar and 1600°C for 15 min [from S. Hirano et al., *J. Am. Ceram. Soc.* 64:734 (1981)]. (a: sample charged with 20 wt% toluene in flow of Ar; b: sample charged in flow of Ar).

mol% AlN. The cubic BN thus synthesized was a typical tetrahedron (grain size ≈ 2 μm). The dense cubic BN-AlN sintered compact with a relative density > 99% was obtained; direct bonding between cubic BN grains was formed. The pressure-temperature diagram for the synthesis of cubic BN was determined at < 70 kbar and T < 1700°C, as shown in Figure 1.2.5.[57] Benzene was found to be a more effective additive for the control of the atmosphere in the high-pressure cell.[58] Borazine was used as the starting material for the synthesis of cubic BN and was found to be the most suitable compound to increase the rate of conversion at a lower temperature under pressure.[59]

A thick film composed only of cubic BN was first synthesized from hBN on AlN substrate by Hirano and co-workers.[60] No intermediate compounds or solid solubility between AlN and BN could be detected, which indicates that AlN does not form a complex or a liquid with BN and does not act as a solvent for hBN under pressure; it is thus different from the known catalysts mentioned above.

Sokolowski and co-workers recently synthesized cubic BN layers under a low pressure of 10^{-4} Pa by a pulsed plasma method.[61] They grew the cubic BN thin layer metastably with a sintered boron electrode in a gas mixture of nitrogen and hydrogen.

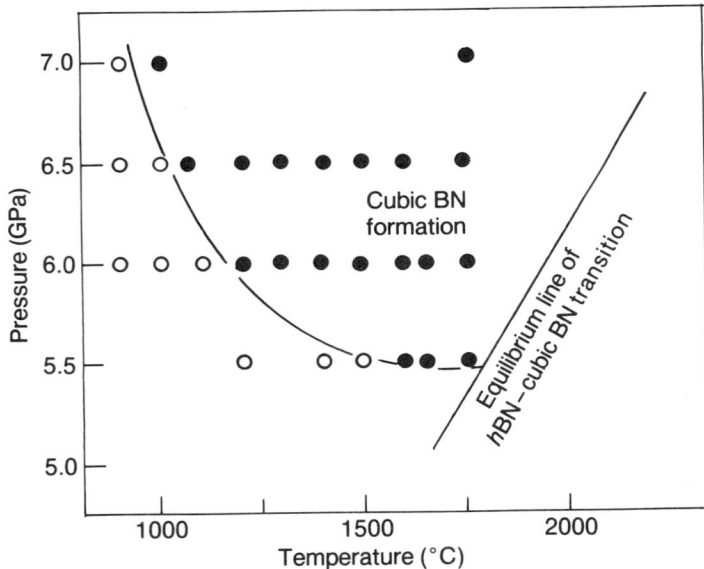

Figure 1.2.5 Pressure-temperature diagram for synthesis of cubic BN with AlN [from S. Hirano et al., *J. Am. Ceram. Soc.* 64:734 (1981); *High Pressure in Research and Industry* 1:376 (1982)].

These new techniques for the synthesis of cubic BN layers have attracted attention, as they create functional advanced materials. Great progress may be expected in these fields, including the recent proposal to synthesize mixed crystals of cubic BN and diamond.[62]

References

1. Moissan, H., *Compt. Rend.* 118:320 (1894).
2. Bundy, F. P., Hall, H. T., Wentorf, R. H. Jr., *Nature* 176:51 (1955).
3. Bundy, F. P., *Science* 137:1057 (1962).
4. Bundy, F. P., Bovenkerk, H. P., Strong, H. M., and Wentorf Jr., R. H., *J. Chem. Phys.* 35:383 (1961).
5. Berman, R., and Simon, F., *Z. Electrochem.* 59:333 (1955).
6. Kennedy, C. S., and Kennedy, G. C., *J. Geophys. Res.* 81:2667 (1976).
7. DeCarli, P. S., and Jamieson, J. C., *Science* 133:182 (1961).
8. Bundy, F. P., *J. Chem. Phys.* 618:631 (1963).
9. Bundy, F. P., and Kasper, J. S., *J. Chem. Phys.* 46:3437 (1967).
10. Bovenkerk, H. P., Bundy, F. P., Hall, H. T., Strong, H. M., and Wentorf Jr., R. H., *Nature* 184:1094 (1959).
11. Strong, H. M., and Hanneman, R. E., *J. Chem. Phys.* 75:1838 (1971).
12. Wentorf Jr., R. H., *J. Phys. Chem.* 75:1833 (1971).
13. Strong, H. M., and Chrenko, R. M., *J. Phys. Chem.* 75:1838 (1971).
14. Strong, H. M., and Wentorf Jr., R. H., *Naturwissenschaften* 59:1 (1972).
15. Kanda, H., Sato, Y., Setaka, N., Ohsawa, T., and Fukunaga, O., *Nippon Kagaku Kaishi* 1981:1349 (1981).
16. Yazu, S., Sato, S., and Nakamura, T., *Huntai Hunmatsu Yakin Kyokai Abstract of 58 Shukitaikai* 154 (1983).
17. Eversole, W. G., U.S. Pat. 3,030, 187 (1962).
18. Eversole, W. G., U.S. Pat. 3,030, 188 (1962).
19. Angus, J. C., Will, H. A., and Stanko, W. S., *J. Appl. Phys.* 39:2915 (1968).
20. Aisenberg, S., and Chabot, R., *J. Appl. Phys.* 42:2935 (1971).
21. Whitmell, D. S., and Williamson, R. W., *Thin Solid Films* 35:355 (1976).
22. Gautherin, G., and Weismetal, C. H. R., *Thin Solid Films* 50:135 (1978).
23. Matsumoto, S., Sato, Y., Kamo, M., and Setaka, N., *J. Appl. Phys.* 21:L183 (1982).
24. Matsumoto, S., Sato, Y., Tsutsumi, M., and Setaka, N., *J. Mat. Sci.* 17:3106 (1982).
25. Bundy, F. P., *J. Chem. Phys.* 38:618, 631 (1963).
26. Naka, S., Horii, K., Takeda, Y., and Hanawa, T., *Nature* 259:38 (1976).

27. Wentorf Jr., R. H., *J. Phys. Chem.* 69:3063 (1965).
28. Kasatochkin, V. I., Strenberg, L. E., Slesarev, V. N., and Nedoshivin, Y. N., *Dokl. Nauk SSSR* 194:801 (1970).
29. Gankevich, L. T., Nagornyi, V. G., and Shipkov, N. N., *Sint. Almazy* 3:6 (1977).
30. Hirano, S., Shimono, K., and Naka, S., *J. Mat. Sci.* 17:1856 (1982).
31. Naka, S., Suwa, Y., Takeda, Y., and Hirano, S., *J. Chem. Soc. Jpn.* 1981:1468 (1981).
32. Naka, S., Suwa, Y., and Hirano, S., High Pressure in Research and Industry, *Proc. 8th AIRAPT Conference,* vol. 1, 1982, p. 365.
33. Naka, S., Tsuzuki, A., and Hirano, S., *J. Mat. Sci.* 19:259 (1984).
34. Tsuzuki, A., Hirano, S., and Naka, S., *Abstract of 58 Shunki Taikai of Huntai Hunmatsu Yakin Kyokai* 94 (1983); *J. Mat. Sci.* 19: (1984).
35. Tsuzuki, A., Hirano, S., and Naka, S., *Abstract of 58 Shuki Taikai of Huntai Hunmatsu Yakin Kyokai* 152 (1983).
36. Wentorf Jr., R. H., *J. Chem. Phys.* 26:956 (1957).
37. Bundy, F. P., and Wentorf Jr., R. H., *J. Chem. Phys.* 38:1144 (1963).
38. Wakatsuki, M., Ichinose, K., and Aoki, T., *Mat. Res. Bull.* 7:999 (1972).
39. Ichinose, K., Wakatsuki, M., and Aoki, T.: *Proc. 4th International Conference on High Pressure,* 1974, p. 436.
40. Wakatsuki M., Ichinose, K., and Aoki, T., *Proc. 4th International Conference on High Pressure,* 1974, p. 441.
41. Sōma, T., Sawaoka, A., and Saito, S., *Mat. Res. Bull.* 9:755 (1974).
42. Corrigan, F. R., and Bundy, F. P., *J. Chem. Phys.* 63:3812 (1975).
43. Wentorf, Jr., R. H., *J. Chem. Phys.* 34:809 (1961).
44. Kudaka, K., Konno, H., and Matoba, T., *J. Appl. Phys.* 4:767 (1965).
45. DeVries, R. S., and Fleischer, J. F., *Mat. Res. Bull.* 4:433 (1969).
46. DeVries, R. S., and Fleischer, J. F., *J. Cryst. Growth* 13/14:88 (1972).
47. Endo, T., Fukunaga, S., and Iwata, M., *J. Mat. Sci.* 14:1375 (1979).
48. Saito, H., Ushio, M., and Nagao, S., *Yogyo Kyokai Shi* 78:7 (1970).
49. Ushio, M., Saito, H., and Nagao, S., *Kogyo Kagaku Zasshi* 74:598 (1971).
50. Susa, K., Kobayashi, T., and Taniguchi, S., *Mat. Res. Bull.* 9:1443 (1974).
51. Kobayashi, T., Susa, K., and Taniguchi, S., *Mat. Res. Bull.* 10:1231 (1975).
52. Kobayashi, T., Isibashi, M., and Susa, K., *Yogyo Kyokai Shi* 86:202 (1978).
53. Kobayashi, T., *Mat. Res. Bull.* 14:1541 (1979).
54. Fischer, A., *Ger. Pat.* 1,131,645 (1962).
55. Kabayama, T., *U.S. Pat.* 3,959,443 (1976).
56. Hirano, S., Yamaguchi, T., and Naka, S., *J. Am. Ceram. Soc.* 64:734 (1981).
57. Hirano, S., Hong, S., and Naka, S., *High Pressure in Research and Industry* 1:376 (1982).

58. Hirano, S., Hong, S., and Naka, S., *Zairyo* (1984) (in press).
59. Hirano, S., Asada, S., Yogo, T., and Naka, S., *Abstract of 58 Shuki Taikai of Huntai Hunmatsu Kyokai* (1983).
60. Hirano, S., and Naka, S., *Abstract of 57 Shuki Taikai of Huntai Hunmatsu Kyokai* (1982).
61. Sokolowski, M., Sokolowska, A., Rusek, A., Romanowski, Z., Gokieli, B., and Gajewska, M., *J. Cryst. Growth* 52:165 (1981).
62. Badzian, A. R., *Mat. Res. Bull.* 16:1385 (1981).

1.3 Hydrothermal Synthesis and Hydrothermal Reaction Sintering

Shin-ichi Hirano

1.3.1 Introduction

The increasing demand for high-quality crystals and ceramics has prompted material scientists and engineers to improve and develop crystalline materials at moderate temperatures. The hydrothermal method has the potential to produce single crystals by low-temperature methods.

The term "hydrothermal reaction" has been accepted as referring to the reaction taking place in the presence of water under high pressure and temperature conditions. The first attempt to synthesize an inorganic material by hydrothermal reaction was made in 1845 by Schafhäutl on the production of quartz crystals from silica gel and water in a high-pressure vessel. Since then, hydrothermal synthesis involving α-quartz has been studied extensively because of the industrial usefulness of grown crystals and the geological and mineralogical importance for confirming predictions concerning the genesis of minerals.

Natural crystals are considered to be grown from magma reacted with mineralizers upon crystallizing. Water is the most common and important mineralizer in nature for accelerating the equilibrium between different crystalline phases. On the one hand, water might act as a catalyst; on the other, water should be considered to be a low-melting-point or volatile constituent in a system, in that it can lower the liquidus temperature of a given compound. In this sense the term "hydrothermal" is appropriate in the category of "high-temperature and high-pressure solutions." Assemblages of constituents in the presence of water under pressure have been reported over a wide range.[1]

Processes to employ the hydrothermal reaction are generally classified as follows:

1. Hydrothermal synthesis — synthesis of a compound by the reaction of starting materials in the presence of a hydrothermal solution.
2. Hydrothermal crystal growth — the crystal growth of a compound that is hardly soluble in an ordinal solution below the boiling temperature, with the aid of the solubility increase in the hydrothermal solution.
3. Hydrothermal treatment — the purification and character improvement of naturally grown crystals or crystals grown by other methods in the presence of a hydrothermal solution.
4. Hydrothermal alteration — modification by the ion exchange of crystals with hydrothermal solutions.

In these systems all hydrothermal reactions are carried out in the presence of active water or in solution above 100°C in a pressure vessel. Thus, a suitable hydrothermal pressure system should be developed.

This section is concerned with the progress made in the growth of single crystals and the new technology for preparing finely dispersed oxide particles and sintered oxide bodies by the hydrothermal method. Well-sintered oxide ceramics can be prepared by the hydrothermal reaction of metallic powders with water under pressure at relatively low temperatures. The technology has the advantage of offering fully dense ceramics. Several examples of hydrothermal crystal growth and hydrothermal reaction sintering are reviewed with reference to the development of the equipment.

1.3.2 Hydrothermal Pressure Vessel

The progress of the hydrothermal method has depended on the development of high-strength alloy materials that are less corrosive under high temperature and pressure conditions. At present the cone-in-cone, seal-type pressure vessel is widely used in laboratories because of its high performance and its ability to hold high pressure with a simple closing system; however, the inner diameter of the vessel is limited to about 20 mm because of difficulties in applying mechanical torque efficiently at the sealing area. In plants the modified

Bridgeman-type pressure vessel has been employed to produce quartz single crystals. However, the required efficiency in crystal production has affected the design of large-scale pressure vessels.

The closing system used to seal the large-diameter, high-pressure tubing in the organic synthesis plant is called the Grayloc seal. There, a high-pressure vessel (autoclave) 40 cm in diameter and about 800 cm long has been safely operating in the commercial production of quartz single crystals. A typical view of the Grayloc seal is shown in Figure 1.3.1a.[2] In the laboratory a modified Grayloc seal system was recently developed in order to improve its operation, as shown in Figure 1.3.1b.[3,4] These improvements in the pressure seal system have allowed great progress in scaling up production and safely operating large-scale pressure vessels.

1.3.3 Representative Hydrothermal Synthesis

Many crystals have been grown hydrothermally, but α-quartz single crystals are the only ones successfully produced on a commercial scale. Alpha-quartz transforms to β-type crystals at 573°C. Crystal growth should be carried out below the transition temperature if highly perfect single crystals are desired. Nagai and co-workers reported on the large-scale production of α-quartz single crystals with the Grayloc-type seal autoclave.[2] Orthophosphate crystals have a modification similar to that of silica. Berlinite, $AlPO_4$, shows piezoelectric properties superior to α-quartz. Extensive studies have re-

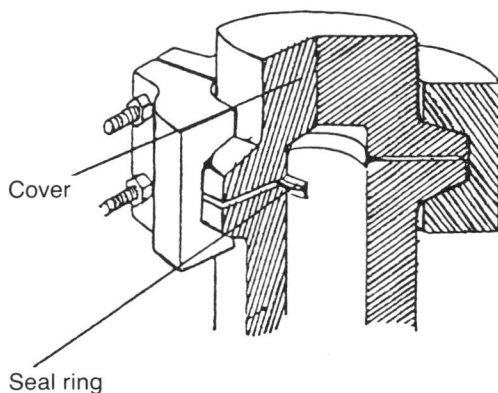

Cover

Seal ring

Figure 1.3.1a Grayloc seal used in industrial production of α-quartz single crystal [from K. Nagai et al., *Abstract of 24th Jinkokobutsu Toronkai* 21 (1979)].

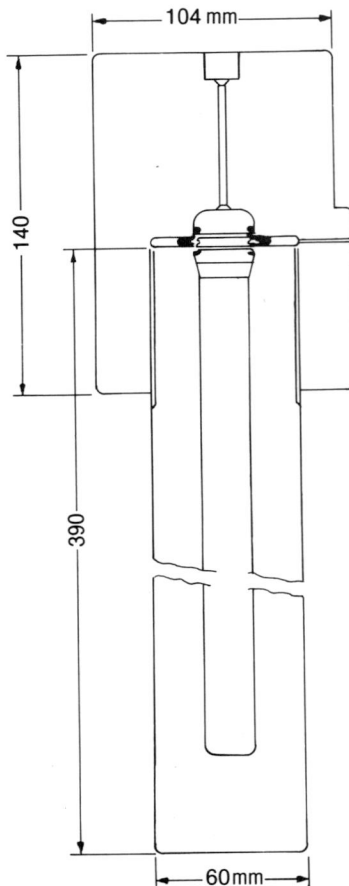

Figure 1.3.1*b* Hydrothermal pressure vessel with modified Grayloc seal [from S. Hirano et al., *High Pressure in Research and Industry* 2:807 (1982); S. Hirano, *Ceramic Datebook* 64:185 (1982)].

cently been made on the growth of large, high-quality single crystals of $AlPO_4$ as a partial substitute for the surface acoustic wave (SAW) device. Stanley first reported the preparation of $AlPO_4$ crystals.[5-9] These single crystals have been prepared in a 6.1 M phosphoric acid solution as a solvent, which is strongly corrosive to the alloy materials of the pressure vessel. This has led to the inevitable disadvantage of needing to protect the inner wall of the pressure vessel with a noble metal liner. The retrograde solubility dependency on temperature also makes it difficult to grow large, high-quality single crystals of $AlPO_4$ on an industrial scale.

Hirano and co-workers found that an ammonium dihydrogen phosphate (ADP) solution had a more advantaneous character for growing highly perfect $AlPO_4$ single crystals. They reported on the transition phenomena and properties of $AlPO_4$ crystals.[10] Single-crystal $GaPO_4$ can also be grown hydrothermally, and further study on the growth of large single crystals is in progress.[11]

Other ferroelectric crystals have also been grown by the hydrothermal method. Representative growth conditions are listed in Table 1.3.1.

The hydrothermal crystal growth of ferrites has not been industrially employed except for the preparation of CrO_2 crystalline powder. Single crystals with controlled composition can be grown at relatively low temperatures, as shown in Table 1.3.2. The hydrothermal growth of thin films of orthoferrite and garnet crystals is under consideration for industrial applications in a few countries. More detailed studies are required on homogeneous doping and composition control of hydrothermally grown single crystals.

Single crystals for laser emission and semiconductors have been grown as shown in Tables 1.3.3 and 1.3.4. These crystals can also be grown by CVD, the flux growth method, or the melt growth method. The hydrothermal growth method, however, has been studied because of its advantages for homogeneous doping, less induced strain, and polymorph control.

Zeolites are alumino-silicate minerals consisting of a $(Si, Al)_n O_{2n}$ framework, with substitution of Al for some of the Si in the SiO_4 tetrahedron giving a framework with a negative charge that is balanced by positive ions in the cavities. A characteristic property of zeolites is the existence of tunnels through the structure and the ease with which they take up and lose water molecules. Intensive attention has been paid to zeolites in order to employ them as molecular sieves, catalysts, ion exchange materials, and porous substrates. The zeolite formation process is very complicated because most synthetic zeolites form as a metastable phase under nonequilibrium conditions. Basic study for understanding the crystallization mechanism is necessary for reproducible controlled formation and improvement of the character of the desired zeolites.

Like zeolites, calcium silicate crystals such as tremolite and xonotlite have also been produced on an industrial scale at relatively low temperatures (below 200°C) by hydrothermal reaction. The

Table 1.3.1 Representative Hydrothermal Growth Conditions of Ferroelectric Crystals

Crystal	Solvent	Growth Zone Temp. (°C)	Dissol. Zone Temp. (°C)	Pressure or Deg. of Fill
α-SiO$_2$	1N Na$_2$CO$_3$	360	400	80%
	1.0M NaOH + 0.025M Li$_2$CO$_3$ + 0.1M Na$_2$CO$_3$	374	397	88%
LiGaO$_2$	3.5M NaOH	385	420	70%
BiTi$_2$O$_{12}$, Bi$_{12}$TiO$_{20}$	KF	550 ~ 600	—	>70 ~ 80%
K(Ta, Nb)O$_2$	15M KOH	650	690	1000 atm
KNbO$_3$, KTaO$_3$	KOH	400 ~ 600	450 ~ 680	70 ~ 80%
PbTiO$_3$, PbZrO$_3$	KF	570	585 ~ 590	50 ~ 55%
Pb(Ti$_x$Zr$_{1-x}$)O$_3$	>10 wt% KF	580	~618	83%
R$_9$Al$_3$(BOH)$_2$Si$_4$O$_{19}$	H$_3$BO$_3$ + NaCl or NaF	400 ~ 700	—	1000 ~ 3000 atm
AlPO$_4$, GaPO$_4$	6.1m H$_3$PO$_4$, 3.8m ADP	150 → 300°C		80%
[Mn, Fe, Zn]$_8$[Be$_6$Si$_6$O$_{24}$]S$_2$	1% NaOH or 8% NH$_4$Cl	450	480 ~ 500	1500 ~ 2000 atm
Na$_2$ZnGeO$_4$	30 wt% NaOH	250 ~ 300	253 ~ 310	50 ~ 90%

Table 1.3.2 Representative Hydrothermal Growth Conditions of Ferrites

Crystal	Solvent	Growth Zone Temp. (°C)	Dissol. Zone Temp. (°C)	Pressure or Deg. of Fill
$NiFe_2O_4$	0.5N NH_4Cl	470 ~ 480	—	70 ~ 75% (1,100 ~ 1,300 atm)
Fe_3O_4	10m NaOH	500	550	1000 atm
$ZnFe_2O_4$	NaOH	400	—	—
$Y_3Fe_5O_{12}$	1 ~ 3M Na_2CO_3 or 1 ~ 3M NaOH	400 ~ 750	—	200 ~ 1,350 atm
	20M KOH	350	360	88%
$Y_3Ga_5O_{12}$	1 ~ 3M Na_2CO_3 or 1 ~ 3M NaOH	400 ~ 500	—	1,000 ~ 3,000 atm
	K_2CO_3	500	550	~1,000 atm

Table 1.3.3 Representative Hydrothermal Growth Conditions of Laser Host

Crystal	Solvent	Growth Zone Temp. (°C)	Dissol. Zone Temp. (°C)	Pressure or Deg. of Fill
α-Al₂O₃	2 ~ 3.4M Na₂CO₃ or 1M K₂CO₃	390 ~ 490	500 ~ 540	75 ~ 82% (1100 ~ 1600 atm)
	10% K₂CO₃ or 10% KHCO₃	530 ~ 600	540 ~ 640	50 ~ 70%
	4M K₂CO₃	370	390	85%
	HCl	—	—	—
Y₃Al₅O₁₂	2M K₂CO₃	550	600	1000 atm
CaWO₄	4 wt% NaOH	380	430	60 ~ 70%
SrWO₄, BaWO₄	7 ~ 10 wt% NaOH	410 ~ 485	450 ~ 500	70%
	5 ~ 7 wt% NH₄Cl or 15 ~ 20 wt% LiCl or 30 ~ 40 wt% NaCl	430 ~ 485	450 ~ 500	65 ~ 70%
CdWO₄	7 wt% NH₄Cl or 16 ~ 25 wt% LiCl	430 ~ 455	450 ~ 470	75%
SrMoO₄, BaMoO₄	5 ~ 7 wt% NH₄Cl or 15 ~ 20 wt% LiCl or 30 ~ 40 wt% NaCl	430 ~ 485	450 ~ 500	65 ~ 70%

Table 1.3.4 Representative Hydrothermal Growth Conditions of Semiconductors

Crystal	Solvent	Growth Zone Temp. (°C)	Dissol. Zone Temp. (°C)	Pressure or Deg. of Fill
ZnO	5.45M KOH + 0.7M LiOH	353	467	83%
PbO	1N LiOH	430	450	60%
ZnS	2 ~ 5M NaOH	350 ~ 380	410 ~ 560	50 ~ 80%
PbS	0.5N RbOH	400	415	750 atm
CdS	H₂O	350	—	50%
HgS	2 ~ 8% HCl	315 ~ 320	355 ~ 340	1800 ~ 2000 atm
Zn-Cd-Hg-S	—	~350	—	700 atm
CuS	9M HBr	420	450	2400 atm
CdTe	20M NaOH or KOH	350	390	85%
CdSe	20M NaOH or KOH	350	350	85%
ZnTe	1M NaOH or KOH	350	390	72%
ZnSe	5m NaOH	350	350	78%
	5m NaOH + 4m LiOH	350	348	78%
HgSe	12M HCl	300	370	83%
HgTe	12N HCl	300	395	80%

crystallization process and phases of the formed crystallite have been found to depend strongly on the crystallinity, grain size, and chemical composition of the starting materials. Here also, basic study of the control of the crystal growth and morphology is required to establish the technology for industrial production.

The hydrothermal reaction can be applicable to direct production of the desired crystalline oxides by the decomposition of natural minerals. Hirano and co-workers developed the direct-synthesis method of fibrous $K_2O \cdot 6TiO_2$ crystals by the hydrothermal decomposition of ilmenite ($FeTiO_3$) in a potassium hydroxide solution.[12] Separation of the formed $K_2O \cdot 6TiO_2$ fibers from the magnetite in the fluid system is accomplished by magnetism.[13] Zirconia fine powders have also been prepared by the same method from zircon sand with hydrochloric acid.[14] Because the process involves hydrothermal reactions that proceed at moderate temperatures and pressures, oxides are precipitated as single fine particles. This hydrothermal precipitation process has been applied to produce fine oxide powders such as HfO_2, TiO_2, Nb_2O_5, Al_2O_3, $BaFe_{12}O_{19}$, and others.[15,16] The fine oxide particles were also synthesized by the hydrothermal reaction of metals with water.[17,18]

Hydrothermal synthesis can be performed for controlled composition crystal growth in a ZrO_2-Y_2O_3 solution.[19] The other advantage of the hydrothermal reaction system is the ease with which the atmosphere can be controlled during the crystal synthesis. A single crystal of the exotic material $Na_x(Ti, Fe)]O_{2-\delta}$ was first grown by adjustment of the cation valence state, which could be carried out by use of hydrogen formed by the hydrothermal reaction of a proper amount of iron and titanium with water.[20]

The hydrothermal syntheses just mentioned are based on the following features originating in the low-temperature homogeneous reaction process:

1. Preparation of crystals that incongruently melt or have a phase transformation.
2. Growth of crystals with high varpor pressure.
3. Synthesis of compounds that decompose even at moderate temperature.
4. Growth of less-strained, high-quality single crystals.
5. Homogeneous doping with foreign ions.
6. Purification in single crystals (the concentration of impurities in

hydrothermally grown crystals is much lower than in the starting materials).

7. Control of the redox condition.

Hydrothermal synthesis meets the increasing demands to prepare the desired crystalline ceramics; as an alternate or new approach, it is essentially less energy-expensive and less polluting. To amplify the capabilities of this technique, basic R&D toward a more efficient system should be further advanced by considering the problem of hydroxide ion uptake in grown crystals. Study is also required on the intermediate states of chemical species in hydrothermal solutions.

1.3.4 Hydrothermal Reaction Sintering

A technique for sintering oxides at low temperatures using hydrothermal reaction of metal powders with water in a capsule permeable to formed hydrogen gas was developed by Hirano.[21] The sealed capsule is squeezed in a hydrothermal pressure vessel by water during the hydrothermal reaction. This sintering method has been found to be very useful in fabricating dense compacts of oxides, wherein the cation valence can be controlled by simultaneously adjusting the redox atmosphere by use of a gas as one of the reaction products. This has been named the hydrothermal reaction sintering method.

This technique first originated accidentally in an experimental failure while iron dispersed in carbon was being prepared. Supercritical water was reacted with formed fine iron powders in a carbon matrix through a pinhole in a gold capsule to leave sintered magnetite agglomerates. Further basic study orientated toward the sintering itself revealed that a fully dense sintered body of magnetite could be obtained at temperatures as low as 550°C at 1000 kg/cm² (100 MPa) pressure by the reaction $3Fe + 4H_2O \rightarrow Fe_3O_4 + 4H_2$.[22] The change in relative density (ρ) with time (t) is shown in Figure 1.3.2.[23] The sintering time necessary for the theoretical density was found to depend strongly on such parameters as the total fill percentage of starting materials, the ratio of starting metal to water, the capsule material, and the pressure and temperature conditions. The dependency of relative density (ρ) upon sintering pressure (p) is shown in Figure 1.3.3. The rate of densification fits the following relation:

$$d\rho/dt = Kp(1 - \rho) \qquad (1.3.1)$$

where ρ = relative density; t = time; K = constant, including the factor of viscosity at infinite shear rate; and p = applied sintering pressure. Equation (1.3.1) can be rewritten as

$$\ln(1 - \rho) = -Kpt + \ln(1 - \rho_0) \qquad (1.3.2)$$

The results probably suggest the partial contribution of the plastic

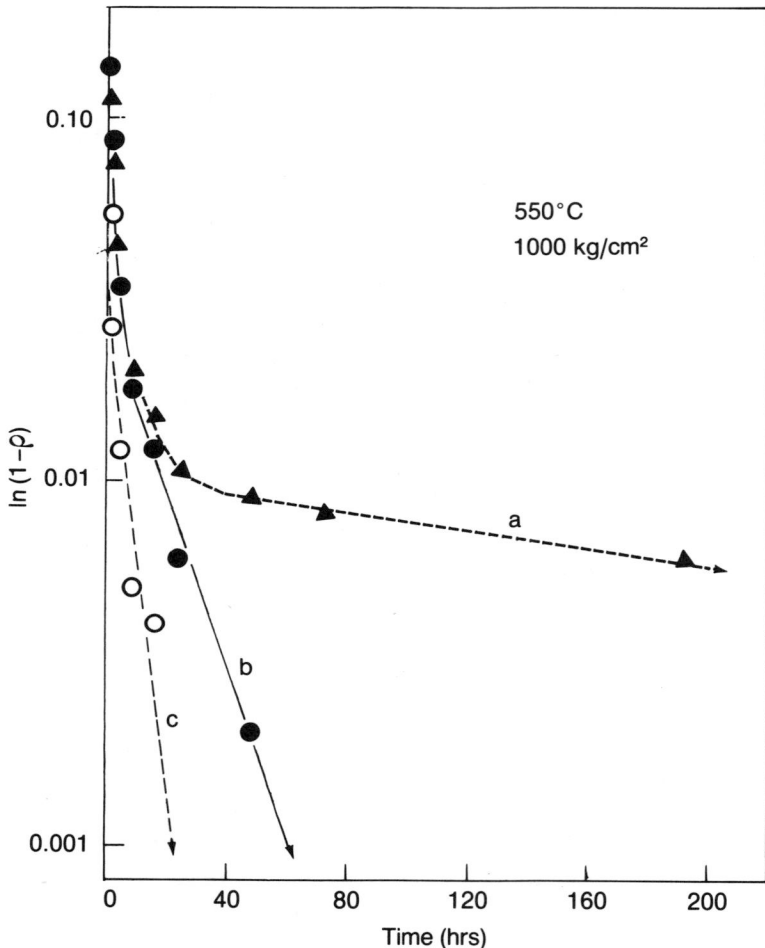

Figure 1.3.2 Plot of $\ln(1 - \rho)$ versus time for magnetite hydrothermally sintered at 550°C and 1000 kg/cm² (ρ: relative density [from S. Hirano, *J. Am. Ceram. Soc.* (forthcoming)]. (a) in gold capsule with mixture of $Fe/H_2O = \frac{3}{6}$ (excess water) (b) in gold capsule with stoichiometric mixture of $Fe/H_2O = \frac{3}{4}$ (c) in platinum capsule with stoichiometric mixture of $Fe/H_2O = \frac{3}{4}$.

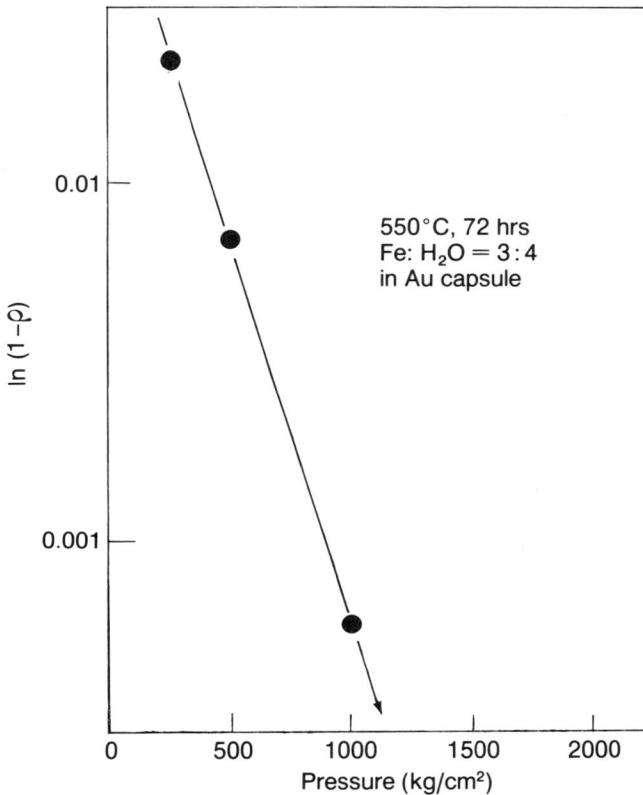

Figure 1.3.3 Plot of ln(1 − ρ) versus pressure for magnetite hydrothermally sintered at 550°C for 72 hours with stoichiometric mixture of Fe/H_2O = $\frac{3}{4}$ (ρ: relative density) [from S. Hirano, *J. Am. Ceram. Soc.* (forthcoming)].

flow mechanism as reported for hot pressings. The deviation from the linear relation in the initial stage must be attributed to the presence of another densification mechanism such as a rearrangement of formed active fine grains by sliding or fragmentation. The densification is also promoted by the grain boundary diffusion of hydrogen formed by hydrothermal reaction in the sealed capsule.

The low sintering temperature tends to greatly hinder grain growth in the sintered body without any inhibiting additive and gives a fully dense sintered body with a homogeneous texture, as shown in Figure 1.3.4. If the amount of water is in excess of the theoretical value for reacting with metal to form the desired oxide, the excess water acts to cause exaggerated grain growth.

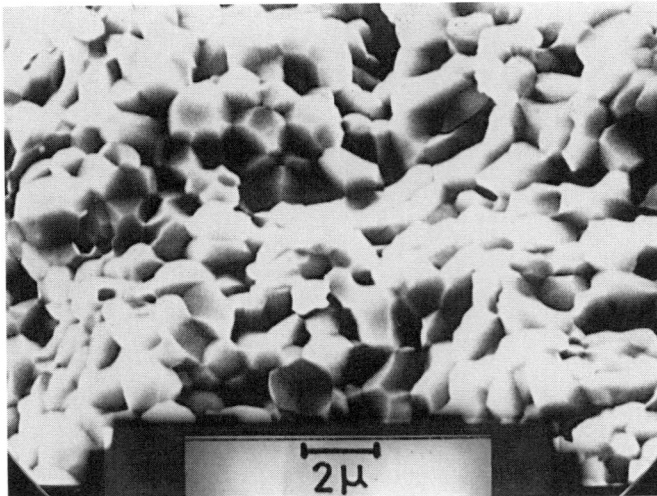

Figure 1.3.4 SEM of fracture surface of magnetite specimen hydrothermally sintered at 550°C and 1000 kg/cm².

This technique was found to be applicable to preparing dense sintered bodies of $MgTiO_3$, $PbTiO_3$, $FeTiO_3$, and $MgAl_2O_4$.[21] Hydroxides were also used in this study as the starting materials to react with metal to form oxides $[Mg(OH)_2 + Ti + H_2O \rightarrow MgTiO_3 + 2H_2]$. A very dense sintered pure chromia (Cr_2O_3) body of 99.2% theoretical density was also prepared by the reaction $2Cr + 3H_2O \rightarrow Cr_2O_3 + 3H_2$ at 1000°C under 1000 kg/cm² pressure, as shown in Figure 1.3.5.[24] Much attention has been given to the sintering of pure Cr_2O_3 because the high volatilization of chromium oxide makes its densification difficult without additives. Nonstabilized ZrO_2 sintered bodies were also prepared using this technique.[25]

The mechanism of hydrothermal reaction sintering is postulated as follows:

1. The reaction of metal powder with supercritical water forms active fine oxide grains in a squeezed capsule.
2. The rearrangement of the grains in the initial, faster densification stage nerves as a major portion of the total sintering.
3. Subsequently, there is a plastic flow process in the final densification stage.

The cooperative mechanism of the plastic flow and the diffusion associated with the formed hydrogen must be taken into considera-

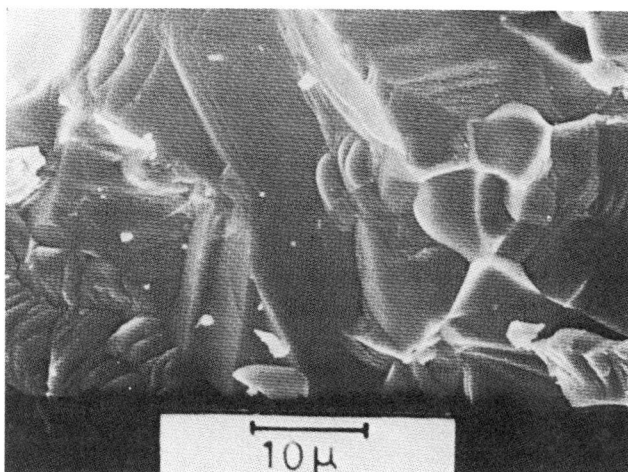

Figure 1.3.5 SEM of fracture surface of pure Cr_2O_3 specimen sintered under hydrothermal condition at 1000°C and 1000 kg/cm².

tion. The combination of these processes is enhanced by exterior pressure through the capsule on the starting materials.

Studies of the mechanism of hydrothermal reaction sintering and its industrial applications are in progress.

References

1. Phase Diagrams for Ceramists *Amer. Ceram. Soc.*
2. Nagai, K., Hara, M., Harada, H., and Asahara, J., *Abstract of 24th Jinkokobutsu Toronkai* 21 (1979).
3. Hirano, S., Ozawa, M., and Naka, S., *High Pressure in Research and Industry* 2:807 (1982).
4. Hirano, S., *Ceramic Databook* 64:185 (1982).
5. Stanley, J. M., *Ind. Eng. Chem.* 46:1684 (1954).
6. Kolb, E. D., and Laudise, R. A., *J. Cryst. Growth* 43:313 (1978); 56:83 (1983).
7. Kolb, E. D., Laudise, R. A., and Grenier, J. C., *J. Cryst. Growth* 50:404(1980).
8. Yoshimura, J., Taki, S., and Maruya, S., *Yogyo Kyokai Shi* 89:433 (1981).
9. Ogawa, T., Nagai, K., Asahara, J., and Taki, S., *Abstract of Jinkokobutsu Toronkai* 9 (1983).
10. Hirano, S., Shibata, K., and Naka, S., *Abstract of 22nd Yogyo Kiso Toronkai* 111 (1984).

11. Hirano, S., Miwa, K., and Naka, S., *Abstract of 28th Jinkokobutsu Toronkai* 25 (1983).
12. Hirano, S., Ismail, M. G. M. U., and Somiya, S., *J. Am. Ceram. Soc.* 59:227 (1976).
13. Hirano, S., *J. Am. Ceram Soc.* (forthcoming).
14. Stambaugh, E. P., and Foos, R. A., U.S. Pat. 3,090,770.
15. Stambaugh, E. P., U.S. Pat. 3,607,006.
16. Foos, R. A., and Stambaugh, E. P., U.S. Pat. 3,065,095.
17. Hirano, S., and Somiya, S., *J. Cryst. Growth* 35:273 (1976).
18. Toraya, H., Yoshimura, M., and Somiya, S., *Comm. Am. Ceram. Soc.* 65:c72 (1982).
19. Nakamura, K., Hirano, S., and Somiya, S., *Am. Ceram. Soc. Bull.* 56:227 (1976).
20. Hirano, S., *J. Min. Soc. Jpn.* 14:161 (1980).
21. Hirano, S., *Jpn. Pat. Kokai* 51-11211.
22. Hirano, S., and Somiya, S., *Abstract of 12th Yogyo Kiso Toronkai* 33 (1974).
23. Hirano, S., *J. Am. Ceram. Soc.* (forthcoming).
24. Yoshimura, M., and Somiya, S., *Am. Ceram. Soc. Bull.* 59:246 (1980).

1.4 Synthesis of Finely Divided Crystalline Oxide Powders and Glasses from Metal-Organic Compounds

Kanichi Kamiya and Shigeharu Naka

1.4.1 Introduction

The fine crystalline or amorphous powders prepared by chemical reaction in the liquid state have been effectively used as sources for preparing high-purity, high-density, controlled-texture ceramic bodies. The preparation of the powders is carried out using metal salts or metal-organic compounds as starting materials through hydrolysis or thermal decomposition. In particular, metal-organic compounds have been regarded from several points of view as preferable origins for fine powders, as will be described below.

The alkoxides of the glass-forming metal elements undergo hydrolysis and polycondensation reactions to form polymerized products, providing transparent gelled masses. Oxide glass has been obtained by heating the gel to remove the included water and other volatile matters. This preparation method for oxide glass has been developed as one of the new glass-making techniques not requiring melting. This section briefly reviews the preparation of fine powders and glass from metal-organic compounds.

1.4.2 Crystalline Powders Made from Metal Alkoxides and Metal Acetylacetonates

Metal alkoxide (sometimes called metal alcoholate) or $M^{n+}(OR)_n$, where M is a metal element and R is an alkyl group, is a compound in which the metal element is bonded to the organic carbon via oxygen. This may be regarded as either a derivative of the corresponding alcohol or metal hydroxide $M(OH)_n$. Metal alkoxides are easily synthesized — for instance, by the direct reaction of metals with alcohols or by the reaction of the corresponding metal chlorides with alcohols. Many elements, enclosed in the heavy solid lines in Table 1.4.1, are able to form alkoxides. The OR^- group in a metal alkoxide is a strong Lewis base undergoing hydrolysis to form a metal oxide or metal hydroxide as follows:

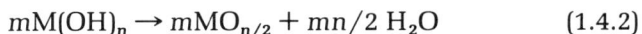

$$M^{n+}(OR)_n + nH_2O \rightarrow M(OH)_n + nROH \qquad (1.4.1)$$

$$mM(OH)_n \rightarrow mMO_{n/2} + mn/2\ H_2O \qquad (1.4.2)$$

Metal acetylacetonates, that is, chelates between metals and acetylacetone (shown in Figure 1.4.1), are stable in air and soluble in any organic solvents, whereas the alkoxides of transition metals other than iron have low solubility in organic solvents. Therefore, it is preferable to use the acetylacetonates of the transition metals as sources of these elements, instead of alkoxides. The acetylacetonates are hydrolyzed to form fine powders as well as metal alkoxides by adjusting the pH value of their solutions to above 7.

The preparation of fine powders from metal alkoxides and acethylacetonates has the following advantages over the conventional mechanical process that uses metal salts such as halides, oxalates, sulphates, and acetates as starting materials:

1. The metal alkoxide is easily purified, leading to oxide powders of high purity and homogeneity. No cations or anions other than the desired metals are incorporated.

2. The heating temperature necessitated to produce crystalline species of the designed composition and structure is relatively low. This results in the formation of low-temperature crystalline species not obtained by the solid-state reactions normally conducted at higher temperatures.

Table 1.4.1 Elements Forming Alkoxides

H																	He
Li	Be											B	C	N	O	F	Ne
Na	Mg											Al	Si	P	S	Cl	Ar
K	Ca	Sc	Ti	V	Cr	Mn	Fe	Co	Ni	Cu	Zn	Ga	Ge	As	Se	Br	Kr
Rb	Sr	Y	Zr	Nb	Mo	Tc	Ru	Rh	Pd	Ag	Cd	In	Sn	Sb	Te	I	Xe
Cs	Ba	La*	Hf	Ta	W	Re	Os	Ir	Pt	Au	Hg	Tl	Pb	Bi	Po	At	Rn
Fr	Ra	Ac**															

*	La	Ce	Pr	Nd	Pm	Sm	Eu	Gd	Tb	Dy	Ho	Er	Tm	Yb	Lu
**	Ac	Th	Pa	U	Np	Pu	Am	Cm	Bk	Cf	Es	Fm	Md	No	Lr

H$_3$C

C —— O

HC   M^{n+}/N

C === O'

H$_3$C

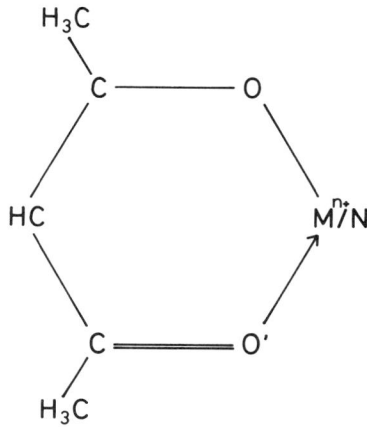

Figure 1.4.1 Metal acetylacetonate.

3. High chemical activity or the highly strained state resulting from the very small particle size gives rise to the appearance of high-pressure crystalline forms even at ambient pressure. The ease in obtaining the highly dense sintered bodies also results from the high chemical activity of the starting powders.

Many powder species prepared from metal alkoxides and acetylacetonates have been reported. Preparation of the fine powders of the BaO-TiO$_2$ system will be described as the first example.[1,2] The isopropanol i-PrOH solution of barium isopropoxide Ba(O·i-Pr)$_2$ and titanium isopropoxide Ti(O·i-Pr)$_4$ or titanium tertiaryamyloxide Ti(O·t-Am)$_4$ was used. Figure 1.4.2 shows the particle size distribution of the BaTiO$_3$ powders prepared by hydrolyzing the mixed alkoxide solution in which the cation ratio Ba/Ti is kept at unity. The relatively sharp distribution feature and the average particle size of about 50 Å can be seen. The as-prepared BaTiO$_3$ powder exhibits cubic symmetry that is metastable under ambient pressure at room temperature, transforming to the stable tetragonal form on heating to 800°C. The powders were sintered to a highly dense, translucent BaTiO$_3$ body. The low-temperature stable crystalline species, BaTi$_2$O$_5$, BaTi$_5$O$_{11}$, and Ba$_2$TiO$_4$, which are not obtained by the conventional solid-state reaction because the processing temperature is too high, could be prepared directly through hydrolysis from the mixed alkoxide solutions having the corresponding Ba/Ti ratios.

Fine powders of barium hexaferrite, BaFe$_{12}$O$_{19}$ (Figure 1.4.3), and manganese zinc ferrite, (Mn, Zn)Fe$_2$O$_4$, have been made by hydrolyzing mixed solutions of barium tetraethoxide, Ba(OEt)$_4$, and

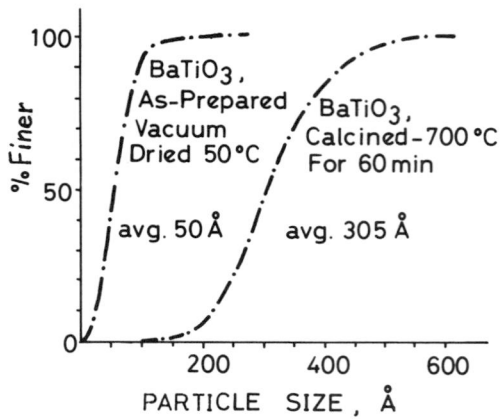

Figure 1.4.2 Particle size distribution of BaTiO$_3$ powders prepared from metal alkoxides [from S. Naka et al., *Bull. Chem. Soc. Jpn.* 41:1168 (1974)].

Figure 1.4.3 Crystalline particles of BaFe$_{12}$O$_{19}$ derived from alkoxide and acetylacetonates.

iron acetylacetonate, $Fe(ACAC)_2$; and zinc, manganese, and iron acetylacetonates, $Zn(ACAC)_2$, $Mn(ACAC)_2 \cdot 2H_2O$, and $Fe(ACAC)_2$ respectively.[3]

Another method for producing ceramic bodies from metal-organic compounds has been developed in which the solution consisting of colloidal oxide particles is gelled by concentration and heated to give a translucent ceramic body.[4] A translucent Al_2O_3 body and TiO_2 plate have been prepared by this method. The solution of colloidal Al_2O_3 particles was extruded continuously through a pin-hole and heated, forming a continuous Al_2O_3 fiber.[5]

This technique for preparing oxide powders or shaped bodies using metal-organic compounds as sources is useful and powerful for basic science as well as for the applications described above — for instance, in determining the low-temperature areas of phase diagrams and in studying the nonstoichiometry of oxides.[6,7] In both, it is difficult to carry out the experiments with the conventional solid-state reaction method, again because of too-high processing temperatures.

1.4.3 Glass Prepared from Metal Alkoxides

The alkoxide of a glass-forming element, such as silicon tetraethoxide, $Si(OEt)_4$, produces colloidal oxide particles on hydrolysis and polycondensation when the pH of the solution is kept above 7. These colloidal particles are linked together to form a gel that in turn forms a monolithic glass on heating.[8] If the hydrolysis and condensation reactions are performed in the acidic solution, linearly or three-dimensionally polymerized products are formed, depending on reaction conditions such as the amount of water added for hydrolysis and reaction temperature.[9] The resulting gel is converted to an oxide glass on heating. This glass-making method is variously called the alkoxide, sol gel, or chemical synthesis method.[10,11] Figure 1.4.4 is a schematic diagram for preparing SiO_2 glass of several shapes from $Si(OEt)_4$. The addition of a small amount of water may lead to the linear alkoxide polymers, bringing about spinnability in the solutions during the course of hydrolysis. From these viscous solutions, fibers can be drawn. Thin gel films are also obtained by spreading the solutions over a nonadhesive plastic plate. Monolithic bulk gels constructed of the three-dimensionally developed polymers result when a large amount of water is added to the alcoholic solution of $Si(OEt)_4$. The heating temperature required to convert the gel to SiO_2 glass is at most 1000°C, a relatively low temperature compared with the con-

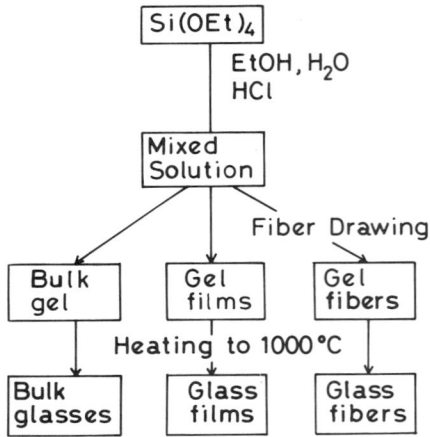

Figure 1.4.4 Schematic diagram for preparing shaped SiO_2 glasses from $Si(O \cdot Et)_4$.

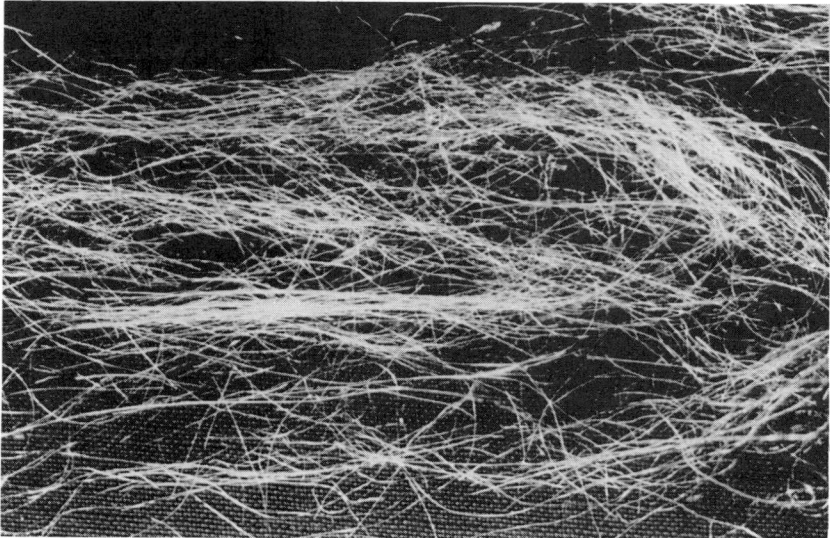

Figure 1.4.5 ZrO_2-SiO_2 glass fibers made from metal alkoxides.

ventional melting method — hence the label "low-temperature synthesis method."

This newly developed method for making oxide glass from alkoxide has the following advantages over the conventional melting method.

1. High purity and high homogeneity are attained in the resulting glass.
2. As in the case of preparing powders, the processing temperature is relatively low; this leads to energy savings and reduced air pollution.
3. Glass of new compositions, which is difficult to obtain by the conventional melting method because of a high tendency toward

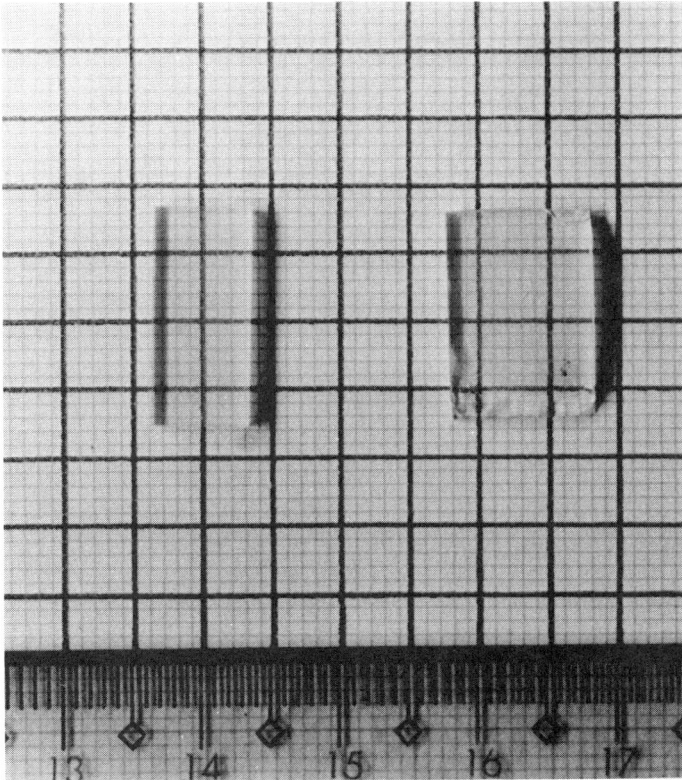

Figure 1.4.6 TiO_2-SiO_2 glasses of ultra-low thermal expansion made from metal alkoxides.

crystallization and phase separation during cooling, can be synthesized.

4. Coating of metals or plastics with thin glass films to improve their surface characteristics (such as chemical durability, color, and hardness) is easily carried out.

ZrO_2-SiO_2 glass and glass fibers containing a large amount of ZrO_2 have been newly made from zirconium normalpropoxide, $Zr(O \cdot n\text{-}Pr)_4$ and $Si(OEt)_4$, through hydrolysis and gelling (Figure 1.4.5). Those glass fibers are very durable toward alkaline solutions. TiO_2-SiO_2 glass with an ultra-low thermal expansion coefficient is conventionally prepared at temperatures as high as 1750°C with a specially designed apparatus. However, TiO_2-SiO_2 glass (Figure 1.4.6) of the same composition and characteristics as that above can be obtained at temperatures as low as 1000°C from gels made in glass beakers with a simple electric furnace. The starting materials used were $Ti(O \cdot i\text{-}Pr)_4$ and $Si(OEt)_4$. Many types of glass other than those just described have been produced as fibers, films, or in bulk from metal alkoxides.[10,11]

References

1. Mazdiyasni, K. S., Dolloff, R. T., and Smith II, J. S., *J. Am. Ceram. Soc.*, 52:523 (1969).
2. Naka, S., Nakakita, F., Suwa, Y., and Inagaki, M., *Bull. Chem. Soc. Jpn.* 41:1168 (1974).
3. Naka, S., Hirano, S., and Suwa, Y., *Preprints of the Annual Meeting of Japan Ceramic Society*, Tokyo, Japan, 1983, p. 131.
4. Yoldas, B. E., *Am. Ceram. Soc. Bull.* 54:286 (1975).
5. Minnesota Mining & Manufacturing Co., Japan Patents 50-39311 (1975), 52-137030 (1977), 57-20409 (1982).
6. Suwa, Y., Kato, Y., Hirano, S., and Naka, S., *Funtai, Funmatsuyakin* 28:28 (1981).
7. Suwa, Y., Inagaki, M., Hayakawa, K., and Naka, S., *Preprints of the 14th Symposium on Powders*, 1976, p. 27.
8. Shoup, R. D., Symposium on Glass Through Chemical Processing, Rutgers University, New Brunswick, N.J., 1983.
9. Kamiya, K., Sakka, S., and Yoko, T., *Yogyo-Kyokai-Shi* (J. Ceram. Soc. Japan) 92:242 (1984).
10. Sakka, S., *Treatise on Materials Science and Technology*, vol. 22, M. Tomozawa and R. Doremus, eds. New York: Academic Press, 1982.
11. Sakka, S., and Kamiya, K., *J. Non-Cryst. Sol.* 42:403 (1980).

1.5 The Solid-Phase Epitaxial Growth Method

Noboru Yamamoto and Soichiro Matsuzawa

1.5.1 Introduction

When a single crystal is brought into direct contact with a polycrystal and the contacted body is heated, the single crystal grows by discontinuous grain growth at the boundary of the single crystal and the polycrystal.[1,2] However, even if a single crystal can be grown by this method, the growth length of the single crystal is not greater than several tens to several hundreds of μm because the grains of the polycrystal grow continuously and inhibit the single crystal's growth.

A method for producing large single crystals by discontinuous grain growth has been proposed,[3] but this method has never been utilized for commercial production. The reason is that discontinuous grain growth is particularly likely to occur when continuous grain growth is inhibited by the presence of pores, and the final single crystal contains a large number of pores that were present in the original polycrystal. Therefore, in order to produce practically usable single crystals through the solid-phase epitaxial growth method, polycrystals that contain few pores and fine grains should be used at the temperature at which the single crystal grows.

In the authors' study of high-density ferrite, ferrite polycrystals suitable for growing single crystals were developed, and a method was established for producing single crystals of Mn-Zn ferrite through the solid-phase epitaxial growth method. Mn-Zn ferrite single crystals produced by this method have homogeneous composition and homogeneous magnetic properties and are widely used in manufacturing superior video tape recorder (VTR) heads. The following discussion relates to the method for producing single crystals of Mn-Zn ferrite and the mechanism of single crystal growth.

1.5.2 Ferrite Polycrystals

Iron oxide having a spinel structure (Fe_3O_4) and purity of 99.99% and containing 0.003% SiO_2 and 0.001% CaO as impurities, along with manganese and zinc oxides, each having a purity of 99.9%, were mixed to make a composition of 31 mol% MnO, 17 mol% ZnO, and 53 mol% Fe_2O_3. The mixture was then calcined, milled, formed, and sintered at 1320°C for 4 hours under an equilibrium oxygen partial pressure to obtain Mn-Zn ferrite polycrystals. The microstructure of the Mn-Zn ferrite polycrystal sintered at 1320°C is shown in Figure

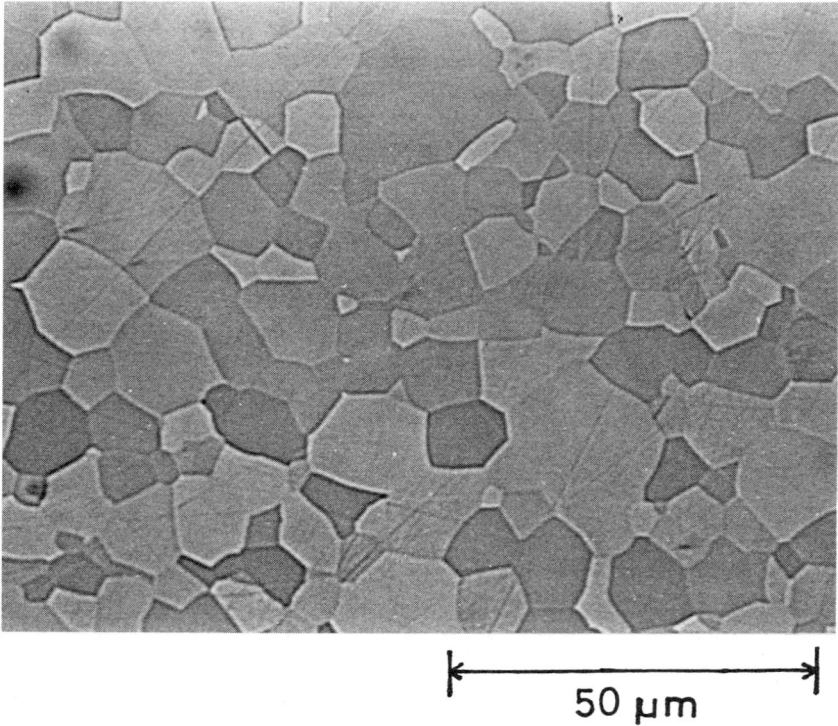

50 μm

Figure 1.5.1 Microstructure of Mn-Zn ferrite polycrystal.

1.5.1. This polycrystal had an average grain size of about 10 μm and a porosity of about 0.02%.

The effect of temperature on the grain size of this ferrite polycrystal is shown in Figure 1.5.2. The grain size of the polycrystal does not substantially change up to about 1390°C. When the temperature reaches about 1390°C, discontinuous grain growth occurs and some grains suddenly grow to become giant grains of about 5 mm. In this polycrystal, grain growth does not substantially occur at a temperature lower than that at which discontinuous grain growth occurs.

1.5.3 Growth of Mn-Zn Ferrite Single Crystal

From the ferrite polycrystal and a single crystal having substantially the same composition, two plates 5 × 25 × 10 mm and 5 × 25 × 1 mm, respectively, were cut off. One of the 5 × 25 surfaces of each plate was polished by diamond abrasive powder on a tin disc to a

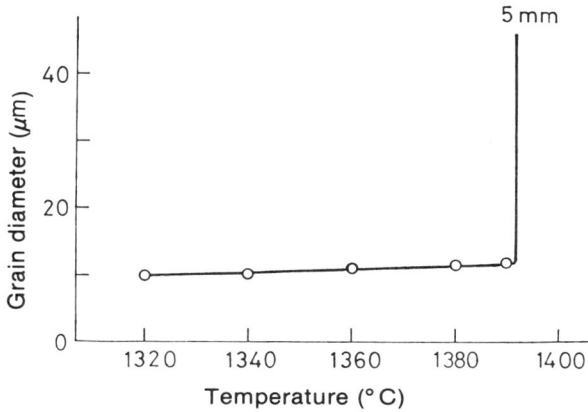

Figure 1.5.2 Effect of temperature on grain size of Mn-Zn ferrite polycrystal heated 4 hours at temperature.

roughness R_{max} of 0.05 μm. A solution of 6N HNO_3 was applied to the polished surfaces, the plates were brought into direct contact and then heated to a temperature at which a solid-phase reaction occurred (1370°C under equilibrium oxygen partial pressure).

A cross section including the single crystal and polycrystal portions of the obtained Mn-Zn ferrite body is shown in Figure 1.5.3. The

Figure 1.5.3 Growth of Mn-Zn ferrite single crystal into a matrix of uniformly sized grains.

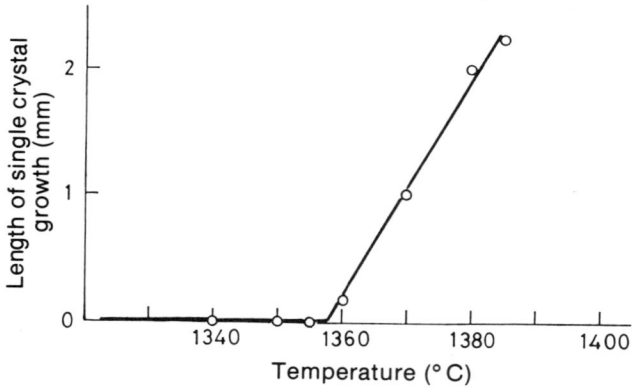

Figure 1.5.4 Effect of temperature on the growth of Mn-Zn ferrite single crystal heated 4 hours.

seed single crystal grew about 1 mm toward the polycrystal portion, and the grain size of the polycrystal did not substantially change.

    The relationship of heating temperature and growth length of the single crystal when the bodies in contact were heated for 4 hours can be seen in Figure 1.5.4. When the temperature is lower than 1350°C, single crystal growth does not substantially occur. When the temperature is higher than 1360°C, substantial single crystal growth occurs. These results indicate that single crystal growth is a discontinuous phenomenon.

    The relationship of heating time and growth length of the single crystal is demonstrated in Figure 1.5.5. Although single crystal

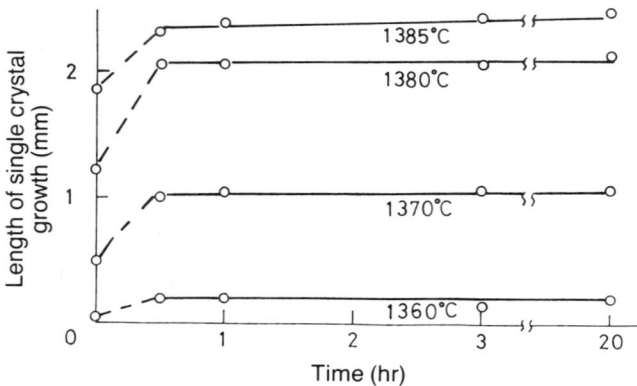

Figure 1.5.5 Effect of heating time on the growth of Mn-Zn ferrite single crystal.

growth continues for up to 30 minutes, after 30 minutes the growth stops.

Usually the growth rate of a single crystal is given by

$$V = AM_0 \, \gamma_b 1/d \, \exp(Q_b/RT) \qquad (1.5.1)$$

where V is the rate of single crystal growth, A is a geometrical factor, M_0 is the boundary mobility, Q_b is the activation energy for boundary movement, γ_b is the boundary surface energy, and d is the polycrystal grain diameter. The phenomenon observed in our experiments, however, cannot be explained by Equation (1.5.1). According to this equation, the growth rate of a single crystal is inversely proportional to its grain size and increases exponentially with temperature, so that the growth rate of the single crystal should be constant as long as the grain size remains unchanged. Moreover, it is impossible to have a discontinuous point in temperature.

Accordingly, the authors consider that the phenomenon observed in their experiments is caused by discontinuous grain growth and that this discontinuous grain growth consists of two processes, a nucleation process and a nuclei growth process. It follows that in the newly developed ferrite polycrystal, the nucleation temperature is higher than the temperature at which the nuclei growth starts.

The effects of heating temperature on the grain size of the polycrystal and the growth length of the single crystal can be seen in Figure 1.5.6. The nucleation temperature of discontinuous grain growth is 1390°C, and the nuclei growth starts at 1360°C. Therefore, the single crystal of the contacted body can be grown at temperatures

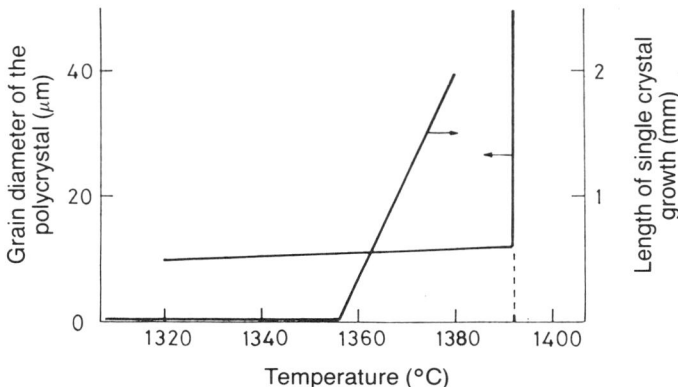

Figure 1.5.6 Effect of heating temperature on the grain size of the polycrystal and the growth length of Mn-Zn ferrite single crystal growth.

between 1360°C and 1390°C without formation of nuclei in the poly-crystal. However, it is impossible to grow the single crystal contin-uously when the heating temperature is kept constant, because single crystal growth stops after 30 minutes as shown in Figure 1.5.6. The reason for this is that the starting temperature of nuclei growth rises with heating time. Hence, in order to grow the single crystal contin-uously, it is necessary to raise the temperature at a suitable rate.

The nucleation temperature also rises with heating time, but the heating rate must be controlled not to exceed the nucleation temper-ature. The length of the single crystal grown by this method is 8 mm.

1.5.4 Conclusion

Discontinuous grain growth consists of two processes, a nucleation process and a nuclei growth process. In the newly developed ferrite polycrystal, the nucleation temperature is higher than that at which the nuclei growth starts.

A single crystal can be caused to grow when brought into direct contact with a ferrite polycrystal and heated at temperatures be-tween the nucleation temperature and the temperature at which nuclei growth starts without formation of nuclei in the polycrystal.

The starting temperature of the nuclei growth rises with heating time, so that in order to grow the single crystal continuously it is necessary to raise the temperature at a suitable rate.

References

1. Kingery, W. D., *Introduction to Ceramics.* New York: John Wiley & Sons, 1960, p. 363.
2. Kinoshita, M., *Yogyo Kyokaishi* 82(5):295–296 (1974).
3. Levesque, P., Gerlach, L., and Zneimer, J. E., *J. Am. Ceram. Soc.* 41(8):300–303 (1958).

1.6 Hot Isostatic Pressing (HIP) of Ceramics and HIP Equipment for Ceramics

Takao Fujikawa

1.6.1 Introduction

Hot isostatic pressing (HIP) is a process to form products of full density by subjecting encapsulated powder bodies or sintered parts with residual porosity to inert gas of isostatic pressure at a high temperature. The process was invented in the United States in the mid-1950s as a technique to clad uranium oxide with zircalloy by diffusion bonding. Today it is used widely on a commercial basis to produce P/M billets for high-speed tool steel or P/M superalloy parts, to heat defects in castings, and to remove residual porosity from cemented carbide parts.[1] The process uses a high isostatic pressure of 100 to 200 MPa and enables manufacture of parts with complicated shapes. For these reasons, it is an excellent technique for making high-density homogeneous products.

For a long time ceramics have been manufactured by pressing and sintering powdered materials. However, this always leaves residual porosity, and ceramics produced by this method unavoidably lack strength and reliability. There is no doubt that the HIP technique, which has been used extensively in the P/M area, could improve existing methods of producing ceramics; as a result, homogeneous high-density ceramics could be obtained. In recent years nonoxide ceramics such as Si_3N_4 and SiC have attracted attention as a material for high-density structural parts. Against this background, interest in HIP techniques for ceramics is increasing dramatically.

This section is concerned with HIP ceramics and HIP equipment for ceramics production.

1.6.2 Methods for Using HIP

There are two techniques for producing high-density parts using HIP. One is to use HIP with green bodies having a density of 50 to 80% of theoretical density (TD) following the sealing of the surface of these green bodies to protect against the pressurizing gas. The other technique is to produce sintered parts of more than 95% TD without open porosity by conventional sintering, and then to densify these parts by HIP. The former technique can be further divided into four subtypes, depending on the sealing methods and the materials used. These are shown in Figure 1.6.1, and the features of each technique are described below.

1.6.2.1 Metal Capsule Method

A powdered material or a green body is packed into a metal capsule, and this capsule is evacuated and sealed; HIP follows. This method can produce a high-density product of simple shape if the capsule is made into the desired shape with some margin for shrinkage of the capsule. If a product with a complicated shape is needed, the powdered material is first cold-pressed and embedded in a sinter-resist-

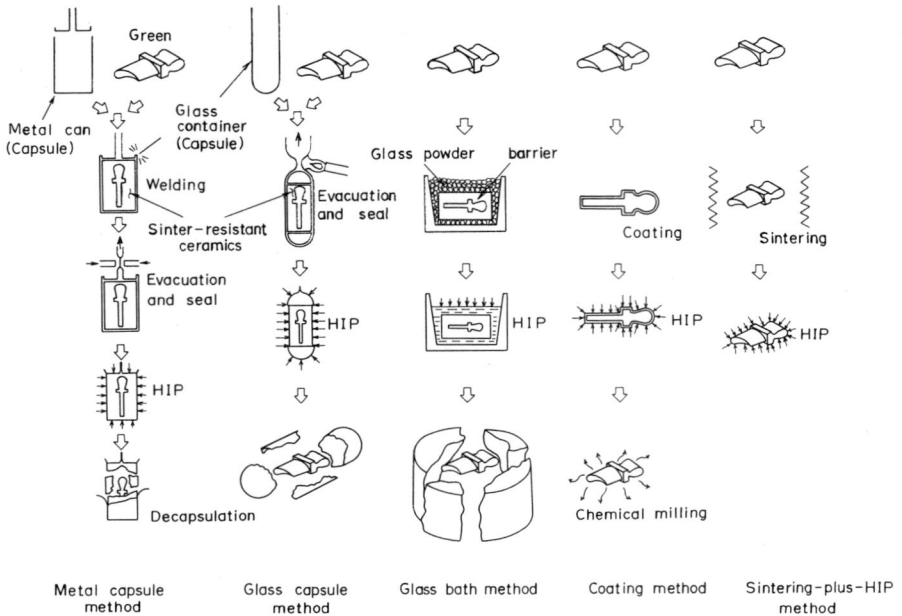

Figure 1.6.1 Methods for using HIP.

ant powder, and then encapsulated. Capsules made of steel are used at temperatures of up to about 1400°C; those made of refractory metals, such as molybdenum and tantalum, are used at higher temperatures.[2,3]

1.6.2.2 *Glass Capsule Method*

In this method, the metal capsules in the foregoing method are replaced by glass capsules. The thermal expansion coefficient of a metal capsule is greater than that of the ceramic contained in the capsule; consequently, it becomes difficult to remove the ceramic without breakage. In addition, at temperatures higher than those suitable for steel, expensive refractory metals must be used in the metal capsule method. Because glass is free from these disadvantages, it has been used experimentally for a long time.[4] However, the disadvantage of glass is that it is brittle. For this reason, handling and pressurizing are difficult, and this is particularly important in the production of larger-sized parts.

1.6.2.3 Glass Bath Method

This method was developed to solve the problems of handling and pressurizing glass capsules. Ceramic green bodies are embedded in a glass powder with a relatively low melting point, and the temperature is raised under reduced pressure to soften the glass. Pressure is raised in the glass bath, and temperature is also increased; HIP follows. The keys to the success of this method are the composition of the glass, and the temperature and pressure profiles. If the melting point of the glass is too low, the ceramic green bodies may float on the surface of the glass bath and the air-tight nature of the capsule may be compromised.

1.6.2.4 Coating Method

With this method, an airtight coating of metal or ceramic is applied to the surface of a sintered part of 80% TD or more by CVD or PVD; HIP follows.[5] It may be technically difficult to use this method with green bodies of 80% TD or less with large open porosities because the coating layer generally is not very thick.

1.6.2.5 Sintering-Plus-HIP Method

With this method, green bodies of ceramics are first sintered by a conventional method to the state of closed porosity (i.e., $>95\%$ TD), and then the remaining closed porosity is eliminated by HIP to produce full-density sintered parts. The complicated process using the sealing techniques described earlier is replaced by the conventional sintering method; in addition, removal of capsules and other extra processes is not needed. For these reasons this method is particularly suitable for production on a commercial basis. In particular, HIP can be used for small parts on a mass production scale, so this method is less expensive than hot pressing. In Japan this method is employed to manufacture soft ferrites for magnetic recording heads[6] or cutting tool inserts of Al_2O_3 and Al_2O_3-TiC.[7]

In the methods discussed in sections 1.6.2.1 through 1.6.2.4, in which sealing techniques are used, the amount of sintering aids can be minimized and the temperature for HIP is the highest of all the procedures. For this reason the microstructure of the finished product depends totally on the temperature control during the HIP. However, none of the sealing techniques is suitable for mass production. As a result, all these methods are now used only for experiments or small-scale production of special items. In contrast, the sintering-plus-HIP method is being increasingly employed in the manufacture of oxide ceramics in Japan. Nitride ceramics, however, may decompose if an inert gas such as Ar is used. For these materials the use of nitrogen gas in HIP is being investigated.

1.6.3 Densification of Sintered Si_3N_4 in Nitrogen

Densification of Si_3N_4 by HIP has been attempted by Yamada[8] and Uy and Hermann[9] using glass capsules. The author and his colleagues were of the opinion that the sintering-plus-HIP method was advantageous in commercial production for the reasons stated in the previous section, and sought a method of densifying Si_3N_4 sintered parts by HIP.[10] First, they used HIP to sinter specimens in Ar gas for densification. However, Si_3N_4 decomposed during the HIP process, and densification did not always result in higher strength. The purpose of the subsequent studies, therefore, was to investigate the effect of using nitrogen gas on suppression of the decomposition of Si_3N_4. The composition of the tested products is shown in Table 1.6.1. HPSN-1 and HPSN-2 were hot pressed, and SSN-1 was made by conventional sintering. SSN-2 was a commercially available sintered product made by a Japanese manufacturer of ceramics.

Figure 1.6.2 shows the flexural strength of each product before and after HIP in relation to the pressurizing gas used. The flexural strength increased markedly after HIP in SSN-1 when nitrogen gas was used. However, some products showed a reduction in flexural strength after HIP in Ar gas. The possible reason for this is the decomposition of Si_3N_4 and the difference in the microstructure before HIP. The flexural strength of SSN-1 was tested before and after HIP in nitrogen gas in about 30 samples, and the mean strength and Weibull modulus were calculated. The mean flexural strength increased from 573 to 805 MPa, and the mean Weibull modulus from 5.2 to 8.0 (see Figure 1.6.3).

The results of this experiment suggest that the sintering-plus-

Table 1.6.1 Composition of Tested Si_3N_4 Products

	Additive(s)	Density (g/cm³)
HPSN-1	6% Y_2O_3-2% Al_2O_3	2.64–3.25
HPSN-2	5% MgO	3.16–3.18
SSN-1	6% Y_2O_3-2% Al_2O_3-3% MgO	3.05–3.22
SSN-2	Unknown	3.16–3.21

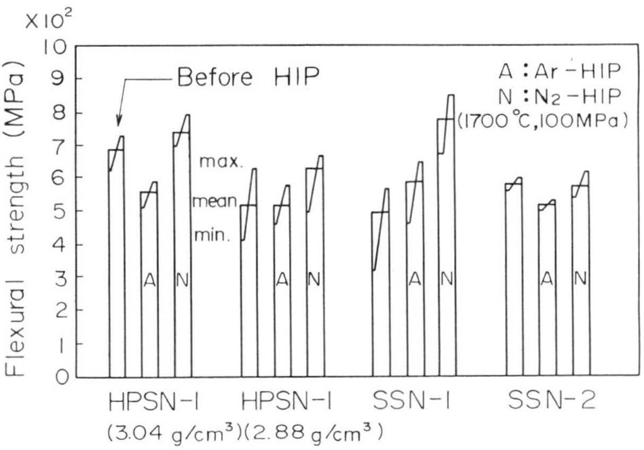

Figure 1.6.2 Flexural strength of tested products.

HIP method, that is, a combination of conventional sintering with HIP, may produce very strong and reliable Si_3N_4 parts. However, the experiment also showed that the microstructure of the sintered product before HIP is crucial in maximizing the effect of HIP. The sintering-plus-HIP method may be widely used in the production of Si_3N_4 parts that need high reliability.

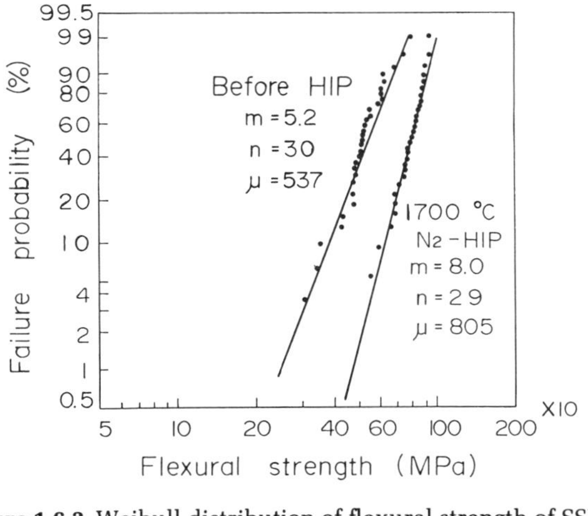

Figure 1.6.3 Weibull distribution of flexural strength of SSN-1.

1.6.4 Structure of HIP Equipment

Conventional HIP equipment consists of a pressure vessel incorporating an electric furnace, a high-pressure gas system to supply inert gas at a high pressure, a pressure-transmitting medium, an electric power system with a control unit to supply power to the electric furnace, and a gas storage unit to store the pressure-transmitting medium[11] (see Figure 1.6.4). The pressure vessel comprises a cylinder, upper and lower closures, and a frame supporting the axial force on the closures. The cylinder and the upper closure have a water cooling system to remove the heat generated by the electric furnace in the vessel and thus keep the temperature of the system below the specification limit. The furnace in the pressure vessel consists of a heating device, a thermal insulating mantle, and a temperature-measuring device. This furnace is the most important part of the entire HIP equipment and is designed to maintain temperature and heat dissipation at certain levels by controlling the natural convection of the pressure-transmitting gas at high pressure. The conventional heating device is divided into several zones, and uniform temperature is kept by natural convection controlled by adjusting the power supply to each zone. The heating device is made of various materials,

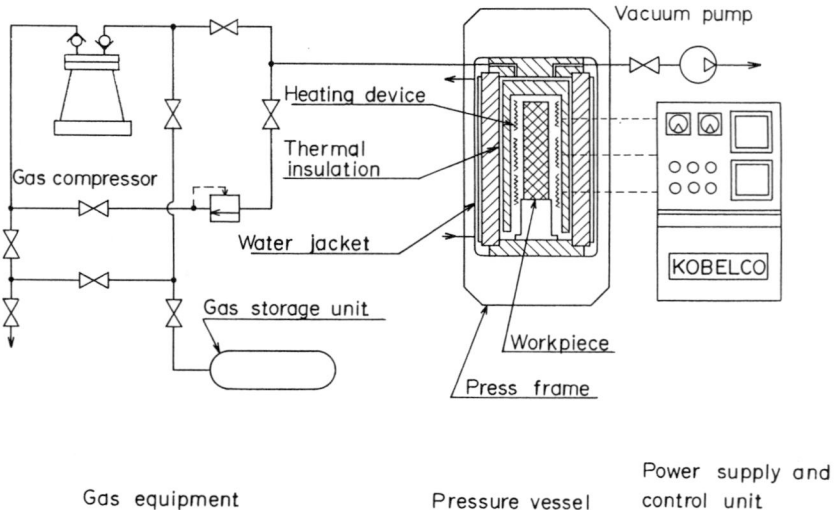

Figure 1.6.4 Schematic of HIP system.

depending on the temperature needed. Fe-Al-Cr alloy is used up to 1250°C, Mo up to 1500°C, and graphite for higher temperatures.

The major part in the high-pressure gas system is the compressor. Inert gas is normally used in HIP equipment; for this reason, heat decomposition occurs if an oily lubricant is used. This may cause carbon to be deposited and electrical breakdown to occur. Oil-free compressors or diaphragm compressors are usually selected to prevent this.

Popular electric supply systems and control units employ thyristor devices. With these systems and units, furnace temperature is controlled by a microprocessor.

The technology for HIP equipment has rapidly advanced in the last few years, and the function of the equipment has diversified. What follows is a brief look at recent developments in HIP equipment for ceramics.

1.6.5 HIP Equipment for Ceramics

Typical temperatures and pressures for ceramic HIP are given in Table 1.6.2. The temperature for ceramic HIP ranges from 1000 to 2000°C. This differs very much from metals, which are mostly given HIP treatment at 1500°C or less. Ceramic HIP on a commercial basis has been used only for soft ferrites, magnetic recording heads, or alumina cutting tool inserts, for which a temperature of 1400°C or less is enough. One of the reasons for this is that the technology for HIP equipment with stable performance at 1500°C or higher has been established only recently; another is the cost of the HIP process. The ceramic parts just cited are all small; therefore, HIP on a commercial

Table 1.6.2 Typical HIP Conditions for Various Ceramics

	Temperature (°C)	Pressure (MPa)	Density (% TD)
Ni-Zn-ferrite	1050–1180	100	>99.5
Mn-Zn-ferrite	1180–1250	100	>99.5
PZT	1000–1100	100	>99.5
Al_2O_3	1350–1450	100	~100
Al_2O_3-30 TiC	1450–1600	100	~100
Si_3N_4-Al_2O_3-Y_2O_3	1700–1800	100 (N_2)	~100
TiN	1850	145	99
BN	1850	145	97
Si_3N_4	1900	145	98
SiC	1950–2050	100	~100

Sintering station   HIP station

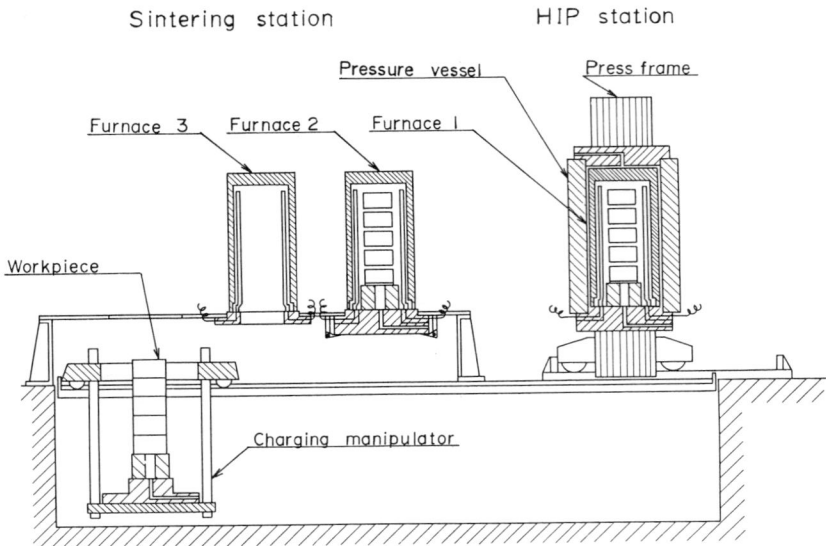

Figure 1.6.5 Typical schematic of a pre-heating modular-type HIP system.

basis is possible, as it is less expensive than hot pressing. Further efforts are being made to reduce HIP cost through modification and improvement of HIP equipment.

HIP equipment for high temperatures has been developed in which the furnace structure is made of solid graphite, flexible graphite sheets, and carbon fibers. This equipment can generate heat up to 2000°C.[12] The major use of this type of equipment is R&D, but equipment 350 mm in diameter and 1000 mm high was installed in 1982 for commercial production.[13]

The major way to reduce HIP costs is to shorten the cycle time. To shorten the cooling time, a rapid cooling type and a modular type in which cooling is done outside the pressure vessel have been developed, and several sets of this equipment are now used on a commercial basis.[11] Recently, in order to shorten the heating time as well, a pre-heating modular type has been developed in which sintering in the sintering-plus-HIP method or sealing processes in the glass bath method are also done in the furnace structure of the modular-type HIP equipment. Figure 1.6.5 is a schematic of such equipment.

1.6.6 Conclusion

In recent years ceramics have been widely recognized as useful for making electronic or high-temperature parts, there is a hope that the features of ceramics will be further improved by densification. In the HIP process a high pressure of 100 to 200 MPa is used at a high temperature. Attention is directed to this technique, as it is very likely that effective densification is available. This technique has already been used in production of some oxide ceramics, and its use will expand; nitride or carbide ceramics will be produced by HIP in the near future.

References

1. Hanes, H. D., Seifert, D. A., and Watts C. R., *MCIC Report,* MCIC-77-34 (1977).
2. Brockway, M. C., and Niesz, D. E., *Research and Development Report,* ECOM-0133-F (1970).
3. Friegesmann, J. et al., *NTIS Report* N81-19128 (1979).
4. Havel, C. J., *SAE Report* 720183 (1972).
5. Ogawa, K. et al., *Nippon Tungsten Review* 11:28 (1978).
6. Takama, E., *IEEE Transaction on Magnetics* MAG-15:1858 (1979).
7. Ogawa, K. et al., *Nippon Tungsten Review* 10:50 (1977).
8. Yamada, T., and Shimada, M., *Am. Ceram. Soc. Bull.* 60:1225 (1981).
9. Uy, J. C., and Hermann, E. R., Ceramics for high performance applications — II:1011 (1978).
10. Homma, K. et al., *Proc. 20th Japan Congress on Material Research,* Kyoto, Japan, 1982, p. 213.
11. Ishii, T. et al., *Proc. 2nd International Conference on Isostatic Pressing,* vol. 1, Stratford-upon-Avon, England, 1982, p. 20–1.
12. Fujikawa, T. et al., *Proc. 2nd International Conference on Isostatic Pressing,* vol. 1, Stratford-upon-Avon, England, 1982, p. 12–1.
13. Fujikawa, T. et al., *Proc. International Symposium on Ceramic Components for Engine,* Hakone, Japan 1983.

1.7 Application of Hot Pressing

Osami Kamigaito

1.7.1 Introduction

Hot pressing is a powerful method for increasing the density of refractory powders as well as powders that tend to decompose under ambient pressure. Products made using this process are of high strength and high density. But its application is limited to ceramics of rather simple shape, as powder can not flow freely even under very high pressure. Therefore, to make dense ceramics with complex shapes by hot pressing, some special methods are needed.

This section discusses the application of the hot pressing technique to some refractory materials, including silicon nitride, sialon, and silicon carbide, as well as the technique's application to complete-shaped ceramics and to joining. Some ceramics, such as those including oxides with transient elements, are very sensitive to atmosphere and decompose or form oxygen deficient oxides under a reductive atmosphere. This suggests that a suitable atmosphere would enhance densification and reduce the hot pressing temperature and pressure. As an example, hot pressing of PZT under an atmosphere containing a small amount of fluorine is presented.

1.7.2 Hot Pressing of Some Refractory Ceramics and Additives for Sintering

In Japan most hot pressing is done using uniaxial or biaxial pressure. In any case the pressing instruments, dies and punches, are ordinarily made of graphite. Because of the limited strength of the graphite material, maximum pressure is limited to about 30 MPa. This pressure is not sufficient to densify most refractory materials of high purity, and some additives are needed to improve densification. Even in pressureless sintering, coercive forces act on powders. When the powders are sintered into a dense body, they lose energy mainly because of the difference between specific surface energy and the specific grain boundary energy. This loss is associated with the reduction of apparent volume of the powders. According to thermodynamic considerations, the mean stress needed to reduce the volume, σ_s, is given as follows:[1]

$$\sigma_s = -\frac{\Delta F}{\Delta V} \tag{1.7.1}$$

where ΔF and ΔV are the energy change and volume change before and after densification, respectively.

Estimated σ_s is determined to be about 3 MPa, given values of 1800 erg/cm² for the specific surface energy and 1000 erg/cm² for the specific boundary energy. The maximum pressure in hot pressing is not high in comparison with the estimated stress in pressureless sintering, in which some additives are needed to enhance densification. Therefore, additives must also be used in hot pressing to enhance sintering.

For the densification of silicon nitride, which is one of the most refractory ceramics, the author studied the influence of adding MgO,[2] Al_2O_3,[2,3] AlN,[3,4] and SiO_2,[5,6] on densification. With any one of these additives, fully densified bodies were obtained under pressures of 20 to 30 MPa and at temperatures of 1700–1750°C. Above 1800°C, large weight losses were observed. This was thought to be due to the decomposition of silicon nitride.

The densification of Si_3N_4 with Al_2O_3 is shown in Figure 1.7.1. The phases detected in the hot pressed bodies depend on the composition of the starting powders. With the addition of less than 30 m/o MgO,[7] the crystalline phase in the hot pressed body was only β-silicon nitride. The lattice constant of the silicon nitride was identical to that of pure silicon nitride. With the addition of MgO in amounts greater than 30 m/o, $MgSiN_2$ was produced in the body. This indicates that some amorphous or glassy phase is produced when silicon nitride

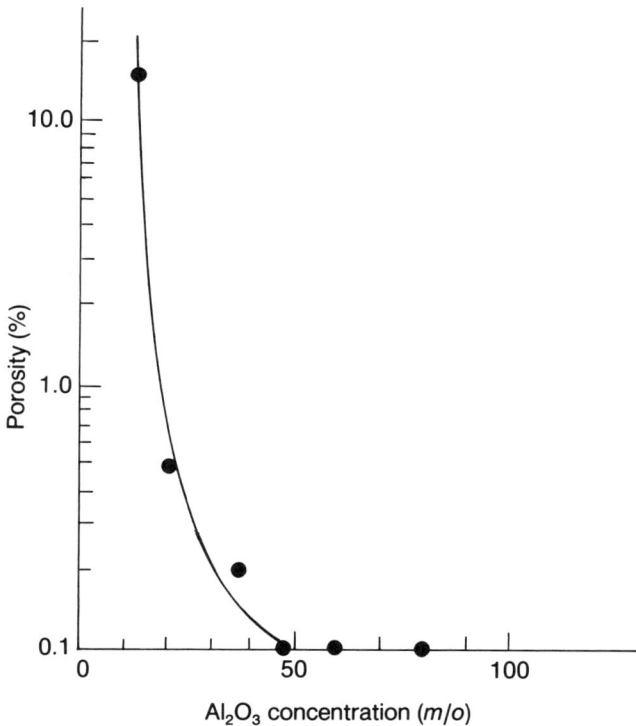

Figure 1.7.1 Densification of Si_3N_4 with addition of Al_2O_3.

containing MgO is heated above 1700°C. Moreover, an exchange of oxygen and nitrogen occurs between silicon nitride and MgO. It is therefore possible that some nitrogen glass is formed in the sintered body.

Some new phases were found with the addition of Al_2O_3, AlN and Al_2O_3, or AlN and SiO_2. One was a solid solution of β-silicon nitride with an expanded lattice constant,[8] and the other was a new crystalline phase whose composition was difficult to determine (X-phase).[2] Today, both are termed "Sialon." It was also found that the formation of the X-phase is associated with a weight loss. The weight loss reaches 40 w/o at a maximum for a composition of 40 m/o silicon nitride and 60 m/o Al_2O_3. The weight loss is thought to result from the vaporization of SiO. The weight loss is reduced by using fine-grain alumina powders or by adding AlN. For example, weight loss in the specimen with 60 m/o alumina with grains 8 μm in diameter is about 30% at 1750°C in comparison with 18% for that with alumina with grains 3 μm in diameter. Addition of AlN enhances rapid formation of the solid solution, which would reduce the loss. Simultaneous addition of AlN and Al_2O_3 in equimolar concentrations results in the slight presence or absence of the X-phase. The solid solubility limit of AlN and Al_2O_3 is estimated to be about 70 m/o. This value has been confirmed by many researchers.

The addition of AlN and SiO_2 also yields a solid solution. The similarity of the Si_3N_4-AlN-SiO_2 system and the Si_3N_4-AlN-Al_2O_3 system can be understood from the following:[5]

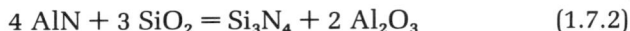

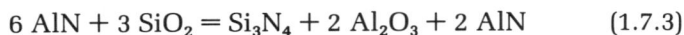

$$4 \text{ AlN} + 3 \text{ SiO}_2 = \text{Si}_3\text{N}_4 + 2 \text{ Al}_2\text{O}_3 \tag{1.7.2}$$

$$6 \text{ AlN} + 3 \text{ SiO}_2 = \text{Si}_3\text{N}_4 + 2 \text{ Al}_2\text{O}_3 + 2 \text{ AlN} \tag{1.7.3}$$

The right-hand side of Equations (1.7.2) and (1.7.3) ($Si_3N_4 - \text{AlN} - Al_2O_3$) gives the solid solution and X-phase, and the left-hand side of Si_3N_4-AlN-SiO_2 gives the same results. Some regions in both systems are identical. The weight loss and properties of the sintered body, however, are not the same. Weight loss is large in the system containing SiO_2, and the hardness of the ceramic is a bit low.

Properties such as oxidation resistance, hardness, and the coefficient of thermal expansion in systems containing the solid solution are superior to those in systems composed of silicon nitride and MgO. One example is shown in Figure 1.7.2 for abrasive resistance of ceramics compared with hot-pressed silicon nitride doped with 5 m/o MgO. The fracture stress of Si_3N_4 with Al_2O_3 is very high (0.8 – 1 GPa) and very useful.

Figure 1.7.2 graph axes: y-axis "Weight loss (g)" with marks 0, 1.0, 2.0; x-axis "Al₂O₃ concentration (m/o)" with marks 0, 50, 100. Labels "Si₃N₄-5MgO" and "Si₃N₄-Al₂O₃".

Sliding velocity: 43 m/min
Averaged pressure: 25 g/cm³
Time: 30 hr
Abrasive powder: Green SiC # 800

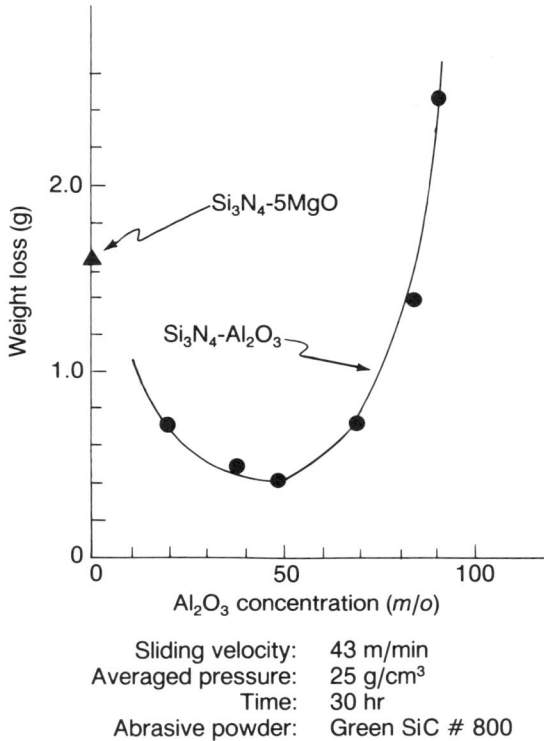

Figure 1.7.2 Abrasive resistivity of hot-pressed Si_3N_4 with addition of Al_2O_3.

Hot pressing of Si_3N_4 containing Y_2O_3 and Al_2O_3 was studied by Tsuge and co-workers.[9] This yielded one of the highest strength ceramics. Their study is presented by Komeya (see Chapter 3, section 3.3). Hot pressing of Sialon was also studied by Mitomo and co-workers, and their results are presented by Mitomo (see Chapter 3, section 3.5). Densification of AlN is achieved by the addition of about 3% Al. AlN densification using Y_2O_3 and SiO_2 additives was also studied by Komeya and co-workers.[10] These additives resulted in high fracture stress. Hot-pressing applications of Al_2O_3 are also reported by many researchers. The addition of MgO is known to inhibit Al_2O_3 grain growth in hot pressing and to yield high-strength bodies. Kagami[11] studied the densification of Al_2O_3 in relation to grain growth, pressure, and temperature.

Hot pressing of SiC has also been studied by many researchers.

Tanaka and co-workers[12] studied SiC with the addition of Al, and Tanaka and Inomata[13] reported results using AlB_2. They obtained high-density SiC.

1.7.3 Applications to Ceramics with Complex Shapes and Joining

As mentioned earlier, powders in hot pressing do not flow freely even under high pressure. This prevents ceramics from being hot pressed in complex shapes, because even if the punch is fashioned in the same profile as that required for the ceramic, the part of the largest dimension in the direction of hot pressing (BB′ in Figure 1.7.3a) is densified first and prevents further densification of other smaller dimension parts (e.g., AA′ in Figure 1.7.3a). The difficulty can be avoided by placing complementary parts[1,14] made of the same powder as the sintered body (in Figure 1.7.3b) in combination with the required ceramic body.

Movement of powders during hot pressing is complicated, and the flow pattern must be known to obtain precision dimensions required for the ceramic body. The flow pattern has been determined by applying a scribing article method to compacted powders. The

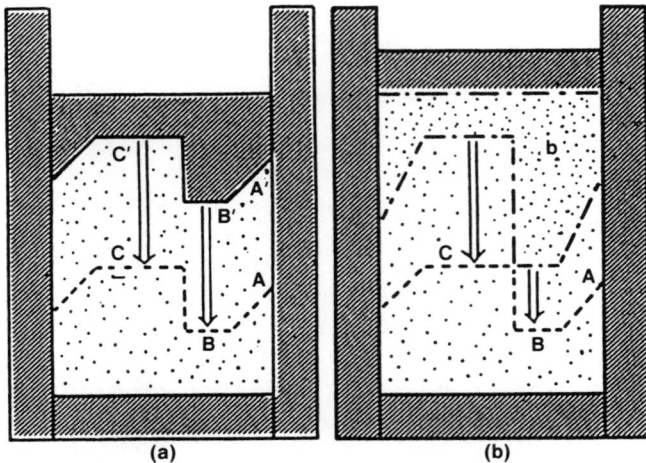

Figure 1.7.3 Schematic of hot pressing of complicated shape ceramics. (a) Ordinary method; the shrinkage to the full density is not the same for A, B, and C. (b) Complementary piece method; the shrinkage is the same.

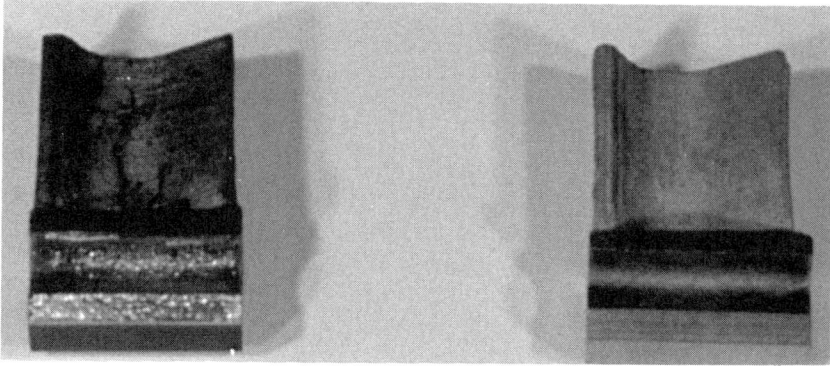

Figure 1.7.4 Model blades made by hot pressing (using complementary pieces).

study revealed that powders move uniformly in hot pressing except for the parts within a 5-mm region of the punch and die. Therefore, the central part of a die must be used for the required ceramic body. As an experiment, model blades for a gas turbine rotor were made by hot pressing. Compacted silicon nitride powder mixed with additives was shaped into the form of the blade using a dimension two times larger in the pressing direction. Two complementary pieces for the blade were made of the same compacted powder. For easy separation of the pieces after hot pressing, all specimens were coated with BN powder. Hot pressing occurred under a pressure of 20 MPa. After cooling, the specimens were separated into three pieces, and a model blade of hot pressed silicon nitride with 98% relative density was obtained. The deviation in dimensions was within 0.2 mm. An example is shown in Figure 1.7.4.

A similar method was developed by Lange.[15] In this method, BN powder is used for pressing media surrounding a specimen. BN powder does not flow freely; therefore, the dimensional accuracy would not be as great in comparison with the method mentioned above.

Also, some researchers attempted to join ceramics with ceramics using hot pressing. Iseki and co-workers[16] studied joining a sintered silicon carbide plate with that of the same material, using silicon carbide powder mixed with a small amount of B and C as the joining media. Joining was accomplished at a pressure of 10 MPa at 1650°C for 30 minutes. The joined specimen proved to have high strength (500 MPa at 20°C and 200 MPa at 1500°C). Tabata and co-workers[17] studied joining dense silicon nitride plates. They joined the plates at 0.1 MPa at 1300–1600°C for 1 hour in N_2. The joined plates had a bending strength of about 500 MPa.

1.7.4 Atmospheric Effects

The atmosphere in an ordinary hot press using a graphite die and punch is composed mainly of N_2 and CO. Therefore, some ceramics decompose or change composition during hot pressing. For such ceramics a nonreductive atmosphere is needed, and Al_2O_3 is used for the punch and die. Moreover, some ceramics decompose at elevated temperatures even under nonreductive atmospheres. For densification of such ceramics, high pressures or suitable atmospheres are needed.

PZT is one of the most widely used ceramics. Densification is needed for its application; however, sintering under an ambient atmosphere is not simple, and hot pressing is applied. In the hot press, a reductive atmosphere must be avoided. In one study an alumina die and punch are used. To reduce the pressure, control of the atmosphere was studied.

Finely powdered PZT was pressed into a 30-mm-diameter disk. The disk was placed into a die with a 40-mm inner diameter. The gap between the disk and the die was filled with a mixture of Al_2O_3 powder and fluor-phlogopite powder of 20–100 w/o. For comparison, a PZT disk was hot pressed in Al_2O_3 powder without fluor-phlogopite. A disk of $BaTiO_3$ doped with fluor-phlogopite (0.2–1 w/o) was also hot pressed. Hot pressing was carried out at 5–20 MPa and 1000–1200°C for 1 hour.

The density of the hot-pressed PZT is shown in Figure 1.7.5. The specimen doped with fluor-phlogopite and that placed into the filling powder could be densified easily at low pressure. The influence of fluor-phlogopite was almost the same for the specimen doped with fluor-phlogopite and that placed into the powder. Another fluorine, BaF_2, yielded a similar effect on the densification of PZT.

Examination of densified PZT revealed that it was composed of only $BaTiO_3$. Even traces of fluorine were detected in PZT placed into the powder with fluor-phlogopite as well as with BaF_2. The easy densification was thought to be caused by the formation of a glassy phase under the influence of a very small amount of fluorine in the atmosphere, through which the solution-precipitation mechanism would occur.

Another important example of the atmospheric effect on the property of sintered ceramics is shown by Komeya and co-workers.

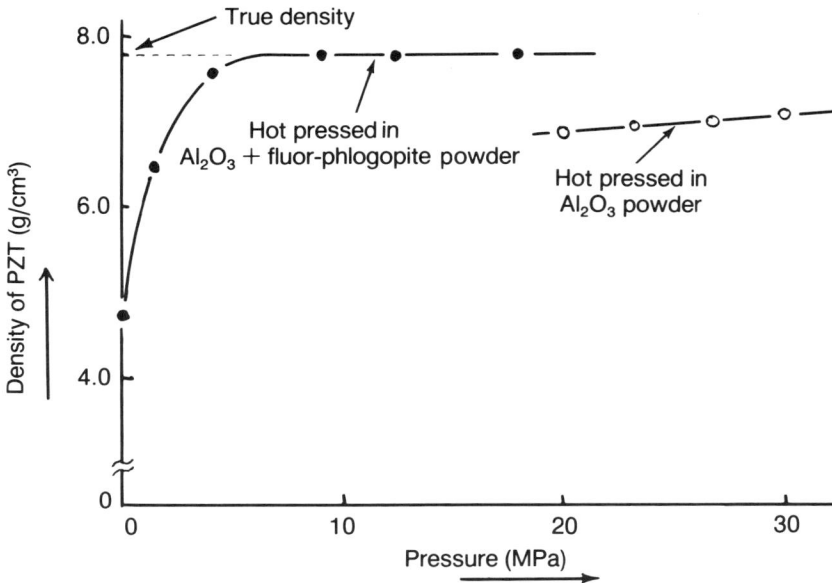

Figure 1.7.5 Density of PZT hot pressed under the influence of fluor-phlogopite.

They found heat-treated Si_3N_4 doped with Al_2O_3 and Y_2O_3 in AlN powder enhances crystallization of the boundary phase and that its strength at elevated temperature is improved.[18] Their study is presented in section 3.3.

Controlling the atmosphere in hot pressing is a very important step in the densification process and represents an improvement in ceramic techniques.

References

1. Kamigaito, O., *J. High Pressure Inst. Jpn.* 16:49 (1978).
2. Oyama, Y., and Kamigaito, O., *J. Ceram. Soc. Jpn.* 80:327 (1972).
3. Kamigaito, O., and Oyama, Y., Jpn. Patent 53-1763 (1978), U.S. Patent 3,903,230 (1975), U.S. Patent 4,066,468 (1978), Dt. Patent 2,262,785 (1978).
4. Oyama, Y., *J. Ceram. Soc. Jpn.* 82:351 (1974).
5. Kamiya, N., Oyama, Y., and Kamigaito, O., *J. Ceram. Soc. Jpn.* 83:553 (1975).

6. Kamigaito, O., and Oyama, Y., Jpn. Patent 51-37656, 51-37657 (1976).

7. Oyama, Y., and Kamigaito, O., *J. Ceram. Soc. Jpn.* 81:292 (1973).

8. Oyama, Y., and Kamigaito, O., Jpn. *J. Appl. Phys.* 10:1637 (1971).

9. Tsuge, A., Nishida, K., and Komatsu, M., *J. Am. Ceram. Soc.* 58:1637 (1975).

10. Komeya, K., Inoue, H., and Tsuge, A., *J. Am. Ceram. Soc.* 57:411 (1974).

11. Kagami, Y., *J. Jpn. Soc. Powder and Powder Metellurgy* 14:353 (1967).

12. Tanaka, H., Inomata, Y., and Kawabata, H., *J. Ceram. Soc. Jpn.* 88:353 (1980).

13. Tanaka, H., and Inomata, Y., *J. Ceram. Soc. Jpn.* 87:541 (1979).

14. Kamigaito, O., and Oyama, Y., Jap. Patent 52-31364 (1977), U.S. Patent 3,845,185 (1977), U.K. Patent 1,356,445 (1977), Dt. Patent 2,135,876 (1978).

15. Lange, F. F., and Terwilliger, G. R., *Am. Ceram. Soc. Bull.* 52:563 (1973).

16. Iseki, T., Arakawa, K., and Susuki, H., *J. Mat. Sci.* 15:1049 (1980).

17. Tabata, H., and Kanzaki, S., Paper Presented at International Symposium on Ceramic Components for Engine, Hakone, Japan, 1983.

18. Tsuge, A., and Nishida, K., *Am. Ceram. Soc. Bull.* 57:424 (1978).

1.8 Coating of Hard Refractory Materials by Chemical Vapor Deposition (CVD)

Kohzo Sugiyama

1.8.1 Carbides, Nitrides, and Carbonitrides

TiC, TiN, TiC_xN_y, SiC, Si_3N_4, BN, and AlN are included in the category of carbides, nitrides, and carbonitrides. Among these TiC is the most widely used, mainly as a coating material for cutting tools.

Lee and co-workers[1] investigated the nucleation and growth of TiC from a gas mixture of $TiCl_4$, CH_4, and H_2 on cemented carbide (WC-Co) in relation to the Co content of the substrate. They found that TiC nucleates at the interfaces of WC-grains and the Co phase followed by secondary nucleation and growth propagation on the WC grains. Except for the initial stage, the growth rate of the TiC layer is not affected by the Co content of the substrate. Lee and colleagues derived a growth rate G in connection with the total pressure p and reaction temperature T as follows:

$$G = Cp^{1/2} \exp\left(-\frac{185 \text{ (kJ)}}{RT}\right) \tag{1.8.1}$$

where C is a constant.

From an analogous viewpoint, the carbon activity of a steel substrate profoundly affects the growth rate of the TiC layer when the gas phase contains $TiCl_4$ and H_2 and the reactant carbon is supplied fully by solid-phase diffusion from carbon-containing steels. Roser[2] reported on the TiC-coating rates related to the carbon activity of the respective alloyed steels.

When TiC layers are coated onto cemented carbide, decarburized interlayers (η-phase) are apt to be formed which cause a lowering of the toughness of the coated insert. Lee and Chun[3] proposed controlling the $CH_4/TiCl_4$ ratio in the reactant gas in order to decrease the η-layer thickness. The η-phase ceases to exist at a $CH_4/TiCl_4$ ratio of 1.25 at 1050°C. Sarin and Lindstrom[4] also reported on the marked η-layer reduction effect of precarburization using 4% CH_4 for 4 hours.

Transmission electron microscopy (TEM) is superior to SEM in magnification. Vuorinen and Horsewell[5] observed interlayers of TiC-coated cemented carbide. Very thin foils, within and parallel to the coating layer, were prepared by sawing, polishing, and finally ion-beam milling. These researchers found that the interlayer is composed of seven sub-interfaces: WC-TiC, Co-TiC, γ(cubic transition metal carbide)-TiC, $M_{12}C$-TiC, $M_{12}C$-WC, $M_{12}C$-Co, and $M_{12}C$-γ.

In the TiN coating process on cemented carbide, the deposition temperature may be markedly lowered in the $TiCl_4$-NH_3-H_2 system compared with that in the $TiCl_4$-N_2-H_2 system. Sjöstrand[6] coated a TiC layer 1.5 μm thick from a $TiCl_4$-CH_4-H_2 atmosphere at 1000–1050°C in order to improve adherence. Then a thin TiN layer was coated from $TiCl_4$-N_2-H_2 at the same temperature, the temperature was decreased to 650–700°C, and the nitrogen source was changed to ammonia. The micrographs of the fracture surface show that the TiN layer is composed of very fine grains, in contrast with the columnar structure of the layer prepared from the $TiCl_4$-N_2-H_2 atmosphere. When the TiB_2 interlayer is undercoated on a carbon steel substance, an amorphous TiN_x film grows on it from a gas mixture of $TiCl_4$, N_2, and H_2 at 800–950°C.[7] The TiN_x film exhibits Vickers microhardness of 1800 under a load of 100 g. Cho and co-workers[8] deposited TiN, TiC_xN_y, and TiC films onto a cemented carbide substrate from a gas mixture of $TiCl_4$, CH_4, N_2, and H_2 in the temperature range of 950–1100°C. Carbon content in the TiC_xN_y films increased with increases in deposition temperature and CH_4 reactant gas concentration. Usually TiC, TiN, and TiC_xN_y films are coated using CH_4 and N_2 or NH_3; however, Bonetti and co-workers[9] examined the use of CH_3CN, $(CH_3)_3N$, $CH_3(NH)_2CH_3$, and HCN as carbon-nitrogen sources for TiC_xN_y deposition.

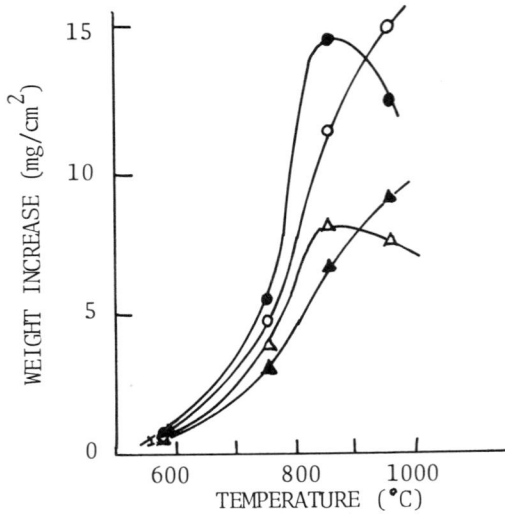

Figure 1.8.1 Dependence of deposition rates of TiC_xN_y on temperature; Gaseous systems (from M. Bonetti-Lang et al., Proc. 8th International Conference on CVD, 1981, p. 606).

○: $TiCl_4$-CH_3CN-H_2 ●: $TiCl_4$-$(CH_3)_3N$-H_2
△: $TiCl_4$-$CH_3(NH)_2CH_3$-H_2 ▲: $TiCl_4$-HCN-H_2

Figure 1.8.1 shows deposition rates as a function of temperature. Except for $(CH_3)N$, TiC_xN_y deposition starts between 550–600°C, and the C/N ratios in the coatings are roughly proportional to those of the gaseous C-N-compounds. Lifetime or toughness tests for tool applications showed that the TiC_xN_y coated from the CH_3CN source was the best choice, and the performance of inserts thus prepared was superior to that obtained using ordinary CVD.

ZrC_xN_{1-x} can also be deposited from a gas mixture of $ZrCl_4$, CH_4, N_2, and H_2 in the temperature range of 950–1150°C. Takahashi and co-workers[10] obtained ZrC_xN_{1-x} coatings on carbon steel or a graphite substrate. The x of ZrC_xN_{1-x} was controlled from zero to unity by varying the CH_4/N_2 ratios in the feed gas and/or by varying the deposition temperature. The relation of x and the lattice constant is shown in Figure 1.8.2. Hexagonal BN(hBN) films were coated from a gas mixture of NH_3, BCl_3, and H_2 in the temperature range of 250–700°C onto copper substrates.[11] Whole films were amorphous and transparent, and films coated at temperatures below 500°C contained BH and NH_2 bonds. From the same reactant system, Takahashi and co-workers deposited hBN onto carbon steel[12] and Ni plate[13] in tem-

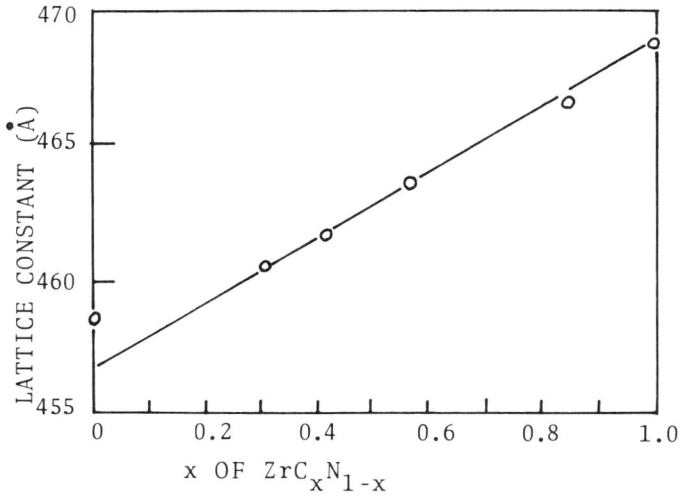

Figure 1.8.2 Lattice constant versus composition of ZrC_xN_{1-x} [from T. Takahashi et al., *J. Less-Common Metals* 80:171 (1981)].

perature ranges of 900–1200°C and 800–1050°C, respectively. Transparent and amorphous films turned into crystalline opaque films by heat treatment at temperatures above 1050°C. The hBN films were thermally stable in air up to 900°C and had a refractive index of 1.65 and electrical conductivity of $4.7 \times 10^{-13} Sm^{-1}$ at 22°C.

AlN has attracted attention because of its refractory and dielectric properties. AlN films are ordinarily coated from a gas system of $AlBr_3$-NH_3-H_2 at 450–850°C. Pauleau and co-workers[14] deposited AlN on a silicon substrate and analyzed the film in terms of Rutherford backscattering spectroscopy. Figure 1.8.3 shows that the numbers of Al and N increase linearly with the duration of deposition; however, Br and O remain independent of the duration, which suggests that Br and O exist only in the surface layer. An attempt to deposit AlN from $[(R_2N)_2AlH]$ (R: Me or Et) was performed by Takahaski and co-workers.[15,16] Although deposition took place in the temperature range of 300–1000°C, carbon was included in the films deposited at high temperature, and the composition of the film obtained at 800°C corresponded to Al_5C_3N. Vickers microhardness increased with increases in deposition temperature and reached a maximum value of 2800 at 900°C.

In the Si ribbon pulling process, a heated die contacts the molten, high-purity Si, and the impurities in the substrate diffuse into the

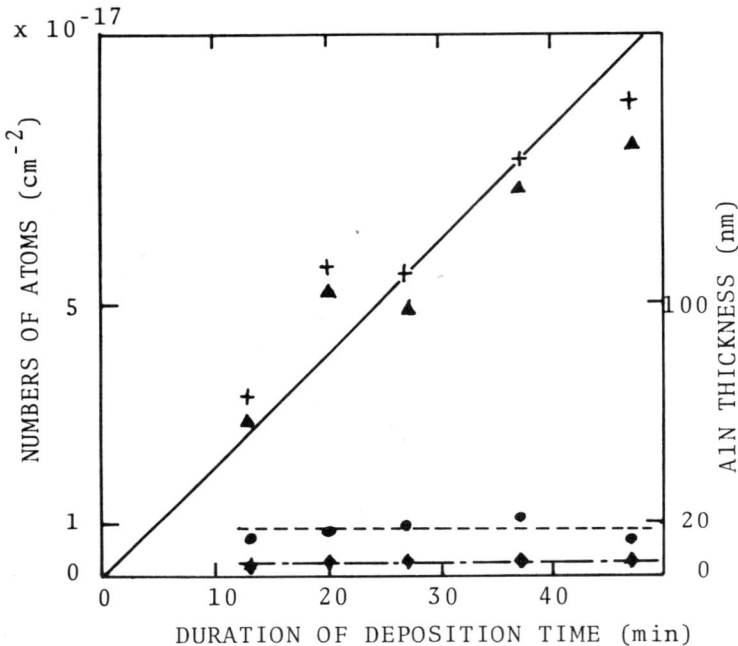

Figure 1.8.3 Numbers of Al, N. O. and Br atoms per cm² in AlN films measured by Rutherford backscattering spectroscopy versus duration of deposition (from Y. Pauleau et al., Proc. 8th International Conference on CVD, 1981, p. 104):

+: Al, ▲: N, ●: 0, ◆: Br(×10)

molten Si. High-purity Si_3N_4 or SiO_xN_y was coated onto reaction-bonded or hot-pressed Si_3N_4 at 1000°C to suppress the impurity diffusion into molten Si.[17] The reactant gas for Si_3N_4 consisted of SiH_4-NH_3, and for SiO_xN_y, SiH_4-NH_3-NO_2. SiO_xN_y coatings were converted to β-rich Si_3N_4 by immersion into molten Si. Oda and co-workers[18] deposited Si_3N_4 onto a graphite substrate from a gas mixture of $SiCl_4$, NH_3, and N_2 using a quartz-glass reaction tube. The phases of the deposits were assigned to β at a deposition temperature of 1300°C, to $\alpha + \beta$ at 1250°C, and to α at 1150°C. Formation of β-phase coatings at relatively low temperatures was ascribed to SiO vapor from the reaction tube, which acted as a catalyst for phase transition. Hirai and Hayashi examined the effect of TiN codeposition with Si_3N_4 on phase selection.[19,20] Normally, amorphous or α-type Si_3N_4 deposits from a gas mixture of $SiCl_4$, NH_3, and H_2 at 1350–1450°C; however, β-Si_3N_4

deposited including 3.5–4.3% TiN from a TiCl$_4$-containing vapor. These researchers observed the TiN dispersions using an electron microscope. TiN in the α-Si$_3$N$_4$ matrix, deposited at 1250°C, consisted of granules with an average size of 10 nm; that in the β-Si$_3$N$_4$ deposited at 1350–1450°C consisted of columns with a diameter of several nm having an axis extending parallel to the direction of the β-Si$_3$N$_4$ crystal's *c*-axis (Figure 1.8.4).

Goto and co-workers[21] measured various thermal properties of amorphous Si$_3$N$_4$-C (C content; 2–6 wt%) composites prepared by CVD on a graphite substrate using SiCl$_4$, NH$_3$, C$_3$H$_8$, and H$_2$ at 1300°C and 4 KPa. The thermal diffusivity of the composite was much smaller than that for amorphous Si$_3$N$_4$, and the specific heat of the composite was independent of the carbon content and increased with

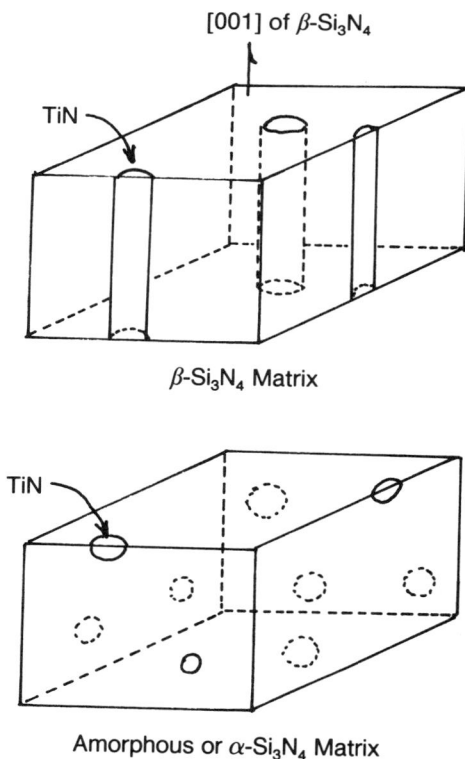

Figure 1.8.4 Schematic representations of the microstructure of the CVD Si$_3$N$_4$-TiN composite [from S. Hayashi et al., *J. Mat. Sci.* 17:3336 (1982)].

increasing temperature. The thermal conductivities of the composite containing 2 to 6 wt% carbon also increased with increasing temperature and decreased with increasing carbon content.

Porous SiC and Si_3N_4 are densified by SiC and Si_3N_4 CVD; also, SiC fiber is impregnated by SiC CVD to form reinforced composites. Fitzer and co-workers[22] deposited SiC from CH_3SiCl_3 onto the various types of reaction-bonded SiC (RB-SiC), and Si_3N_4 from $SiCl_4$ and NH_3 onto the RB-Si_3N_4. The higher the deposition temperature, the more the impregnation was limited to the outer zone. Newkirk and co-workers[23] coated carbon yarn with Ta from a gas mixture of $TaCl_5$ and H_2 at 950°C. The coated yarn was then densified by hot pressing, during which the Ta layer reacted with carbon filament to form TaC. TiC-coated fiber was examined in terms of comparability with Al.[24] TiC-coated fiber showed no loss in strength after heat treatment at 673–873°K for 25 hours, and also at 973–1273°K for 30 minutes.

1.8.2 Borides and Silicides

TiB_2 is as hard and refractory a material as TiC. Pierson and Mullendore[25] examined the optimum conditions for depositing thick and uniform films onto graphite substrates from a gas mixture of $TiCl_4$, BCl_3, and H_2. They proposed as optimum conditions a deposition temperature of 900–950°C and source gas ratios of Ti/B = 0.5 and H/Cl = 6. The coatings were as hard as 3700 kg/mm² (Vickers microhardness) and contained an excess of boron over stoichiometry. Takahashi and Itoh[26] applied an ultrasonic vibrator directly to the steel substrate in TiB_2 deposition from the same reactant gas as above. Ultrasound affected the film, resulting in a fine-grained structure, and the effect increased with increases in the power of decreases in the frequency of ultrasound. Copper has the effect of lowering the temperature of TiB_2 deposition and also has an accommodation effect of thermal stress in the substrate. Motojima and co-workers[27] deposited TiB_2 on copper plate from the system $TiCl_4$-BCl_3-H_2-Ar at 600–800°C. The coated plate had a microhardness of 3300–3800 Kg/mm², oxidation resistance in air of up to 700°C, and corrosion resistance to concentrated HCl and 3N HNO_3. Newkirk and co-workers[28] infiltrated graphite woven cloth with TiB_2 or B_4C by CVD to produce fusion reactor materials. TiB_2 was also deposited from a $TiCl_4$-BCl_3-H_2 system at 700–1000°C under a reduced pressure of 2–3 KPa, followed by hot pressing at 2350°C and 28 MPa. The resulting composite showed a flexure strength of 108 MPa. B_4C was deposited from the BCl_3-C_3H_8-H_2 system at 900°C, and the B_4C-impregnated graphite cloth was hot pressed at 2100°C and 32 MPa. The resultant composite had an electrical conductivity of 441 and 204 $(\Omega\text{-cm})^{-1}$ for 27 and 43 vol% B_4C, respectively.

TaB_2 was coated from a $TaCl_5$, BCl_3, H_2, and Ar gas mixture onto a quartz-glass substrate at 900–1300°C[29], and TaB was coated onto copper substrate at 540–800°C.[30] Microhardness values of TaB_2 and TaB layers were measured as 3500–4100 and 3250 kg/mm², respectively. TaB-coated copper was satisfactorily resistant to 36N H_2SO_4 and 48N HNO_3 at 60°C. AlB_{12} is one of the promising materials for wear-resistant or refractory use. AlB_{12} could be deposited from the gaseous $AlCl_3$-BCl_3H_2-Ar system onto a Mo or W filament at 800–1400°C.[31] The B/Al atomic ratio in deposits varied from 8 to 24, depending on the $BCl_3/AlCl_3$ ratios in the source gas. X-ray diffraction of the deposits suggested that the layer was composed of α-AlB_{12} and tetragonal B. A maximum microhardness of 3900 kg/mm² was obtained on the coated layer deposited at 1000°C with a $BCl_3/AlCl_3$ source gas ratio of about 2.

Usually, elementary B is chemically vapor-deposited from a BCl_3-H_2 mixture. Pierson and Mullendore[32] used B_2H_6 as a B source and decomposed it to form a B layer up to 60 μm thick on a graphite substrate. Vickers microhardness on a cross section of the coating deposited at 500°C was 3400 kg/mm².

1.8.3 Oxides

Brown and co-workers[33] reported coating SiO_2 onto high-alloyed steels formed from a gas mixture of $Si(OEt)_4$, H_2O, and N_2 at 700–900°C. Preoxidation of the steel substrate was an essential feature of the process to maintain coating adherence. The coating rate increased with increases in deposition temperature with an activation energy of 214 kJ/mole and also with increases in $Si(OEt)_4$ concentration of up to 0.3%. This technique could be successfully applied to coating the inner surface of tubes, and protection performance was confirmed in air and CO_2 at 800–1000°C. Al_2O_3 film is usually coated as the uppermost layer of cutting tools, such as Al_2O_3/TiN-cemented carbides. Kim and co-workers[34] examined the effect of reactant gas concentration of CVD of Al_2O_3 in the temperature range of 900–1150°C. The deposition rate was limited by both the $AlCl_3$ concentration and the H_2/CO_2 ratio. The maximum rate was attained when the concentrations of H_2 and $AlCl_3$ were 60 and 1–1.5%, respectively.

Cubic ZrO_2 can be stabilized by the addition of Y_2O_3. Wahl and co-workers[35] directly chlorinated Y and Zr metals and examined the optimum conditions of ZrO_2, Y_2O_3, and $Zr(Y)O_{2-x}$ deposition using the reactions of chlorides with O_2. ZrO_2 deposited at temperatures above 700°C, and Y_2O_3 above 1070°C. Then codeposition of ZrO_2 and Y_2O_3 was carried out at 1100°C, in which the maximum deposition rate was 5 μm/h. Kamata and co-workers[36] deposited cubic-stabilized $Zr(Y)O_{2-x}$ films onto Si substrates from a gas mixture of $Y(C_{11}H_{19}O_2)_3$ and $Zr(C_{11}H_{19}O_2)_4$ at 735°C ($C_{11}H_{19}O_2$: 2,2,6,6-tetramethyl-3,5-heptanedione).

References

1. Lee, C. W., Nam, S. W., and Chun, J. S., *Thin Solid Films* 86:63 (1981).
2. Röser, K. *Proc. 8th International Conference on CVD*, 1981, p. 586.
3. Lee, C. W., and Chun, J. S., *Thin Solid Films* 86:73 (1981).
4. Sarin, V. K., and Lindstrom, J. N., *J. Electrochem. Soc.* 126:1281 (1979).
5. Vuorinen, S., and Horsewell, A., *J. Mat. Sci.* 17:585 (1982).
6. Sjöstrand, M. E., *Proc. 7th International Conference on CVD*, 1979, p. 452.
7. Itoh, H., *J. Cryst. Growth* 57:456 (1982).
8. Cho, J. S., Nam, S. W., and Chun, J. S., *J. Mat. Sci.* 17:2495 (1982).
9. Bonetti-Lang, M., Bonetti, R., and Hintermann, H. E., *Proc. 8th International Conference on CVD*, 1981, p. 606.
10. Takahashi, T., Itoh, H., and Fukao, K., *J. Less-Common Metals* 80:171 (1981).
11. Motojima, S., Tamura, Y., and Sugiyama, K., *Thin Solid Films* 88:269 (1982).
12. Takahashi, T., Itoh, H., and Kuroda, M., *J. Cryst. Growth* 53:418 (1981).
13. Takhashi, T., Itoh, H., and Ohtake, A., *Yogyo-Kyokai-Shi* 89:63 (1981).
14. Pauleau, Y., Bouteville, A., Hantzpergue, J. J., and Remy, J. C., *Proc. 8th International Conference on CVD*, 1981, p. 104.
15. Takahashi, Y., Yamashita, K., Motojima, S., and Sugiyama, K., *Surface Sci.* 86:238 (1979).
16. Takahashi, Y., Mutoh, K., Motojima, S., and Sugiyama, K., *J. Mat. Sci.* 16:1217 (1981).
17. Duffy, M. T., Berkman, S., Cullen, G. W., D'Aiello, R. V., and Moss, H. I., *J. Cryst. Growth* 50:347 (1980).
18. Oda, K., Yoshio, T., and O-oka, K., *Comm. Am. Ceramic Soc.* C-8 (1983).
19. Hirai, T., and Hayashi, S., *J. Am. Ceram. Soc.* 64:C-88 (1981).
20. Hayashi, S., Hirai, T., Hiraga, K., and Hirabayashi, M., *J. Mat. Sci.*, 17:3336 (1982).

21. Goto, T., Hayashi, S., and Hirai, T. *Sci. Rep. Research Inst. Tohoku Univ.* A29:176 (1981).
22. Fitzer, E., Hegen, D., and Strohmeier, H., *Proc. 7th International Conference on CVD*, 1979, p. 525.
23. Newkirk, L. R., Riley, R. E., Sheinberg, H., Valencia, F. A., and Wallace, T. C., *Proc. 7th International Conference on CVD*, 1979, p. 488.
24. Obara, T., Mutoh, N., and Imanishi, Y., *Nippon Kinzoku Gakukai-Shi* 43:589 (1979).
25. Pierson, H. O., and Mullendore, A. W., *Thin Solid Films* 95:99 (1982).
26. Takahashi, T., and Itoh, H., *J. Cryst. Growth* 49:445 (1980).
27. Motojima, S., Yamada, M., and Sugiyama, K., *J. Nucl. Mat.* 105:335 (1982).
28. Newkirk, L. R., Riley, R. E., Scheinberg, H., Valencia, F. A., and Wallace, T. C., *Proc. 7th International Conference on CVD*, 1979, p. 515.
29. Motojima, S., and Sugiyama, K., *J. Mat. Sci.* 14:2859 (1979).
30. Motojima, S., Kito, K., and Sugiyama, K., *J. Nucl. Mat.* 105:262 (1982).
31. Motojima, S., Takai, K., and Sugiyama, K., *J. Nucl. Mat.* 98:151 (1981).
32. Pierson, H. O., and Mullendore, A. W., *Proc. 7th International Conference on CVD*, 1979, p. 360.
33. Brown, D. E., Clark, J. T. K., Foster, A. I., McCarroll, J. J., Richards, M. S., Sims, M. L., and Swidzinski, M. A. M., *Proc. 8th International Conference on CVD*, 1981, p. 699.
34. Kim, J-G., Park, C-S., and Chun, J. S., *Thin Solid Films* 97:97 (1982).
35. Wahl, G., Schlosser, S., and Schmaderer, F., *Proc. 8th International Conference on CVD*, 1981, p. 536.
36. Kamata, K., Matsumoto, S., and Shibata, Y., *Yogyo Kyokai-Shi* 91:46 (1982).

1.9 Deposition of Metal Oxide Films by Reactive Evaporation

Yoshichika Bando and Toshio Takada

1.9.1 Introduction

Much attention has been given to metal oxide films used as transparent conducting films, dielectric films, optical coating films, and magnetic films. The semiconducting oxides that have been used as transparent conductors include SnO_2, In_2O_3, CdO, ZnO, and Cd_2SnO_4. These films are used as transparent heaters and electrodes for display devices. In addition to insulating films' conventional use for passivation of semiconductor devices and as capacitors, such films as SiO_2, TiO_2, and Al_2O_3 are needed in a number of electronic technologies. Optical films such as TiO_2, SiO_2, SnO_2, and so on are applied to reflecting, antireflecting, and absorbing coats. Magnetic iron oxide films have been developed for high-density digital magnetic recording. Recently, lower oxide films such as TeO_x, GeO_x, and MoO_x have been reported to be applicable to optical disk memories.

Numerous methods have been employed to deposit oxide films. Four are discussed below.

1. *Chemical Vapor Deposition (CVD).* Reviews of CVD have been performed by Powell and co-workers[1] and Feist and co-workers.[2] The CVD contains hydrolysis of metal chlorides and pyrolysis, which is defined as thermal decomposition of such compounds as metal-organic compounds.
2. *Oxidation of Thin Metal Films by Evaporation or Sputtering.* The oxidation process is not often used because of cracks and disruption of films resulting from volume change during oxidation.
3. *Reactive Sputtering and Sputtering of Oxide Targets.* Oxide films can be formed by sputtering metals in an argon-oxygen atmosphere. This reactive sputtering process is similar to that in reactive evaporation. Sputtering from oxide targets to form oxide films is significantly different from that of the reactive sputtering of metal targets. The control of stoichiometry of oxides has been found to be much easier with oxide targets.
4. *Reactive Evaporation (RE).* RE is defined as oxide film deposition onto a substrate by evaporation of a metal or lower metal oxide in a low-pressure reactive-gas atmosphere of 10^{-3}–10^{-1} Pa.

Selection of the appropriate materials and processes for a given application is complex. Vossen shows an attempt to rate the commonly used decomposition processes.[3]

1.9.2 Deposition Parameters for Oxide Formation by the RE Process

In RE at low partial pressures of the evaporant species, oxidation occurs during condensation of the evaporated metal onto the substrate. The main control parameters for oxide formation are the deposition rate, the oxygen background pressure, the substrate temperature, and the substrate material. The deposition rate is a function of the metal evaporation rate, the source-substrate separation, and the total gas pressure. The total gas pressure is related to the mean free path of the metal vapor. A careful balance must be maintained between the amounts of metal vapor and oxygen arriving at the substrate at any given temperature to ensure stoichiometry of the oxide.

1.9.2.1 *Influence of Oxygen Pressure on Condensation of Metal Oxides*

Kerner[4] investigated the proportion of oxygen incorporated in condensates of oxides as a function of the ratio of the numbers of molecular impacts on the condensation surface. The incorporation of oxygen in the vapor deposition of Al, Cr, or SiO could be measured by means of two quartz-crystal oscillators exposed to different partial pressures of oxygen as the difference in the rate of deposition onto the two crystals. The incorporated mass depends on the impact ratio on the condensation surface. To oxidize aluminum to Al_2O_3, an oxygen/aluminum impact ratio of 50 times that stoichiometrically predicted is required. For silicon monoxide a ratio of 100 times and for chromium a ratio of twice that stoichiometrically predicted must be available to oxidize them to Si_2O_3 and Cr_2O_3. The quantity of the reactive gas must exceed the stoichiometric amount to attain a given degree of oxidation. This was first explained by Ritter[5] on the basis of the chemisorption of oxygen gas. These results were obtained in deposition on a condensation surface kept at room temperature, and the obtained oxides were amorphous.

1.9.2.2 *Effect of Substrate Temperature on Oxidation Degree and Crystallization*

A summary of the results of depositing various oxides using the RE process is given in Table 1.9.1. The substrate temperature has effects on the oxidation degree, crystallization, and grain size of the oxide. The deposits on substrates at room temperature are amorphous except for CoO, NiO, Fe_3O_4, and Mn_3O_4. A post-deposition annealing is required to crystallize the oxides and control their physical properties. Crystalline oxide films have been directly obtained by deposition on substrates at high temperatures.

The dependence of the crystal phase of tin oxide films on oxygen pressure and substrate temperature is shown in Figure 1.9.1.[6] The oxidation degree of the films increases with increasing oxygen pressure at a constant temperature. Crystalline SnO_2 deposits directly onto a glass substrate at temperatures above 300°C. Amorphous tin oxide films crystallized to the rutile-like SnO_2 phase by heating to above 400°C. This indicates that the crystallization temperature of

Table 1.9.1 Summary of Composition and Crystalline State of Various Oxides Deposited by RE Process (A: Amorphous; C: Crystalline)

Evaporated Material	Substrate Temperature		
	Room Temperature	200°C	Higher than 300°C
Al[4,13]	Al_2O_3 (A)	Al_2O_3 (A)	α-Al_2O_3 on α-Al_2O_3
SiO[4]	Si_2O_3 (A)		
Ti[18,19,20]	TiO_2 (A)	TiO_2 (A)	TiO_2 rutile (1100°C)
Cr[4]	Cr_2O_3 (A)		
Mn[11]	Mn_3O_4 (C)	Mn_3O_4 (C)	Mn_3O_4 (C)
Fe[9,10]	Fe_2O_3 (A)	Fe_2O_3 (A)	α-Fe_2O_3 (C)
	Fe_3O_4 (C)	Fe_3O_4 (C)	Fe_3O_4 (C)
Co[11]	CoO (C)	Co_3O_4 (C)	Co_3O_4 (C)
		CoO (C)	CoO (C)
Ni[11]	NiO (C)	NiO (C)	NiO (C)
In	In_2O_3 (A)	In_2O_3 (A)	In_2O_3 (C)
Sn or SnO[6]	SnO_{2-x} (A)	SnO_{2-x} (A)	SnO_2 (C)
	SnO	SnO (C)	SnO (C)
Rh[17]	RhO_{1-x} (A)		

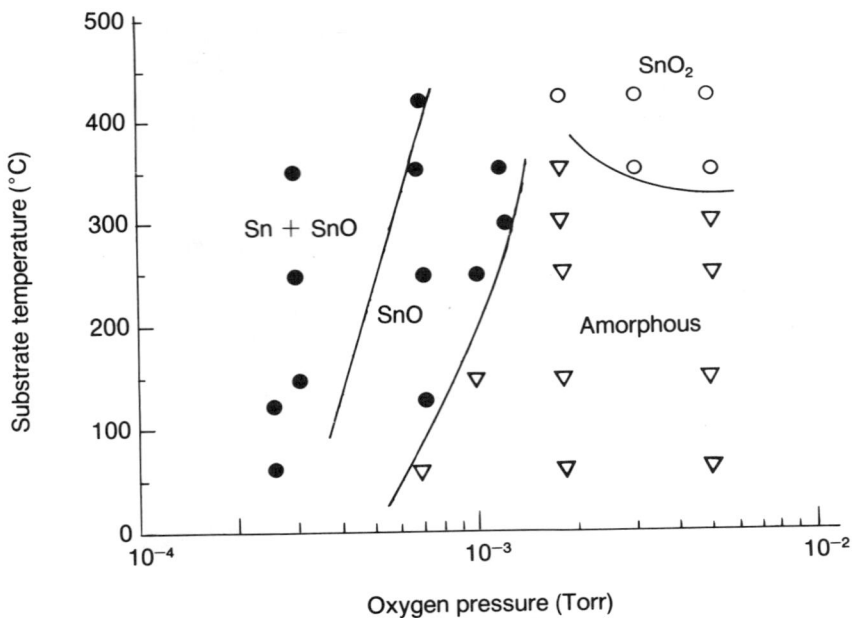

Figure 1.9.1 Formation range of tin oxides as a function of oxygen pressure and substrate temperature [from S. Muranaka et al.[18]].

the amorphous tin oxide is higher than the substrate temperature at which crystalline SnO_2 deposits.

The evaporant species from the RE of tin metal contain Sn and SnO, which form on the molten tin surface at the evaporation source. The deposition rates in oxygen and in inert gas at a constant source temperature ($1190 \pm 2°C$) were experimentally compared. The deposition rate in oxygen has a tendency to increase with increasing gas pressure, opposite to that in inert gas. This phenomenon indicates that the more volatile SnO forms on the molten tin surface and is evaporated. Therefore, tin oxide films form by deposition of SnO, oxidation of SnO, and also oxidation of tin atoms.

Formation of Fe_3O_4 thin films by RE was described by Schneider and co-workers[7] and the present authors.[8] The formation ranges of Fe_3O_4 and Fe_2O_3 films were determined as functions of the substrate temperature and the deposition rate at an oxygen partial pressure of 5×10^{-2} Pa, as shown in Figure 1.9.2.[9] The impact ratio of oxygen molecules to iron atoms on the condensation surface decreases with

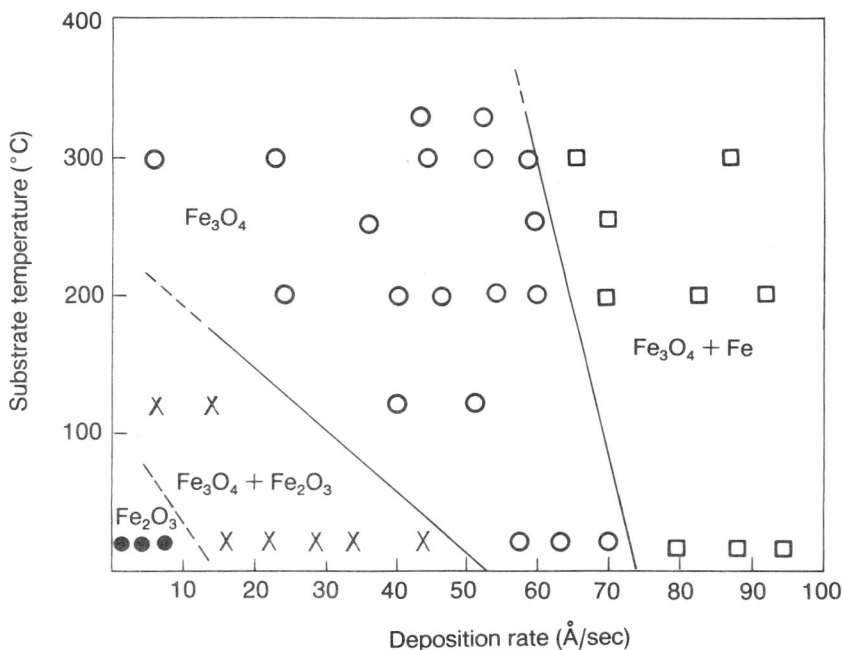

Figure 1.9.2 Formation range of iron oxides as a function of deposition rate and substrate temperature at an oxygen pressure of 5×10^{-2} Pa [from Y. Bando et al., *Jpn. J. Appl. Phys.* 19:1037 (1978)].

an increasing deposition rate at a constant oxygen partial pressure. Therefore, it is reasonable to assume that the oxidation degree of iron oxide decreases with an increasing deposition rate.

At a constant deposition rate the oxidation degree of the film decreases as the substrate temperature increases. At higher substrate temperatures the sticking coefficient of O_2 on the condensation surface is lower and the oxidation rate of Fe decreases, as the sticking coefficient of Fe may be unity. The formation range of Fe_3O_4 is wider with increasing substrate temperature; this is due to a large shift of the amorphous Fe_2O_3/crystalline Fe_3O_4 boundary to a lower deposition rate. In the Fe_3O_4-phase range the oxidation degree x, represented as $(1 - x)Fe_3O_4 \cdot xFe_2O_3$, increases as the deposition rate decreases.

Fe_2O_3 films deposited at substrate temperatures below 300°C are amorphous. The magnetic properties of amorphous Fe_2O_3 were investigated by magnetic susceptibility and Mössbauer effect measurements.[10] The Néel temperatures of amorphous Fe_2O_3 deposited at substrate temperatures of 20 and 60°C are 48 and 62°K, respectively, and are much lower than that of crystalline α-Fe_2O_3 (950°K).

In the cases of both iron and tin, the oxidation degree has a tendency to decrease with increasing substrate temperature. However, this tendency is not true in the deposition of cobalt oxides. Cobalt monoxide deposits on glass at room temperature. However, cobaltite (Co_3O_4) deposited at between 200 and 250°C when cobalt metal was evaporated in an oxygen atmosphere of 6.5×10^{-2} Pa at a deposition rate of 1 Å/s.[11] Furthermore, in the RE of indium, mixtures of amorphous indium oxide, crystalline In_2O_3, and indium metal deposited on glass at temperatures of 50 to 150°C, but crystalline In_2O_3 required temperatures of 250 to 450°C, when indium metal was evaporated in an oxygen atmosphere of 1.3×10^{-2} Pa at a deposition rate of 1.5 Å/s.[13] Because indium metal melts at 159°C, indium metal deposited as a liquid and therefore did not form a metal film on the substrate above 160°C. Liquid metal, which is not oxidized, may depart from the condensation surface.

Korikorian and Sneed[6] carried out an investigation of the condition required for growth of Al_2O_3 using both reactive sputtering and evaporation. They found that the oxygen pressure required to form stoichiometric Al_2O_3 was sensitive to the substrate temperature and the deposition rate, decreasing with increasing substrate temperature and decreasing deposition rate.

As shown in Table 1.9.1, oxides with the NaCl and spinel structures have a tendency to deposit as crystalline substances, and corundum type oxides, such as α-Al_2O_3, α-Fe_2O_3, and Cr_2O_3, deposit as amorphous substances when the substrate temperature is low. A substrate temperature above 300°C is necessary for crystallization of oxides with a corundum structure. In_2O_3 and SnO_2 form crystalline films at substrate temperatures above 200 and 300°C, respectively.

1.9.3 Epitaxial Growth

The formation range and crystal orientation of iron oxides deposited on the (001) plane of rock salt as a function of substrate temperature and deposition rate are shown in Figure 1.9.3. The formation range of magnetite on NaCl is wider than that on glass.

The deposits of magnetite on NaCl show three types of orientation. These are the (100) orientation, the seven-orientations, and random orientation. The formation condition of the (100)-oriented deposit (single-crystal film) indicated as region I in Figure 1.9.3 exists between two critical values of deposition rate. With a deposition rate lower than 22 Å/s at a substrate temperature of 200°C, the deposits of magnetite show the seven-orientations.

The composition x of the magnetite phase, represented as $(1 - x)Fe_3O_4 \cdot xFe_2O_3$, increases with decreasing deposition rate. The seven-orientations appearing in the lower deposition rate side may involve deviations from stoichiometry. NiO and CoO deposit epitaxially on (001) NaCl at room temperature and 150°C, respectively, and

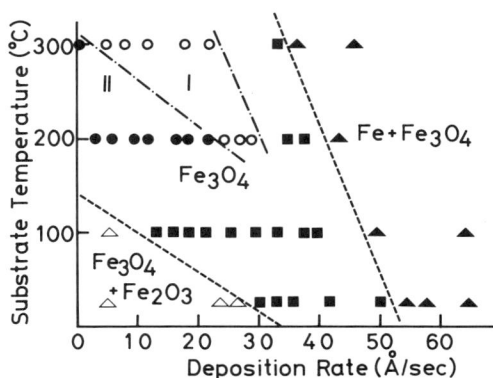

Figure 1.9.3 Formation of iron oxides as a function of deposition rate and substrate temperature at an oxygen pressure of 6×10^{-2} Pa. The films obtained in the regions I (O) and II (●) are defined as epitaxial films of type I and II, respectively. The films (■) indicate nonoriented Fe_3O_4 films.

CoO films are epitaxially grown on (001) CoO and (001) NiO at room temperature, which is lower than the temperature of epitaxial growth on NaCl. The authors obtained an artificial superlattice composed of ultra-thin layers (below 100 Å) of NiO and CoO by epitaxially depositing these oxides alternately.[7]

1.9.4 Magnetic Films

Magnetic films for high-density recording have been developed by many investigators. With regard to applications for high-density digital recording, iron oxide films seem promising because of their resistance to corrosion and wear. The magnetic iron oxides are Fe_3O_4 and γ-Fe_2O_3. Preparation techniques for magnetic iron oxide films include vacuum evaporation, sputtering, reactive evaporation, and chemical deposition. Magnetic iron oxide (Fe_3O_4) films can be directly prepared by reactive evaporation as well as reactive sputtering, by heat diffusion of Fe/α-Fe_2O_3 composites and heat treatment of α-Fe_2O_3 in a reducing atmosphere. γ-Fe_2O_3 films can be obtained by oxidation of Fe_3O_4 films. Reactive sputtering has been one of the most intensively investigated methods.[14] As for Fe_3O_4 films, it has been reported that the RE process is more advantageous, as magnetite can be directly deposited at higher deposition rates (60–100 Å/s). Nishimoto and Aoyama[15] reported preparation conditions for γ-Fe_2O_3 thin-film disks by Re and also the read/write characteristics of Co- and Cu-doped γ-Fe_2O_3 disks. As a result of theoretical and experimental evaluations of the disks, a recording density feasibility as high as 2.4×10^7 bit/in^2 has been confirmed.

Recording media of iron oxide films have made significant progress in the 1980s. Now, recording densities above 6×10^7 bit/in^2 are considered reasonable for practical use, when continuous-film recording media are employed. Replacement in the future of longitudinal magnetic recording by perpendicular recording has been proposed.

1.9.5 Conclusion

Of the control parameters involved in RE, the most difficult is the evaporation rate, because the oxidation of the evaporant in the source retards or enhances the evaporation rate. This problem is especially severe when doped films are to be deposited.

The sputtering rate can be more easily controlled than the evaporation rate, and the composition of doped films can be controlled easily when sputtering alloy targets. The RE process involves disadvantages but also has the advantages of a faster evaporation rate and a lower equipment cost. The substrate temperature must be maintained high enough to ensure the desired degrees of reaction, crystallization, and grain growth, but the thermal stability required severely restricts the choice of substrate materials. For the NaCl-type or spinel-type oxides, the substrate temperature to ensure crystallization and epitaxial growth is as low as $150-200°C$. Epitaxial growth generally needs single crystals as substrate materials. This restricts the use of single-crystal films. Recently, an atomic layer epitaxy using vapor deposition was proposed to realize an epitaxial growth on an amorphous substrate.[16] If such a new technique of epitaxial growth on amorphous materials is developed, the use of oxide thin films will further expand.

References

1. Powell, C. F., Oxley, J. H., and Blocher, J. M. eds., *Vapor, Deposition*, New York: John Wiley & Sons, 1966.
2. Feist, W. M., Steele, S. R., and D. W. Ready, *Physics of Thin Films*, vol. 5, G. Hass and R. E. Thun, eds. New York: Academic Press, 1969, p. 105.
3. Vorun, J. L., *Physics of Thin Films*, vol. 9, G. Hass, M. H. Francombe, and R. W. Hoffman, eds. New York: Academic Press, 1977, p. 63.
4. Kerner, K. O. J., *Jpn. J. Appl. Phys.*, suppl. 2(1):463 (1974).
5. Ritter, E., *Monatshaft fur Chemie* 95:795 (1964).
6. Muranaka, S., Bando, Y., and Takada, T., *Thin Solid Films* 86:11 (1981).
7. Schneider, J. W., Stoffel, A. M., and Trippel, G., *IEEE Trans. Magn.* MAG-9:183 (1973).
8. Terashima, T., and Bando, Y., *J. Appl. Phys.* 56:3445 (1984).
9. Bando, Y., Horii, S., and Takada, T., *Jpn. J. Appl. Phys.* 19:1037 (1978).
10. Shigematsu, T., Bando, Y., and Takada, T., *J. Physique, Colloq. C2, Suppl. Tome* 40:C2-153 (1979).
11. Bando, Y., unpublished ms.
12. Hirooka, H., Muranaka, S., Bando, Y., and Takada, T., Paper presented at 45th Spring Annual Meeting of the Chemical Society of Japan, Summary I, Tokyo, 1982, p. 496.
13. Francombe, M. H., *Epitaxial Growth*, Part A, J. W. Matthews, ed. New York: Academic Press, 1975, p. 163.
14. Yoshii, S., *Ferrites, Proceedings of the ICF3*, H. Watanabe, S. Iida, and M. Sugimoto, eds. Tokyo, Japan, Center for Academic Publications Japan, 1981, p. 579.

15. Nishimoto, K., and Aoyama, M., *Ferrites, Proceedings of an International Conference*, H. Watanabe, S. Iida, and M. Sugimoto, eds., Tokyo, Japan, Center for Academic Publications Japan, 1981, p. 588.

16. Ahonen, M., Pessa, M., and Suntra, T., *Thin Solid Films* 65:301, 1980.

17. Hoffman, D. M., *J. Vac. Sci. Techn.* 13:122 (1976).

18. Yoshida, S., *Thin Solid Films* 56:321 (1979).

19. Grossklaus, W., and Bunshah, R. F., *J. Vac. Sci. Tech.* 12:593 (1975).

20. Pulker, H. K., Paesold, G., and Ritter, E., *Appl. Optics* 15:2986 (1976).

2

CHARACTERIZATION

2.1 Overview

Shin-ichi Shirasaki

For many years investigators have been attempting to establish the relations among the preparation history, structure, and properties of ceramics. Yet knowledge of these relations is not completely satisfactory in the case of many ceramics and almost nonexistent for others. This lack of knowledge generates difficulty in understanding ceramics. But if these relations can be established, it will become possible to determine what structure provides the optimal properties for a given use and to tailor ceramics to specific applications. Thus, the importance of knowing such relations cannot be overemphasized. To establish them, many structures must be properly characterized, including point defect structure, metastable structure, dislocation, grain boundary and surface structure, compositional fluctuation, segregation and precipitation structure, and layered structure.

Small amounts of impurities are often intentionally added to ceramics to control their sinterability and other properties. Therefore, understanding the point defect structure of doped materials is particularly important. Unfortunately, there is at present no satisfactory guiding principle as to the choice of impurities to add for specific purposes. A concept has been proposed by Verwey and Kroger as to the relationship of impurity and point defect structure. It seems, however, that much more concrete information on thermally formed and extrinsic point defects as influenced by additives must be accumulated before impurity and point defect-related phenomena can be completely understood. Moreover, even if excellent properties can be achieved, the material in question cannot be used commercially unless its properties are reliable and reproducible. The relations among fabrication, metastable structure, and properties may be the basis of understanding reproducibility. Point defect structures of a metastable nature appear particularly often in ceramics, depending on their preparation histories.

A knowledge of different types of defects such as dislocation and stacking faults is important to understanding the mechanical properties of ceramics. The special need at present is to accumulate data on the piling up of dislocations and the resulting formation of microcracks under stress in bulk with and without a second phase, grain boundaries, and surfaces. More macroscopic defects such as surface flaws, pores, and microcrystals must also be characterized and controlled if excellent mechanical properties are to be achieved in structural ceramics. Attention has also been focused recently on the mechanical properties of many functional ceramics. For practical uses of optical glass fibers, for example, mechanical performance and long-term reliability are very important. The mechanical strength of the fiber is also significantly affected by a variety of defects.

Many useful functional ceramics have recently been developed through active use of their grain boundaries. Typical examples are ZnO varistors, positive temperature coefficient (PTC) thermistors, and Ca- and Si-doped Mn-Zn ferrites with a very low level of eddy current loss. There are, however, several examples in which the existence of grain boundaries has a negative effect on ceramic properties. Instances are SiC and Si_3N_4 ceramics, for which there is at present a rapidly increasing need as materials for a new type of turbine blade capable of functioning at very high temperatures. These materials sinter well with the aid of additives such as Y_2O_3 and MgO. However, these additives precipitate and/or segregate along grain boundaries, forming a glassy phase that denies the materials sufficient mechanical strength for high temperature. Lack of suitable characterization of grain boundaries also causes difficulty in further developing the useful properties of such structural and functional ceramics.

Studies of surfaces are important in catalysis, semiconductor devices, and thermal and field emission technology. Little is known about the details of surfaces. Fortunately, many spectroscopical techniques, such as ultraviolet and X-ray photoemission spectroscopy (UPS and XPS) and electron energy-loss spectroscopy (EELS), are currently being developed to characterize surfaces.

Much attention has recently been given to layered inorganic materials. Studies have also been made with a view to applications making active use of the layered structure. Beta-Al_2O_3 is a layered material famous as a fast ionic conductor. TiS_2 is a candidate material for secondary battery cathodes, as both the electrical conductivity and lithium diffusivity in its interlayer are relatively high. $K_2Ti_4O_9$ (or $H_2Ti_4O_9H_2O$) and $Na_2Ti_3O_7$ (or $H_2Ti_3O_7$) with layered structures have excellent properties for cation exchange and are therefore under consideration for application in treating high-level radioactive liquid waste. However, knowledge of the relations in these materials between properties, such as selectivity and capacity for cation exchange, and layered structures is insufficient.

It has become possible to see many structures, including point defect, layered, and interface structures, by means of high-resolution transmission electron microscopy (HRTEM). The use of this technique will undoubtedly lead to the accumulation of a large amount of data on these structures in the future, although many other techniques are also necessary for a complete understanding of them.

Although a knowledge of instrumental relations among fabrication, structure, and properties in ceramics is difficult to obtain, discussions in this chapter indicate that some progress has been made to date in Japan. Continued advances in this area are anticipated.

2.2 Structure/Property Relationships for Layered Inorganic Materials

Shinichi Kikkawa and Mitsue Koizumi

2.2.1 Introduction

In recent years there has been much progress in the field of layered inorganic materials. Intercalation and related phenomena constitute a large area of development.[1] Intercalation has been applied as the cathode reaction of secondary batteries.[2] Many layered compounds having electronic conduction have been extensively surveyed as possible cathode materials. Electron transport in low-dimensional conductors has attracted the attention of solid-state physicists. Periodic lattice distortions have sometimes been found as a result of the formation of charge density waves.[3] These activities in electrochemistry and physics have stimulated the development of solid-state chemistry for layered materials.[4]

New methods have been developed in the preparation of layered compounds. The high-pressure technique has been applied to the preparation of layered chalcogenides by confining the high chalcogen vapor pressure in a reaction vessel.[5-8] Deintercalation has also been established as a new preparation technique. It has been investigated on ternary alkali transition metal oxides,[9,10] chalcogenides,[11,12] and also on $CaSi_2$.[13] In addition, ion exchange can lead to the preparation of new compounds. Ion exchange, organic intercalation, and dehydration have been investigated on layered $Na_2Ti_3O_7$ and $K_2Ti_4O_9$.[14-17] Dehydration of tetratitanate has opened a new route to the preparation of octatitanate. Formation of inorganic porous materials has also been attempted by modifying layered compounds. Several kinds of inorganic pillars have been made in the interlayer region of clay minerals.[18-20] Furthermore, organics have been grafted to the interlayer surface of inorganic layered compounds in attempts to obtain porous materials having rigid frameworks.[21-23] These developments in solid-state chemistry in Japan are introduced in the following sections.

2.2.2 High-Pressure Syntheses of Layered Chalcogenides

Transition metal trichalcogenides are normally prepared by heating the elements in fused silica glass tubes. Their crystal structures basically consist of infinite chains of MX_6 trigonal prisms. They show marked low-dimensional electron transport characteristics in the chains. However, their behaviors are quite different from each other as a result of slight differences in their crystal structures, as shown in Figure 2.2.1. Both $TaSe_3$ and $NbSe_3$ are metallic conductors having monoclinic unit cells. $TaSe_3$ becomes a superconductor below 2°K, but $NbSe_3$ shows a peculiar change in electrical conductivity with temperature. There are four MX_3 chains in a unit cell for $TaSe_3$ and six for $NbSe_3$. $TaSe_3$ shows a Peierls transition around 218°K and has an orthorhombic unit cell containing a variety of TaS_3 chains. Metal-metal distances in the NbS_3 chain are not equal, and $5d^1$ electrons localize on every two niobium atoms in the NbS_3 chains. The reasons for the difference in structure and properties between these MX_3 compounds was the subject of further investigation.

The transition metal trichalcogenides $TaSe_3$, TaS_3, $NbSe_3$, and NbS_3 were prepared under high chalcogen vapor pressure in a high-pressure reaction vessel.[5,6] The preparations were performed under

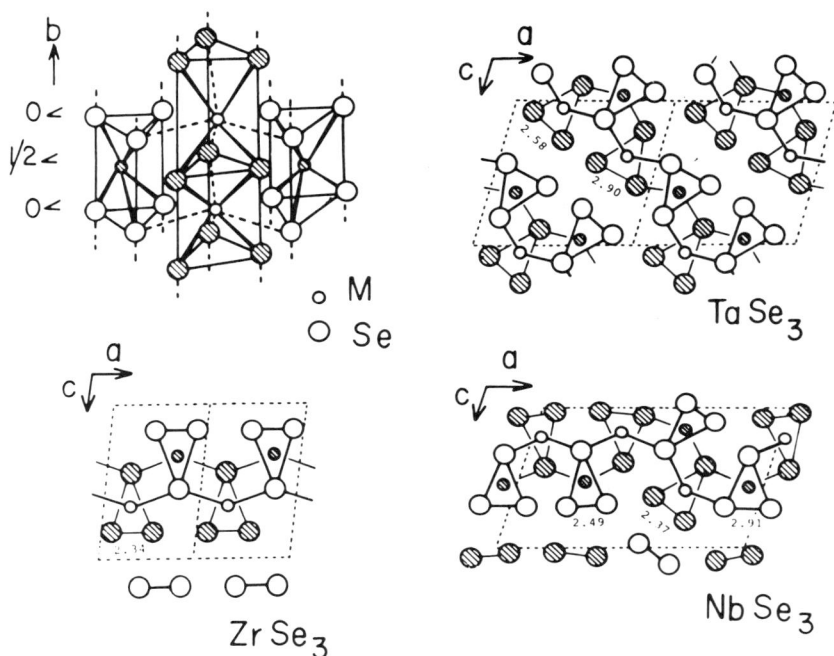

Figure 2.2.1 Schematic crystal structure of triselenides. Stacking of prisms along the *b* axis and projections of ZrSe$_3$, TaSe$_3$, and NbSe$_3$ structures in the *ac* plane are represented. Open and shaded circles are at 0 and *b*/2, respectively [from S. Kikkawa et al., *J. Solid State Chem.* 41:315 (1982)].

reaction conditions of 2 GPa at 700°C for 30 minutes. NbSe$_3$ prepared under pressure had the same structure as already reported.[24] However, the other three compounds were different from those prepared in a fused silica tube.[25,26] Using the high-pressure technique, TaSe$_3$, TaS$_3$, and NbS$_3$ were prepared as the compounds having NbSe$_3$-type crystal structures.

The selenide systems of niobium and tantalum were investigated under high pressure in the compositional range of MX$_2$ to MX$_3$.[7] Three phases were observed in the tantalum selenide system with increasing amounts of selenium: TaSe$_2$, "TaSe$_3$," which could be obtained by the usual sealed-tube method, and a new TaSe$_3$ phase. The ratio of Se/Ta in the nominal "TaSe$_3$" was assumed to be 2.8. The stoichiometric TaSe$_3$ decomposed to "TaSe$_3$," releasing Se when it was heated at 250°C for 1 day in an evacuated glass tube.[7] A similar situation was also observed on the high-pressure form of TaS$_3$.[5] At present the high-pressure phases cannot be related to the normal products by their crystal structure; however, they probably contain more chalcogen than the normal phases. They could be obtained by confining high chalcogen vapor pressure in a small reaction vessel in high-pressure equipment.

TiS_2 is a promising candidate for secondary battery cathode material because the electrical conductivity and lithium diffusion characteristics in its interlayer are relatively high.[2] High energy density can also be expected because of its low atomic weight among the transition metal dichalcogenides. However, it normally has the non-stoichiometric composition of $Ti_{1+x}S_2$ ($x > 0$). The excess titanium is in the interlayer region and reduces battery performance. Rigid control of the chemical composition is required to prepare TiS_2 as a cathode material.

Preparation of stoichiometric TiS_2 was also attempted under high pressure at 1000°C.[8] TiS_3 accompanying nonstoichiometric TiS_2 was formed first from the starting stoichiometric mixture of Ti and S. Stoichiometric TiS_2 could be obtained only after 4 hours' duration. Grains of TiS_2 grew during the reaction; the average grain size was 50 μm. Such large grains are not favorable because lithium must diffuse into the TiS_2. To reduce this grain growth, the mixture of Ti and TiS_3 was equilibrated for 2 hours. The grain size was then only 20 μm.

2.2.3 Deintercalation of Layered Alkali Transition Metal Dioxides AMO_2

Layered compounds such as VS_2 and $CrSe_2$ have recently been prepared by extraction of alkali metals from the interlayer region of $LiVS_2$ and $KCrSe_2$.[11,12] The starting materials were oxidized with iodine in acetonitrile on deintercalation. Alkali metals were almost completely removed from these ternary chalcogenides. Deintercalation is interesting not only as a model reaction for the battery-charging process but also as a technique to prepare a metastable phase that cannot be obtained by the direct combination of elements.

Alkali metals are probably more tightly bound to their host lattices in alkali transition metal oxides, AMO_2, than in chalcogenide because there are more ionic bonds between the alkali metal and the host lattice. Thus, it seems more difficult to remove alkali metal from the interior of solid oxides than from that of chalcogenides. Goodenough and Mizushima tried to extract lithium from $LiCoO_2$ electrochemically;[27] however, the deintercalated products were not well characterized, probably because of the shortage of sample. It is useful to accomplish the deintercalation in a nonaqueous solvent in order to prepare a sufficient amount of homogeneous sample.

Chemical deintercalations were attempted on AMO_2 in series. $NaCrO_2$ was oxidized to $Na_{0.75}CrO_2$ with iodine acetonitrile solution.[9] $Na_{0.5}CrO_2$ was obtained from $NaCrO_2$ when a stronger oxidizing agent, bromine, was used instead of iodine. From measurements of the magnetic and electrical properties and lattice parameters of the products, the investigators detected that a portion of the chromium ions were oxidized from Cr^{3+} to Cr^{4+}. The interlayered sodium ions were octahedrally coordinated by six oxygens of the CrO_2 layers in the $NaCrO_2$ and $Na_{0.75}CrO_2$. Electrostatic interaction between the CrO_2 layer and the Na slab was reduced. The interlayer distance expanded with the deintercalations. The coordination of sodium was trigonal prismatic in the $Na_{0.5}CrO_2$. The CrO_2 layers rotated from each other by about $60°$ with the deintercalation to $Na_{0.5}CrO_2$. Then $NaCrO_2$ was antiferromagnetic, but ferromagnetic interaction appeared with $Na_{0.75}CrO_2$ and $Na_{0.5}CrO_2$. Half of the sodium could be removed from $NaCoO_2$ and $NaNiO_2$ as in the case of $NaCrO_2$. A peculiar temperature dependence of the magnetic susceptibility was observed with $Na_{0.5}CoO_2$. This might be related to the formation of a charge density wave in the CoO_2 layer. The reaction rates of deintercalation were different between these compounds.[10] Alpha-$NaFeO_2$ gave a deintercalated product having the approximate composition of $Na_{0.9}FeO_2$. It was not possible to remove lithium from the lithium compounds.

The oxidation potentials of these compounds for deintercalation were measured using an electrochemical cell. The difference in reactivity of the chemical deintercalation was related to the oxidation potentials of the compounds, as shown in Figure 2.2.2.[10] The cell potentials of Na_xCoO_2/Na and Na_xNiO_2/Na were lower than the oxidation potential of iodine in the range of $0.5 \leq x \leq 1$. Thus, about half of the sodium was easily removed from the $NaCoO_2$ and $NaNiO_2$ by using iodine as their oxidizing agents. The Na_xCrO_2/Na cell had a slightly higher potential than those of the cobalt and nickel cells at $x = 1.0$, so the rate of deintercalation using iodine was much slower in the case of $NaCrO_2$. However, half of the sodium was also extracted from $NaCrO_2$ when equilibrium was attained. The open-circuit voltage OCV of the Na_xFeO_2/Na cell was higher than the oxidation potential of iodine and comparable to that of bromine. Therefore, the sodium ion in α-$NaFeO_2$ was not removed by the oxidation using iodine but was slightly deintercalated by bromine. Lithium ions could not be removed from $LiCoO_2$ and $LiCrO_2$ by chemical oxidation

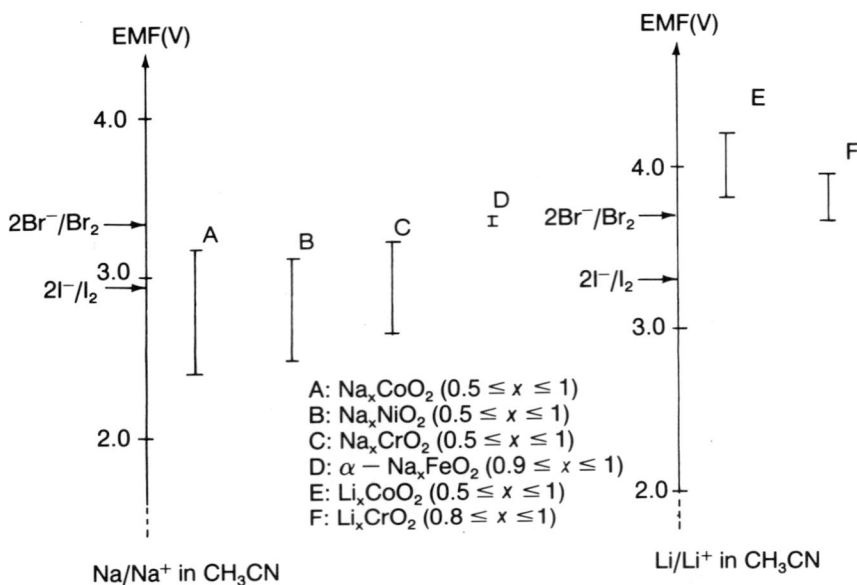

Figure 2.2.2 Open circuit voltage of A_xMO_2/A cells in comparison with the oxidation potentials of iodine and bromine [from S. Miyazaki et al. *Synth. Metal.* 6:211 (1983)].

because their lithium batteries showed higher OCV than the oxidation potentials of iodine and bromine.

Formation of layered Si was attempted by deintercalation from $CaSi_2$.[13] Ca could be removed by electrochemical oxidation of $CaSi_2$ in acetonitrile. Characterization was difficult because the quality of the product was not good. Electron spin resonance (ESR) measurements showed the presence of dangling bonds in the layered Si.

2.2.4 Ion Exchange and Related Phenomena on Layered Titanates

$Na_2Ti_3O_7$ and $K_2Ti_4O_9$ have layered structures with alkali metals in their interlayer regions. $H_2Ti_3O_7$ and $H_2Ti_4O_9 \cdot H_2O$ were obtained by extraction of the alkali metals of these titanates in HCl solution. The protonated forms could take alkali ions and long-chain alkyl-ammonium ions into their interlayer regions much more easily than the $Na_2Ti_3O_7$ and $K_2Ti_4O_9$ themselves.[14,15]

Cation exchanges were investigated on $H_2Ti_3O_7$ and $H_2Ti_4O_9 \cdot H_2O$ in solutions having various pH values. The amounts of potassium were less than 10% in the products prepared from $H_2Ti_4O_9 \cdot H_2O$ below pH = 10. However, they rapidly increased with higher pH values in the region of pH $\geqq$ 11 and attained the value of 84% above pH = 12. The amount of sodium in $H_2Ti_3O_7$ similarly increased in the higher pH region, but only to about 54%. Exchange reactions in both kinds of titanates occur in solutions having high pH values.

Exchange reaction rates were investigated in solutions of 0.1M LiOH, NaOH, and KOH, where the pH of the solutions was above 12. The reaction rate of $H_2Ti_3O_7$ was greatly influenced by the kind of alkali metal.[17] Among the alkali ions, Li^+ was the most quickly exchanged into $H_2Ti_3O_7$. The amount of Li^+ was about 45% of the total exchangeable cations in the case of the sample soaked in 0.1M LiOH solution for 1 hour. This value increased with duration and was 63% after 3 days. In NaOH solution the Na^+ content was 11% for a duration of 1 hour and increased to 43% after 3 days. Exchange to K^+ was very slow, and only 11% of the K^+ was attained in 3 days. The rate of the exchange reaction seems to be related to the ionic radii of the alkali metals. The reaction rate decreased in the order of $Li^+ > Na^+ > K^+$. The estimated ionic radii are 0.60 Å for Li^+, 0.95 Å for Na^+, and 1.33 Å for K^+. Trititanate has interlayered cations without hydrations.

Saturations of tetratitanate were very rapidly attained in cation exchanges with alkali. There were few differences in the reaction rates and in the amounts of absorbed alkali among the three kinds of alkali ions. The amounts were 76% for Li^+, 75% for Na^+, and 82% for K^+ after a duration of 3 days. The products contained alkali with some amount of water. Thus, the size of the hydrated ion is important in an exchange reaction. It has not yet been determined how ions are hydrated within the interlayers. The radii of hydrated ions in solution were estimated to be Li^+(3.82 Å), Na^+(3.58 Å), and K^+(3.31 Å). The difference between Li^+ and K^+ was less than 20%. Accordingly, the size effect could not be as well defined as with trititanate. Diffusion of interlayered cations is probably the most important process for exchange reactions.

Cation exchanges of $H_2Ti_3O_7$ and $H_2Ti_4O_9 \cdot H_2O$ were studied in 0.1M mixed solutions prepared from equal amounts of LiOH, NaOH, KOH, and CsOH. The molar ratios of Li : Na : K : Cs in the products were 1.00 : 0.40 : 0.07 : 0.01, respectively, in the case of trititanate. $H_2Ti_3O_7$ generally absorbs smaller cations into its interlayer regions, so the smaller cations diffuse more easily into the tight interlayer of trititanate. The molar ratios of Li:Na:K:Cs were $1.00:0.17:0.56:0.17$ in tetratitanate. $H_2Ti_4O_9 \cdot H_2O$ contains various amounts of water with alkali ions in its widely opened interlayer. Thus, it did not show a sharp cation preference based on the size of the alkali ions.

$H_2Ti_4O_9 \cdot H_2O$ dehydrated to several new phases in three steps.[14] It lost its interlayered water below 250°C. The $Ti_4O_9^{2-}$ layer is uneven, and the convex and concave surfaces are just opposite in the neighboring layers, as shown in Figure 2.2.3. In the dehydrated product, the distance betwen the neighboring layers across the narrow interlayer space is too close to keep the layer structure as it was. Thus, the second step of dehydration occurred almost instantaneously. The $Ti_4O_9^{2-}$ layers shifted by an amount $\vec{c}/4$ in the structure of $H_2Ti_4O_9$. They shared the free corners of the $4TiO_6$ units. They gradually condensed to form $H_2Ti_8O_{17}$ having the structure shown in Figure 2.2.3. Half of the oxygen located at the free corners of the $4TiO_6$ unit was removed; the interlayered proton remained from the first dehydration step. The unit cell b and c parameters were not much different from those of $K_2Ti_4O_9$ and $H_2Ti_4O_9 \cdot H_2O$. This suggested that the linkage of the $4TiO_6$ unit in the yz-plane remained through the dehydrations. $H_2Ti_8O_{17}$ dehydrated further to TiO_2 (B), which had already been reported by Marchand and co-workers.[16]

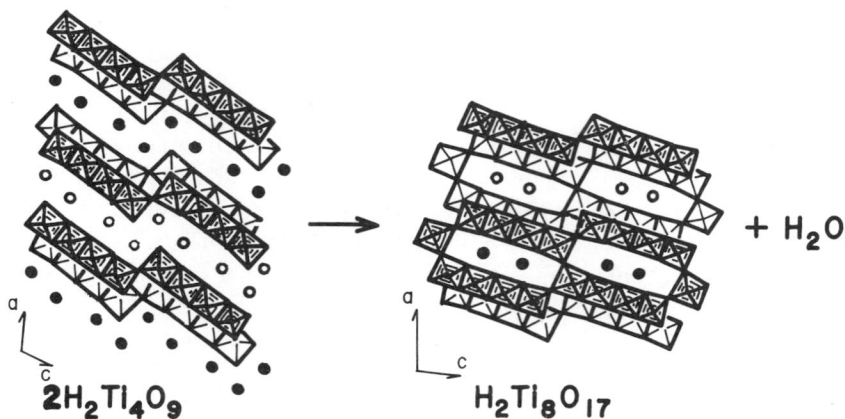

Figure 2.2.3 Schematic representation of the dehydration step from $H_2Ti_4O_9$ to $H_2Ti_8O_{17}$.

2.2.5 Formation of Inorganic Porous Materials Using Layered Materials

Micropores can be made within the interlayer space of clay minerals when bulky ternary ammonium ions are intercalated.[28] Recently, several kinds of inorganic pillared clay minerals have been made which can be used at temperatures higher than 300°C. Spherical cations $[Al_{13}O_4(OH)_{24}(H_2O)_{12}]^{7+}$ having diameters of about 9 Å were formed in an aluminum hydroxide solution of OH/Al < 2.5. The clay minerals, such as montmorilonite, exchanged their interlayer cations for the bulky aluminum hydroxide cation and expanded the interlayer distance to about 19 Å.[18] The aluminum hydroxide cation converted to aluminum oxide when the clay minerals were heated above 550°C. The interlayer distance did not change much at dehydration. The product had a very large surface area of about 500 m²/g and micropores about 9 Å in diameter. Pillared interlayered clays were also prepared having ZrO_2 or SiO_2 instead of Al_2O_3 as the pillars.[19,20]

Grafting of guest species to the host layer is necessary to obtain porous materials in which the interlayer distance does not expand as a result of later gas absorption. There have been no reports on clay mineral grafting. Two kinds of organic grafting have been observed on synthetic layered inorganic compounds.

Zirconium phosphate, $Zr(HPO_4)_2$, has OH groups both below and above the two-dimensional $Zr(HPO_4)_2$ layer. Gamma-$Zr(HPO_4)_2$ intercalates some kinds of organic molecules. Ethylene oxide was also intercalated.[21] The interlayer spacing expanded with the intercalation, and ethylene oxide was grafted to each $Zr(PO_4)_2$ layer following the equation:

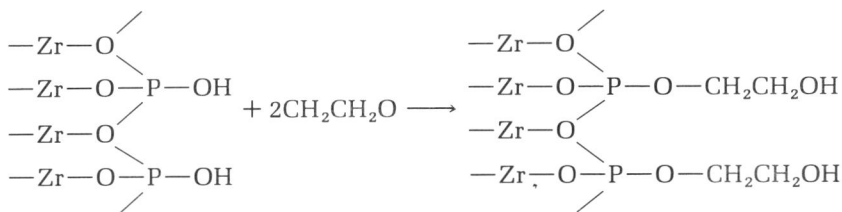

$$
\begin{array}{l}
-Zr-O \diagup \\
-Zr-O-P-OH \\
\quad\quad\quad \diagup \\
-Zr-O \diagup \\
-Zr-O-P-OH \\
\quad\quad\quad \diagup
\end{array}
+ 2CH_2CH_2O \longrightarrow
\begin{array}{l}
-Zr-O \diagup \\
-Zr-O-P-O-CH_2CH_2OH \\
\quad\quad\quad \diagup \\
-Zr-O \diagup \\
-Zr-O-P-O-CH_2CH_2OH \\
\quad\quad\quad \diagup
\end{array}
$$

Iron oxychloride has a structure similar to γ-FeOOH, and it can intercalate alkali ions, pyridine derivatives, and organo-metallic compounds such as ferrocene. FeOCl (pyridine derivative)$_{1/n}$ complex reacted with methanol and gave another grafted type complex:[22]

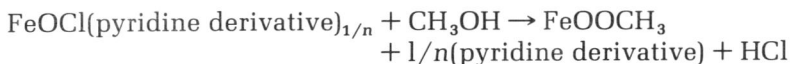

$$FeOCl(\text{pyridine derivative})_{1/n} + CH_3OH \rightarrow FeOOCH_3$$
$$+ 1/n(\text{pyridine derivative}) + HCl$$

This compound, FeOOCH$_3$, could not be obtained by a direct reaction of FeOCl with methanol. It was necessary to expand in advance the interlayer spacing of FeOCl with the intercalation of pyridine derivatives. The intercalated methanol molecule substituted the chlorine of the FeOCl layer with a CH$_3$O$^-$ ion to give FeOOCH$_3$. The structure of the product was derived by the replacement of Cl$^-$ with CH$_3$O$^-$ without any reconstruction of the FeO layer in FeOCl. Similar kinds of compounds were obtained in the reactions of FeOCl (pyridine derivative)$_{1/n}$ with alcohols having longer alkyl chains and with diols. It may be possible to link the neighboring host layers by grafting with organic molecules such as diols having more than two functional groups. The ethylene glycol molecule was grafted to the same FeO layer with its two terminal oxygens.[23]

References

1. Levy, F., ed., *Intercalated Layered Materials*. Dordrecht, Holland: Reidel Publishing Co., 1979.
2. Whittingham, M. S.: *Prog. Solid State Chem.* 12:41 (1978).
3. Wilson, J. A., DiSalvo, F. J., and Mahajan, S., *Advances in Phys.* 24:117 (1975).
4. Whittingham, M. S., and Jacobson, A. J., eds., *Intercalation Chemistry*. London: Academic Press, 1982.
5. Kikkawa, S., Koizumi, M., Yamanaka, S., Onuki, Y., Inada, R., and Tanuma, S., *J. Solid State Chem.* 40:28 (1981).
6. Kikkawa, S., Ogawa, N., Koizumi, M., and Onuki, Y., *J. Solid State Chem.* 41:315 (1982).
7. Kikkawa, S., Shinya, K., and Koizumi M., *J. Solid State Chem.* 41:322 (1982).
8. Yamamoto, T., Kikkawa, S., and Koizumi, M., *Mat. Res. Bull.* 18:1451 (1983).
9. Miyazaki, S., Kikkawa, S., and Koizumi, M., *Rev. Chem. Min.* 19:301 (1982).
10. Miyazaki, S., Kikkawa, S., and Koizumi, M., *Synth. Metal.* 6:211 (1983).
11. Murphy, D. W., Cros, C., DiSalvo, F. J. D., and Waszczak, J. V., *Inorg. Chem.* 16:3027 (1977).
12. Van Bruggen, C. F., Hange, R. J., Wiegers, G. A., and Debeor, D. K. G., *Physica* 99B:166 (1980).
13. Yamanaka, S., Suehiro, F., Sasaki, K., and Hattori, M., *Physica* 105B:230 (1981).
14. Izawa, H., Kikkawa, S., and Koizumi, M., *J. Phys. Chem.* 86:5023 (1982).

15. Izawa, H., Kikkawa, S., and Koizumi, M., *Polyhedron* 2:741 (1983).
16. Marchand, R., Brohan, L., and Tournoux, M., *Mat. Res. Bull.* 15:1129 (1980).
17. Izawa, H., Kikkawa, S., and Koizumi, M., *J. Solid State Chem.* 60:264 (1985).
18. Brindley, G. W., and Yamanaka, S., *Am. Min.* 64:830 (1979).
19. Yamanaka, S., and Brindley, G. W., *Clays Clay Miner* 27:119 (1979).
20. Endo, T., Mortland, M. M., and Pinnavaia, T. J., *Clays Clay Miner* 28:105 (1980).
21. Yamanaka, S., *Inorg. Chem.* 15:2811 (1976).
22. Kikkawa, S., Kanamaru, F., and Koizumi, M, *Inorg. Chem.* 15:2195 (1976).
23. Kikkawa, S., Kanamaru, F., and Koizumi, M., *Inorg. Chem.* 19:259 (1980).
24. Meerschaut, A., and Rouxel, J., *J. Less Common Metals* 39:197 (1975).
25. Bjerkelund, E., and Kjekshus, A., *Z. anorg. allg. Chem.* 328:235 (1964).
26. Kadijk, F., and Jellinek, F., *J. Less Common Metals* 19:421 (1969).
27. Mizushima, K., Jones, P. C., Wiseman, P. J., and Goodenough, J. B., *Mat. Res. Bull.* 15:783 (1980).
28. Barrer, R. M., *Zeolites and Clay Mineral as Sorbents and Molecular Sieves*. New York: Academic Press, 1978, p. 407.

2.3 Fine Structures in Inorganic Materials Examined by High-Resolution Transmission Electron Microscopy (HRTEM)

Shigeo Horiuchi

2.3.1 Introduction

A number of inorganic compounds have been found to have excellent properties, and some have recently been used as "new ceramics." The properties of these materials strongly depend on their crystal, defect, or interface structures, here referred to as "fine structures," because they relate closely to the nature of the chemical bonds in the materials. It is therefore important to clarify the fine structures in order to understand and further develop the properties of the materials.

The resolving power of the transmission electron microscopes has been significantly improved in the last decade. It has become possible to observe the fine structures in materials by means of high-resolution transmission electron microscopy (HRTEM).[1] This section presents some examples of HRTEM images to show their role in these materials' properties.

2.3.2 Interpretation of HRTEM Images

The method of direct imaging of atoms in crystals is based on the principle that the contrast of HRTEM images approximately reflects the potential projected in the direction of the incident electron beam when they are taken under the so-called Scherzer's optimum defocus condition. The resolving power under this condition, d_{res}, is described by[2]

$$d_{res} = 0.65\ C_s^{1/4}\lambda^{3/4}$$

where C_s is the spherical aberration coefficient of the objective lens and λ is the wave length of the incident electrons. From this, it follows that higher resolutions will be obtained from electrons with shorter wave lengths. The authors have constructed a high-voltage, high-resolution electron microscope usually operated at an accelerating voltage of 1 MV. It enabled our first observation of individual cations in inorganic compounds in 1976.[3]

HRTEM images showing the correspondence between a crystal and its image contrast can be seen in Figure 2.3.1. The crystal is TiO_2 with a rutile-type structure. The positions of the Ti atoms are indicated by closed circles and those of the O atoms by open ones in (a). A small piece of sintered block was lightly crushed in an agate mortar. A fragment with a sharp wedge form was selected in the microscope and its edge, thinner than 50 Å, was observed. The projected sites of cation rows are schematically represented by small dots in (b) and (c) at the same scale. A comparison of the inset with the image contrast shows that each position in the cation rows, which have the highest projected potential, is imaged as a dark spot.

The positions of oxygen ions are not clear in the figure. They can, however, be estimated from those of cations obtained previously. Because these images enable us to intuitively construct the projection of a crystal structure (although only approximately), we call them "crystal structure images" or simply "structure images."[4] Although each structure image provides two-dimensional information, we can envision the three-dimensional atom positions if we compare two photos taken from different directions of the identical area. This is the principle behind crystal structure analysis, which has become possible through the higher resolving power of the high-voltage electron microscope.[5]

The theory behind the interpretation of image contrast has almost been completed.[6] At present, image contrast can be computed even for thick crystals.[7] Examples of such calculation are found in

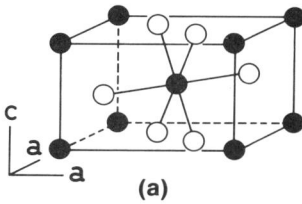

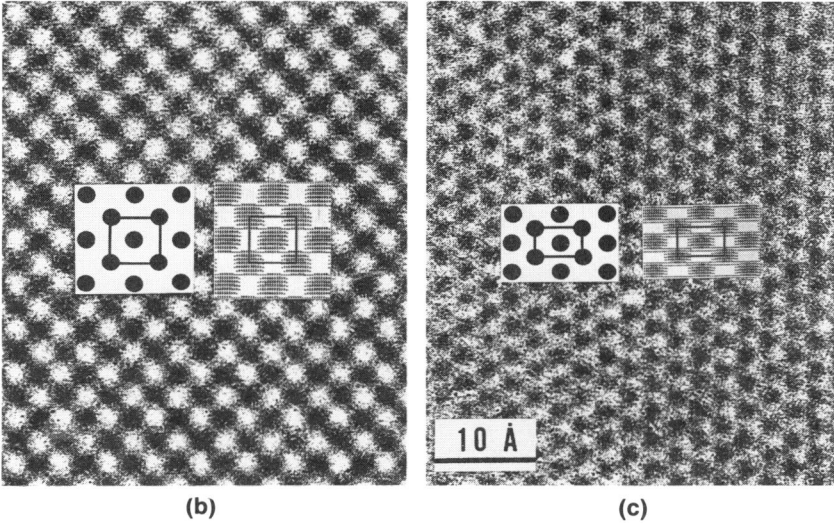

Figure 2.3.1 (a) The unit-cell of TiO_2, tetragonal. $a = 4.59$ and $c = 2.96$ Å. (b) and (c) are the 1 MV HRTEM images, in which electrons are incident along [001] and [100], respectively.

Figure 2.3.1*b* and *c*. Here the spherical aberration coefficient of the objective lens is taken as 5 mm, the underfocus value as 600 Å, the mean focus spread resulting from chromatic aberration as 200 Å, the divergent angle of the incident beam as 8×10^{-4} radians, and the objective lens aperture radius as 0.67 Å^{-1} in reciprocal space.

2.3.3 Fine Structures Affecting the Property of Inorganic Materials

Ceramics are formed by sintering the powders of the starting materials. The properties of ceramics are strongly influenced by the existence of microcracks and second phases that arise during sintering.

Figure 2.3.2 is 1-MV HRTEM image showing a second phase.[8] The compound has been prepared by heating mixed powders of Nb_2O_5 and WO_3. Most of the region is composed of a $2Nb_2O_5 \cdot 7WO_3$ phase. In the region indicated by the arrows, a second phase is formed. From the contrast this phase was identified as WO_3, which must have remained without reacting with the Nb_2O_5.

There are many factors that affect the properties of ceramics. They are related to the fine structures in HRTEM images, examples of which follow.

2.3.3.1 Electrically Conductive Materials

Many oxide crystals become electrically conductive when point defects such as foreign atoms or vacancies are introduced. For example,

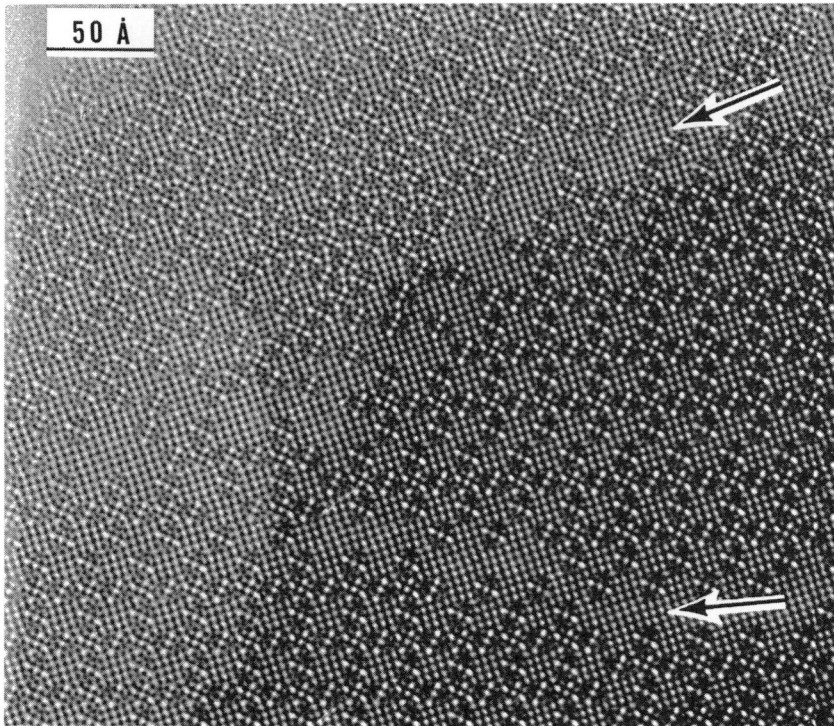

Figure 2.3.2 An HRTEM image of $2Nb_2O_5 \cdot 7WO_3$, showing the incomplete stage of sintering. Unreacted WO_3 remains at the arrows. [After H. Horiuchi[8].]

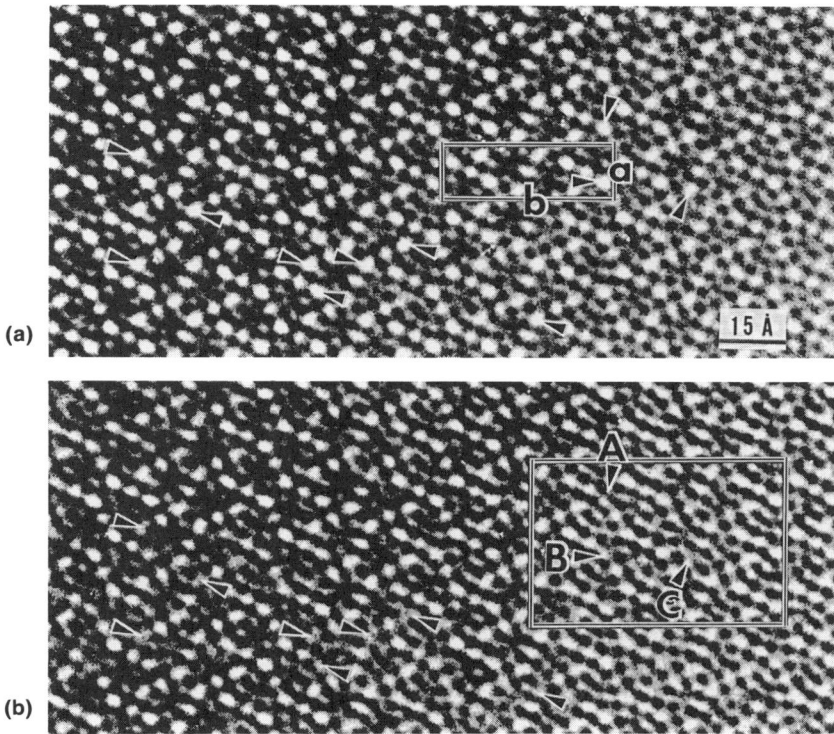

Figure 2.3.3 1 MV HRTEM images of $4Nb_2O_5 \cdot 9WO_3$. (a) and (b) are the same area before and after long time electron irradiation. The contrast change at the arrows is due to the movement of atoms. $a = 12.3$ and $b = 36.6$ Å. [After S. Horiuchi et al.[9]]

SnO_2 behaves as an n-type semiconductor when a small amount of Sb is added.

Figure 2.3.3 is an HRTEM image of $4Nb_2O_5 \cdot 9WO_3^9$ prepared at 1300°C. In (a) individual sites of cation rows are resolved as dark spots. In (b) the same area as (a) is shown after irradiation by 1-MV electrons for about 20 minutes. From the change in contrast between (a) and (b) we may conclude that some fraction of the atoms is shifted as a result of the collision with electrons. The movement of atoms is schematically shown by arrows in Figure 2.3.4a. It is known for an ideal crystal (b) that the atom rows of -M-O-M-O-, where M denotes a cation, occupy the pentagonal tunnels whose positions are indicated by dots in (a). In a real crystal, however, there must be an

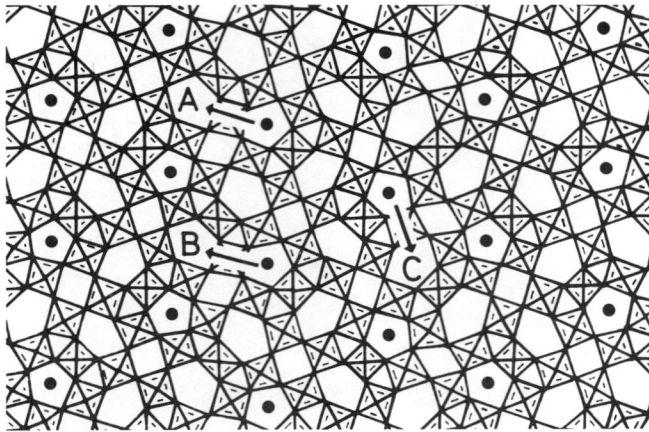

(a)

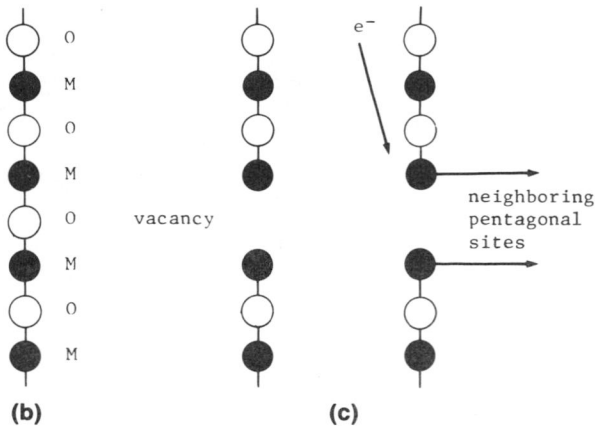

(b)   **(c)**

Figure 2.3.4 A schematic explanation of contrast change in Figure 2.3.3. (a) The atom rows in the pentagonal tunnel are shown after and before oxidation, respectively in (b) and (c).

oxygen vacancy, as indicated in (c). When the highly energetic electrons hit the cations near the vacancy, they must be knocked out because the chemical bond is weak. It is then supposed that adjoining oxygens and cations are shifted successively.

The model in (c) presumes the existence of oxygen vacancies. These must have been formed during crystal growth under the reducing atmosphere. This presumption is supported by the fact that the compound increases in weight when oxidized in air at a temperature lower than 900°C. The weight change measured has suggested that 1/10 of the oxygen sites in the atom rows in the pentagonal tunnels are vacant in the reduced state, that is, before oxidation.

The compound becomes electrically nonconductive after oxidation. The electrical conduction before the oxidation must be related to oxygen vacancies. Here, the electrons released on the formation of vacancies can form a donor level.

Another type of electrical conduction in oxides arises from the movement of ions. In a β-alumina, as a typical example, Na^+ ions migrate through the crystal. Because of its high ionic conductivity, β-Al_2O_3 is anticipated to be useful as a solid electrolyte for electric cars. The bright spots in Figure 2.3.5 show the holes in which Na^+ ions migrate. Incident electrons are along the [110] direction. The dark-contrast layers between the rows of the bright spots consist of a spinel-type structure. Some investigators have studied β''- and β''''-Al_2O_3 by HRTEM and have reported images similar to those in Figure 2.3.5.[10]

Figure 2.3.5 A 1 MV HRTEM image of β-Al_2O_3. Bright spots show the holes, in which Na^+ ions migrate through the crystal.

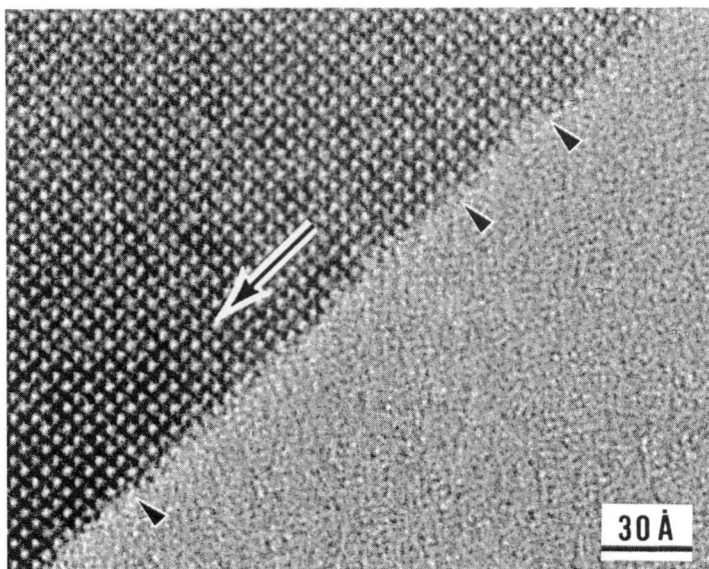

Figure 2.3.6 Interface between crystalline and amorphous phases in $Si_3N_4 \cdot Y_2O_3$. Small steps are seen at the arrows. [After S. Horiuchi and M. Mitomo[11].]

2.3.3.2 High-Temperature Structural Materials

Some covalently refractory ceramics show excellent mechanical properties at temperatures near 1000°C. Typical examples are SiC and Si_3N_4. Because volume diffusion is not easy with these materials, it is rather difficult to sinter the starting powders. In order to promote sintering, another powder, like Y_2O_3, is added to the Si_3N_4. However, an amorphous phase produced at the grain boundaries often causes mechanical strength deterioration at high temperatures. It is then necessary to decrease the amount of additive or to crystallize the glassy phase produced. Figure 2.3.6 is an HRTEM image of the interface between the crystalline and amorphous phases in $Si_3N_4 : Y_2O_3$.[11] The interface is parallel to the [110] plane of Si_3N_4, and there are many steps with atomic scale height at the regions indicated by the small arrows. It is probable that the crystalline region increases in volume when the steps move simultaneously in the direction of the large arrow.

The diffusion rate is generally higher in oxides than in nitrides or carbides. This means that oxides are deformed more easily by creep at high temperature. Some oxide materials are, however, strengthened by the formation of complex structures produced by heat treatment. Accordingly, this provides another type of high-temperature structural material. A typical example is partially stabilized zirconia. Figure 2.3.7 is an image of CaO- (7.9 mol%) stabilized ZrO_2 that is commercially available.[12] Here, the tetragonal phase exhibits geometrically defined habit planes produced on transformation from the cubic phase; a small amount of monoclinic phase is indicated by the narrow fringe pattern.

2.3.3.3 A Hydrogen Storage Material

Rhenium trioxide, ReO_3, was thought to be stable in air at room temperature. Electron diffraction patterns from a crystal exposed in air have, however, given weak but clear extra reflections.[13] This suggests that ReO_3 rapidly reacts with H_2O in air according to the following equation:

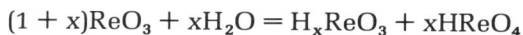

$$(1 + x)ReO_3 + xH_2O = H_xReO_3 + xHReO_4$$

where $x < 0.1$. The chemical reaction causes hydrogen to be ab-

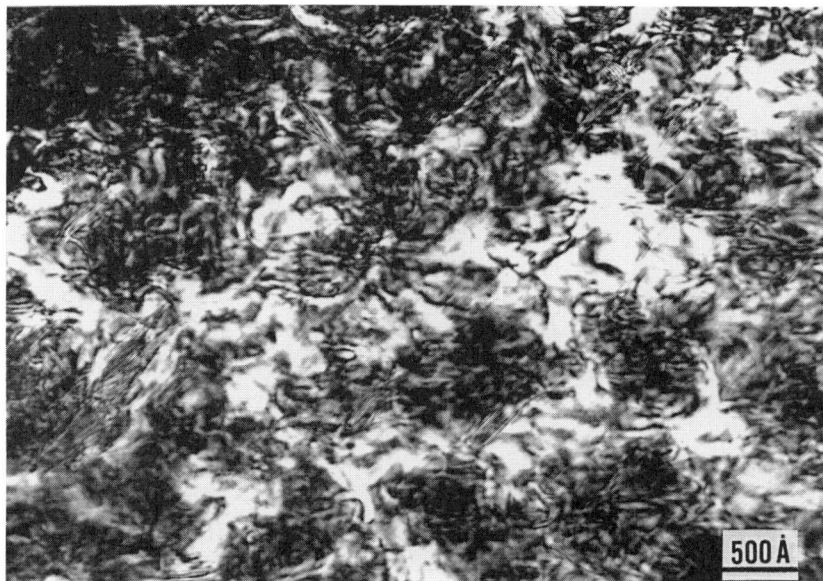

Figure 2.3.7 Complex structure in ZrO_2 partially stabilized by CaO.

sorbed by the ReO_3. The extra reflections are considered to be from the resulting H_xReO_3 crystal in which a superstructure with a dimension $\approx 2a \times 2a \times 2a$ is formed, where a is the lattice parameter of the initial ReO_3.

In the cubic unit cell of ReO_3, the Re ions are indicated by dark circles in Figure 2.3.8a and the O ions by open ones. Figure 2.3.8b is a 1-MV HRTEM image taken with the incident electrons along the [100] direction. The dark spots correspond to the position of the Re ions projected along the [100] direction. $HReO_4$, formed by the chemical reaction above, can be recognized as a thin amorphous layer at the crystal surface indicated by the arrow in Figure 2.3.8b.

The optical diffraction of the image in Figure 2.3.8b gives a simple pattern consisting only of fundamental spots from a normal ReO_3. Here, no extra reflections are observed. This suggests that the superstructure mentioned above owes its origin to the displacement of oxygen ions. The displacement direction must be [011], first because of the stabilization of hydrogens absorbed in the crystal (as will be mentioned) and second because such a displacement is reported for $D_{0.53}WO_3$, whose unit cell dimension and excitation rule are the same as those of H_xReO_3.[14]

The potential in ReO_3 has been calculated, and the result given in Figure 2.3.9 shows that a shallow potential well is formed along the periphery around an oxygen in the [200] plane. The radius of the

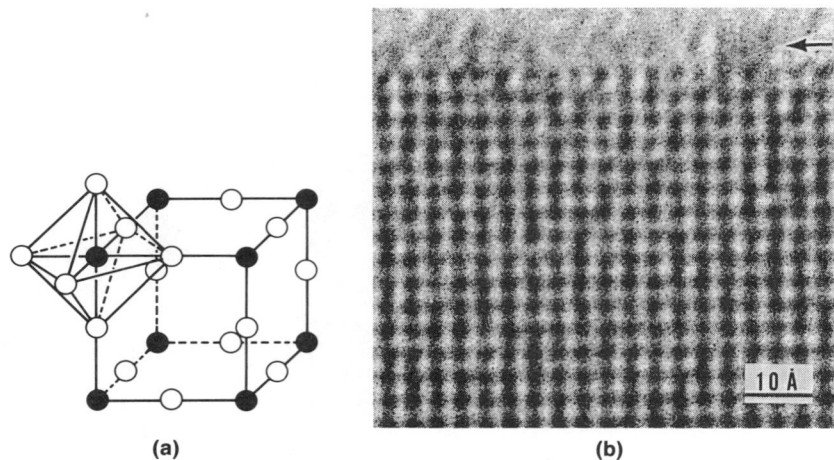

(a)　　　　　　　　　　　(b)

Figure 2.3.8 The unit-cell of ReO_3, $a = 3.75$ Å (a). A 1 MV HRTEM image of "ReO_3." (b) At the edge of the fragment there is a thin amorphous layer of $HReO_4$. [After S. Horiuchi et al.[13]]

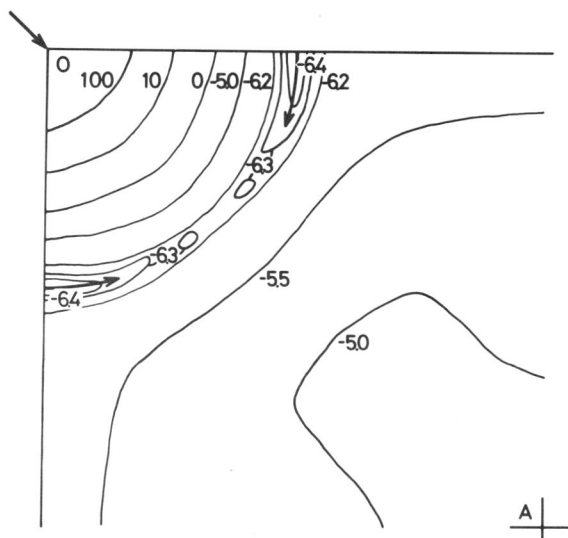

Figure 2.3.9 A calculated potential map in ReO_3 (volt). One quarter of the (200) plane is shown. [After S. Horiuchi et al.[13]]

circle is almost equal to the conventional bond length between 0 and H (0.94 Å). The hydrogen absorbed is considered to exist as H^+ in the crystal. Because the amount is very small, the protons must be localized in the potential well and must move around the central oxygen.

When the oxygens move slightly in the [011] direction, the potential minima become deeper and shift along the well (as indicated by arrows in Figure 2.3.9), with the distance between O-H remaining constant. The displacement direction of [011] can be reversed in every second oxygen layer. This must be the origin of the superstructure.

When the volume of the absorbed hydrogen is increased, the phase transforms from cubic to monoclinic.[15] When it is heated, the transformation in the opposite direction occurs easily and releases hydrogens. It has recently been reported that a much larger amount of dueterium can be included to form $D_{1.36}ReO_3$,[16] whose structure is essentially the same as that of the cubic H_xReO_3 mentioned above.

2.3.4 Conclusion

Fine structures in inorganic materials, which are being used practically in new ceramics, are characterized on an atomic level by

HRTEM images. It is noted that fine structures are related to such excellent properties as electrical conductivity in reduced Nb-W oxide and β-Al$_2$O$_3$, mechanical strength at high temperatures for Si$_3$N$_4$ and CaO-stabilized ZrO$_2$, and hydrogen storage for ReO$_3$.

References

1. Kihrborg, L., ed., *Proc. Nobel Symposium 47*, "Direct Imaging of Atoms in Crystals and Molecules," 1979.
2. Eisenhandler, C. B., and Siegel, B. M., *J. Appl. Phys.* 37:1613 (1966).
3. Horiuchi, S., Matsui, Y., and Bando, Y., *Jpn. J. Appl. Phys.* 15:2483 (1976).
4. Buseck, P. R., and Iijima, S., *Am. Mineralog.* 59:79 (1974).
5. Horiuchi, S., Kikuchi, T., and Goto, M.: *Acta Crystallog.* A33:701 (1977).
6. Frank, J., *Optik* 38:519 (1973).
   Fejes, P. L., *Acta Crystallog.* A33:109 (1977).
7. Ishizuka, K., *Ultramicroscopy* 5:55 (1980).
8. Horiuchi, S., *Ultramicroscopy* 10:229 (1982).
9. Horiuchi, S., Muramatsu, K., and Matsui, Y., *Acta Crystallog.* A34:939 (1978).
10. Matsui, Y., and Horiuchi, S., *Acta Crystallog.* A37:51 (1981).
    Matsui, Y., Horiuchi, S., and Ohta, T., *J. Solid State Chem.* 32:181 (1980).
11. Horiuchi, S., and Mitomo, M., *J. Mat. Sci.* 14:2543 (1979).
12. Horiuchi, S., and Suzuki, T. (forthcoming).
13. Horiuchi, S., Kimizuka, N., and Yamamoto, A., *Nature* 279:226 (1979).
14. Wiseman, P. J., and Dickens, P. G., *J. Solid State Chem.* 6:374 (1973).
15. Kimizuka, N., Akahane, T., Matsumoto, S., and Yukino, K., *Inorg. Chem.* 15:3178 (1976).
16. Dickens, P. G., and Weller, M. T., *J. Solid State Chem.* 48:407 (1983).

2.4 Characterization of Aluminosilicate Glass Containing Rare Earth Oxides

Akio Makishima

2.4.1 Introduction

Rare earth oxides, including Sc$_2$O$_3$ and Lu$_2$O$_3$, are some of the less common oxides. Very few studies have been reported on the effects of rare earth oxides on the properties and structure of silicate glass. Izumitani and Sagara[1] recently summarized the application of rare

earth oxides for various kinds of optical glass, such as borate- and phosphate-based glass. Their review reveals that application of rare earth oxides is a relatively new field and that many new kinds of glass containing rare earth elements could be developed.

Because Y_2O_3 has the highest melting temperature (2410°C) of the rare earth oxides, melting an aluminosilicate glass containing Y_2O_3 is expected to require a high temperature. Russian workers[2] reported that small amounts of glass in the system Al_2O_3-Y_2O_3-SiO_2 were obtained by melting the composition at 1800 to 2000°C for 15 minutes. They reported refractive indices for the vitrification region, but their exact experimental procedures were not described. The present author and co-workers[3] discovered that many variations of aluminosilicate glass containing large amounts of Y_2O_3 could be obtained by conventional melting. Fifty grams of glass were melted at 1550°C, and La_2O_3 and TiO_2 were added to expand the glass formation region. All of them were hard and showed high elastic modulus, refractive index, and alkaline durability values. The physical properties of an aluminosilicate glass containing a large amount of Y_2O_3, TiO_2, and La_2O_3 have been described by the author and co-workers.[3] They also discuss the relation between physical properties and chemical composition for these glass variations,[3,4] which do not contain alkali or alkaline earth oxides.

Glass fibers with high elastic modulus are useful for composite materials in combination with carbon fibers. The high-modulus fiber or so-called S glass fiber, has a Young's modulus of ~ 800 kbar, but some current glass has a much higher value (~ 1100 kbar) for Young's modulus. High-alkaline-durability glass fibers are used for reinforcement of cement (GRC). At present ZrO_2 containing silicate fibers developed by Pilkington Brothers Co. has sufficient alkaline durability for the high-alkaline environment of cement, but glass fibers with higher alkaline durability need to be developed.

Recently many types of silicate glass containing both rare earth elements and nitrogen atoms, called oxynitride glass, have been produced.[5] It has been found that the incorporation of nitrogen atoms changes a wide range of glass properties, and glass of high hardness and elastic modulus has been developed. The relations between the structure and properties of some oxynitride glasses are discussed.

2.4.2 Glass Formation

The glass formation region in the system Al_2O_3-Y_2O_3-SiO_2 has been studied, and it has been shown that aluminosilicate glass containing large amounts of Y_2O_3 and/or La_2O_3 can easily be obtained by melting 50 g quantities in an electric furnace with SiC heating elements at 1550°C for 3 hours. Some of the chemical compositions of the glass variations produced are shown in Table 2.4.1. It is noteworthy that a glass of low silica content (~30 mol%) could be prepared. Glass formations in the systems Re_2O_3-Al_2O_3-SiO_2 and Re_2O_3-Y_2O_3-Al_2O_3-SiO_2 (RE = Ce, Pr, Nd, Eu, Gd, Tb, Dy, Ho, Er, Yb, and Sc) were studied by the author and co-workers.[6] It has been shown that except for Ce_2O_3, the upper limit of the amount of rare-earth oxide that can be incorporated into the aluminosilicate glass decreases as the atomic number increases from 57 (La) to 70 (Yb). This behavior is related to the lanthanide contraction. Chemical analysis of the Ce-containing aluminosilicate glass showed Ce^{3+} and Ce^{4+} in amounts of 89% and 11%, respectively. The ionic radius of Ce^{3+} is larger than that of Ce^{4+}, so the coexistence of Ce^{3+} and Ce^{4+} in the Ce-containing glass may influence the glass formation.

The preparation of oxynitride aluminosilicate glass containing rare-earth oxides such as Si-Y-Al-O-N has been reported by several workers.[7] Messier and Broz.[8] formed glass in the system Si-Y-Al-O-N containing up to 15 at% N. They used Si_3N_4 powder as a part of the batch compositions. The author and co-workers[9,10] prepared an oxynitride glass in the system La-Si-O-N containing 18 at% N. The glass has been melted under high N_2 pressure at about 3 MPa.

Table 2.4.1 Glass Compositions and Observed Young's Modulus [from A. Makishima and Shimohira, *J. Non-Cryst. Solids* 38–39:661 (1980)

Glass No.	Oxide (in mol)					Young's Modulus (Kbar)
	SiO_2	Al_2O_3	Y_2O_3	La_2O_3	TiO_2	
GL-1	58.0	24.4	—	17.6	—	949
GY-1	58.0	24.4	17.6	—	—	1123
GY-2	55.0	22.7	22.3	—	—	1145
GYLT-4	50.0	20.0	10.0	10.0	10.0	n.d.
GYT-1	43.2	25.4	18.4	—	13.0	1145
GLT-1	43.2	25.4	—	18.4	13.0	1066
GYT-2	42.0	22.7	23.3	—	13.0	1213
GYL-3	46.0	32.0	11.0	11.0	—	1109
GLT-3	40.0	22.7	—	22.3	15.0	1070
GR-20	77.1	0.6	ZrO_2 (8.5)		Na_2O(11.6)	
						~700
			Li_2O(2.2)			

2.4.3 Observed and Calculated Elastic Modulus

The elastic modulus of aluminosilicate glass containing Y_2O_3 and/or La_2O_3, determined by the ultrasonic method, ranges from 949 to 1213 kbar. Young's modulus for silica glass is 730 kbar, so the current glass can be considered to have a high Young's modulus.

Theoretical elastic moduli of glasses were discussed by Makishima and Mackenzie,[11,12] who considered the dissociation energy per unit volume, G_i, and packing density of atoms in glass, V_t. They derived an equation to calculate Young's modulus, shear modulus, bulk modulus, and Poisson's ratio from chemical composition as

$$E = 83.6V_t\Sigma G_i x_i \qquad (2.4.1)$$

where x_i is the mol fraction of component i. Equation (2.4.1) gives good agreement between the observed and calculated values of Young's modulus for silicate glass containing alkali or alkaline earth oxide. The authors have used the equation to calculate the Young's modulus of the current glass types; Figure 2.4.1 compares the calculated and observed values. As shown by the straight line in this figure, fairly good agreement was obtained between the observed and calculated values for the Young's moduli. The same agreements were obtained for shear and bulk moduli.

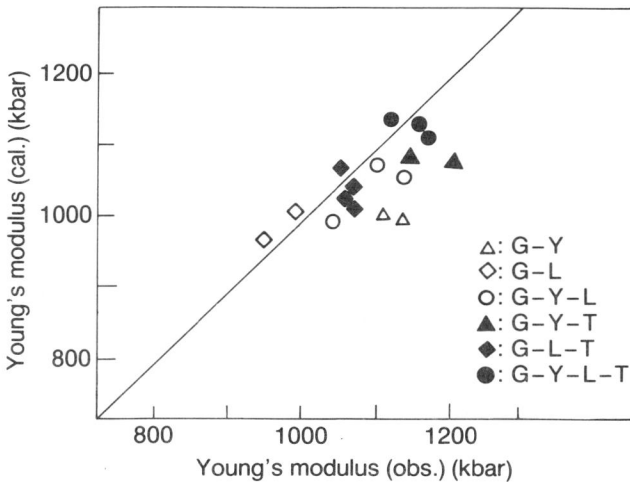

Figure 2.4.1 Agreement between measured Young's moduli and those calculated from Equation (2.4.1) for aluminosilicate glasses containing Y_2O_3 and/or La_2O_3 [from A. Makishima et al., *J. Am. Ceram. Soc.* 61:247 (1978)].

The high values of the elastic modulus for the current glass can be explained by the high dissociation energy of La_2O_3 and Y_2O_3 and the high packing density of the atoms — for example, 0.62 — because most ordinary glass has values of 0.54 to 0.57.[12] Comparison of the Young's modulus of G-Y-1 glass with that of G-L-1 glass, which contains the same amount of Al_2O_3 and SiO_2, shows that Y_2O_3 is more effective than La_2O_3 in increasing the modulus of an aluminosilicate glass. This result is expected because the dissociation energy of Y_2O_3 (17.7 kcal/cm^3) is greater than that of La_2O_3 (16.2 kcal/cm^3). However, this may not always be true, because the packing density factor (V_i) of La_2O_3 is higher (28.4) than that of Y_2O_3 (24.8), and E is determined by the product of $\Sigma G_i x_i$ and $V_t = (\rho/M)\Sigma V_i x_i$ (where ρ is the density and M is the molar volume).

The incorporation of nitrogen atoms into aluminosilicate glass increases the Young's modulus values. The author reported values of 1150 kbar for an aluminosilicate glass containing Y_2O_3, but Messier and Broz[8] reported values of about 1800 kbar for oxynitride aluminosilicate glass containing Y and N, which are comparatively high values for glass.

2.4.4 Vickers Hardness and Refractive Index

Conventional glass is as a whole hard and has a high refractive index. The ranges for the Vickers hardness value and refractive index are 789 to 860 kg/mm^2 and 1.658 to 1.821, respectively. Many types of high-refractive-index optical glass contain PbO but are not as hard. The hardness of an optical glass, SF13, has been reported as 456 kg/mm^2, which is only half that of the current G-Y-T-2 glass (830 kg/mm^2). Their refractive indices are nearly the same (1.74 and 1.77, respectively). In general, the current glass types are comparatively hard when compared with PbO-containing optical glass. Because the empirical coefficients for La_2O_3 and Y_2O_3 for calculating the refractive index of glass are greater than those for common oxides, the high refractive indices of the current glass types are the result of successfully preparing glass having low silica content and large amounts of La_2O_3 and Y_2O_3.

The Vickers hardness values of oxynitride glass are in general higher, and the author and co-workers[10] reported a value of 1220 kg/mm^2 for La-Si-O-N glass containing 18 at% N. This value is much higher than in the La-Si-O oxide glass studied by Mukherjee and co-workers[13] who reported hardness values in the system La_2O_3-SiO_2 of 650 to 700 kg/mm^2. Vickers hardness versus nitrogen content is

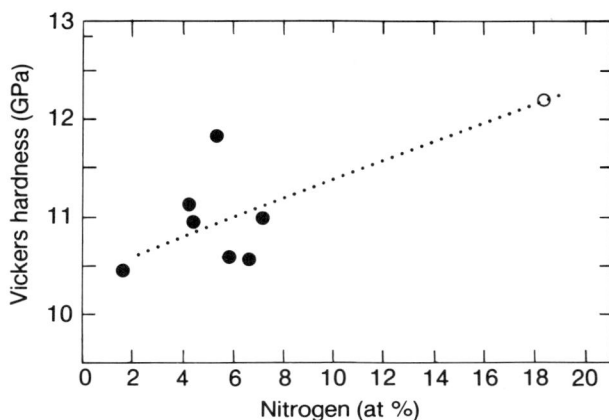

Figure 2.4.2 Vickers hardness versus nitrogen content for oxynitride glasses containing Y or La: (O) La-Si-O-N, (●) Si-Y-Al-O-N [from A. Makishima et al., *J. Am. Ceram. Soc.* 66:C55 (1983)].

plotted in Figure 2.4.2 along with data for oxynitride glass in the system Si-Y-Al-O-N obtained by Loehman.[7] The hardness increases with increasing nitrogen content, which is consistent with the trend in Knoop hardness reported by Messier and Broz.[8]

The coexistence of Si-O and Si-N bonds in the structure of the La-Si-O-N glass was confirmed by their infrared absorption spectra. The Si-N absorption band at 900 cm^{-1} is consistent with those observed for Si-Al-Y-O-N glass and amorphous Si_3N_4. The replacement of O by N in the glass structure tightens the structure via the formation of more bonds than would be present in a similar oxide. This tightening of the glass structure by the formation of Si-N bonds would be a primary reason for the high hardness value of La-Si-O-N glass containing 18 at% N or the Si-Al-Y-O-N oxynitride system glass.

2.4.5 Alkaline Durability

Alkaline durability of silica, borosilicate (Pyrex), and GY-1 glass in 2N NaOH solution at 95 °C has been determined; the results are plotted in Figure 2.4.3. The weight loss of borosilicate and silica glass changes linearly with soaking time, indicating the corrosion proceeds by the dissolution of the network structure. The result also indicates that GY-1 glass containing a large amount of Y_2O_3 has high alkaline durability. The authors determined the alkaline durability of the current aluminosilicate glass types and ZrO_2-containing glass

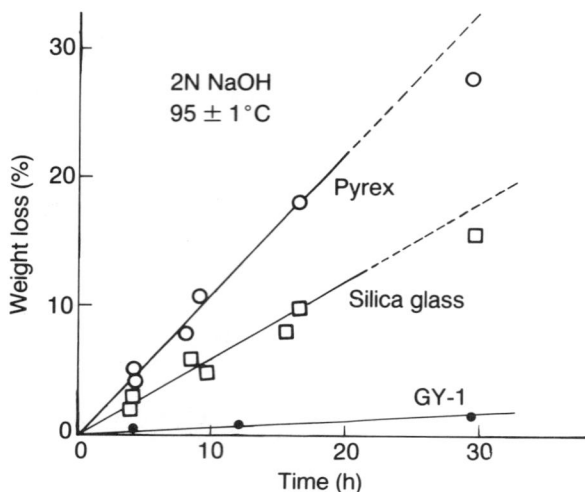

Figure 2.4.3 Alkaline durability of silica, borosilicate (Pyrex), and GY-1 glasses in a 2N NaOH solution at 95°C, powder method [from A. Makishima and T. Shimohira, *J. Non-Cryst. Solids* 38–39:661 (1980)].

(GR-20)[14] for long-soaking-time periods in 2N NaOH solution at 95°C. The results are shown in Figure 2.4.4. The chemical compositions of these glass types are shown in Table 2.4.1 in the order of their alkaline durability. The result for Gr-20 is omitted.

It was found that some of these aluminosilicate glass variations have very high alkaline durability, higher than that of ZrO_2-containing glass. The Young's modulus for these is greater than that for ZrO_2-containing glass, as shown in Table 2.4.1. The present results show that alkaline durability increases with decreasing SiO_2 content, and this can be interpreted by considering the solubility of the component oxide in alkaline solution. Y_2O_3 and La_2O_3 act as components to increase both alkaline durability and elastic modulus; Al_2O_3 lowers the alkaline durability but increases the elastic modulus and is an important oxide for stable glass formation.

2.4.6 Conclusion

Several types of aluminosilicate and oxynitride glass containing large amounts of rare earth oxides, such as Y_2O_3 and/or La_2O_3, have been investigated. Glasses having high elastic modulus, hardness, refractive index, and alkaline durability have been developed. Y_2O_3,

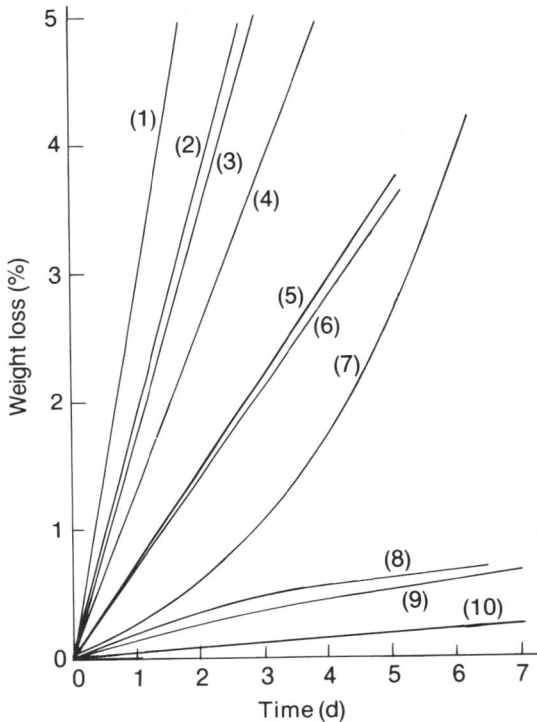

Figure 2.4.4 Alkaline durability of high-modulus aluminosilicate glasses containing Y$_2$O$_3$, La$_2$O$_3$, and TiO$_2$ in 2N NaOH solution at 95°C. (1) GL-1, (2) GY-1, (3) GR-20, (4) GY-2, (5) GYLT-4, (6) GYT-1, (7) GLT-1, (8) GYT-2, (9) GYL-3, (10) GLT-3 [from A. Makishima and T. Shimohira, *J. Non-Cryst. Solids* 38–39:661 (1980)].

La$_2$O$_3$, and N act as agents to increase the elastic modulus, hardness, refractive index, and alkaline durability. Al$_2$O$_3$ lowers the alkaline durability but increases the elastic modulus and is an important oxide for glass formation. The observed Young's moduli of these various types of glass show good agreement with theoretical values.

References

1. Izumitani, T., and Sagara, H., in *Rare Earths—Properties and Applications*. T. Kanho and H. Yanagida, eds. Tokyo: Gihoodou-shyutsupan, 1980, p. 153.

2. Sedykh, T. S., Pustil'nik, A. I., and Mikheikin, V. I., Izv. Akad. Nauk SSSR, *Neorg. Mater.* 11:1153 (1975).
3. Makishima, A., Tamura, Y., and Sakaino, T., *J. Am. Ceram. Soc.* 61:247 (1978).
4. Makishima, A., and Shimohira, T., *J. Non-Cryst. Solids* 38–39:661 (1980).
5. Jack, K. H., *J. Mat. Sci.* 11:1135 (1976).
6. Makishima, A., Kobayashi, M., Shimohira, T., and Nagata, T., *J. Am. Ceram. Soc.* 65:C210 (1982).
7. Loehman, R. E., *J. Am. Ceram. Soc.* 62:491 (1979).
8. Messier, D. R., and Broz, A., *J. Am. Ceram. Soc.* 65:C123 (1982).
9. Makishima, A., Mitomo, M., Tanaka, H., Ii, N., and Tsutsumi, M., *Yogyo-Kyokai-Shi* 88:701 (1980).
10. Makishima, A., Mitomo, M., Ii, N., and Tsutsumi, M., *J. Am. Ceram. Soc.* 66:C55 (1983).
11. Makishima, A., and Mackenzie, J. D., *J. Non-Cryst. Solids* 12:35 (1973).
12. Makishima, A., and Mackenzie, J. D., *J. Non-Cryst. Solids* 17:147 (1975).
13. Mukherjee, S. P., Zarzycki, J., and Traverse, J. P., *J. Mat. Sci.* 11:341 (1976).
14. Larner, L. J., Speakman, K., and Majumdar, A. J., *J. Non-Cryst. Solids* 20:43 (1976).

2.5 Characterization of Dislocations

Yuusuke Moriyoshi

2.5.1 Introduction

MgO is an ionic material with a simple face center cubic structure with a [100] cleavage face. Because of its high solubility in acids, it is easy to make thin films for a transmission electron microscope (TEM) by chemical thinning. Therefore, basic studies of dislocation-related phenomena such as mechanical and thermal properties in MgO have been conducted using a TEM. The authors' experimental data concerning high-temperature creep[1] and thermal properties of dislocations in MgO single crystals[2] are briefly presented in this section.

2.5.2 High-Temperature Creep in MgO

Since Nabarro-Herring[3] and Coble,[4] steady-state creep of polycrystal MgO has been studied extensively.[5-10] The creep theories associated with dislocation climb, compression creep, and [110] tensile creep in MgO single crystals have been reported by Weertman,[11] Bilde-Sorensen,[12] and Clauer and Wilcox,[13] respectively. The authors have also studied dislocation structure developed in MgO single crystals during [100] tensile creep in air using TEM.[1]

MgO single crystals with major impurities of Si $\sim$ 300, Ca $\sim$ 330, Al $\sim$ 650, and Fe $\sim$ 70 ppm were cleaved on [100] faces to 20 $\times$ 10 $\times$ 0.5 mm. The sheets were further thinned by mechanical polishing on a grinding wheel with diamond powder. Then the sheets were coated with lacquer and treated in a hot phosphoric acid solution as shown schematically in Figure 2.5.1. The resultant specimen was set between alumina holders for creep tests that were carried out at 1250–1450°C under stresses ranging from 10 to 350 kg/cm².

The creep data obtained showed the usual primary and steady-state creep stages. The steady-state creep region was very short, and it may be that creep takes place nonuniformly. Tertiary creep was hardly observed. The relationship of strain rate $\dot{e}$ and stress σ can be expressed as $\dot{e} \approx \sigma^{2.2}$ at every experimental temperature from 1250–1450°C at stresses higher than 80 kg/cm². The effect on the creep rate of 1000 ppm of cobalt was indiscernible in this experiment.

The dislocation density in the specimens tested at 1400°C was measured by etch pitting as well as by TEM. The stress dependence of the dislocation density, ρ, is almost similar to that of the strain rate. That is, the dislocation density changes little over the stress ranges from 10–80 kg/cm² and increases at stresses higher than 80 kg/cm².

Dislocation structures during creep at 1400°C at various stresses are shown in Figure 2.5.2. In comparison with the specimen obtained from cleavage, there was no distinct dislocation structure feature in

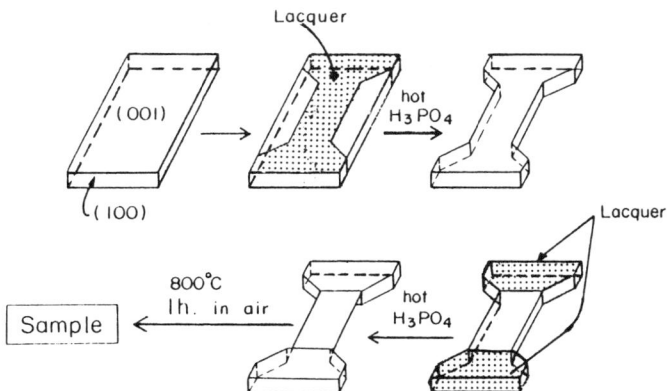

Figure 2.5.1 Schematic for preparing a tensile creep sample [from Y. Moriyoshi et al. *J. Phys. Chem.* NF119:239 (1980)].

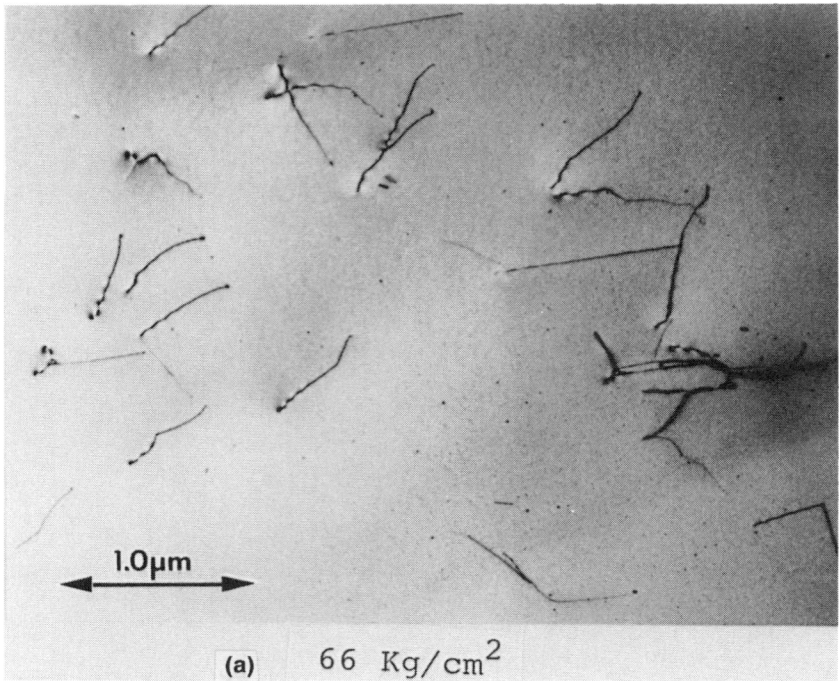

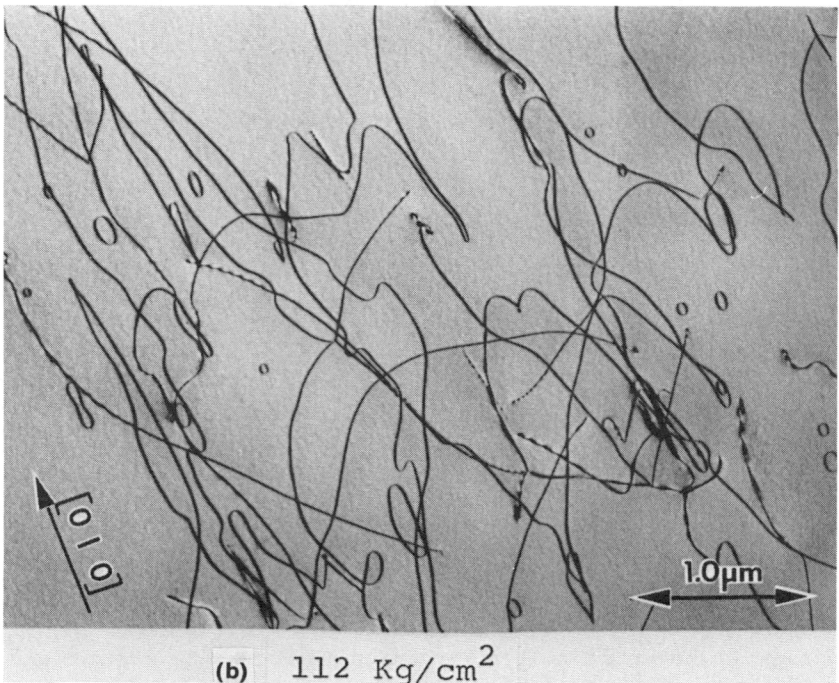

Figure 2.5.2 Dislocation structures developed during tensile creep of MgO at 1400°C at 66 (*a*), 112 (*b*), 190 (*c*), 250 (*d*), 245 (*e*), and 350 Kg/cm² (*f*) [from Y. Moriyoshi et al., *J. Phys. Chem.* NF119:239 (1980)].

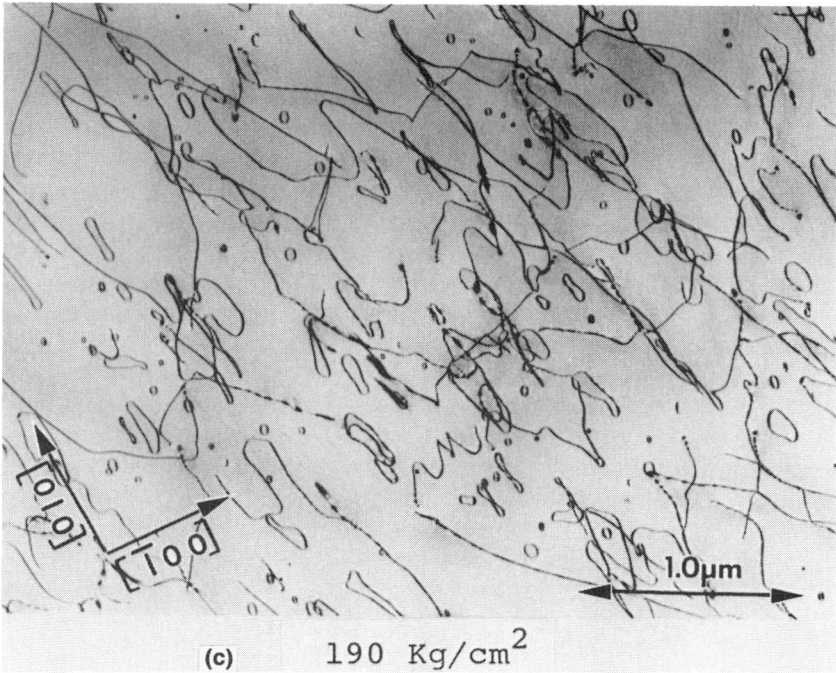

(c)   190 Kg/cm^2

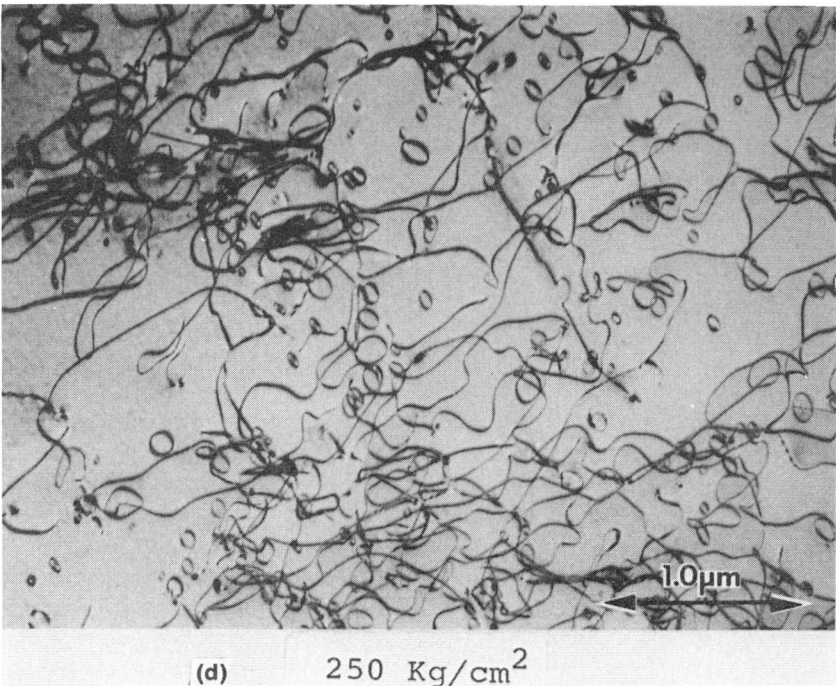

(d)   250 Kg/cm^2

115

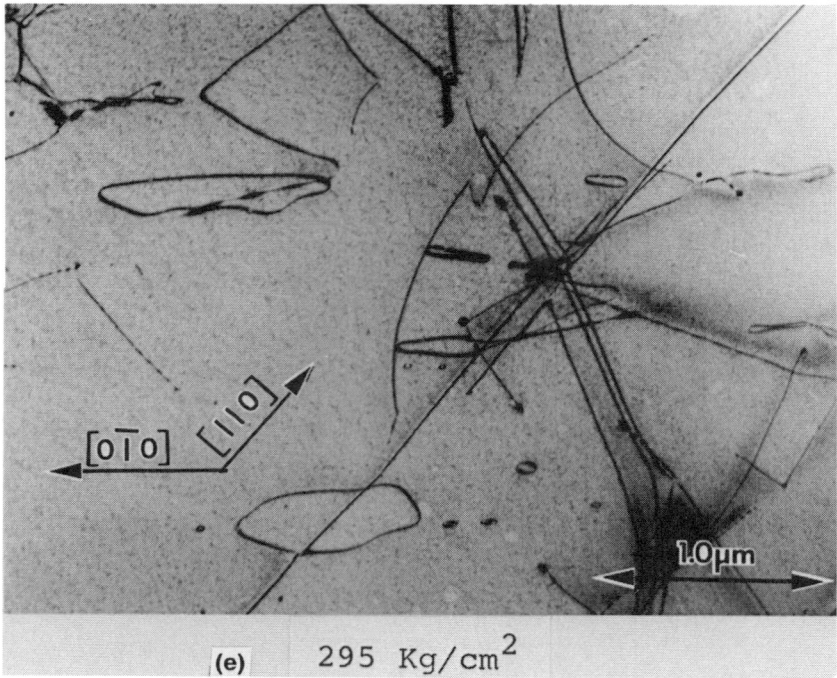

(e)   295 Kg/cm^2

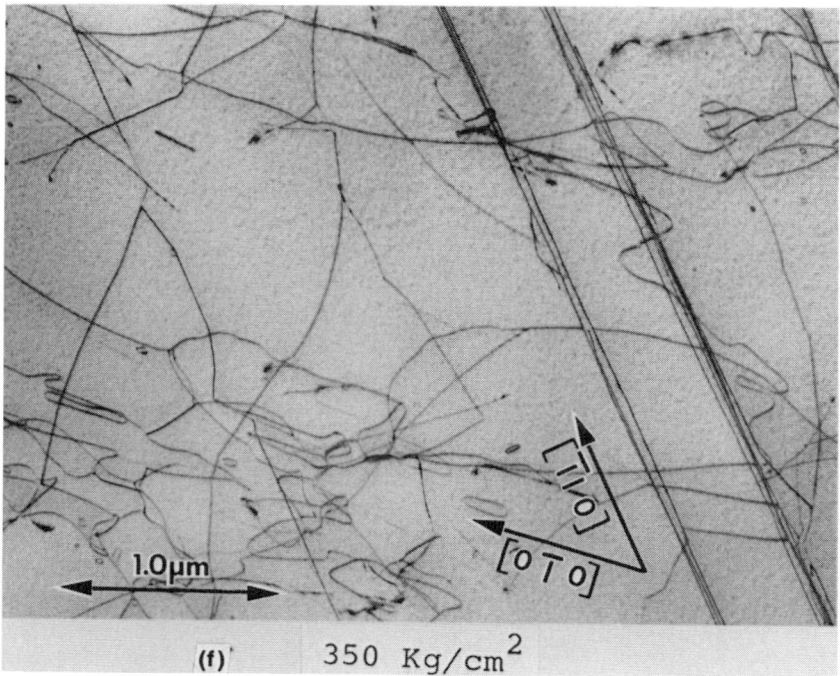

(f)   350 Kg/cm^2

Figure 2.5.2 (Continued)

the specimen tested at 66 kg/cm². At stresses lower than 80 kg/cm², no distinct dislocation structural features were found in the specimens tested. At stresses higher than 80 kg/cm², where dislocation density increases proportionally with the applied stress, long curved dislocations appeared at 112 kg/cm², and a large number of dislocation loops existed in the specimen tested at 190 kg/cm² and 250 kg/cm². At stresses higher than about 290 kg/cm², long straight dislocations appeared.

Both dislocation density and creep rate changed little over the stress ranges from 10–80 kg/cm². This suggests that the creep rate in single-crystal MgO correlated well with dislocation density, and it is assumed that no glide would occur in this stress range because there are no characteristic changes in the dislocation structure or dislocation density. At this stage creep takes place by dislocation climb, that is, by diffusional processes through grown-in dislocations in the crystal.

In the range from 80–250 kg/cm², creep rates as well as dislocation densities increased with an increase of stress. The characteristic feature of dislocation structures in this range is the presence of many dislocation loops. Groves and Kelly[14] have reported that plastic deformation introduces elongated-edge dislocation loops in MgO crystals and that relatively large circular loops are derived from the elongated loops by annealing at 1200–1500°C. According to the present authors' observations, dislocation loops are created by the motion of screw dislocations with jogs. Elongated-edge dislocation dipoles are produced by screw dislocation motion, and then the elongated dipole is seen to break up into a loop as shown in Figure 2.5.3. A circular loop would be derived from this.

Analysis of the Burgers vector **b** shows that most of the dislocation loops have the same Burgers vector and are out of contrast for the diffraction vector $\mathbf{g} = [\bar{2}02]$. They are on the planes of the same slip system. Impurity precipitations may also have some influence on the formation of dislocation loops. Precipitations along the dislocations were often observed. Fundamentally, these dislocation loops are created by initial dislocation glide and subsequent dislocation climb. The question is this: Which is the rate-determining step in the various stress ranges? As clarification, the temperature dependence of strain rates at a constant stress showed an activation energy of 73 kcal/mol, which is in fairly good agreement with that of the extrinsic 0^{2-} diffusion coefficients in MgO, 62 kcal/mol, obtained by Oishi and Kingery.[15] This may indicate that creep in these stress ranges is controlled mainly by dislocation climb.

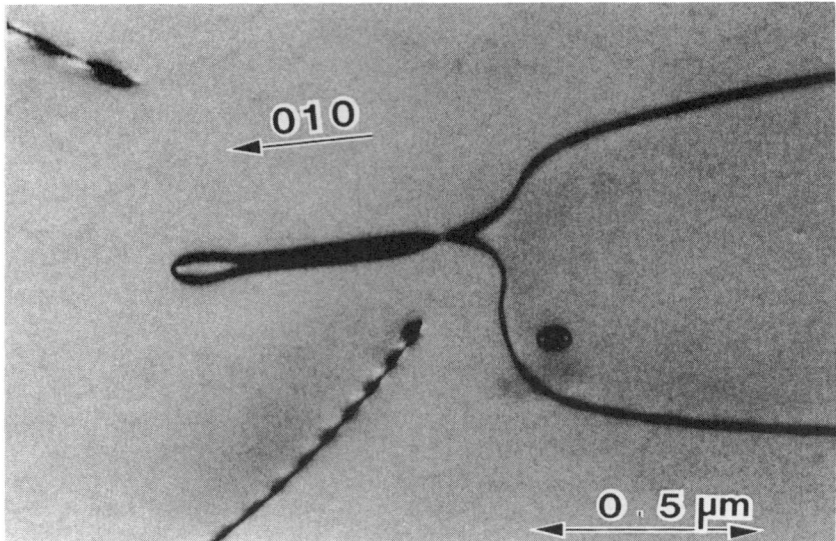

Figure 2.5.3 Dislocation loop generated from a dislocation dipole in an MgO sample tested at 1400°C and 112 kg/cm² [from Y. Moriyoshi et al., *J. Phys. Chem.* NF119:239 (1980)].

2.5.3 Thermal Properties of Dislocations

Dislocation behavior at high temperatures is very interesting. Narayan and Washburn[16] indicated that the diffusion coefficients obtained from the change of dislocation loop radii agree fairly well with those of oxygen diffusion coefficients reported by Oishi and Kingery. Narayan and Washburn[17] also reported a diffusion coefficient for the breaking up into rows of prismatic dislocation loops by pipe diffusion.

The authors have recently studied the thermal properties of dislocations in MgO single crystals.[2] Thin sheets of MgO (mentioned previously) were mechanically polished on a diamond disk to introduce dislocations into the crystals. The resultant sheets were ultrasonically washed in water, alcohol, and acetone. Then the sheets were fired in air in a LaCrO₃ furnace at 1400–1750°C for given firing times. The heat-treated sheets were thinned by the procedure developed by Washburn and co-workers[18] in which a jet of orthophosphoric acid is directed at the area to be thinned. The resultant thin foil specimen, to which a carbon coating was applied, was observed with a TEM. The dislocation density was measured by both the etch-pit method and with a TEM. The determination of the Burgers vector was carried out by analysis of diffraction patterns and images. The thickness of the foils was estimated by the projected length of the linear screw dislocations on the [110] faces in the foils.

A typical micrograph taken before heat treatment is shown in Figure 2.5.4. The average dislocation density value is about $10^{10}/cm^2$, which was determined by both etch pits and an electron micrograph. As can be seen from the micrograph, these dislocations are randomly oriented, and dipoles are visible. When the thin sheets were heat treated at a given temperature for various times, subgrain boundaries, as shown in Figure 2.5.5, were formed. Their size depends on the dislocation density. High dislocation density results in small subgrains; low density forms large subgrains. This indicates that the subgrain boundaries were formed by interactions among the various dislocations in the sheet. If unheat-treated foils are compared with heat-treated ones, the dislocation densities are similar. After subgrain boundaries were formed in the crystal, dislocations associated with the boundaries were virtually immobile for a long time. Therefore, the diffusion coefficient can be estimated by this process if a

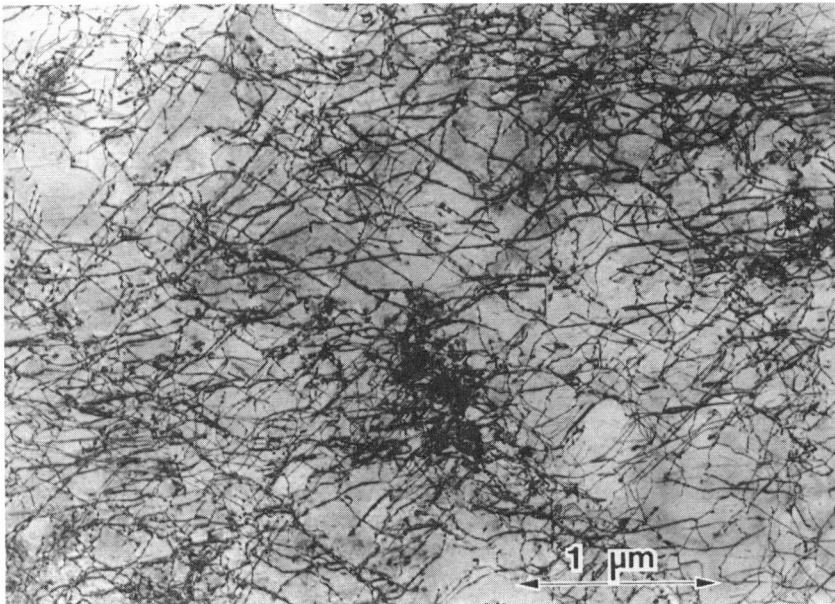

Figure 2.5.4 Dislocations in MgO single crystals introduced by mechanical polishing.

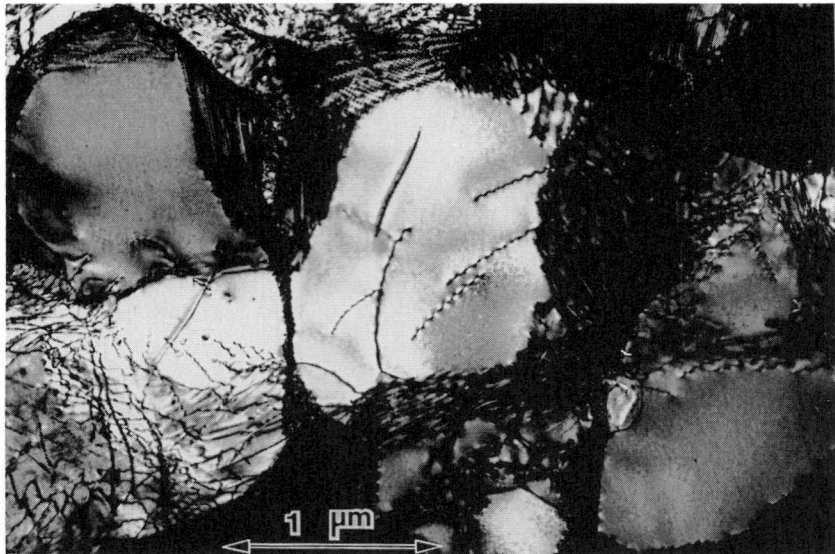

Figure 2.5.5 Subgrain boundary in a heat-treated sample of MgO.

relation exists between heating times and the subgrain formation temperature. The diffusion coefficient obtained from mathematical treatment of the data is

$$D = 1.35 \times 10^{-5} \exp(-75.5 \times 10^3/RT)$$

This value was compared with those obtained by other authors. Our data are one order of magnitude lower than that of Oishi and Kingery.[15] The activation energy of oxygen ion diffusion is 62.4 kcal/mol, which is a little different from our data, 75.5 kcal/mol. The discrepancy between the two is not large. Therefore, the formation process of subgrain boundaries is rate-determined by the slowest diffusion species, the oxygen ion, in MgO.

The electron micrographs, shown in Figure 2.5.6, indicate typical dislocation nets at boundaries. A figure like this is very often found in heat-treated specimens. The character of dislocations at subgrain boundaries has been determined from the out-of-contrast conditions corresponding to $b \cdot g = 0$ and $b \cdot gxu = 0$ elsewhere.

As mentioned before, dislocations are thermodynamically unstable. However, heat treatment at very high temperature, such as 1700°C, for 24 hours is not sufficient to eliminate them. Clauer and

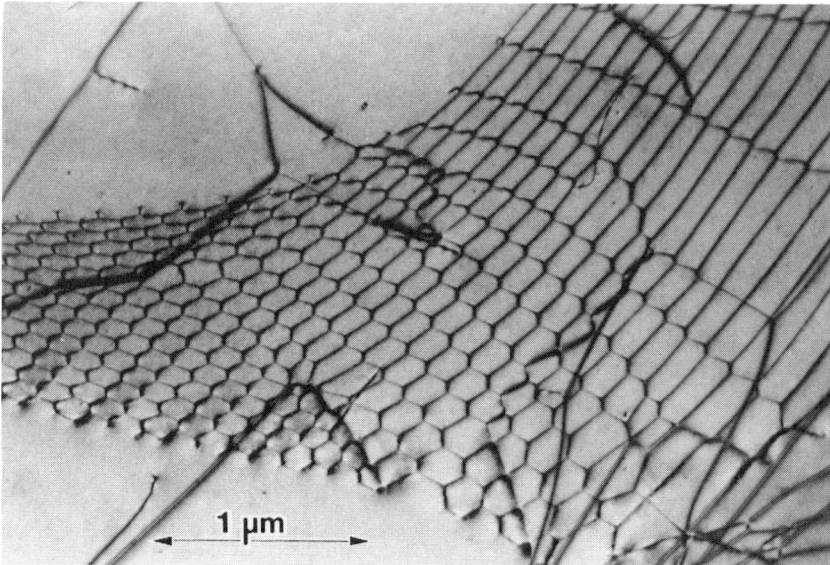

Figure 2.5.6 Dislocation network at a subgrain boundary in a sample of MgO heat treated at 1900°C for 180 minutes [from Y. Moriyoshi et al., *J. Phys. Chem.* NF118:187 (1979)].

Wilcox[13] have reported the elimination of disloctions in MgO in the case of heat treatment at a very high temperature for 30 minutes in an argon atmosphere. Our data of 1900°C for 180 minutes, however, indicate that subgrain boundaries clearly exist. Thus, the dislocations associated with the formation of subgrain boundaries are very stable. It is difficult to eliminate them by heat treatment.

It has been reported that impurities were precipitated preferentially at dislocations and at nodes of the dislocation network, and that impurity segregation is found at the subgrain boundaries of MgO.[19] However, the segregation and precipitation of impurities at the subgrain boundaries was seldom observed in our data. Dislocation loops also could not be found.

2.5.4 Conclusion

Dislocation-related phenomena, high temperature creep, and thermal properties of dislocations in MgO single crystals have been briefly presented. These problems are thoroughly discussed in an article entitled "Dislocation in MgO" submitted for publication in *Ceramic Advances.*[20]

References

1. Moriyoshi, Y., Ikegami, T., Shirasaki, S., and Sekikawa, Y., *J. Phy. Chem.* NF119:239 (1980).
2. Moriyoshi, Y., Ikegami, T., Matsuda, S., and Shirasaki, S., *J. Phys. Chem.* NF118:187 (1979).
3. Nabarro, F. R. N., *Report of the Conference on Strength of Solids,* University of Bristol, England, 1947, p. 75; Herring, C., *J. Appl. Phys.* 21:437 (1950).
4. Coble, R. L., *J. Appl. Phys.* 34:1679 (1963).
5. Gordon, R. S., *J. Am. Ceram. Soc.* 56:147 (1973).
6. Gordon, R. S., and Hodge, J. D., *J. Mat. Sci.* 10:200 (1975).
7. Ashby, M., *Acta Metall.* 20:887 (1972).
8. Evans, H. E., and Knowles, G., *Acta Metall.* 26:141 (1978); 25:963 (1977).
9. Hodge, J. D., Lessing, P. A., and Gordon, R. S., *J. Mat. Sci.* 12:1598 (1977).
10. Ikuma, Y., and Gordon, R. S., *J. Am. Ceram. Soc.* 66:139 (1983).
11. Weertman, J., *J. Appl. Phys.* 26:1213 (1955); 28:362 (1957).
12. Bilde-Sorensen, J. B., *Acta Metall.* 21:1495 (1973).
13. Clauer, A. H., and Wilcox, B. A., *J. Am. Ceram. Sci.* 59:89 (1976).
14. Groves, G. W., and Kelly, A., *J. Appl. Phys.* 34:3104 (1963).
15. Oishi, Y., and Kingery, W. D., *J. Chem. Phys.* 33:480 (1960).
16. Narayan, J., and Washburn, J., *Acta Metall.* 21:533 (1973).
17. Narayan, J., and Washburn, J., *Cryst. Lattice Defects* 3:91 (1972).
18. Washburn, J., Groves, G. W., Kelly, A., and Williamson, G. K., *Philos. Mag.* 5:991 (1960).
19. Kingery, W. D., *J. Am. Ceram. Sci.* 57:1 (1974).
20. Moriyoshi, Y., *Ceramic Advances* 10:258 (1985).

2.6 Grain Boundary Structure of Mn-Zn Ferrite

Yoshichika Bando and Tsuneo Akashi

2.6.1 Introduction

High-purity Mn-Zn ferrite exhibits high permeability at low frequencies but shows a marked frequency dependence. Eddy current losses are pronounced in this ferrite, although they are negligible in other common ferrites having very low electrical conductivity.

Mn-Zn ferrite containing Fe^{2+} ions has a high permeability and a high conductivity. The conductivity of iron-rich Mn-Zn ferrite containing Fe^{2+} ions has been reduced by the addition of small amounts of foreign oxides such as CaO, SiO_2, and TiO_2. It has been found that the grain boundary segregation of additives forms insulating layers.

Paulus and Guilland[1] showed by autoradiography and a chemical etching technique that Ca is concentrated in the grain boundary regions. Akashi[2] found that the addition of CaO and SiO_2 even in small amounts resulted in low conductivity in the Mn-Zn ferrite. Adding CaO and SiO_2 has the same effect on the conductivities of various iron-rich ferrites.[3] On the basis of frequency-dependent conductivity measurements, Akashi suggested that ferrites containing CaO and SiO_2 have an inhomogeneous dielectric structure of highly conductive grains and insulating layers separating grains. The grain boundary segregating of CaO and SiO_2 has been confirmed by various analytical techniques.

Akashi found that the discontinuous (exaggerated) grain growth in Mn-Zn ferrite was caused by the addition of CaO and SiO_2.[3] The microstructures depended on a complicated relation of the amounts of CaO and SiO_2. It was shown that segregation of CaO and SiO_2 at grain boundaries and exaggerated grain growth could be explained from the view of liquid phase sintering.[4,5] These results were described from an examination of equilibrium phase diagrams, liquid formation, and wettability in the Mn-Zn ferrite-CaO-SiO_2 system.

This section reviews the role of CaO and SiO_2 in Mn-Zn ferrite sintering and its grain boundary structure.

2.6.2 Phase Diagram of Mn-Zn Ferrite-CaO-SiO_2

Figure 2.6.1 is a phase diagram of the Mn-Zn ferrite-CaO system.[6] A compound of the brownmillerite phase represented as $Ca_1Fe_{2-2x}Mn_xZn_xO_{5+y}$ ($x = 1/3$) where the manganese ions were tetravalent was found in this system.[7]

CaO solubility in the ferrite is 10 mol% at 1277°C, which is a eutectic temperature as determined from variations of the ferrite lattice constant. When the ferrite contains no SiO_2, CaO of less than 10 mol% can dissolve in the ferrite at high temperatures but may segregate at grain boundaries during cooling.

Liquidus curves in the Mn-Zn ferrite-CaO-SiO_2 system are shown in Figure 2.6.2.[4] The liquidus temperature of 1100°C was lowest at a composition of 30 mol% CaO, 60 mol% SiO_2, and 10 mol% ferrite. As the liquid in this system can be quenched to glass, it can be

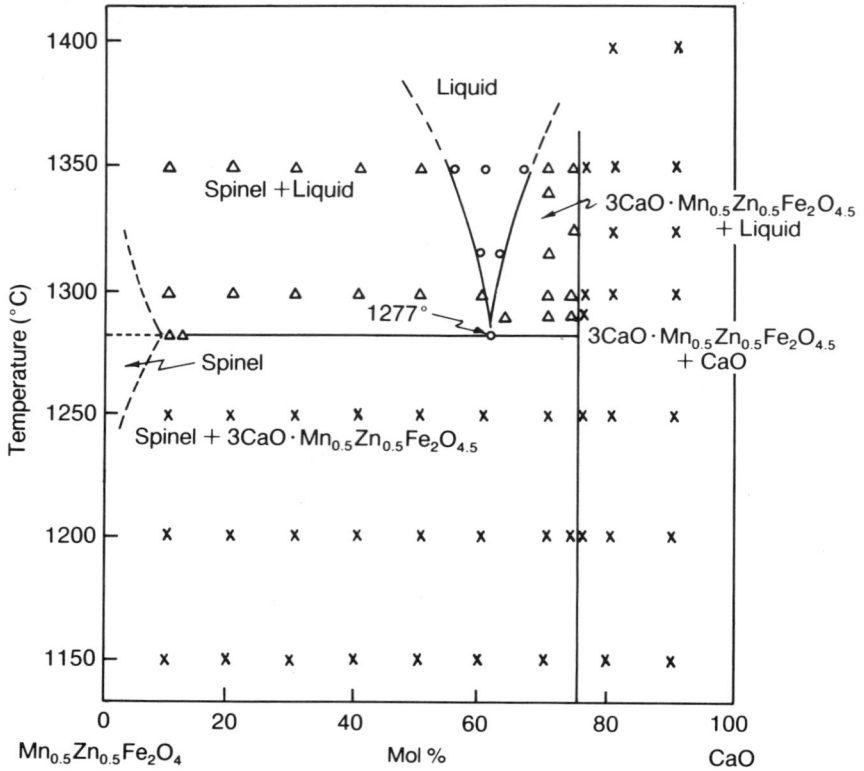

Figure 2.6.1 Phase from diagram of CaO-Mn$_{0.5}$Zn$_{0.5}$Fe$_2$O$_4$ in air [from Y. Bando et al., *Bull. Inst. Chem. Res. Kyoto Univ.* 46:289 (1971)].

distinguished from ferrite crystallites in the microstructure; therefore, the liquid formation can be detected by microscopic examination.

Figure 2.6.3 shows the microstructures of mixtures of CaO, SiO$_2$, and the ferrite quenched from 1200°C. In this figure the crystals are ferrite and the matrix is glass containing CaO, SiO$_2$, ZnO, and manganese and iron oxides.

The solubility of CaO in the Mn-Zn ferrite depends on the SiO$_2$-to-CaO ratio. The distribution coefficient of CaO in the ferrite is zero above the SiO$_2$-to-CaO ratio of unity and about 0.2 at a ratio of 0.25 at 1250°C. Therefore, CaO distributes between the liquid and solid phases of ferrite at low ratio values. When an SiO$_2$-rich CaO mixture is added, CaO scarcely dissolves in the ferrite.

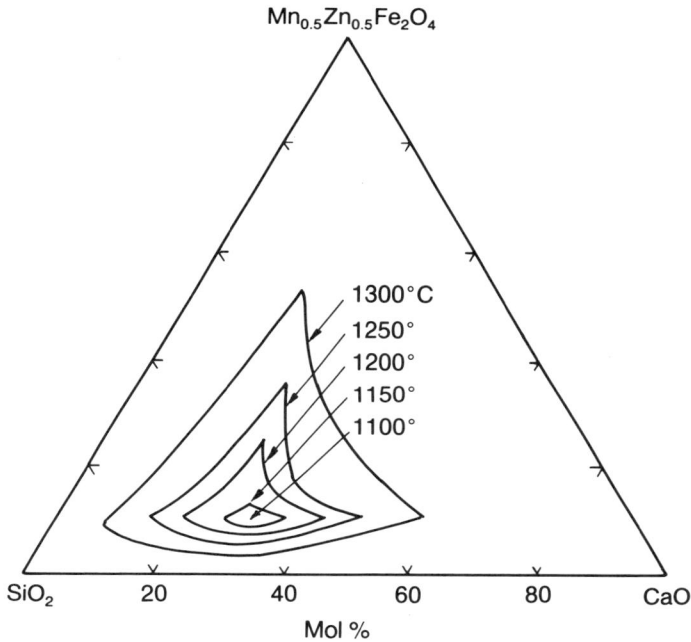

Figure 2.6.2 Isothermal liquidus curves in CaO-SiO_2-$Mn_{0.5}Zn_{0.5}Fe_2O_4$ system at temperatures below 1300°C in air (from Y. Bando et al., *Modern Developments in Powder Metallurgy*, H. H. Hausner, ed. New York: Plenum Press, 1971, p. 339).

2.6.3 Wettability of the Ferrite

The relation between liquid-solid and solid-solid interfacial energies

$$\gamma_{ss} = 2\gamma_{ls} \cos (\theta/2) \qquad (2.6.1)$$

is applicable to a microstructure that contains a liquid and a solid. Each symbol is shown in Figure 2.6.4. The high wettability, that is, lower γ_{ls}, decreases the dihedral angle θ, and complete grain boundary wetting finally occurs if $\gamma_{ss} \geqq 2\gamma_{ls}$ as shown in Figure 2.6.4*b*. Grain boundary energy γ_{ss} depends on the angle between the crystal directions of two grains. For small-angle tilt grain boundaries, γ_{ss} is small and θ becomes high. Even if γ_{ls} is small, the microstructure includes small-angle tilt boundaries and grains enveloped by liquid.

Wettability can be examined by the infiltration method. Eutectic glass powder, a CaO and SiO_2 powder mixture, or a CaO, SiO_2, and Mn-Zn ferrite powder mixture was placed on high-density ferrite,

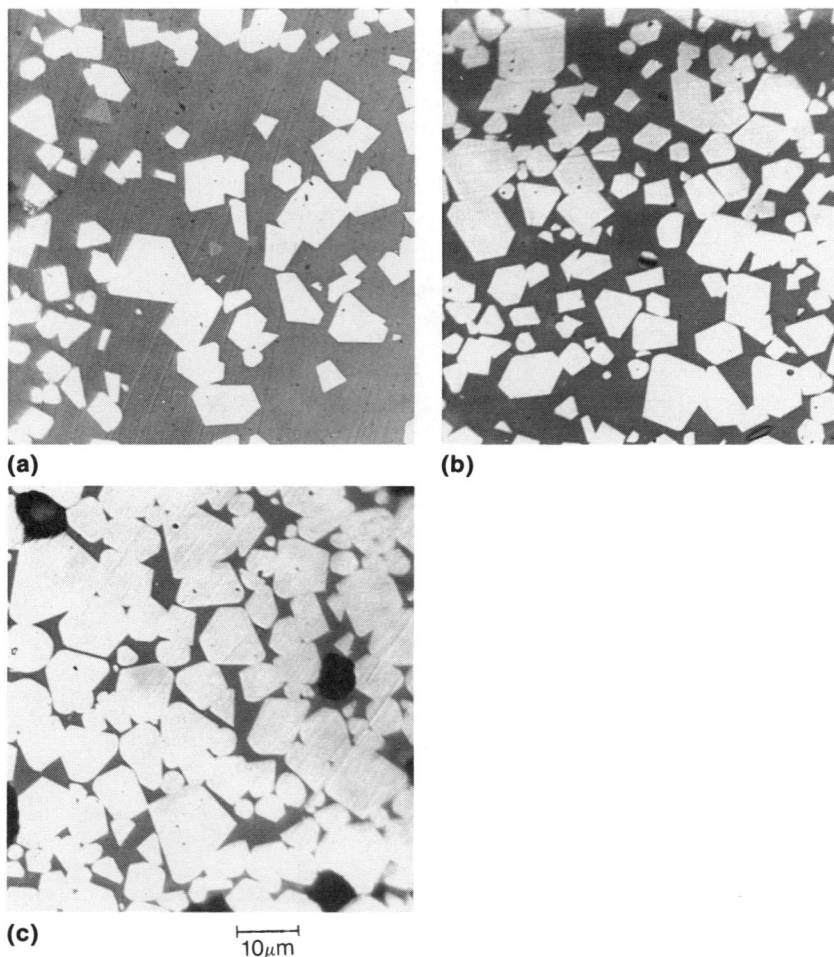

(a)

(b)

(c)

$\overline{10\mu m}$

Figure 2.6.3 Microstructures of specimens obtained by heating mixtures of CaO-SiO$_2$-Mn-Zn ferrite at 1200°C. (a) 27% CaO, 53% SiO$_2$, 20% ferrite; (b) 20% CaO, 40% SiO$_2$, 40% ferrite, and (c) 13% CaO, 27% SiO$_2$, 60% ferrite (mol%) etched by hydrofluoric acid.

heated at 1250°C for 5 minutes and then quenched. All the powders infiltrated as liquid into the high-density ferrite.

The microstructure of the sample infiltrated with the eutectic glass is shown in Figure 2.6.5. A great number of ferrite grains were individually separated by the glassy phase, but few grains showed small-angle tilt boundaries.

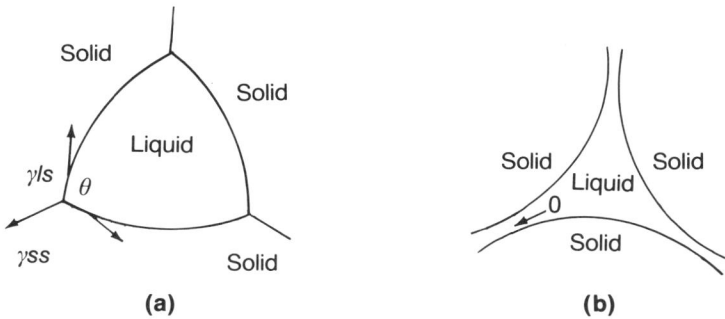

Figure 2.6.4 Liquid-solid microstructures: (a) $\gamma_{ss} = \gamma_{ls}$ dihedral angle $\theta = 120°$; (b) complete boundary wetting, $\theta = 0$ (from Y. Bando et al., *Modern Developments in Powder Metallurgy*, vol. 4, H. H. Hausner, ed. New York: Plenum Press, 1971, p. 339).

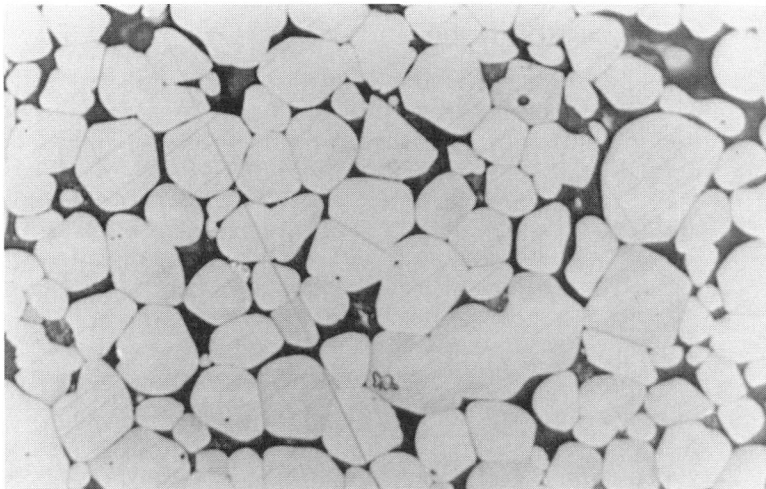

10μm

Figure 2.6.5 Microstructure of Mn-Zn ferrite infiltrated by a glass consisting of 30% CaO, 60% SiO_2, and 10% Mn-Zn ferrite (mol%), etched by hydrofluoric acid.

It is clear from the microstructure that liquid penetrates through grain boundaries by dissolving them. When a powder mixture of CaO and SiO$_2$ is placed on the ferrite, the liquid forms as a reaction of the oxide powders with the ferrite and penetrates through the grain boundaries. The initial infiltration velocity is above 60 μm/sec at 1300°C for either powder-mixture infiltrant or the eutectic powder. The formation of liquid is assumed to occur as quickly as the melting of the eutectic glass.

2.6.4 Formation of Liquid During Sintering

Mn-Zn ferrite powder mixed with 1 wt% eutectic glass was pressed, sintered at 1250°C for 2 hours, and quenched. The microstructure of the specimens revealed that a glassy phase existed at the grain boundaries, as compared with that of high-purity Mn-Zn ferrite sintered under the same conditions. The glassy phase was also observed when CaO and SiO$_2$ powders were added in place of the eutectic glass.

The Mn-Zn ferrite mixed with additives as low as 0.04 wt% CaCO$_3$ and 0.08 wt% SiO$_2$ was sintered at 1250°C and quenched. A glassy phase was again observed at the grain boundaries.

2.6.5 Liquid Phase Sintering and Exaggerated Grain Growth

Grains of Mn-Zn ferrite sintered at 1250°C without additives or with only CaO or SiO$_2$ additives are uniform and several microns in size. Exaggerated grain growth to above 50 μm is, however, observed in microstructures containing both CaO and SiO$_2$.

In the present experiment, high-purity Mn-Zn ferrite including CaO less than 0.002 wt% and SiO$_2$ less than 0.001 wt% were used. The microstructure depended on the SiO$_2$-to-CaO ratio and also on the total amount of additives. The proportion of the number of large grains increased with increasing amounts of liquid within the limit of several vol% liquid. The volume of liquid formed at 1250°C by adding 0.16 wt% CaO (0.7 mol%) and 0.336 wt% SiO$_2$ (1.3 mol%) was estimated to be 2% from the liquidus temperature curves, where the density of the liquid is assumed to be 4. The amount of liquid was considerably greater than that expected from the additives only, because the liquid also contained the host material. Generally speaking, however, amounts of liquid less than several vol% are not sufficient for liquid phase sintering but are enough for exaggerated grain growth. Microstructures of ferrites containing CaO and SiO$_2$ show planar grain boundaries between the large grains and the fine-grained matrix, which are similar to those caused by the well-known liquid phase dopants such as Sb_2O_3, V_2O_5.[8] The exaggerated and fine grains are separated by a liquid film, and exaggerated grain growth occurs by dissolution and precipitation in the liquid medium to form the planar grain boundaries.

Yan and Johnson[8] investigated impurity-induced exaggerated grain growth in Mn-Zn ferrites at 1300°C. In ferrite samples with TiO_2-doped layers, the exaggerated grains are nucleated by a liquid phase, but no liquid phase is involved in further growth to the exaggerated grains. CaO and SrO caused exaggerated grain growth in ferrites in which a liquid phase was involved.

2.6.6 Grain Boundary Segregation and Electrical Properties

Examination of grain boundaries of Mn-Zn ferrites has been carried out by autoradiography, X-ray microanalysis, Auger electron spectroscopy, and transmission electron microscopy (TEM). Some of these techniques have found a Ca- and Si-rich segregation layer at the grain boundaries. Paulus[1] suggested that the high resistivity of grain boundaries might be due to segregation of CaO during cooling.

Akashi[2] showed that the resistivity of Mn-Zn ferrite depended on oxygen partial pressure during sintering, the SiO_2-to-CaO ratio, and the composition of the ferrite itself. It was also suggested that the insulating film consisting of CaO, SiO_2, and ferrite was a glassy phase. Franken and Stacy[9] reported that the presence of an intergranular film in Mn-Zn ferrite had not been established by TEM. They argued against the presence of a high-resistivity glassy layer and supported Paulus's hypothesis. However, using TEM combined with X-ray microanalysis they found two glassy phases and one crystalline phase at multiple-grain junctions.

It is certain that the grain boundary segregation of CaO and SiO_2 occurs as the result of liquid phase sintering and that the liquid consists of CaO, SiO_2, and the ferrite. Liquid is apt to vitrify even during cooling in a furnace. The ferrite-dissolving CaO may be precipitated from a liquid and a glassy phase by very slow cooling.

Akashi investigated the effects of oxygen partial pressure and temperature during heat treatment on the resistivity of a $(Ca_{1-x}Si_xO_z)_{1-y}(ferrite)_y$ system corresponding to the grain boundary phase. It was found that the resistivity increased by several orders of magnitude with increasing oxygen partial pressure and varied according to composition. This means that the Fe^{2+} ion content in the glassy phase and in the precipitated ferrite-dissolving CaO depends on composition, heating temperature, and atmosphere. As diffusion is predominant along grain boundaries, it is obvious that the oxidation or reduction of the grain boundary phase is more sensitive to atmosphere and temperature than is the grain interior.

2.6.7 Conclusion

Considering liquid phase sintering and electrical properties of the CaO-SiO$_2$-ferrite mixture, it appears likely that glassy phase films enveloping grains are responsible for the high resistivity of Mn-Zn ferrite. However, because of their complexities the structure and composition at the grain boundaries are not yet clear in spite of many investigations. The key to the solution of additive segregation at grain boundaries may be to investigate liquid and glassy phase behavior during cooling rather than observing the resultant grain boundary structures.

References

1. Paulus M., and Guillaud, C., *J. Phys. Soc. Jpn.* 17:Suppl. B1, 632 (1962).
2. Akashi, T., *J. Jpn. Soc. Powd. Powd. Metall.* 8:101, 195 (1961) (in Japanese); *NEC Res. Dev.* 8:89 (1966); *NEC Res. Dev.* 19:66 (1970).
3. Akashi, T., *Trans. Jpn. Inst. Met.* 2:171 (1961).
4. Bando, Y., Ikeda, Y., Akashi, T., and Takada, T., *Modern Developments in Powder Metallurgy*, vol. 4, H. H. Hausner, ed. New York: Plenum Press, 1971, p. 339.
5. Bando, Y., *J. Jpn. Soc. Powd. Metall.* 14:378 (1967); 15:414 (1969) (in Japanese).
6. Bando, Y., Kato, T., Ikeda, Y., and Takada, T., *Bull. Inst. Chem. Res. Kyoto Univ.* 46:289 (1968).
7. Bando, Y., Takada, T., and Akiyama, T., *Bull. Inst. Chem. Res. Kyoto Univ.* 49:342 (1971).
8. Yan, M. F., and Johnson Jr., D. W., *J. Am. Ceram. Soc.* 61:342 (1978).
9. Franken, D. E. C., and Stacy, W. T., *J. Am. Ceram. Soc.* 63:315 (1980).

2.7 Surface Structure of Oxide Ceramics

Eizo Miyazaki

2.7.1 Introduction

Oxide surface characteristics constitute an important and interesting area of ceramics science and technology and are also important in surface passivation, catalysis, semiconductor device technology, and so on. However, little is known about oxides' microscopic surface detail. Among the oxides, transition metal oxides have received a great deal of attention and have been extensively studied both experimentally[1] and theoretically[2]. So-called well-defined single-crystal surfaces have been studied experimentally using currently developed surface spectroscopic techniques such as ultraviolet and X-ray photoemission spectroscopy (UPS and XPS) and electron energy-loss spectroscoopy (EELS), all under ultra-high-vacuum (UHV) conditions. Several different theoretical models have been applied; in particular, the Hartree–Fock–Slater molecular orbital (Xα-MO) calculations[2] seem to have been successfully applied to these problems. This section reviews several different oxides (including NiO, MnO, FeO, TiO, CoO, TiO_2, MgO, and ZnO), focusing mainly on their surface electronic structure.

2.7.2 Zinc Oxide (ZnO)

ZnO has a crystal structure of the wurtzite type and shows typical polar characteristics. The ideal polar faces have only one atomic species within the surface, that is, O atoms at the $(000\bar{1})$O face and Zn atoms at the (0001)Zn face, as shown in Figure 2.7.1. This suggests

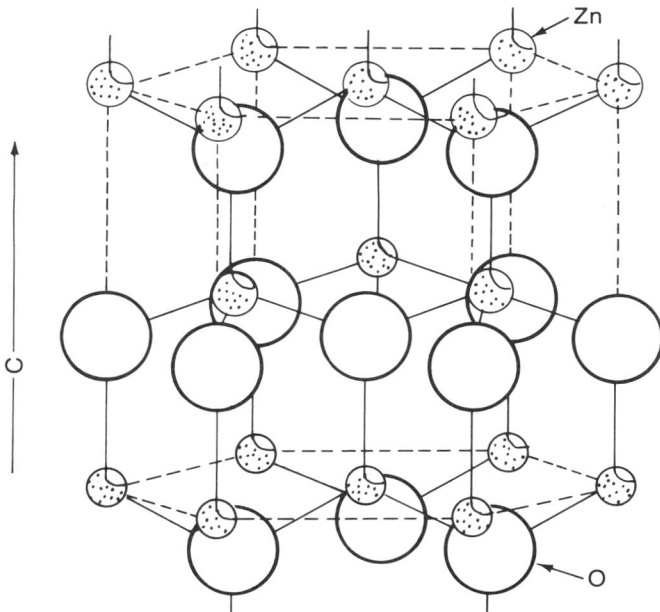

Figure 2.7.1 Crystal structure of ZnO.

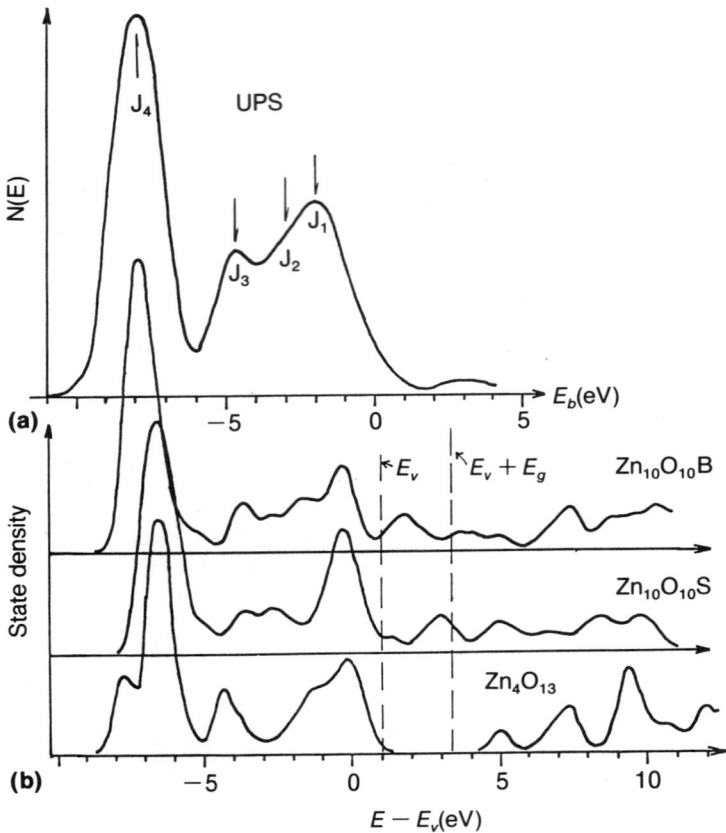

Figure 2.7.2 (a) UPS spectrum of ZnO(0001)Zn surface with the photon energy 48.7 eV; (b) total state densities of three clusters.

that a drastic difference exists in the surface electronic structure and charge state from that of the bulk ions.

ZnO UPS spectra have been reported by several workers. In Figure 2.7.2a the spectrum by Ranke[3] shows four main structures, $J_1 \ldots J_4$. The peak J_4 is the emission of the Zn-3d band, and the J_1-J_3 are the superposition of Zn-4s and O-2p electrons. This interpretation is experimentally confirmed by an increase of the Zn-3d emission relative to the s-p emission with increasing $h\nu$ and the spectra of adsorbed oxygen on metallic zinc.[4] According to the excitation probability of the spectra in Figure 2.7.2a, the Zn-3d peak is expected to contain ten electrons and no contribution of s- or p-electrons. The

UPS spectra of the (0001)Zn- and (000$\bar{1}$)O-faces showed no striking differences.[5]

More detailed surface structure and reactivity with other atoms can be deduced by the calculations.[6] The model clusters for calculations by the discrete-variational Xα (DV-Xα) method are shown in Figure 2.7.3. Cluster (a), Zn_4O_{13}, shows no polar surface. Clusters (b) and (c) show polar surfaces, but the electrostatic potential of the polar surface is more enhanced in the $Zn_{10}O_{10}S$ than in the $Zn_{10}O_{10}B$. The total state density for these clusters is compared with the UPS spectrum (see Figure 2.7.2b).

A sharp peak appearing at about 7 eV below E_v (E_v is taken to be the middle point between the highest occupied level and lowest unoccupied level) corresponds to the narrow Zn-3d band, and there the admixture of O-2p or Zn-4s and Zn-4p components into the 3d band are of only several percent. The oxygen valence band extends 4–5 eV below E_v. Similar results have also been obtained with the [Zn_4 + O] cluster.[4] The main features of the DOS correspond well with observed UPS spectra. For the cluster Zn_4O_{13} without the polar Zn surface, the conduction band is separated from the band by a gap of about 3 eV. While the DOS for other clusters extends continuously from E_v toward the upper energy, the state in this region was found to result mainly from the 4s and 4p orbitals of the Zn ions on the polar Zn surface or on the corner of the clusters. These gaps states are dangling bond states as a result of the absence of the nearest-neighbor O ions. In addition, for cluster (b) the bulk-like O ion, O(4), has the charge of −1.31, and the bulk-like Zn ion, Zn(1), has a charge of 1.33. However, the charges of the Zn(3) and O(6) surface ions are +1.07 and −1.00, respectively; that is, the absolute values of the surface charges are reduced from those for the bulk ions by about 20–25%. This trend is

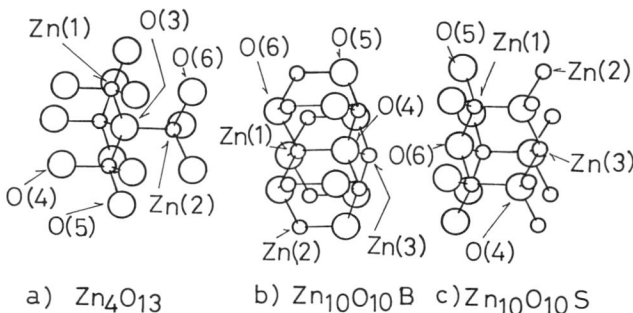

a) Zn_4O_{13} b) $Zn_{10}O_{10}$ B   c) $Zn_{10}O_{10}$ S

Figure 2.7.3 Structure of model clusters for DV-Xα calculations.

more noticable at the corner atoms of the cluster; in other words, the charges on the O(5) and Zn(2) ions are only -0.87 and $+0.83$, respectively.

Similar properties of the ionic charge distribution are also found in the cluster $Zn_{10}O_{10}S$. The marked reduction of these ionic charges is caused by the level crossing between the O dangling bond states and the Zn dangling bond states, resulting in electron flow from the former into the latter. The bonding characteristics of the Zn-O bond was studied using the $[Zn_4 + O]$ cluster;[4] the bonds between the O-2p orbital and the Zn-4s (σ bond) and -4p (π bond) orbitals have a strong bonding character, whereas the bond between the O-2s and Zn-4s orbitals has an antibonding character, canceling in part the Zn-O bond. The contribution of the Zn-3d orbital is not important to the Zn-O bond. The charge of the chemisorbed oxygen atom is -0.53, which is much smaller than that of the bulk-like or surface oxygen ions. The local-state density of the surface Zn(3) in the $Zn_{10}O_{10}S$ cluster drastically changes when an oxygen atom is attached to it; the large-state density in the gap disappears, and the overall shape approximates that of the bulk Zn(1). The charge of the chemisorbed hydrogen on top of the surface O(6) ion becomes $+0.36$, and this charge is almost completely transferred from the O(6) ion. When the hydrogen atom is chemisorbed on the surface Zn(3) atoms, the hydrogen atom is in a negatively charged state, -0.38, in contrast to the chemisorption onto the O surface.

2.7.3 Magnesium Oxide (MgO)

Crystalline MgO has the cubic structure of rock salt. Mg ions in bulk are sixfold coordinated, and the surface ions are fivefold coordinated, The EELS spectra[7] for MgO(100) are shown for the incident electron energy in Figure 2.7.4a. The two loss peaks at 6.2 and 2.3 eV are of surface origin, as is seen by the decrease in their intensity with increasing primary electron energy. The 2.3 eV peak is thought to arise from an electron trapped at an O surface vacancy as the peak disappears when the surface is annealed at about 1000°K or after exposure to oxygen (Figure 2.7.4b). The peak at 6.2 eV is intrinsic and is believed to result from transitions of the valence band to the surface-shifted Mg-3s electric field levels.

These results were studied theoretically by the DV-Xα method using surface $[(MgO_5)^{8-}]$ and bulk $[(MgO_6)^{10}]$ clusters.[8] Calculated energy levels are shown in Figure 2.7.5. In the bulk cluster a set of occupied levels between -5.0 and -7.3 eV is predominantly composed of ligand 2p character and is separated from the lowest unoc-

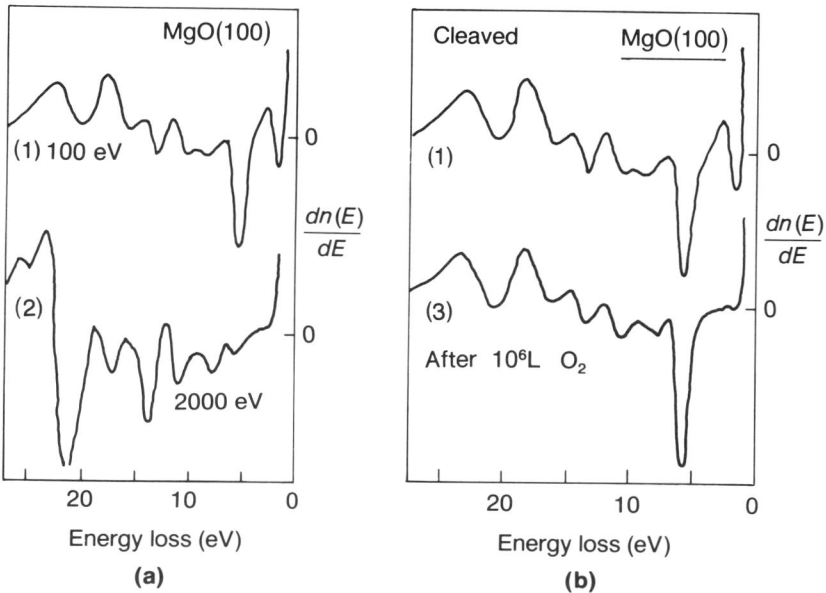

Figure 2.7.4 EELS spectra for vacuum-cleaved MgO(100) for an incident-electron energy E_I of 100 eV (1), $E_I = 2000$ eV (2) and after exposure to O_2 (3).

cupied $MO(6a_{1g})$ by an energy gap of 9.7 eV. This compares well with experimental values of 7.8 eV. The $6a_{1g}$ and $6t_{1u}$ for the bulk cluster are composed mainly of the Mg-3s and 3p orbitals, respectively. For the surface clusters, comparable amounts of Mg-3s and 3p orbitals are admixed in the $11a_1$ and $12a_1$ states. The large shift of the $11a_1$ level from the bulk $6a_{1g}$ level and the above admixture is due to the strong electric field at the surface. This level will correspond to the surface state observed at 2.3 eV above the bottom of the conduction band. The net charge of an Mg ion at the surface is less than that in the bulk as seen in the case of ZnO surfaces. Because of the polarization, the lowering of the unoccupied Mg-3s level changes the mixing with the occupied 2p level so that the electron charge transfers from the O atoms to the Mg atoms. In addition, the localized electronic states resulting from surface defects are important for chemisorption.

2.7.4 NaCl-Type Transition-Metal Oxides (MeO, Me = Ni, Co, Mn, Fe, and Ti)

In these metals the 3d cations are in an octahedral crystal field. This removes the degeneracy of the ground state to yield two upper (e_g)

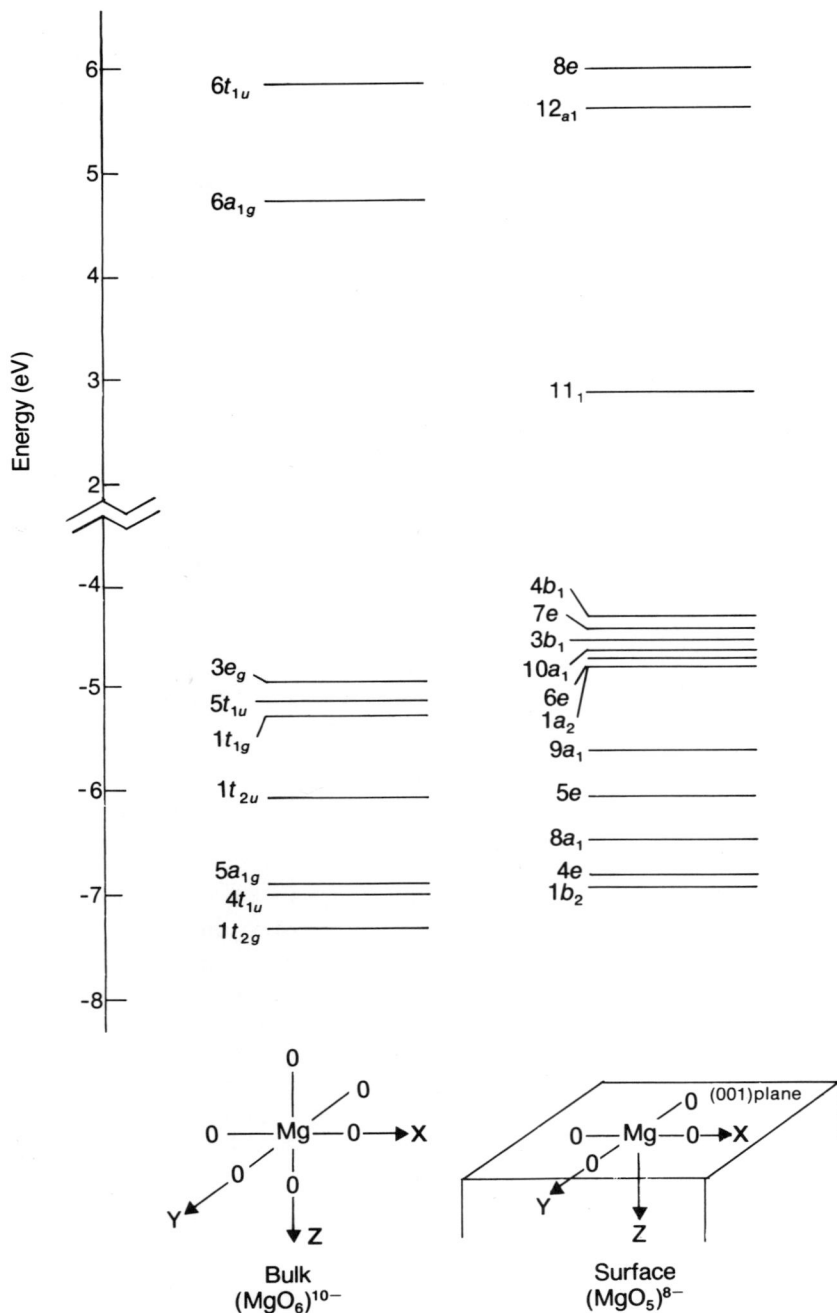

Figure 2.7.5 DV-Xα electronic energy levels for bulk $(MgO_6)^{10-}$ and surface $(MgO_5)^{8-}$ clusters.

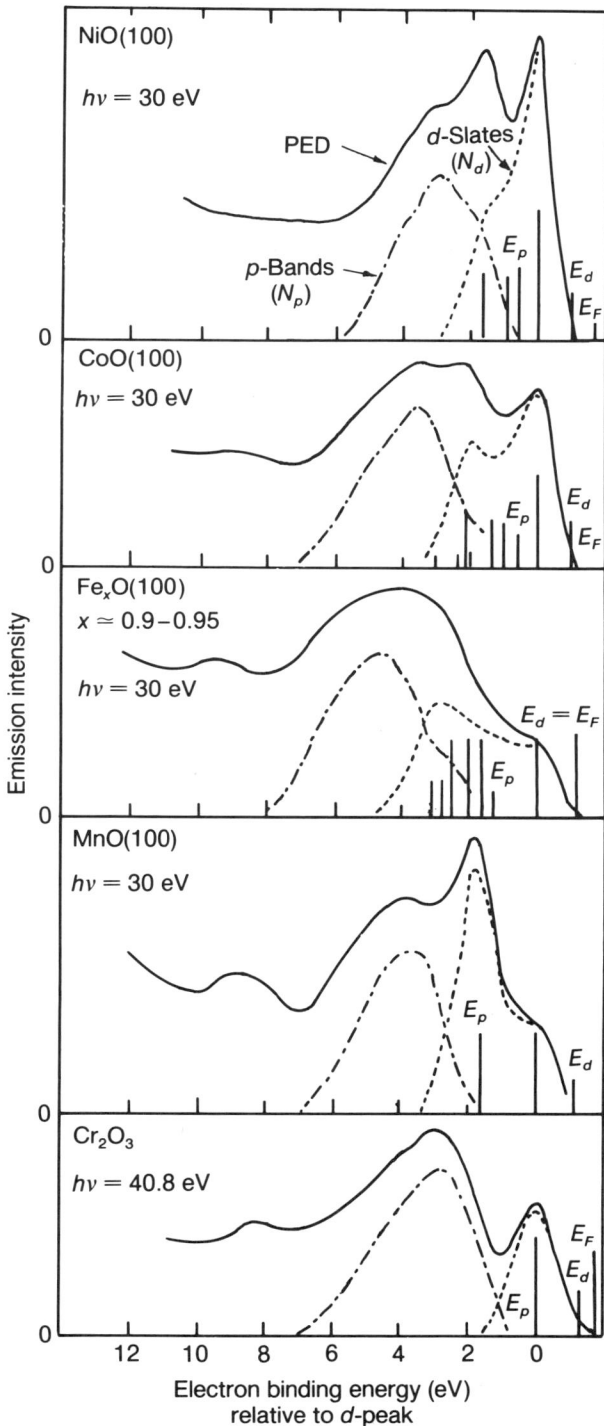

Figure 2.7.6 Photoemission energy distributions (PED), partial d-state intensities N_d, and p-band intensities N_p. The vertical lines denote calculated $3d^{n-1}$ ionization potentials.

and three lower (t_{2g}) levels. The difference is about 1 eV. In the solid, the filled 2p oxygen orbitals and the empty 4s levels broaden and interact to form bonding and antibonding states. These are separated by about 5 eV in these oxides. The 3d states line up with this forbidden band. Several UPS or XPS measurements have been reported.

Results by Eastman and Freeouf[9] are shown in Figure 2.7.6, where the d- and p-state partial emission intensities are shown by

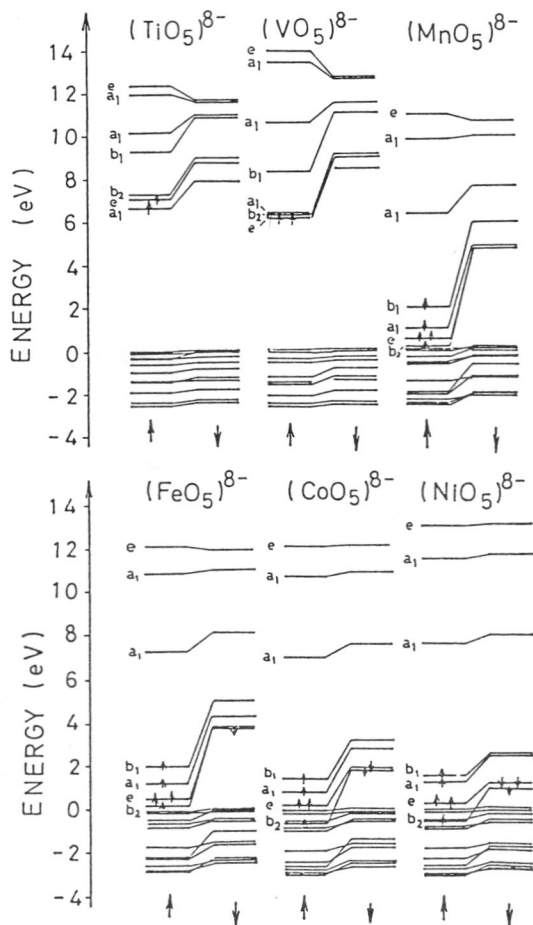

Figure 2.7.7 The energy levels of the surface clusters of NaCl-type transition d-metal oxides. The occupation of d-levels is shown by small arrows corresponding to electron spins.

dashed and broken lines, respectively. All p-band spectra are about 3 eV wide, with a p-band peak from 3 to 5 eV below the highest d-state level.

The results calculated by the similar DV-Xα method are shown in Figure 2.7.7.[2,10] The d-levels shift downward from TiO to NiO with increasing metal atomic number, and the Me-3d–O-2p energy gap becomes smaller. The position of the metal 4s level is nearly constant for all metal oxides. As a high electric field is applied at the metal site on the surface, the surface electronic configuration is different from the bulk configuration; in the former, the $3d_{z^2-r^2}$ orbital is unoccupied, and the TiO surface electronic properties may be quite different from the bulk properties. In addition, the surface atoms are more neutral than the bulk atoms. At the surface the mixing of the metal d-orbital with O-2p in the antibonding state is stronger than that in the bulk, because the energy gap of the former between the d- and p-orbitals is smaller than that of the latter. As the antibonding levels have partially unfilled d-orbitals, the back-donation from the metal to the oxygen is partially missing.

2.7.5 Titanium Dioxide (TiO$_2$)

In the rutile form of TiO$_2$, each atom is coordinated to six O atoms and each O atom coordinated to three Ti atoms. Figure 2.7.8a is a typical UPS spectrum from an ordered TiO$_2$(001) surface that has not been bombarded as well as the spectrum from the same [001] surface after Ar$^+$-ion bombardment.[11] For the ordered [001] surface, the O-2p-derived portion of the spectrum is characterized by a large peak at -5.2 eV accompanied by a smaller shoulder at -7.8 eV. However, when this surface is reduced and disordered by bombardment, a new peak appears at -6.8 eV and grows in intensity; the peak at -6.8 eV coincides with the decrease in the surface O-to-Ti Auger ratio, which decreases from 1.74 for the annealed surface to 1.31 for the surface after 5 minutes of bombardment. A more characteristic feature is the appearance of a new peak at -0.7 eV. When this bombarded surface is exposed to O$_2$ molecules, the spectrum of the ordered surface appears again. The UPS spectrum of the bombarded TiO$_2$ is comparable to the spectrum of fractured Ti$_2$O$_3$ in *vacuo*, and the Auger ratio is also consistent with that of Ti$_2$O$_3$.[12] Thus, the narrow peak at -0.7 eV in the band gap assigned to Ti^{3+}-3d and the spectra after Ar$^+$-ion bombardment can be explained by desorption of oxygen species from the ordered TiO$_2$ surface. These results present an interesting problem for theoreticians.[13,14]

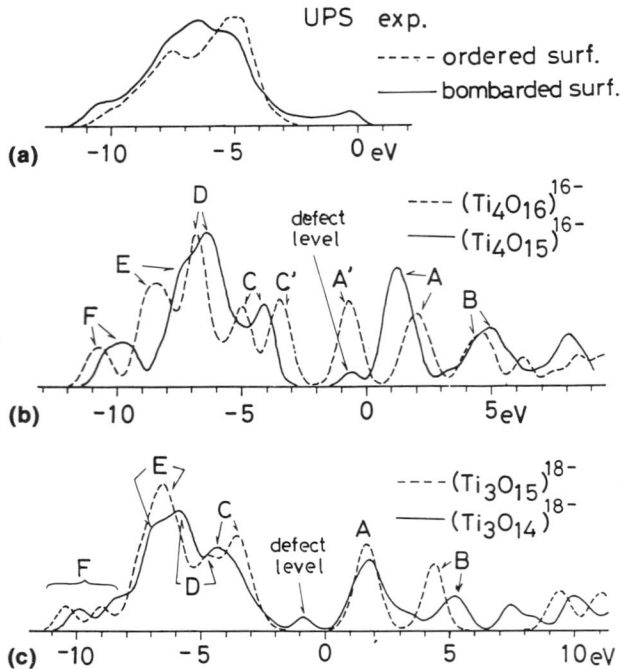

Figure 2.7.8 The state densities of the surface clusters (a), bulk clusters (b), and the UPS spectra for the ordered (dashed line) and the bombarded (full-line) [110] rutile surface.

The model clusters for the calculations[13] of the surface cluster $(Ti_4O_{16})^{16-}$ and the surface defect cluster, which is derived from the Ti_4O_{16} cluster by the removal of the outermost oxygen, are shown in Figure 2.7.9. For the state density (Figure 2.7.8b), it is remarkable that with the O ion removal, the peaks A′ and C′ of the cluster $(Ti_4O_{16})^{16-}$ representing the intrinsic surface state disappear, and a partly occupied defect level appears at about 1.8 eV below the lowest Ti d-band. For comparison, the electronic structure of the bulk $(Ti_3O_{15})^{18-}$ cluster has also been calculated (Figure 2.7.8c). It was seen that the broadening of the d-levels as a result of the interaction among those on different Ti ions is relatively small compared with the crystal field splitting. In addition, the local electronic structure associated with the bulk oxygen vacancy was studied by the Ti_3O_{14} obtained from Ti_3O_{15} (Figure 2.7.8c). The defect level is clearly found to be induced near the gap center and occupied by two electrons. The defect clusters both in the bulk and on the top layer exhibit the localized defect

O(8)

O(9)

Ti(2)

Ti(1)

O(3)

O(4)

O(7)

O(5)

O(6)

Ti$_4$O$_{16}$ CLUSTER

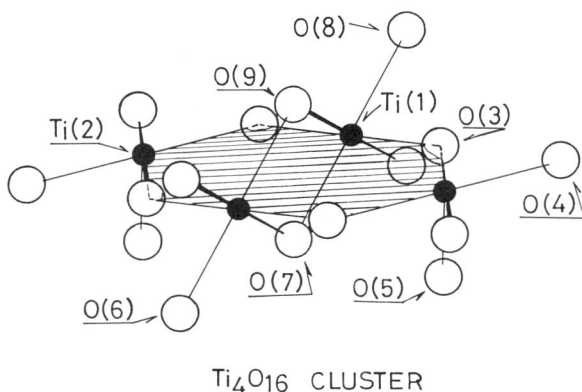

Figure 2.7.9 Structure of Ti$_4$O$_{16}$ model cluster for the ideal [110] rutile surface. White and black circles represent oxygen and titanium ions, respectively. The shadowed plane shows the [100] surface.

state, which explains the UPS spectrum in the gap region when the surface was bombarded. The EELS peak[15] at 2.4 eV for the ordered [110] surface is assigned to the transition from the oxygen intrinsic surface state to the titanium intrinsic surface state (C' → A'). Similar calculations of the state density have also been made by LCMTO (Linear Combination of Muffin-Tin Orbitals),[14] and similar results have been obtained.

Finally, Koma and Tamura[16] have recently reported the first observation of two intrinsic surface states on the clean single crystal of α-Al$_2$O$_3$(0001) using a highly sensitive EELS; the first peak seems to come from an electron transition from the Al-$2p$ core level to the vacant intrinsic surface state, and the second one is observed in the valence region.

2.7.6 Conclusion

The surface electronic structure of metal oxides is influenced by the following: (a) a reduction in the Madelung potential near the surface, (b) variations in charge transfer between the cation and anion as compared with the bulk, and (c) polarization of the wave functions of the surface ions resulting from the potential gradient. Effect (a) causes a narrowing of the energy gap, while effect (b) exerts the opposite influence. Effect (c) reduces the energy gap, which is important for chemical reactivity because the protrusion of the wave functions from the surface by the large polarization effect generally increases

the reactivity of the surface. Localized electronic states associated with impurities and surface lattice defects may play the role of an active center.

References

1. Henrich, V. E., *Progress in Surf. Sci.* 14:175 (1983).
2. Tsukada, M., Adachi, H., and Satoko, C., *Progress in Surf. Sci.* 14:113 (1983).
3. Ranke, W., *Solid State Comm.* 19:685 (1976).
4. Miyazaki, E., Tsukada, M., and Adachi, H., *Surf. Sci.* 131:L390 (1983).
5. Schmeisser, D., and Jacobi, K., *Surf. Sci.* 88:138 (1979).
6. Tsukada, M., Miyazaki, E., and Adachi, H., *J. Phys. Soc. Jpn.* 50:3032 (1981).
7. Henrich, V. E., and Kurtz, R. L., *J. Vac. Sci. Tech.* 18:416 (1981).
8. Satoko, C., Tsukada, M., and Adachi, H., *J. Phys. Soc. Jpn.* 45:1333 (1978).
9. Eastman, D. E., and Freeouf, J. L., *Phys. Rev. Lett.* 34:395 (1975).
10. Satoko, C., and Tsukada, M., *IMS Ann. Rev.* (1979):32.
11. Kasowski, R. V., and Tait, R. H., *Phys. Rev.* B20:5168 (1979).
12. Lo, W. J., Chung, Y. W., and Somorjai, G. A., *Surf. Sci.* 71:199 (1978).
13. Tsukada, M., Satoko, C., and Adachi, H., *J. Phys. Soc. Jpn.* 47:610 (1979).
14. Tait, R. H., and Kasowski, R. V., *Phys. Rev.* B20:5178 (1979).
15. Chung, Y. W., Lo, W. J., and Somorjai, G. A., *Surf. Sci.* 64:588 (1977).
16. Koma, A., Tamura, T., *Proc. 5th International Conference on Solid Surfaces*, Madrid, Spain, 1983, p. 62.

2.8 Defect/Interface Structure of Optical Glass Fiber

Shigeki Sakaguchi and Shiro Takahashi

2.8.1 Introduction

Substantial progress has been made recently in the development of low-transmission-loss glass fiber for optical communications.[1,2] With its advantages such as low transmission loss, broad bandwidth, lack of electromagnetic interference, small diameter, and light weight, optical glass fiber is applicable for use in various public transmission systems, including trunk lines and subscriber and submarine cable.

The practical use of optical glass fiber depends on its mechanical performance and long-term reliability as well as on its transmission characteristics. Unfortunately, the mechanical strength of fiber made of silica glass, a typically brittle material, is very sensitive to defects. Moreover, it is subject to static fatigue, which causes it to break easily under small strain after a long period of time.

The strength of glass was determined by Griffith to be a function of surface flaws,[3] which exist constitutionally in the glass and proportionally to its surface area. However, the study of optical fiber strength has confirmed that strength dependence upon surface area is not intrinsic but extrinsic in character, arising from the macroscopic defects generated after drawing, and that the strength of fibers with no macroscopic defects is very high, more than 6 GPa. Thus, the most important feature for optical fiber is a plastic coating that plays a very important role in protecting the fiber surface from damage.[4] The plastic coating also affects time-dependent change in strength.

This section describes defects characteristics of the glass-plastic interface in high-silica optical fibers, with an emphasis on mechanical performance.

2.8.2 Optical Fiber Drawing

Optical fibers are produced by the combination of two processes: synthesis of preforms and the drawing of these preforms. The former process aims to make high-quality glass without impurities, voids, and the like, which cause optical attenuation, and a precise waveguide structure by controlling the dopant concentration. In the latter process the preform is drawn into a fiber, with the diameter controlled to keep it uniform, and coated in line with organic material to provide good mechanical and transmission properties.

Figure 2.8.1 is schematic of the drawing process. To be drawn into a fiber, the preform must be heated to 2000°C, because the temperature at which high-silica glass softens is very high. Several kinds of heat sources are available, including oxy-hydrogen flame,[5] CO_2 lasers,[6] and zirconia induction[7] and carbon resistance furnaces.[8] Furnaces are widely used in industrial production because of their utility in mass-producing the fiber and in maintaining uniform diameter.

The majority of macroscopic defects, so-called Griffith flaws, are formed during the drawing process as a result of many factors, such as contamination in the furnace and abrasion, as shown in Figure 2.8.1. It is important to reduce these defects if long-length, high-strength fibers are to be produced.

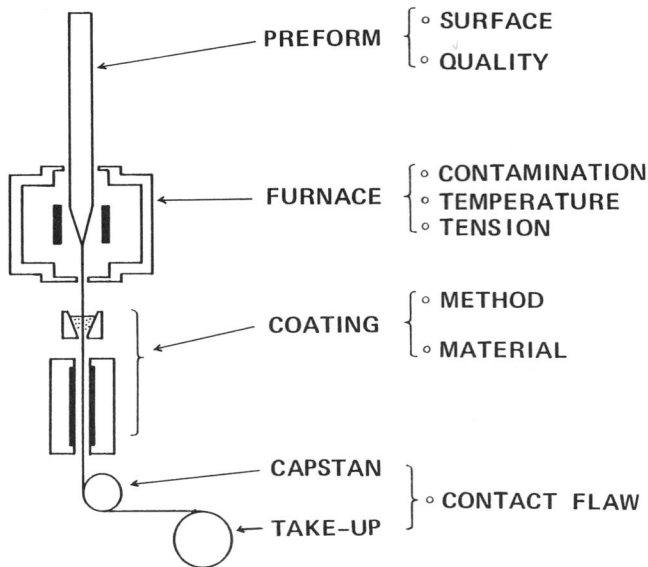

Figure 2.8.1 Schematic of optical fiber drawing process in relation to factors affecting formation of macroscopic defects.

2.8.3 Defects and Strengths

2.8.3.1 Strength Distribution

The tensile strength of glass fibers is characterized by the Weibull plot.[4] Figure 2.8.2 is an example of strength distribution in plastic-coated fibers.[9] The distribution curve is expressed in conventional Weibull form as[10]

$$F = 1 - \exp\{-L(\sigma/\sigma_0)^m\} \qquad (2.8.1)$$

where L is fiber length and σ_0 and m are constants. The strength distribution generally exhibits three modes: high- and low-strength regions with a steep slope and a median region with a gentle slope, as shown in Figure 2.8.2. This indicates that the distribution curve arises from the superposition of two groups, the high-strength region and the low-strength region.

2.8.3.2 Defect Size

The fracture mechanics concept[11] gives the critical condition of brittle fracture as

$$K_{IC} = Y\sigma c^{1/2} \qquad (2.8.2)$$

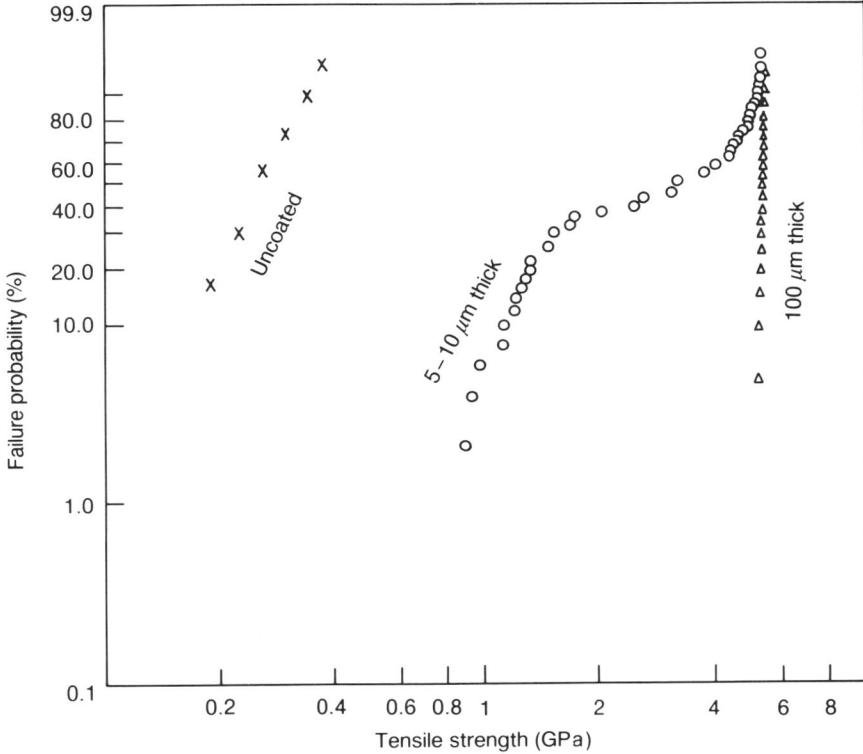

Figure 2.8.2 Strength distribution of plastic coated fibers [from S. Sakaguchi and M. Nakahara, Rev. ECL 27:188 (1979)].

where K_{IC} is the fracture toughness (0.8 MPam$^{1/2}$), Y is a geometric parameter, and c is half the critical defect size. Based on Equation (2.8.2), the defect size for high-strength fiber of 6 GPa is estimated to be on the order of 10^{-7} mm, whereas that for low-strength fiber of 0.3 GPa is 10^{-3} mm. That is, strength distribution indicates that there are two groups of defects dominating fiber strength. The latter are macroscopic defects (Griffith flaws) that do not exist constitutionally but are formed after drawing. The former should be considered intrinsic, because their size is on the same order as that of the average diameter for the glass network structure.

The defect size in weak fibers is estimated through fracture surface analysis. The fracture surfaces of weak fibers exhibit typical mirror, mist, and hackle features. Mirror radius is related to strength as expressed in the following equation:

$$R^{-1/2} = \sigma/M \qquad (2.8.3)$$

where M is the mirror constant for silica fibers (2.18 MPam$^{1/2}$).[13] A comparison of Equations (2.8.2) and (2.8.3) shows that the mirror radius is related to the critical defect size, as $c = 0.088 \times R$ for silica fibers.

2.8.3.3 Factors Affecting Macroscopic Defect Formation

Plastic Coating. Plastic coating, which was developed originally in order to form a waveguide structure by cladding a pure silica core with low-index plastic,[14] is very effective in protecting the fiber surface from abrasion. The effect of coating thickness on strength is shown in Figure 2.8.2. Fiber with a relatively thin coating of $5 - 10\,\mu m$ exhibits a widely scattered strength distribution. In contrast, the fiber with a sufficiently thick coating is a high-strength one with a distribution curve exhibiting no weak points at all. This indicates the importance of the coating as protection against abrasion.

Surface Treatment. Cracks and impurity particles existing on the preform surface may remain on the fiber surface after drawing at temperatures higher than 2000°C, resulting in the formation of macroscopic defects such as flaws and microcrystals. Thus, surface treatment with hydrofluoric acid and an oxy-hydrogen flame prior to drawing leads to the production of a uniformly strong fiber.[15] This indicates that surface quality affects strength. Polishing with a CO_2 laser is also effective in smoothing the preform surface.

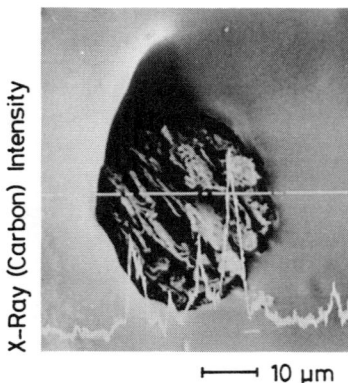

FLAW FORMATION DUE TO CARBON DUST

Figure 2.8.3 Macroscopic defect formed by embedding a carbon particle assigned by X-ray intensity along the dashed line [from S. Sakaguchi et al., *J. Non-Cryst. Solids* (forthcoming)].

Cleanliness of Drawing Atmosphere. In a carbon furnace, dust particles are generated by combustion in the heater and formation of SiC resulting from the reaction of carbon and silica. These particles are easily trapped on the fiber surface, which is activated at high temperature. An example of a defect formed by an embedded carbon particle, assigned by X-ray intensity along the dashed line, is shown in Figure 2.8.3. Strength is expressed as a function of dust particle radius as[13]

$$r^{-1/2} = \sigma/D \tag{2.8.4}$$

where D is a constant given as 0.474 MPam$^{1/2}$.

In a drawing furnace the fiber is in danger of being contaminated with dust particles. Thus, these furnaces are specially designed to expel such particles. For example, the gas flow in the suscepter tube is controlled in zirconia induction furnaces,[16] and a gas exhaust port is designed into carbon resistance furnaces.[13]

2.8.4 Effects of Glass-Plastic Interface on Strength

The glass-plastic interface also plays an important role in determining time-dependent changes in strength, especially in cases where the fracture begins at microscopic defects. Time-dependent changes in strength for fibers coated with different materials and soaked in distilled water are shown in Figure 2.8.4. The fiber coated with silicone shows no strength degradation after 10,000 hours of soaking,[17] whereas the strength of the fiber coated with epoxyacrylate clearly decreases after only one day.[18] This difference is due primarily to differing resistances to water corrosion at the glass-plastic interface.

When external stress acts on a defect, the defect begins to grow because of the corrosive reaction of glass and water. Its growth rate is expressed by[19]

$$dc/dt = AK^n \tag{2.8.5}$$

where K is the stress intensity factor and A and n are constants dependent on the material and the environment. This fatigue phenomenon is mainly characterized by the parameter n. The n value obtained from high-strength silica fibers with no macroscopic defects, regardless of whether they are coated[20] or not,[21] is around 20. However, the n value differs slightly with the coating material, especially with fibers obtained in humid air.[22,23] In addition, the n value for low-strength fibers is about 40, the same as that obtained from bulk glass.

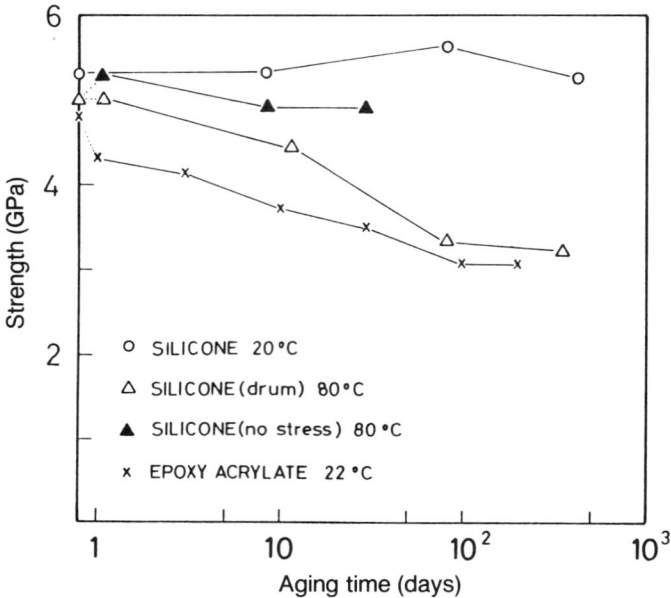

Figure 2.8.4 Time-dependent change in strength for fibers coated with silicone [from T. Kimura et al., *Trans. IECE* J64-C:157 (1981)] and epoxyacrylate in water [from T. T. Wang and H. M. Zupko, *J. Mat. Sci.* 13:2241 (1978)].

This indicates that defect initiation and growth are dependent on the surface state of the fiber.

It has been established that water corrosion on glass surfaces initiates at the silanol group on the surface, which acts as a water adsorption site. Infrared inspection of silica surfaces reveals that surface OH groups remain even after heating at temperatures higher than 800°C.[24] Water molecules are easily trapped at these surface OHs, breaking the neighboring Si-O bonds. A schematic of this cleavage process is shown in Figure 2.8.5.

Silicone resin with a structure composed of Si-O bonds similar to glass forms a hydrogen bond with surface OHs; as a result, they are stabilized against water adsorption. Compared with silicone, epoxyacrylate[25] contains only a small number of functional groups, such as OH and CO, with the ability to form hydrogen bonds with surface OHs. As a result, not every surface OH can form the stabilizing hydrogen bond that prevents a corrosion reaction. This is why a degradation in strength occurs in epoxyacrylate-coated fiber.

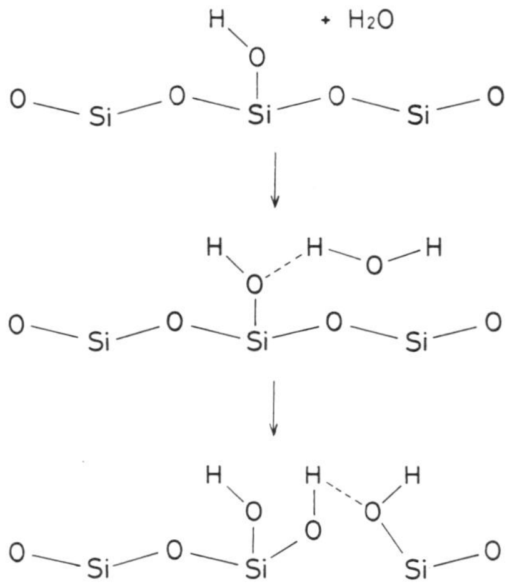

Figure 2.8.5 Schematic of cleavage process resulting from the corrosion reaction of glass and water.

Surface OHs can also be stabilized through treatment with a silane coupling agent.[26]

2.8.5 Conclusion

The defect and interface structures of high-silica optical fiber have been described above in relation to its mechanical strength. Two groups of defects dominate fiber strength: intrinsic defects on the order of 10 Å and extrinsic defects formed after drawing. The interface structure affects the initiation and growth of intrinsic microscopic defects. The chemical activity of the surface silanol group is influenced by the coating material. Thus, optical fibers should be considered a composite of glass and plastic. More detailed study in this area is needed to determine the fracture mechanism in glass, which would lead to a more precise understanding of glass structure.

References

1. Kapron, F. P. et al., *Appl. Phys. Lett.* 17:423 (1970).
2. Miya, T. et al., *Electron. Lett.* 15:106 (1979).
3. Griffith, A. A., *Phil. Trans. R. Soc. London* 221:163 (1920).
4. Maurer, R. D., *Appl. Phys. Lett.* 27:220 (1975).
5. French, W. G. et al., *Ann. Rev. Mat. Sci.* 5:373 (1975).

6. Schonhorn, H. et al., *Ann. Rev. Mat. Sci.* 29:712 (1977).
7. Dimarcello, F. V. et al., *Electron. Lett.* 14:578 (1978).
8. Payne, D. N., and Gambling, W. A., *Ceram. Bull.* 55:195 (1976).
9. Sakaguchi, S., and Nakahara, M., Rev. ECL 27:188 (1979).
10. Olshansky, R., and Maurer, R. D., *J. Appl. Phys.* 47:4497 (1976).
11. McClintock, F. A., and Irwin, G. R., *ASTM STP* 381:87 (1965).
12. Mecholsky, J. J. et al., *Ceram. Bull* 56:1016 (1977).
13. Sakaguchi, S. et al., *J. Non-Cryst. Sol.* (forthcoming).
14. Kaiser, P. et al., *Appl. Opt.* 14:156 (1975).
15. Mirror, T. J. et al., *Electron Lett.* 14:603 (1978).
16. Dimarcello, F. V. et al., *IOOC* 81:MG6 (1981).
17. Kimura, T. et al., *Trans. IECE* J64-C:157 (1981) (in Japanese).
18. Wang, T. T., and Zupko, H. M., *J. Mat. Sci.* 13:2241 (1978).
19. Wiederhorn, S. M., *Fracture Mechanics to Ceramics*, vol. 2. New York: Plenum Press, 1974, p. 613.
20. Schonhorn, H. et al., *J. Appl. Phys.* 49:4783 (1978).
21. Proctor, B. A. et al., *Proc. R. Soc. London* A297:534 (1967).
22. Kalish, D., and Tariyal, B. K., *J. Am. Ceram. Soc.* 61:518 (1978).
23. Sakaguchi S., and Kimura, T., *J. Am. Ceram. Soc.* 64:259 (1981).
24. Hair, M. L., and Hertl, W., *J. Phy. Chem.* 73:2372 (1969).
25. Schonhorn, H. et al., *J. Appl. Polym. Sci.* 23:75 (1979).
26. Schonhorn, H., *J. Appl. Polym. Sci.* 23:687 (1979).

2.9 Structure/Property Relationships in Perovskite Electronic Ceramics

Shin-ichi Shirasaki and Kazuyuki Kakegawa

2.9.1 Introduction

Impurities are often intentionally added to ceramics to control their properties and sinterability. Therefore, an understanding of point defect structures and diffusion characteristics in doped materials is particularly important. Unfortunately, not enough is known about how impurities influence point defect structures in ceramics.

Wagner,[1] Verwey,[2] and Kröger and Vink[3] have proposed the concept of a controlled valence mechanism to explain variations in point defects, electrons, and holes when aliovalent impurities are incorporated in oxides. However, sufficient recognition has not been given to the variations in oxygen defects in the concept. In addition, no systematic studies have been undertaken of the role of impurity doping in the thermal formation of point defects in oxides.

It is well known that n-type semiconduction can be achieved by doping a typical ferroelectric material, barium titanate, with rare earths such as La^{3+}, Y^{3+}, and Gd^{3+} and then firing the doped material at about 1400°C. This type of semiconductor material has been widely used in thermistors having a positive temperature coefficient of resistivity and a barrier-layer-type capacitor with quite high apparent permittivity. In an early explanation of conduction, Saburi[4] proposed a hopping model for limited La doping in an assumed composition of $Ba^{2+}_{1-x}La^{3+}_xTi^{4+}_{1-x}Ti^{3+}_xO_3$. Other researchers[5] believed that the carriers in the doped material originated essentially from donor rare earths replacing Ba^{2+}. Both models took no account of variations in the oxygen vacancy level caused by La doping.

This section presents a new idea regarding the impurity/point defect relationship in this La-doped barium titanate system. The role of oxygen vacancies on semiconduction in doped titanate is also discussed.

For many years researchers have been making efforts to establish the relations among fabrication, structure, and properties in ceramics. The importance of these relations cannot be overemphasized. To establish them, it is necessary to appropriately characterize many different structures, especially point defect structure. If these relations in ceramics can be clearly established, it will then be possible to determine what structure yields a desired property for a given application.

In relation to the discussion of the point defect structure and semiconduction in La-doped barium titanate, this section also describes the successful fabrication of a high-capacitance monolithic ceramic capacitor using a base metal electrode.

2.9.2 La-Doped Barium Titanate Semiconductor Studies

Previous reports have shown that when rare earth-doped barium titanate was fired at elevated temperatures, electroneutrality could be maintained without altering the number of oxygen vacancies. The basic idea was first proposed by Saburi,[4] who described a controlled valence mechanism represented by

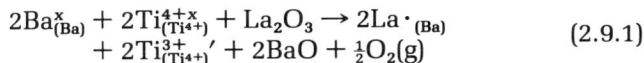

$$2Ba^x_{(Ba)} + 2Ti^{4+}_{(Ti^{4+})} + La_2O_3 \rightarrow 2La^{\cdot}_{(Ba)}$$
$$+ 2Ti^{3+}_{(Ti^{4+})}{}' + 2BaO + \tfrac{1}{2}O_2(g) \tag{2.9.1}$$

This means that the excess positive charge formed by replacing La^{3+} for Ba^{2+} is compensated for by the occurrence of a mixed valence state of Ti, that is, Ti^{3+} and Ti^{4+}. Other researchers[5] believed that carriers in the doped materials originated from the donors obtained from rare earths replacing Ba^{2+}. This can be written as

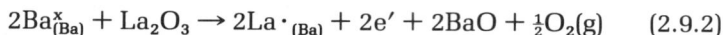

$$2Ba_{(Ba)}^x + La_2O_3 \rightarrow 2La \cdot_{(Ba)} + 2e' + 2BaO + \tfrac{1}{2}O_2(g) \qquad (2.9.2)$$

It was also found that doping with monovalent cations such as Ag, Na, K, Rb, and Cs instead of rare earths resulted in n-type semiconducting behavior.[6] This fact seems difficult to explain in conjunction with the foregoing two mechanisms [Equations (2.9.1) and (2.9.2)].

Another interesting behavior of La-doped $BaTiO_3$ is that semiconduction can be achieved by doping with rare earths of a concentration of about 0.2 at%; insulation again results at dopant levels higher than about 0.2%.[4] In interpreting this peculiar overdoping phenomenon, Saburi[4] considered the possibility of crystal strain, in which electron exchange between Ti^{4+} and Ti^{3+} may be inhibited. Gallagher,[7] in contrast, assumed precipitation of an insulating material along grain boundaries to explain this peculiarity. Moreover, Jonker[8] considered that in La overdoping the formation of partial Ba-site cation vacancies as acceptor traps causes conductivity to decrease. The latter has been accepted as a reliable model, although there is no concrete supporting evidence.

2.9.3 Macroscopic View of Defect Structure[9,10]

Two compositions, $(1 - x)BaO \cdot TiO_2 \cdot \tfrac{1}{3}xLa_2O_3$ and $0.9\,BaO \cdot TiO_2 \cdot \tfrac{1}{2}yLa_2O_3$, were chosen to clarify the origin of the semiconducting behavior of La-doped barium titanate. As far as X-ray diffraction is concerned, the materials under study were monophasic perovskite. In the fired materials with composition $(1 - x)BaO \cdot TiO_2 \cdot \tfrac{1}{3}xLa_2O_3$, the formation of vacancies can be expected in the 12-coordinated Ba site to maintain electroneutrality. The general expected defect formula can be written as $(Ba_{1-x}La_{2x/3}\square_{x/3})TiO_3$, where $\square$ denotes a vacancy. Examples are $(Ba_{0.9}La_{0.0667}\square_{0.0333})TiO_3$ for $x = 0.1$ and $(Ba_{0.8}La_{0.1334}\square_{0.0667})TiO_3$ for $x = 0.2$. To test whether the postulated defect structure was actually formed, the density of the powdered solid was measured pycnometrically and compared with the corresponding density calculated from the composition and unit-cell volume with the postulated defect structure. The results are shown in Figure 2.9.1. The two corresponding densities showed good agreement in this system, indicating the formation of a perovskite containing only Ba-site vacancies.

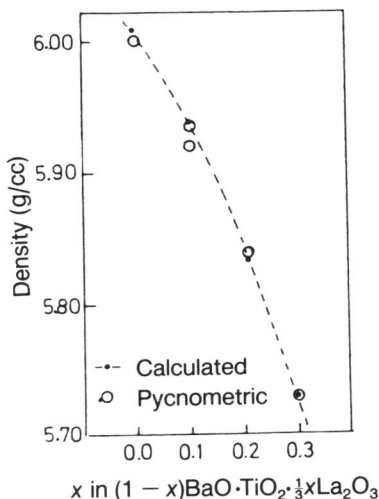

Density (g/cc) axis: 6.00, 5.90, 5.80, 5.70

x-axis: 0.0 0.1 0.2 0.3

x in $(1 - x)\mathrm{BaO \cdot TiO_2 \cdot \frac{1}{3}xLa_2O_3}$

-•- Calculated
○ Pycnometric

Figure 2.9.1 Calculated and observed density as a function of x in $(1 - x)\mathrm{BaO \cdot TiO_2 \cdot \frac{1}{3}xLa_2O_3}$.

In the other type of fired La-doped material with a composition of $0.9 \ \mathrm{BaO \cdot TiO_2 \cdot \frac{1}{2}yLa_2O_3}$, $0.1 \leqq y \leqq 0.13$ possible defect structures were determined on the basis of the following two requirements: maintenance of electroneutrality and equality in the number of the two different cation sites. Two assumptions were also made: valency $+3$ for La and $+4$ for Ti. The latter is supported by the fact that Ti^{3+} was not detected in the ESR spectra of La^{3+}-doped $BaTiO_3$, ruling out the occurrence of mixed valence states. The calculated results are summarized in Table 2.9.1.

As can been seen, the materials concerned can be generally expressed by the defect structure formula $(Ba_{x'}^{2+}La_{y'}^{3+}\square_{x'})(Ti_{u'}^{4+}\square_{v'})O_3$. To

Table 2.9.1 Possible Types of Defect Structure for Monophasic Compositions $0.9\mathrm{BaO \cdot TiO_2 \cdot \frac{1}{2}yLa_2O_3}$ and Their Calculated and Observed Densities as a Function of y

y in $0.9\mathrm{BaO \cdot TiO_2 \cdot \frac{1}{2}yLa_2O_3}$		0.100	0.115	0.120	0.125	0.130
x'		0.885	0.879	0.876	0.875	0.872
y'		0.0984	0.1123	0.1169	0.1215	0.126
z'	in $(Ba_{x'}^{2+}La_{y'}^{3+}\square_{z'})(Ti_{u'}^{4+}\square_{v'})O_3$	0.0164	0.0088	0.0065	0.0037	0.0017
u'		0.984	0.976	0.974	0.972	0.967
v'		0.0164	0.0234	0.0260	0.0280	0.0308
Calculated density (g/cm³)		5.98	6.00	5.99	5.99	6.00
Observed density (g/cm³)		5.97	5.99	5.99	6.02	5.98

test whether the postulated defect structure was actually formed, the densities of the powdered solids were also determined by pycnometry and X-ray diffractometry. The results are also given in Table 2.9.1. The two corresponding densities also agree well, indicating that this type of perovskite can contain both Ba-site vacancies and Ti-site vacancies. An important point, however, is that semiconducting behavior cannot be explained in terms of such cation vacancies alone.

2.9.4 Relationship of Resistivity and Cation Vacancy Concentration[9]

Special attention was directed to the number of Ba-site vacancies in the La-doped materials. This number was plotted as a function of the compositional parameter y in an attempt to correlate this with room-temperature resistivity (Figure 2.9.2). The number of the vacancies decreases monotonically with increasing y, reaching zero at $y = 0.1325$. The y value of about 0.1325 corresponds to a distinct boundary between semiconductors and insulators. Therefore, semiconduction should, either directly or indirectly, be associated with the presence of Ba-site vacancies.

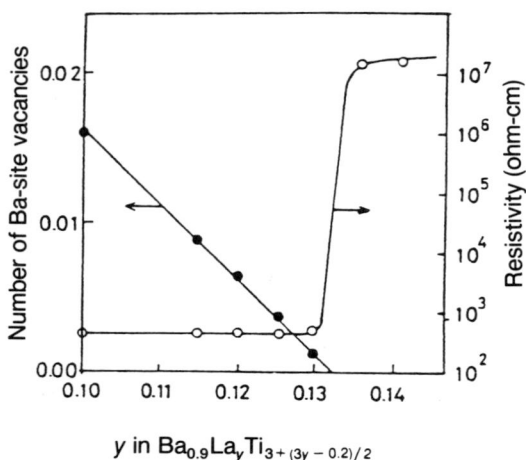

y in $Ba_{0.9}La_yTi_{3+(3y-0.2)/2}$

Figure 2.9.2 The number of Ba-site vacancies and room temperature resistivity as functions of y in composition $Ba_{0.9}La_yTiO_{3+(3y-0.2)/2}$.

2.9.5 Oxygen Diffusion Characteristics[10]

Oxygen self-diffusion coefficients were determined by measuring the exchange rate of oxygen between a gas phase and the heated polycrystalline aggregate over a temperature range of 770–1430°C. Oxygen gas enriched with about 20% O^{18} was used as the tracer. The reaction chamber used for the exchange was made of transparent silica glass whose outer surfaces were cooled by circulating water to minimize the exchange between the constituent oxygen of the chamber and the enriched oxygen. Details of the experimental setup and procedure have been described elsewhere.[11]

The Crank relation[12] was used to calculated D, the oxygen diffusion coefficient:

$$\frac{Mt}{M_\infty} = 1 - \sum_{n=1}^\infty \frac{6\alpha(\alpha+1)\exp\left(-Dq_n^2 t/a^2\right)}{9 + 9\alpha + q_n^2\alpha^2} \qquad (2.9.3)$$

where the q_n's are the nonzero roots of $\tan q_n = 3q_n/(3+q_n^2)$, a is the solid sphere radius, α is the gram-atom ratio of oxygen present in the solid particles to that in the gas phase, and Mt/M_∞ is the total amount of solute in the sphere after time t as a fraction of the corresponding quantity after an infinite time.

Figure 2.9.3 shows the oxygen diffusion coefficient as a function of reciprocal temperature for La-0.0667 $((Ba_{0.9}La_{0.0667}\square_{0.0333})TiO_3)$ and BT($BaTiO_3$) polycrystalline materials with various particle sizes. All calculations were made taking the grain radius to be equal to the sphere radius a in the Crank relation. As shown in the figure, diffusion is independent of particle size for both materials. The diffusivity of polycrystalline barium titanate is represented by

$$D = 2.9 \times 10^{-10} \exp\left[(-10500 \pm 3000)/RT\right] \qquad (2.9.4)$$

The diffusivities of polycrystalline La-0.0667 in the low and high temperature regions are expressed respectively by

$$D = 8.0 \times 10^{-12} \exp\left[(-14500 \pm 3000)/RT\right] \qquad (2.9.5)$$

$$D = 2.0 \times 10^3 \exp\left[(-102200 \pm 4000)/RT\right] \qquad (2.9.6)$$

Figure 2.9.3 shows that when the D calculations are made with a = grain radius, the resultant D is independent of particle size. This indicates that the grain boundary diffusion coefficient D_g is so large in comparison with the volume diffusion coefficient D_l that the concentration of O^{18} in the gas phase is always equal to that of the grain boundary region throughout a diffusion anneal.[13,14,15] In this case the

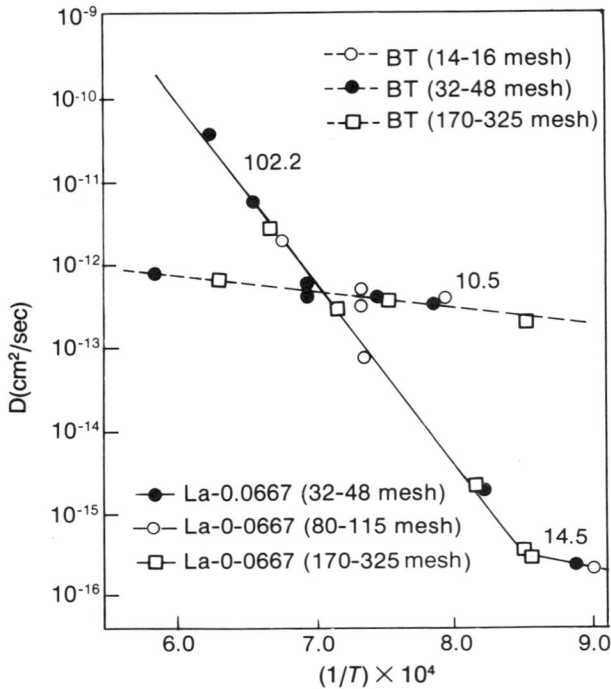

Figure 2.9.3 Temperature dependence of oxygen diffusion coefficient of polycrystalline BT and La-0.0667, in which the calculations of D were made with sphere radius a = grain radius. The results for specimens with various particles with different mesh sizes are indicated. The numbers on the curves show activation energies (kcal/mol).

calculated diffusion coefficient can be regarded as D_l in these polycrystalline aggregates.

The oxygen volume diffusion coefficient level can be used as a measure of the oxygen vacancy concentration if the diffusion actually progresses by a vacancy mechanism. The pre-exponential factor, 2.0×10^3 cm^2/sec, for La-0.0667 strongly indicates that a vacancy mechanism is likely.[16]

In summary, appreciable oxygen vacancies form in La-0.0667 with respect to barium titanate as the temperature increases (Figure 2.9.3).

2.9.6 Origin of Semiconducting Behavior[9,10]

Until recently the origin of semiconducting behavior in doped materials was thought to result from electron formation described by

Equation (2.9.2). A very different interpretation of the origin can be given in light of the current data. First, the major fraction of La-doped into barium titanate is available for the formation of cation vacancies (see Table 2.9.1 and Figure 2.9.1). Moreover, the existence of Ba-site vacancies may weaken the bond strength of TiO_6 octahedra adjacent to the cation vacancies. Therefore, when material containing a large number of Ba-site vacancies is fired at elevated temperatures, oxygen vacancies plus electrons could thermally form with ease according to the following equation:

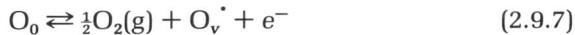

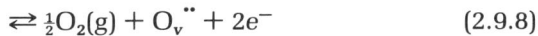

$$O_0 \rightleftarrows \tfrac{1}{2}O_2(g) + O_v^{\cdot} + e^- \tag{2.9.7}$$

$$\rightleftarrows \tfrac{1}{2}O_2(g) + O_v^{\cdot\cdot} + 2e^- \tag{2.9.8}$$

where $O_v^{\cdot}$ and $O_v^{\cdot\cdot}$ are the oxygen vacancies with effective charges of $+1$ and $+2$, respectively. The resultant electrons could cause n-type semiconducting behavior in doped barium titanate. It is necessary to point out that oxygen vacancies formed by Schottky equilibrium are generally difficult to correlate with electrical conductivity.

   This new concept should be taken to be reliable on the basis of other experimental factors. Perhaps most important is that even when a completely monophasic perovskite with a composition of $(Ba_{0.9}La_{0.0667}\square_{0.0333})TiO_3$ was prepared by firing the mixture at high temperatures around 1100°C, the resultant material did not exhibit semiconduction. To achieve semiconduction, it was necessary to raise the firing temperature to at least 1380°C. If a controlled valence mechanism expressed by Equations 2.9.1 and 2.9.2 is likely, n-type semiconducting should be achieved by firing the doped material at temperatures around 1100°C, because this is the temperature at which La is incorporated into the host lattice. However, the results contradict the expectations. The firing temperature-dependence behavior of conduction agrees with the present concept concerning the origin of semiconducting behavior.

   It thus seems that the present concept can apply to many other doped oxides.[17]

2.9.7 Conduction Behavior in Rare Earth Overdoping

An interesting characteristic of rare earth-doped barium titanate is the insulating effect of overdoping the host with rare earths or other oxides. As shown in Figure 2.9.4, the amount of rare earth necessary for semiconducting is approximately 0.2 at% when stoichiometric $BaTiO_3$ is used as the host. In the present study using

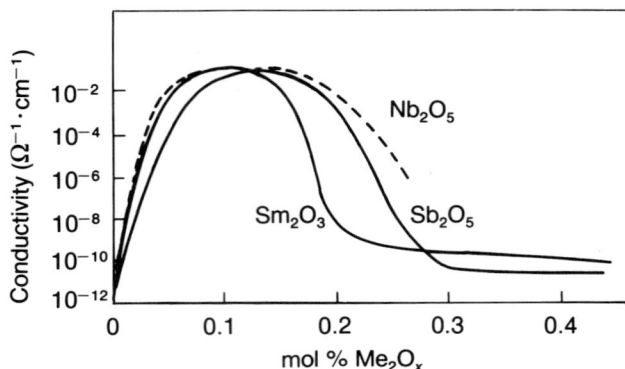

Figure 2.9.4 Electrical conductivity as a function of additive (Sm_2O_3, Nb_2O_5, and Sb_2O_5) concentration.

$0.9BaO \cdot TiO_2 \cdot \frac{1}{2}yLa_2O_3$, the limited amount was found to be $y \approx 0.1325$ (Figure 2.9.2).

If the foregoing interpretation on the origin of semiconduction is valid, such peculiar behavior is of interest because semiconduction after overdoping should also be explained by this new concept.

The measurement of perovskite oxygen diffusion coefficients for $y > 0.1325$ showed that D_l of these materials was always below D_l of barium titanate up to at least 1400°C.

Insulating behavior resulting from overdoping can therefore be explained as follows. The overdoping results in the disappearance of Ba-site vacancies, by which the bond strength of the TiO_6 octahedra again increases, compared with perovskites with Ba-site vacancies. When this material without Ba-site vacancies is fired at elevated temperatures, therefore, the formation of oxygen vacancies plus electrons may be considerably inhibited, resulting in insulating effects.

2.9.8 Structural Design of Perovskite for Monolithic Ceramic Capacitor with Ni Inner Electrode

Functional materials are generally required to achieve a higher grade of function with smaller size of materials. This is also the case with ceramic capacitors. Monolithic capacitors consisting of inner electrodes embedded in dielectrics have been developed for this purpose. Inner electrodes, shown in Figure 2.9.5, are separated by several tens of μm; therefore, a high capacitance in the range of 10–100 μF can be achieved.

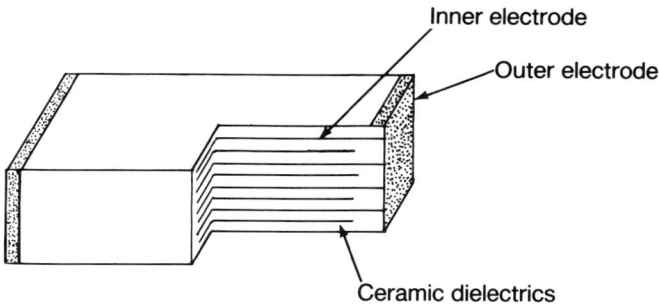

Inner electrode

Outer electrode

Ceramic dielectrics

Figure 2.9.5 Construction of monolithic ceramic capacitor.

Materials used for internal electrodes should meet the following requirements: (1) the melting points of electrode materials must be higher than the sintering temperature of the composite materials, and (2) they should neither be oxidized nor react with the dielectric materials in sintering in air up to 1300°C. These requirements are satisfied by using Pt and Rd for electrodes.

Recently there has been a great demand for utilizing base metals such as Ni and Co rather than precious metals in order to substantially reduce the cost of monolithic capacitors. In this case a green sheet consisting of dielectrics and the printed inner electrodes should be sintered at a low Po_2 to prevent electrode oxidation. However, commercial dielectrics like perovskite compounds are generally reduced in low Po_2, resulting in semiconduction.

The point defect structure of perovskite can be designed so that the material does not exhibit semiconduction even after sintering at a low Po_2. To this end, the present proposed relationship of point defect structure and semiconduction is useful. The conclusion is that perovskite semiconduction could be easily achieved by the introduction of Ba-site cation vacancies. If Ba-site cation vacancy concentration is as low as possible, insulation would be expected. Such a structure design for capacitor use was successful in the $[(Ba_{1-x}Ca_x)O]_m$ $[(Ti_{1-y}Zr_y)O_2]$ system.[18] Resistivity as a function of m for material sintered in a $Po_2 = 5.0 \times 10^{-6}$ atmosphere is shown in Figure 2.9.6. As can be seen, a high resistivity in the range of $m > 1.00$ can be achieved. One can strongly expect a very low level of Ba-site cation vacancies in this range, by which oxygen vacancies plus electrons, as the origin of conduction, can be greatly inhibited even upon sintering these materials at low Po_2 at elevated temperatures.

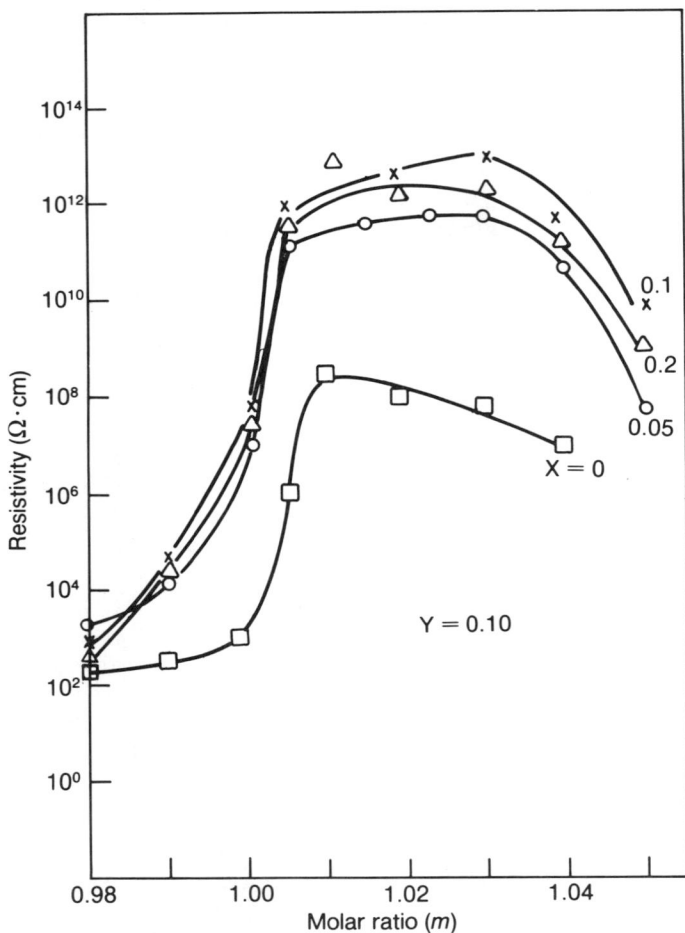

Figure 2.9.6 Resistivity versus molar ratio m under the conditions of $y = 0.1$, $x = 0 -$ 0.20 and $P_{O_2} = 5 \times 10^{-6}$ atm.

References

1. Wagner, C., *Z. Phys. Chem. Abt.* B22:199 (1933).
2. Verwey, E. J. W., *Philips Res. Rep.* 51:1731 (1950).
3. Kröger, F. A., and Vink, H. J., *Solid State Physics*, vol. 3. New York: Academic Press, 1956, p. 310.
4. Saburi, O., *J. Phys. Soc. Jpn.* 14:1159 (1959).

5. Harman, G. G., *Phys. Rev.* 106:1358 (1967); Takeda, T., and Watanabe, A., *Jpn. J. Appl. Phys.* 7:232 (1968).

6. Ikushima, H., and Hayakawa, S., *Jpn. J. Appl. Phys.* 4:328 (1965).

7. Gallagher, P. K., *J. Am. Ceram. Soc.* 46:359 (1963).

8. Jonker, G. H., *Solid State Electron.* 7:895 (1964).

9. Shirasaki, S., Tsukioka, M., Yamamura, H., Oshima, H., and Kakegawa, K., *Solid State Commun.* 19:721 (1976).

10. Shirasaki, S., Yamamura, H., Haneka, H., Kakegawa, K., and Moori, J., *J. Chem. Phys.* 73:4640 (1980).

11. Hall, R., Justand, D., and Dumbgen, G., *Proc. 4th International Symposium on the Reactivity of Solids*, J. H. de Boer, ed. Amsterdam: Elsevier, 1960, p. 65.

12. Crank, J., *The Mathematics of Diffusion.* London: Oxford University Press, 1957, p. 88.

13. Kijima, K., and Shirasaki, S., *J. Chem. Phys.* 65:2668 (1976).

14. Hashimoto, H., Hama, H., and Shirasaki, S., *J. Appl. Phys.* 43:4828 (1972).

15. Shirasaki, S., Shindo, I., and Haneda, H., *Chem. Phys. Lett.* 50:3459 (1978).

16. O'Keefe, M., *Material Science Research*, vol. 6. New York: Plenum Press, 1975, p. 57.

17. Shirasaki, S., Matsuda, S., Yamamura, H., and Haneda, H., *Advances in Ceramics* 10:474 (1985).

18. Wakino, K., Minai, K., and Sakabe, Y., *Proc. US-Japan Study Seminar on Dielectric and Piezoelectric Ceramics*, K. Okazaki, ed., Tokyo, Japan, p. w-1.

CHAPTER

3

STRUCTURAL CERAMICS

3.1 Overview

Osami Kamigaito

In Japan there is great interest in fine ceramics for structural use. Because almost all fuel is imported, energy saving is one of the most important industrial requirements. High-temperature structural materials in various types of heat engines and power plants can contribute to energy savings through the elevation of operating temperatures. Metallic alloys are not thought to be promising, as they seem to have nearly reached their thermal limits; however, structural fine ceramics are thought to be promising because of their intrinsic high strength in elevated temperatures as well as their high chemical stability. The application of structural fine ceramics to heat engines for automobiles, especially heavy-duty engines, is expected to result in considerable fuel savings because such materials are lightweight, have high operating temperatures, and save or eliminate cooling energy requirements. Applications to small engine parts, such as pre-ignition chambers and turbine wheels for supercharging, are also expected to improve engine performance.

Applying fine ceramics to high-temperature structures is also thought to be valuable from the point of view of saving precious metals, such as cobalt, nickel, and chromium, used in high-temperature alloys. In addition, fine ceramics can be useful in various types of

163

tools. In industry there is a great demand for tool materials for high-speed, high-reliability machining. High-speed machining results in cheap mass production, and high reliability results in trouble-free tool exchanging accomplished in every fixed machining period (depending on machining conditions). The application of fine ceramics to tools represents an effort to meet these requirements.

Some oxide ceramics, including alumina, partially stabilized zirconia (PSZ), mullite, and so on, are widely used as structural ceramics in such applications as spark plug insulators, machining tools, valves, and mechanical seals. Sintered alumina and mullite are not so strong, but they are still important materials as they are cheap and there is much experience in their use. Efforts are being made to improve their mechanical properties by refining their microstructure and (in the case of zirconia) by dispersing small particles; this is expected to improve these materials' fracture stress and thus enhance their importance.

PSZ is attracting interest because of its high fracture stress and fracture toughness. Its fracture strength is now being improved by refinements in the production process and by addition of some oxides. PSZ is applied in catalytic-converter-system oxygen sensors for automobile exhaust-gas cleaning and in steel making. Its application to dies for cold-drawing soft metal, nonmagnetic tools for cutting magnetic recording tape, and so on is being attempted. It is expected to become a more important ceramic material in the future.

Nonoxide ceramics such as silicon nitride, silicon carbide, and Sialon are attracting great interest as the most important ceramics for structural use. Silicon nitride has been strengthened by doping with Y_2O_3 and Al_2O_3 as well as by boundary crystallization. This process was developed in Japan, and great improvement has resulted in the mechanical properties of sintered silicon nitride. The study of silicon nitride ceramics is continuing on a large scale in Japan. Also, the preparation of silicon nitride powder is being studied seriously.

Silicon carbide has been used mainly as an abrasive powder and in fire bricks for steel making. Recent study of silicon carbide has focused mainly on developing high-strength sintered bodies by pressureless sintering as well as on applying silicon carbide to mechanical parts such as heat engine parts. Also, the preparation of silicon carbide powder is being studied to achieve high sinterability.

Both β'- and X-phase Sialon were developed in Japan at almost the same time as in Great Britain, and several varieties of Sialon, including the glassy phase, have been studied. As a result, dense, strong sintered Sialon is available, and it is expected to be used as a structural material as well as a cutting tool material and in other applications.

There is also interest in a carbon-carbon composite as a high-temperature structural material as well as an implantable material —for example, in nuclear and fusion reactors—and as a bio-engineering material, space-engineering material, aircraft brake material, and so on. To develop this composite, basic studies on carbonization, graphitization, and microstructure as well as process studies such as CVD are now in progress.

Evaluation of structural failures in ceramics to ensure high reliability is being carried out in a national project. Ceramics failure, including that of glass, is being studied on the basis of slow crack growth, and prediction of ceramic lifetime and proof testing are being pursued on the same basis. The prediction technique and the proof test are expected to be widely applied to ceramic structural parts in the near future. The evaluation of ceramics offers a basis for the design of ceramic structural parts, but it is not being used because of the complicated nature of ceramic failures. The study of failures on the basis of slow crack growth is strengthening analytical capability. Additionally, bending strength, tensile strength, and fatigue life of ceramics under static as well as cyclic load are being studied. The results are expected to be very useful in ensuring the high reliability of structural ceramics. Because of these efforts, structural fine ceramics are expected to be used widely and safely in industry in spite of their inherent brittleness.

3.2 Fabrication and Properties of Some Oxide Ceramics: Alumina, Mullite, and Zirconia

Isamu Fukuura and Toshiyasu Asano

3.2.1 Introduction

Among the various so-called new ceramics for industrial uses, materials currently in wide use are oxide ceramics such as Al_2O_3, MgO, ZnO, BeO, mullite, and spinel. These ceramics are mechanically stable at higher temperatures, resistant in both active and inert atmospheres, superior in terms of corrosion resistance and wear resistance because of their strong chemical bonding, and easily available because their constituents are abundant.

3.2.2 Strengthening Methods

In order for ceramics to be strong, they must possess the following:

1. Strong chemical bonds and relevant crystal structures.
2. Dense and fine microstructures.
3. Homogeneous microstructures.

In the manufacturing processes, emphasis is placed on producing dense ceramics with a fine microstructure. However, other factors such as chemical composition (purity), the nature and distribution of impurities, crystal structure, grain size, and pores are important. Because the mechanical properties of ceramics are characterized by brittle fracture, it is necessary to develop materials with the following characteristics:

1. Large K_{1C} and few cracks.
2. Small strength degradation at high temperatures and low crack propagation rate.
3. Small scattering in crack size — that is, high reliability.

The following sections describe several examples of strengthening with alumina and zirconia.

3.2.3 Mechanical Properties of Alumina

3.2.3.1 *Microstructure and Strength*

In general the strength of alumina is largely dependent on composition (alumina content), porosity, grain size, and finishing conditions. Also, a large body of data is available on the mechanical properties of alumina at higher temperatures, 1000°C.

Figure 3.2.1 shows the relation between alumina content and strength. It can be seen that the bending strength is higher for a higher alumina content. Above 800°C an abrupt decrease in strength is observed for 96%, 93%, and 90% alumina. The decrease in strength for 99% alumina is also marked but not abrupt. This increase in strength with temperature is thought to result from two factors. First, the internal stress generated by the thermal expansion mismatch between the crystalline and glassy phases is relieved at higher temperatures because of differences in thermal expansion of the two phases and the local plastic deformation of the glassy phase. Second, sharp cracks become blunt, which results in smaller stress concentrations.

The strength of sintered products with the same compositions

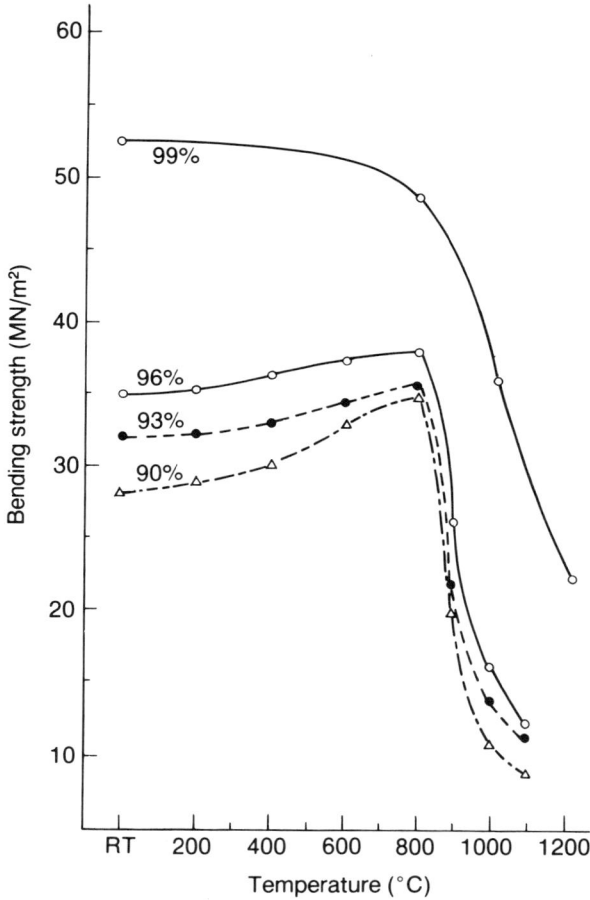

Figure 3.2.1 Bending strength of various alumina ceramics (alumina content: 90%, 93%, 96%, and 99%).

varies with the manufacturing process and the raw materials as a result of differences in microstructure. The relation between strength, porosity, and grain size has been thoroughly studied. The typical equations are as follows:

$$\sigma = KG^{-a}e^{-bp} \qquad (3.2.1)[1]$$

$$\sigma = Ke^{-bp}G^{a+cp} \qquad (3.2.2)[2]$$

Passmore and co-workers[3] hot pressed 99.9% alumina powder

(mean particle size of 0.3 μm) and prepared bodies with various porosities and grain sizes. From the measurements of bending strength at 25°C and 1000°C, constants K, a, b, c were determined as follows:

$$S_{25} = 142,500e^{-11.83P} \cdot G^{-0.60+3.33P} \qquad (3.2.3)$$

$$S_{1200} = 73,000e^{-11.83P} \cdot G^{-0.60+3.33P} \qquad (3.2.4)$$

3.2.3.2 Scattering of Strength and Its Analysis

Thus far only the relation between average strength and microstructure has been discussed; however, there is a scattering of strength, generally about 20%, in a given product. This is because fractures originate from inhomogeneous regions such as grain boundaries, pores, large grains, and impurity inclusions. Fractures not only originate inside ceramic bodies but are also affected by machining conditions.

The effects of pores and large grains on strength have been studied by Rice,[4,5] Kirchner,[6] and Gruver.[7] The authors measured the strength of sintered Al_2O_3 and hot-pressed Al_2O_3-TiC; the results are described below.[8] The mechanical properties of the two materials used in the study are listed in Table 3.2.1; measured fracture strength is plotted in Figure 3.2.2. The fracture surfaces of each specimen were

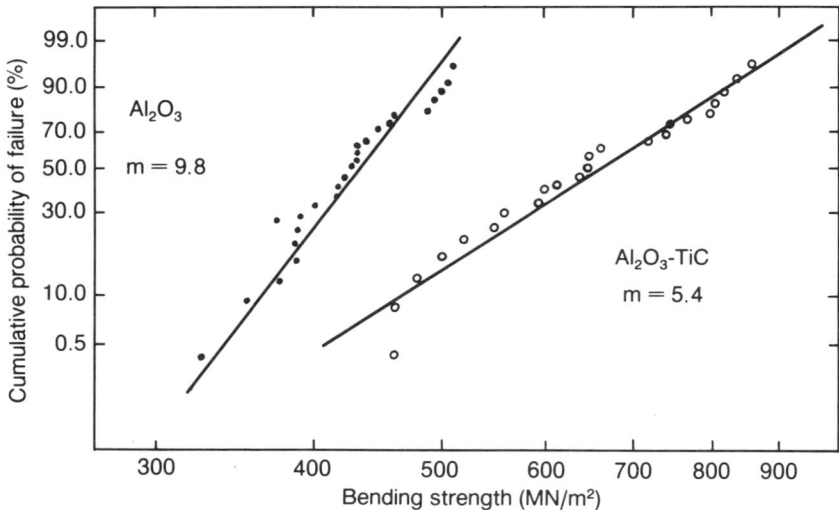

Figure 3.2.2 Weibull distribution of bend strength of Al_2O_3 and Al_2O_3-TiC.

Table 3.2.1 Mechanical Properties of Al_2O_3 and Al_2O_3-TiC

Property	Material	Al_2O_3	Al_2O_3-30% TiC
Density	g/cm³	3.93	4.25
Strength	MN/m²	440	670
Fracture toughness	MN/m³/Z	4.85	7.12
Weibull modulus m		9.8	5.4
Hardness, H_{RA}		93.5	94.5
Thermal expansion	$10^{-6}/°C$	7.8	7.9
Thermal conductivity	W/mk	17	21

examined, and fracture origins, flaw sizes, and strength were correlated. The data obtained were analyzed by the following equations:

$$\sigma_d = \sigma_m (1 - Z\Delta t/t)(1 - 2\Delta t/t) \qquad (3.2.5)$$
$$\sigma_o = \sigma_d (1 + Z\sqrt{a/\rho}) \qquad (3.2.6)$$

where

σ_m = bend strength

σ_d = external stress acting on a defect

$2a$ = length of major axis of defect

ρ = effective radius of curvature

σ_o = ideal strength

$1 + \sqrt{a/\rho}$ = stress concentration factor

Defect size and bend strength are plotted in Figure 3.2.3. By the least
squares fit,

$$\sigma_m = 0.176\sqrt{a} + 1.12 \times 10^{-3} \qquad (3.2.7)$$

was obtained. The ideal strength and strength change as a function of
defect size are summarized in Table 3.2.2.

3.2.3.3 Machined Surface Conditions and Strength

Alumina ceramics generally shrink about 20% upon firing. Therefore, sintered products are diamond machined if high tolerance is
required. Fractures can originate from defects induced by surface
machining, as maximum stress is usually at the surfaces. Strength is
therefore largely dependent on surface conditions.

Figure 3.2.4 is an example of strength measurements as a function of surface roughness for diamond-machined 99% alumina. Furukawa and co-workers[9] have studied the relation of strength and

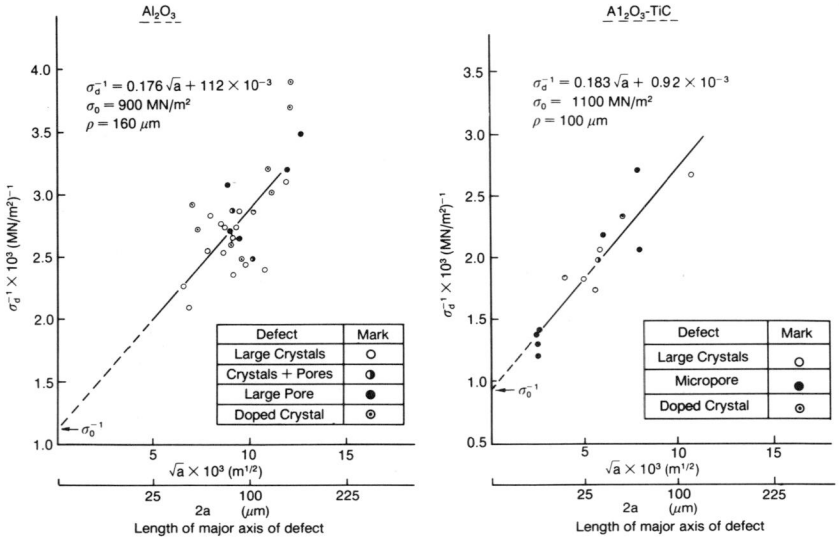

Figure 3.2.3 Relation of σ_α^{-1} and $\sqrt{a}$.

Table 3.2.2 Relation of Defects and Strength

Length of Defects	Al$_2$O$_3$	Al$_2$O$_3$-TiC
	Bending Strength — Calculated	
0$_\mu$	88 MN/m^2	108
0$_\mu$	90 kg/mm	110
1	80	95
1	82	97
10	66	76
10	67	77
100	42	45
100	43	46
	Bending Strength — Experimental	
—	43	66
—	44	67

surface cracks and how strength is recovered by annealing. Their results are shown in Figure 3.2.5. Specimens with $H_{max} = 1$ μm are stronger than those with 5 μm by 10 MN/m^2. As-sintered specimens have $H_{max} = 15 - 30$ μm and a strength of 40 MN/m^2, equivalent to the strength of the specimens with $H_{max} = 5$ μm. They explained that this was caused by blunt-shaped surface defects for the as-sintered

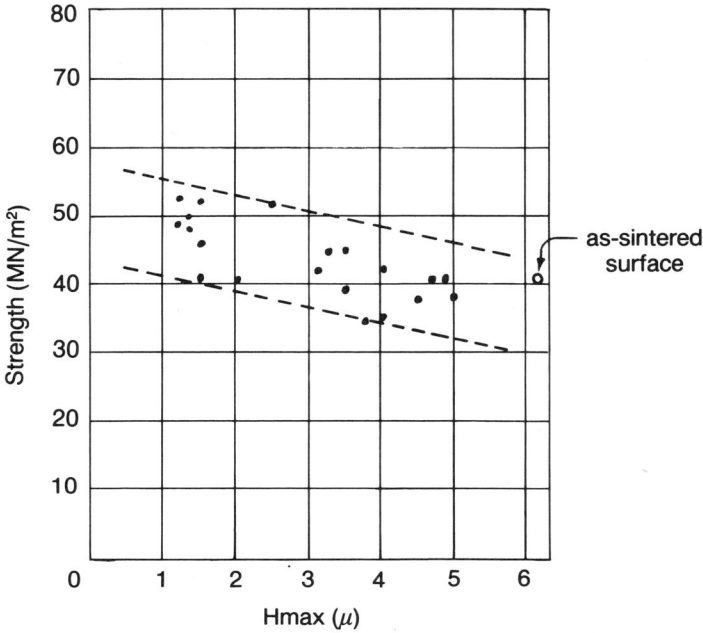

Figure 3.2.4 Strength versus surface roughness.

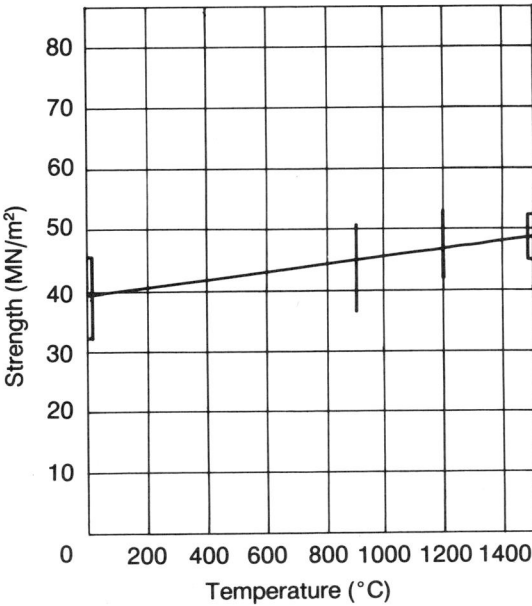

Figure 3.2.5 Strength versus annealing temperature.

specimens. The annealed surfaces show a flattening trend above 1000°C. Machined defects have been reported to flatten at 900°C and were annihilated at 1500°C.

3.2.4 Partially Stabilized Zirconia

ZrO_2 has a monoclinic structure (*m*) at room temperature. It transforms to a tetragonal structure (*t*) above 1100°C and to a cubic structure (*c*) at higher temperatures (about 2370°C). When pure ZrO_2 is sintered, it spontaneously falls to pieces during cooling because of the $t \rightarrow m$ transformation. Therefore, oxides such as MgO, CaO, and Y_2O_3 are added to stabilize the cubic structure. These additives are called stabilizers, and the doped ZrO_2 is called stabilized ZrO_2.

Recently, partially stabilized ZrO_2 (PSZ) has attracted attention because of its improved strength and toughness. It contains less stabilizer than fully stabilized ZrO_2, and the metastable *t*-phase is retained after sintering. In 1963, Wolten[10] suggested that the $t \rightleftarrows m$

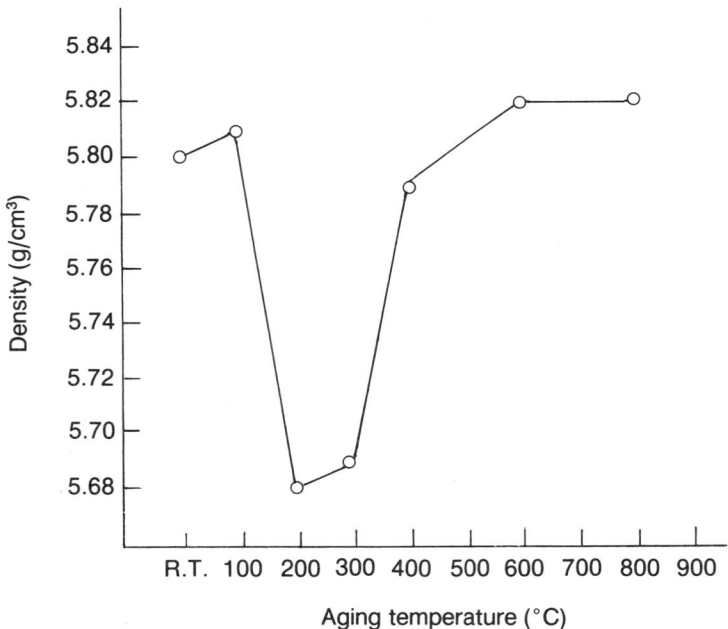

Figure 3.2.6 Density versus aging temperature in PSZ containing 4 mol% Y_2O_3 (held for 100 hours).

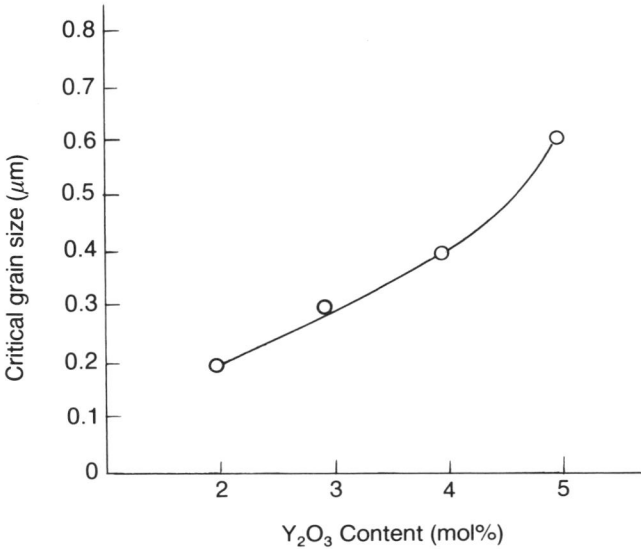

Figure 3.2.7 Critical grain size as a function of Y_2O_3 content (after holding for 1000 hours at 300°C).

transformation is martensitic. In 1975, Garvie and co-workers[11] noted that the transformation absorbs crack propagation energy, and developed toughened, partially stabilized ZrO_2 utilizing stress-induced transformation. By appropriate heat treatment, these investigators succeeded in producing fine t-ZrO_2 precipitates (0.1 μm) in the CaO-PSZ. As a result of this treatment, the strength increased from 250 to 650 MPa.

Gupta and co-workers[12] produced a Y_2O_3-PSZ sintered body having a tetragonal phase by appropriate selection of the starting powder, quantity of Y_2O_3, and sintering temperature. This Y_2O_3-PSZ has a different microstructure from CaO-PSZ. Y_2O_3-PSZ consists of fine t-phase grains, whereas fine precipitates are dispersed in a cubic matrix in CaO-PSZ. Kawanami and co-workers[13] studied the same system and obtained a sintered body having a strength higher than 100 MN/m^2. Masaki and co-workers[14] reported that hot-pressed PSZ with 3 mol% Y_2O_3 had a strength of 150 MN/m^2.

The research group of one of the present authors[15] has studied the effects of adding Al_2O_3 (0–40%) to PSZ with 2–5 mol% Y_2O_3. They found that Al_2O_3 was effective in retarding grain growth and the

$t \rightarrow m$ transformation. However, strength degradation at higher temperatures was not improved.

The thermal stability of the t-phase was also studied in the Y_2O_3-PSZ. Marked decreases in density and strength resulting from the $t \rightarrow m$ transformation were observed for some materials around 200 – 300°C. The t-phase instability was found to be related to the Y_2O_3 content and the grain size. Critical grain sizes were determined to be 0.2 μm for 2 mol% Y_2O_3 and 0.6 μm for 5 mol% Y_2O_3.

Research and development is underway to apply the PSZ to piston crowns, cylinder liners, and piston head plates in diesel engines aiming at thermal insulation. Metal wire drawing dies and cutlery made of PSZ are already commercially available in Japan. Developments of other industrial parts such as corrosion resistant nozzles and wear resistant parts are also underway.

References

1. Knudsen, F. P., *J. Am. Ceram. Soc.* 42:376 (1959).
2. Passmore, E. M., Spriggs, R. M., and Vasilos, T., *J. Am. Ceram. Soc.* 53:232 (1970).
3. Passmore, E. M., Spriggs, R. M., and Vasilos, T., *J. Am. Ceram. Soc.* 48:1 (1965).
4. Rice, R. W., *Bull. Am. Ceram. Soc.* 51:335 (1972).
5. Rice, R. W., U.S.-Japan Joint Symposium on Fine Ceramics 6:18 (1974).
6. Kirchner, H. P., and Gruver, R. M., *Phil. Mag.* 27:1433 (1973).
7. Gruver, R. M., Scotter, W. A., and Kirchner, H. P., *Bull. Am. Ceram. Soc.* 55:198 (1976).
8. Fukuura, I., and Watanabe, S., Ceramic Science and Technology at the Present and in the Future, Japan, (1981) pp. 193, 201.
9. Furukawa, M. et al., *Seimutsu Kikai* 35:634 (1969).
10. Wolten, G. M., *J. Am. Ceram. Soc.* 46:418 (1963).
11. Garvie, R. C. et al., *Nature* 258:703 (1975).
12. Gupta, T. K. et al., *J. Mat. Sci.* 13:1464 (1978).
13. Kawanami, T. et al., *Kogyo Zairyo* 30(8):100 (1982).
14. Masaki, T., Kobayashi, K. et al., *Abstracts of '81 Annual Meeting of the Ceramics Society of Japan*, 1981, pp. 2, 4.
15. Watanabe, M., Iio, S., and Fukuura, I., *Advances in Ceramics* 12.

3.3 Fabrication and Properties of Silicon Nitride Ceramics

Katsutoshi Komeya

3.3.1 Introduction

At present, nitrogen ceramics have generated great interest as a group of attractive new ceramic materials. Some nitrogen ceramics can be characterized by a covalent chemical bond structure between the metallic element and nitrogen. Typical light materials such as boron nitride (BN), aluminum nitride (AlN), and silicon nitride (Si_3N_4) have attracted attention.

In particular, silicon nitride is recognized as a highly useful material in structural engineering applications. Its high strength over a wide temperature range, good thermal shock resistance, and strong wear and corrosive resistance make it suitable for use in engine components, metallurgical and chemical plant components, wear-resistant parts, heat jigs, and cutting tools, among other things. However, there are many problems to be overcome in the development from raw powders to application.

In the initial stage of this study, the author and his co-workers developed high-strength silicon nitride by adding yttria (Y_2O_3) and alumina (Al_2O_3). Nitride properties were then improved by means of raw powder synthesis and precise process control. This section describes the development of these silicon nitride ceramics.

3.3.2 Fundamental Description of Silicon Nitride

Silicon nitride consists of α- and β-phase hexagonal crystal structures. Electronegativity analysis indicates that the Si-N bond exhibits approximately 30% ionicity. As a result, components consisting of silicon nitride are more resistant than metals and oxide ceramics to high temperatures, thermal shock, wear, erosion, and chemical corrosion. However, as silicon nitride is typically unsinterable because of its strong covalent bond structure, it is very difficult to obtain full densified masses from the pure raw powder. Silicon nitride ceramics have been fabricated by a number of techniques, including hot pressing, reaction bonding, pressureless sintering, and hot-isostatic pressing. These are classified as pressures and additive parameters, as shown in Figure 3.3.1. Of these techniques, hot pressing and pressureless sintering have become the focus of attention in high-strength

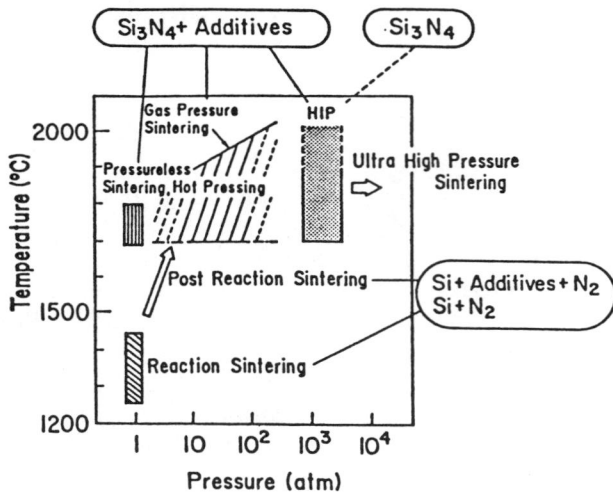

Figure 3.3.1 Sintering methods of silicon nitride.

silicon nitride development. In these processes, the characteristics of raw silicon nitride powder are also critical parameters.

What follows is a description of the powder synthesis of silicon nitrides as a sintering source and the development of a highly reliable material by hot pressing and pressureless sintering.

3.3.3 Synthesis of Silicon Nitride Powder

There are basically four synthesis methods for silicon nitride raw powders, as shown in Table 3.3.1. These include (1) direct silicon nitridation, (2) silica reduction, (3) vapor phase reaction, and (4) silicon imide decomposition. Of these, direct silicon nitridation is

Table 3.3.1 Synthesis Methods of Silicon Nitride Powders

1. Silicon direct nitriding method	$3\,Si + 2\,N_2 \rightarrow Si_3N_4$
2. Silicon reduction method	$3\,SiO_2 + 6\,C + 2\,N_2 \rightarrow Si_3N_4 + 6CO$
3. Pyrolysis method	$3\,Si(NH)_2 \rightarrow Si_3N_4 + 2\,NH_3$ $3\,Si(NH_2)_4 \rightarrow Si_3N_4 + 8\,NH_3$
4. Epitaxial synthesis method	$3\,SiCl_4 + 16\,NH_3 \rightarrow Si_3N_4 + 12\,NH_4Cl$

widely used because it is the simplest method of silicon nitride formation. However, it is difficult to control particle shape and size, as well as the high α-phase content, because of an intrinsic reaction mechanism in the silicon and nitrogen. Recent research has attempted to resolve these difficulties.

Vapor phase reaction has been widely used in the semiconductor industry as a synthesis method for pure silicon nitride. The silicon imide decomposition method is a recent development in which pure α-silicon nitride can be obtained.

Although sufficient evaluation data have not yet been obtained for the powder formed by methods (3) and (4), these processes are quite suitable for forming high-purity powder. However, it has occasionally been pointed out that chroline contamination in the powder is a critical problem in practical use. At present, silicon nitride powder produced by methods (1), (3), and (4) has been sold as commercial-grade raw powder for silicon nitride ceramic fabrication.

The silica reduction method (2) has been studied since a German patent for it was obtained in 1896.[1] The reaction is complicated because of several reaction steps and the simultaneous formation of silicon oxynitride (Si_2N_2O) and silicon carbide, the presence of residual silica, and the uncontrollable nature of the grain shape. However, high-purity, fine-sized silica and carbon powders are preferred for producing high-purity, fine-grained silicon nitride. It is especially meaningful that the crystal structure for silicon nitride powder prepared by the silica reduction method is mainly α-type.[2] Controlling raw powder particle size and shape is also important in fabricating high-performance ceramics.

The relations among synthesized powder properties, starting materials, and nitriding conditions were investigated. It was found that the addition of silicon nitride to the SiO_2-C mixture affected the grain morphology and reaction rate.[3] Figure 3.3.2 shows the relation of the nitrogen content of synthesized powder and the SiO_2/Si_3N_4 ratio in the starting raw-powder system, SiO_2-C-Si_3N_4. Figure 3.3.3 shows typical micrographs of Si_3N_4 powders synthesized from SiO_2-C-Si_3N_4,[4] as compared with powder synthesized without Si_3N_4. Figure 3.3.4 is a typical X-ray diffraction pattern for the powder. The pattern indicates that the synthesized powder consists mainly of α-silicon nitride. It was thought that silicon nitride in the SiO_2-C-Si_3N_4 system acts as a "seed" to promote the nitriding reaction and is effective in controlling powder size and shape. During consolidation experiments, it was proved that synthesized silicon nitride powder was preferable for obtaining high-strength silicon nitride ceramics.[5]

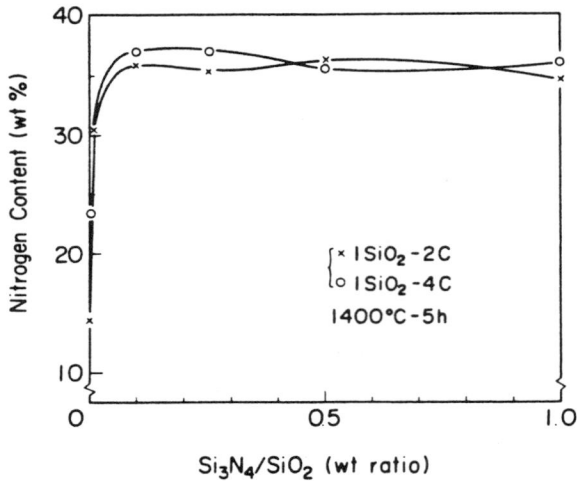

Figure 3.3.2 Nitrogen content of synthesized powders versus Si_3N_4/SiO_2 ratio in the system SiO_2-C-Si_3N_4.

3.3.4 Development of High-Strength Silicon Nitride Ceramics

Silicon nitride is a typical unsinterable material because of the strong chemical bond in Si-N. In the initial developmental stage, available sintering aids were investigated for the full densification. Lumby and

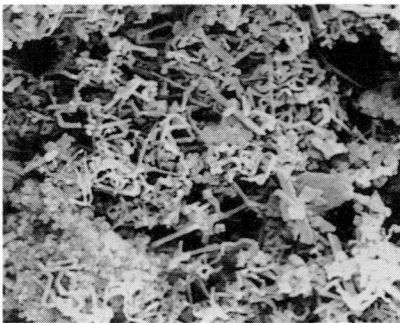

Figure 3.3.3 Silicon nitride powder from the silica reduction method.

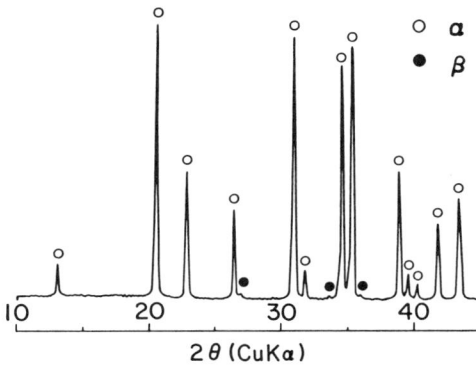

Figure 3.3.4 Typical x-ray diffraction pattern of the synthesized Si_3N_4 powder.

co-workers[6] developed high-strength silicon nitride ceramics by hot pressing a Si_3N_4-MgO system. However, additives form lower melting compounds that cause strength degradation at elevated temperatures. The development of silicon nitride ceramics with still greater strength over a wide temperature range was pursued by the author and his co-workers.

It was found that rare earth oxides, especially yttria, show good densification and high strengthening.[7] In 1974 the existence of a highly refractory Si_3N_4-Y_2O_3 compound was shown using the Si_3N_4-Y_2O_3 system. The phase relationships were later confirmed by Jack.[8] It was also found that the addition of alumina to silicon nitride with yttria promoted densification. Thus, from these fundamental studies, silicon nitride with high strength over a wide temperature range was developed by Tsuge and co-workers.[9] The characteristics are shown in Figure 3.3.5.

In general, the fracture strength of ceramics is shown in Equation (3.3.1):[10]

$$\sigma_f = \frac{1}{Y} \sqrt{\frac{2\gamma_i E}{\pi C}} \, \alpha \, \frac{K_{1C}}{\sqrt{C}} \qquad (3.3.1)$$

where σ_f is fracture strength, γ_i is fracture energy, E is Young's modulus, K_{1C} is fracture toughness, C is flaw size, and Y is a geometrical factor. Therefore, in high-strength silicon nitride development, it is necessary to increase the K_{1C} value and decrease the flaw size C.

Today, it is well known that the following conditions must be

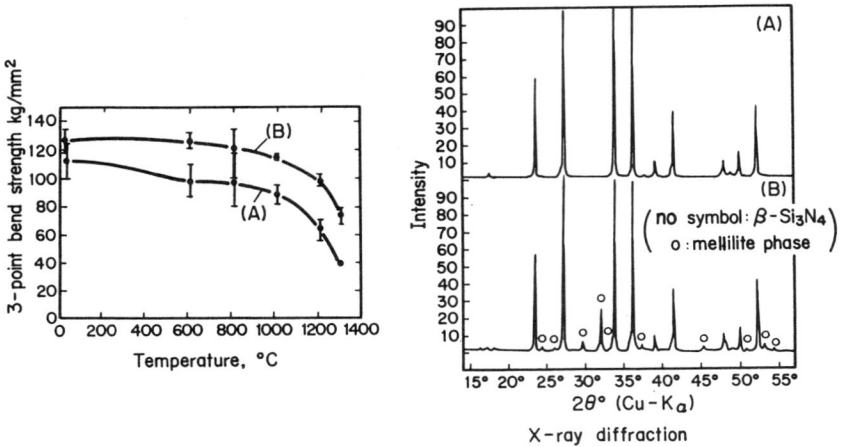

Figure 3.3.5 Flexural strength of hot-pressed silicon nitride as a function of temperature:
(A) Grain boundary, glass phase existence structure (no crystallization).
(B) Grain boundary crystallization structure to mellilite phase.

satisfied to obtain high-quality structural silicon nitride ceramics:

1. High-purity, fine-grained, α-silicon nitride powder must be used.
2. All available sintering aids must be used.
3. Refractory grain boundary phases must be improved or eliminated.
4. Large flaws and/or inclusions, which cause strength degradation, must be eliminated; that is, microstructure must be homogenized.

A combination of (1) and (2) increases the K_{1C} of Equation (3.3.1), and (4) yields lower and homogeneous flaw sizes. The effect of adding yttria on α-silicon nitride powder can be explained as follows. Alpha-silicon nitride powder compaction with yttria additives results in an elongated grain structure during the sintering process (Figure 3.3.6),[4] which cause higher K_{1C}. The mellilite phase derived from Si_3N_4-Y_2O_3, the K, H, and J phases in the sialon is useful for improving high-temperature strength.

Figure 3.3.7 shows typical bend strength values for pressureless sintered and hot-pressed silicon nitride with yttria and alumina recently developed in the laboratory.[4,5]

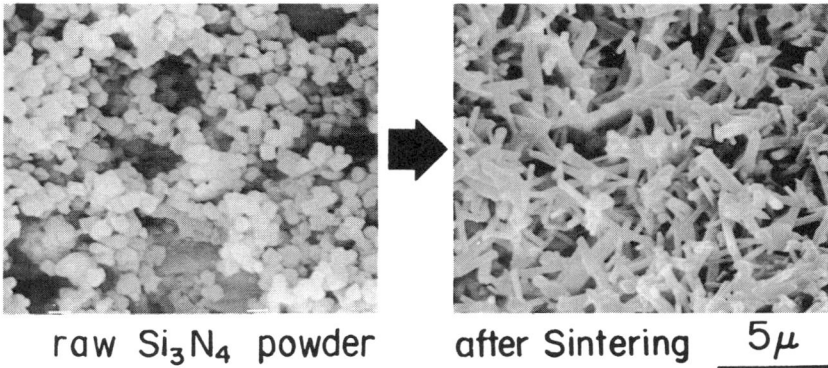

raw Si_3N_4 powder   after Sintering 5μ

Figure 3.3.6 Changes of grain morphology by sintering powder compaction of α-Si_3N_4 with Y_2O_3 and Al_2O_3.

3.3.5 Strength Reliability Improvement of Silicon Nitride Ceramics[11]

Among the various factors responsible for strength degradation, porosity has been demonstrated to have a pronounced effect. Figure 3.3.8 shows the relationship of the relative density and strength of

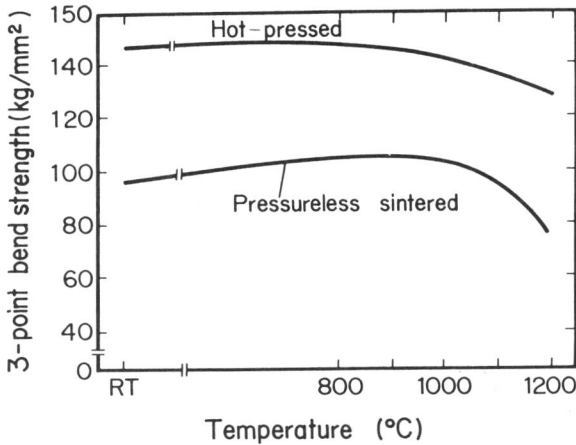

Figure 3.3.7 High-temperature strength of developed silicon nitride ceramics in laboratory scale.

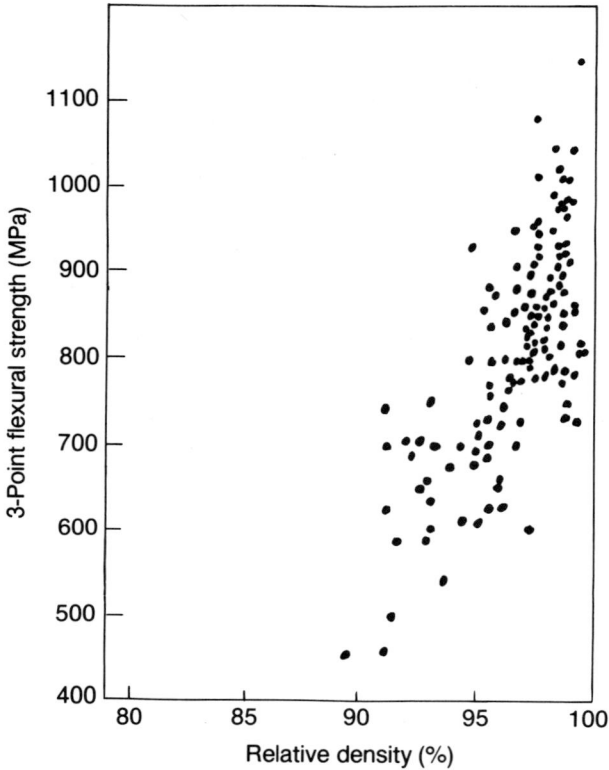

Figure 3.3.8 Relationship of density and strength of pressureless sintered silicon nitride.

silicon nitride with yttria and alumina produced by pressureless sintering, indicating that strength varies over a wide range depending on the total volume and/or size of the pores.

As shown in Figure 3.3.8, variations in strength degradation arise even at the same porosity, primarily because of the distribution in the shapes of grains. It is also recognized that the K_{1C} value (Vickers indentation method) corresponds well with the respective strengths. Figure 3.3.9 shows the relationship of K_{1C} and strength on pressureless sintered material.

Figure 3.3.10 is an example of interior impurity debris that belongs to the category of process defects. These defects can be eliminated by removing foreign substances contained in the raw material

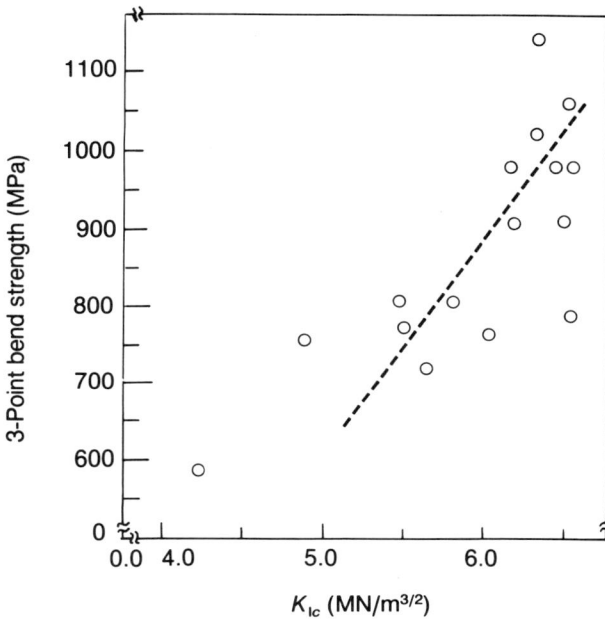

Figure 3.3.9 K_{1c} and strength of pressureless sintered silicon nitride.

or by removing the contaminating impurities in the manufacturing process.

Meanwhile, the size of the surface defects, including pores formed during the pressureless sintering process, are strongly related to strength. Machining must be also performed carefully. It is important that these defects are eliminated by process control; consequently, acceptable minimum strength values can be obtained. Figure 3.3.11 is an example of the bend strength Weibull plot for pressureless sintered silicon nitride. Figure 3.3.12 presents recent improvements in pressureless sintered silicon nitride ceramics.

As described above, high-temperature strength is controlled by grain boundary characteristics. Strength scattering is reduced by control of porosity and grain characteristics from the point of view of intrinsic factors. However, porosity and grain characteristics are investigated because the grain boundary is examined in relation to the added sintering aids, so the entire problem revolves around grain boundary engineering.

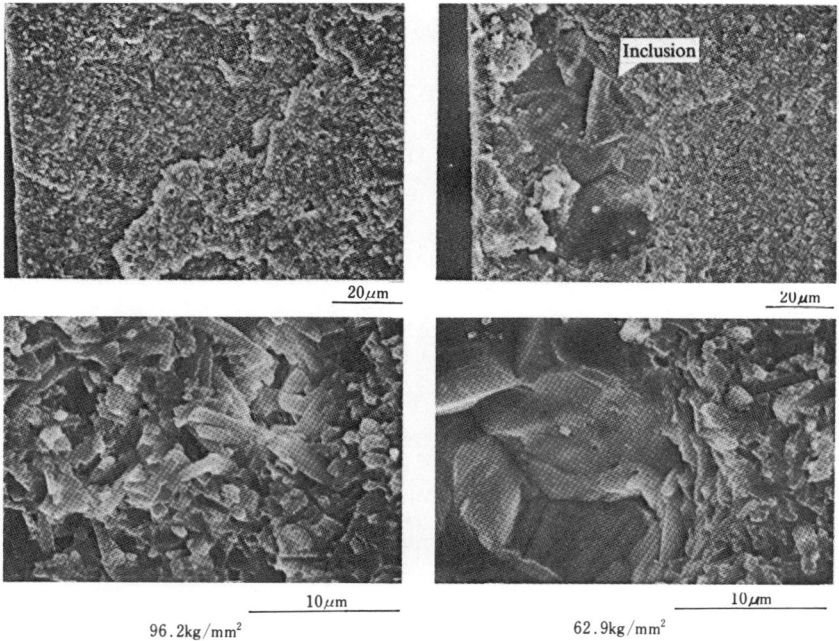

Figure 3.3.10 Typical fractographs of pressureless sintered silicon nitride as a function of fracture stress.

Figure 3.3.13 and Table 3.3.2 show typical fabricated silicon nitride components, including other materials, and expected fields of application of silicon nitride ceramics. At present, some heat- or wear-resistant components such as mechanical seals, cutting tools, and glow plugs are being used. However, the most important applications are engine components and engineering plant materials. Table 3.3.3 gives typical materials data for the developed hot-pressed and pressureless silicon nitrides.

3.3.6 Conclusion

Recently, high-performance ceramics are being developed worldwide. Nitrogen ceramics are representative of these materials. High-strength silicon nitride ceramics have been developed from raw powder synthesis. This section has described materials development for silicon nitride strengthening. Important factors include making actual high "reliability and reproducibility" components in a cost-effective manner.

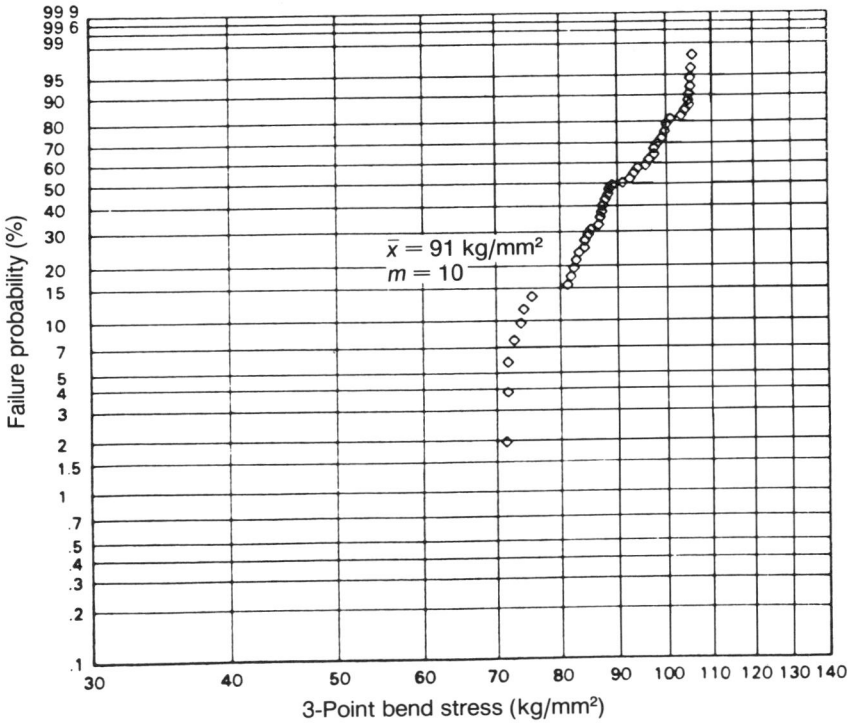

Figure 3.3.11 Typical strength distribution of pressureless sintered silicon nitride.

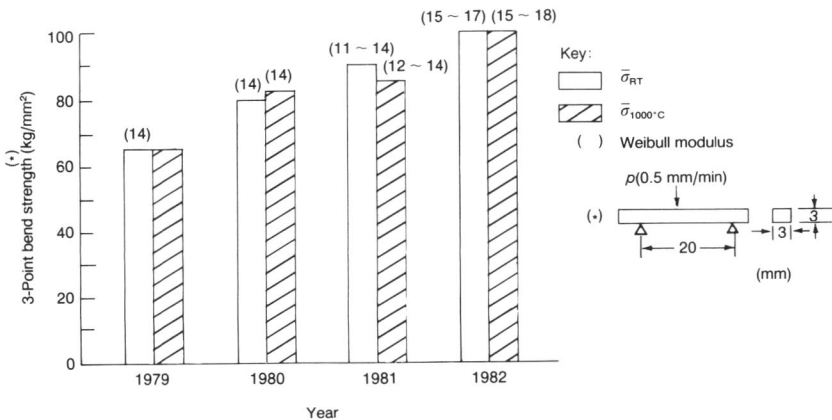

Figure 3.3.12 Recent improvement of pressureless sintered silicon nitride (laboratory scale).

Figure 3.3.13 Silicon nitride components, including other materials [partially stabilized zirconia (white) and aluminum nitride substrates (thin plates)].

Table 3.3.2 Expected Fields of Application of Silicon Nitride Ceramics

Application Fields	Components
Engine components:	
Diesel	Pistons, cylinder liners, precombustion chambers, plugs, tapets, turbocharger rotors
Gas turbine	Combustors, rotors, stator vanes, shrouds
Wear- and corrosion-resistant components	Bearings, mechanical seals, blast honing nozzles, vane pump parts, chemical pump parts
Metal treatment components	Aluminum diecast parts (metal melt guides, plungers, cylinders, and piston cylinders); wire-drawing roller pulleys and dies; steel forming parts
Tools	Cutting tools
Heat-resistant jigs:	
Heat-protecting parts	Thermal-insulation ceramic tiles, heat-shielding plates, plasma insulators
High-temperature test jigs	Strength test jigs (bend and tensile)

Table 3.3.3 Typical Materials Data for Developed Hot-Pressed and Pressure-less Sintered Silicon Nitrides[a]

Material Item	Hot Pressed Si_3N_4	Pressureless Sintered Si_3N_4
Density (g/cm³)	3.26	3.20
Thermal conductivity (W/mk)	29.3	15.5
Specific heat (cal/g·°C)	0.17	0.17
Flexural strength (MPa)	1200	1000
Compressive strength (MPa)	4500	4000
Thermal expansion ($\times 10^{-6}/°C$)	3.2	3.4
Young's modulus ($\times 10^4$ Kg/mm²)	3.2	2.8
K_{1c} (MNm³/²)	8.3	5.4

[a] Room temperature data.

Thus, although ceramic materials were initially used in lower-stress applications, much work still remains to be done in the development of engineering plant and practical ceramic engine components. Material properties require improvement; fabrication techniques for complicated shapes and high-volume components need to be developed along with materials evaluation technology; and design methodology and component tests need refinement. For all these problems, further study is needed.

References

1. Mehner, H., German Pat. 88999 (September 30, 1896).
2. Komeya, K., and Inoue, H., *J. Mat. Sci.* 10:1243 (1975).
3. Inoue, H., Komeya, K., and Tsuge, H., *J. Am. Ceram. Soc.* 65(12):C-205 (1982).
4. Komeya, K., *Am. Ceram. Soc. Bull.* 63(9):1158 (1984).
5. Tsuge, A., Inoue, H., and Komeya, K., Paper presented at the Annual Meeting of the American Ceramics Society, 1979.
6. Lumby, R. J. et al., *Proc. British Ceramics Society* 15:91 (1970).

7. Tsuge, A., Nishida, K., and Komatsu, M., *J. Am. Ceram. Soc.* 58:323 (1975).

8. Jack, K. H., *Final Technical Report*, European Research Office, United States Army, London W.I., England (1977).

9. Tsuge, A., Kudo, H., and Komeya, K., *J. Am. Ceram. Soc.* 57:259 (1975).

10. Davidge, R. W., and Evans, A. G., *Mat. Sci. Eng.* 6:281 (1970).

11. Tsuge, A., Inoue, H., and Komatsu, M., *Toshiba Rev.* 38(1):39 (1983).

3.4 Fabrication and Properties of Silicon Carbide Ceramics

Takayoshi Iseki and Teizo Hase

3.4.1 Introduction

For many years silicon carbide has been extensively used as an abrasive, a refractory material, and for such applications as heating elements, setter tiles, and so on; however, its use has been somewhat restricted because it cannot be sintered to high density. Although it has excellent physical and chemical properties for high-temperature materials, full use of its ability has not been possible because of its lower sinterability.

In 1974 Prochazka[1] first reported that submicron powder of β-SiC with concurrent B and C addition could be sintered to near theoretical density without applied pressure. Since then, R&D with regard to the preparation of sinterable SiC powder, sintering aids, and sintering techniques has also been carried out in Japan. Additionally, forming and machining techniques have been developed for the practical use of SiC ceramics in products ranging from leisure goods to engineering components.

Japanese R&D on SiC is on a high level, and several unique materials have been developed: continuous β-SiC fiber invented by Yajima and co-workers,[2] hot-pressed SiC having high thermal conductivity and high electrical resistivity, and high-strength, pressureless sintered SiC having a bending strength of 800–1000 MPa from room temperature to 1600°C. This section describes the state of the art of fabrication and the products of SiC ceramics in Japan. It concentrates on the preparation of sinterable SiC powder, sintering aids, SiC whisker and fiber, fabrication methods for SiC ceramics, and the properties and applications of SiC.

3.4.2 Sinterable SiC Powder

3.4.2.1 Preparation of Submicron β-SiC Powder

Submicron β-SiC powders have been prepared on a laboratory scale in the following ways:

1. Siliciding of carbon black with SiO.
2. Thermal decomposition of organosilicon such as CH_3SiCl_3 or $(CH_3)_4Si$.
3. Arc discharge between a carbon electrode and Si metal.
4. Thermal decomposition of an organosilicon polymer.

Hase and Suzuki[3] reported that submicron β-SiC powder was prepared by the reaction of carbon black with SiO under reduced pressure at 1340, 1440, and 1570°C, and that the specific surface area of the powders was 32.2, 13.7, and 4.4 m²/g, respectively. These powders could be sintered in the as-prepared state and without any further treatment. In the usual case, it is necessary to remove free carbon by oxidation and to remove free SiO_2 by acid treatment. The weight gain of the powders by heating in air is shown in Figure 3.4.1 as an indicator of chemical properties. The temperature of the initial weight gain decreases with increasing specific surface area. For fine powder the weight gain initiates at as low a temperature as the ignition temperature of ordinary carbon (300–550°C). Surprising to say, 40–50 wt% of these powders dissolved in a 1 : 1 mixture of HF and HNO_3. Powder 1-FN in Figure 3.4.1a, which had a specific surface area of 200 m²/g, was obtained from powder 1 (specific surface area, 32.2 m²/g) by treatment with mixed acid. The increase of the specific surface area was due more to the increase of surface irregularity than to a decrease in grain size. The acid treatment also caused a change in the infrared absorption spectra and a deviation from stoichiometry as the Si content was reduced by about 3%, whereas the C content did not change. The details of these phenomena have not yet been clarified.

Hase and co-workers[4] obtained sinterable submicron SiC powder by reaction between SiO and carbon black with the addition of Al metal. The powder consisted of both β and 2H polytypes and could be sintered at lower temperature than usual (as will be described). The resulting sintered specimen consisted of β and 4H polytypes.

Hojo and co-workers[5] synthesized β-SiC powder with an average grain size of 0.01 to 0.06 μm by chemical vapor deposition (CVD) of

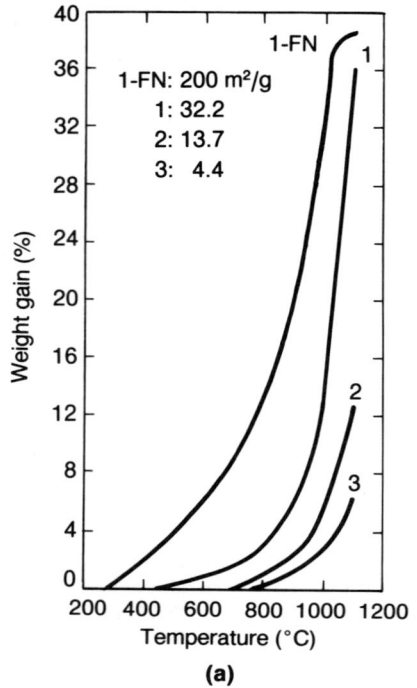

Figure 3.4.1 (a) Weight gain of house-made β-SiC powder heated in air at a heating rate of 5.8°C/minute. (b) Shrinkage curves of SiC fine powder with the addition of 1% of B and C heated in He at a heating rate of 5.5°C/ minute.

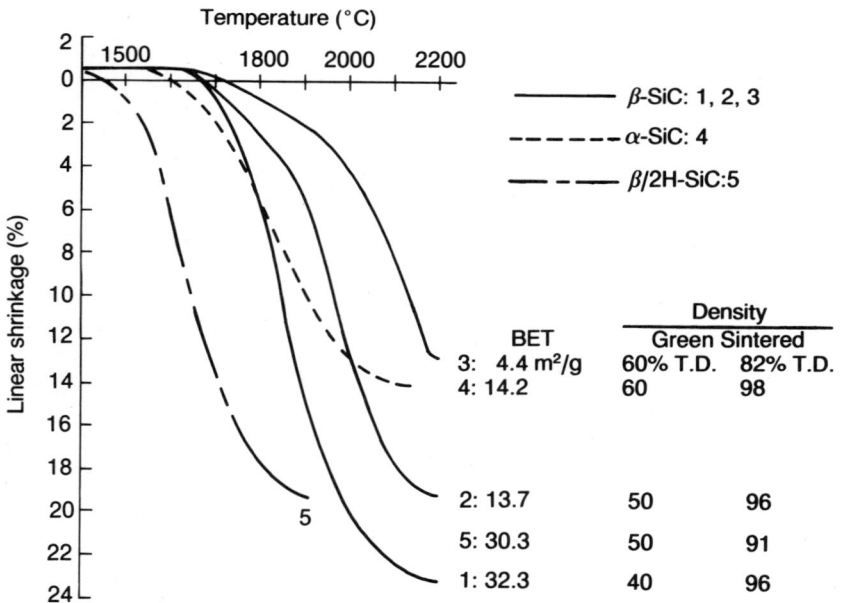

$(CH_3)_4Si-H_2$. They obtained a sintered body with 95% theoretical density (TD) at 2050°C in the presence of 1 wt% B when these powders contained enough carbon to remove the impure oxygen.

Ohokochi and Ando[6] also synthesized β-SiC powder of an average grain size of 0.01–0.05 μm by arc discharge between a carbon electrode and Si in a flow of CH_4 under reduced pressure. Using the powder, they obtained a green density of 41 and 50% TD with molding pressures of 200 and 800 MPa, respectively.

The late Prof. Yajima and co-workers prepared a uniform β-SiC fine powder having an average particle size of 0.1 μm by heating polyborosiloxane, an organosilicon polymer. The polymer was heated above 1500°C in a nonoxidizing atmosphere. Then, after the free carbon was removed by heat treatment in air and after treatment with HF, the powder was obtained.[7]

3.4.2.2 Commercial Powder

Two types of SiC powder, β- and α-SiC, are now commercially available. Ibiden Co., Ltd., one of the suppliers of β-SiC, makes submicron β-SiC by a continuous process wherein a mixture of coke and SiO_2 is introduced into the top of a vertical furnace. The reaction within the mixture proceeds as it falls, and the product is collected from the bottom of the furnace. Alpha-SiC powder, however, is manufactured by crushing and classifying coarse grains made by the Acheson method. Sinterable α-SiC powders are thus supplied by several companies who make SiC abrasive grains. Typical properties of these powders are given in Table 3.4.1.

3.4.3 Whisker and Fiber

There has been remarkable development of SiC whisker and fiber. These materials are essential for making composites that offer high strength and great toughness. In 1982, commercial manufacture of SiC whisker (0.5–1.0 μm in diameter and 50–500 μm long) was undertaken by Tokai Carbon Co., Ltd., and Tateho Chemical Industries Co., Ltd. Yajima and co-workers[2] first developed β-SiC fiber from an organosilicon polymer. Polycarbosilane was formed into a fiber and heated to 1300°C, and SiC fiber with high tensile strength was obtained. At present the fiber, which is more than 300 m long, is produced by Nippon Carbon, Ltd., on a pilot-plant scale. Since the beginning of manufacturing, samples of the fiber have been distributed throughout the world, and the fiber has been tried in various applica-

Table 3.4.1 Typical Properties of Commercial SiC Powders for Pressureless Sintering

	Manufacturer	
Property	Showa Denko K. K.	Ibiden Co., Ltd.
Grade	A-1	Ultrafine
Major polytype	α	β
Chemical composition (wt%)		
SiC	97	>98
Free C	0.8	0.4
Free SiO_2	0.7	0.3
Free Si	0.02	—
Total Al	0.01	0.03
Total Fe	0.06	0.04
Particle size		
Mean size (μm)	0.4	0.27
Cumulative <1 μm (wt%)	>90	96
Maximum size (μm)	2.0	2.0
True density (g/cm³)	3.2	3.2
Packing density (g/cm³)	1.9	1.9
Specific surface area (m²/g)	14	17.5

tions. It has been found suitable as a reinforcing element for composite materials.

3.4.4 Fabrication of SiC Ceramics

Dense SiC bodies can be prepared by (1) reaction sintering or reaction bonding, (2) pressureless sintering, (3) hot pressing, (4) CVD, and (5) repeated impregnation of polycarbosilane in a SiC compact and firing.

In reaction sintering, little or no shrinkage occurs during siliciding; thus, the technique can be applied to the fabrication of complex or high-precision components and larger components. In particular, tubes, rods, or slabs that are not very thick can be made by this technique. It is used to make inner tubes for diffusion furnaces for semiconductor production and various components for trial vehicular engines.

SiC has been considered for application as a structural ceramic, and for this purpose pressureless or normal sintering has been most extensively investigated. Curves 1 to 3 in Figure 3.4.1b show densification curves for the ultrafine β-SiC described in subsection 3.4.2.1. Curve 4 is that of a commercial α-SiC powder with particle size of less than 0.55 μm and which underwent further treatment with HF.[8] The particles of this α-SiC included impurities of 0.05 wt% of Al and 0.008 wt% of Fe. The result shows that α-SiC powder containing such impurities is sinterable at lower temperatures than ordinary high-purity β-SiC powder. Isothermal sintering experiments showed that α-SiC powder can be sintered to 98% TD at 2000°C and β-SiC powder to 96% TD at 2100°C. Curve 5 is a densification curve of the powder that contained Al on the surface of the particle, which originated in the powder preparation, and consisted of about equal amounts of β and 2H polytypes. This powder can be densified at a temperature about 300°C lower than usual. During sintering, 2H polytype was converted to 4H.

As sintering aids for pressureless sintering, the B-C system[1] and the Al-C system[9] are well known. Omori and Takei[10] used a Y_2O_3-Al_2O_3 system in the aqueous state as a sintering aid and obtained a dense SiC body. For the role of B and C, Suzuki and Hase[11] explained that B and C existed at the grain boundary between β-SiC particles and enhanced material transport during densification, but at higher temperatures and at the final stage of densification, B and C were soluble in the β-SiC particle and the grain boundary phase disappeared. Bourdillon and co-workers[12] reported that the grain boundary phase was not detected, but B precipitated as a B-rich inclusion, and most of the secondary phase was graphite. Ogbuji[13] found a grain boundary phase in hot-pressed SiC with the addition of Al_2O_3 but did not find it in B-doped SiC. In Al-doped SiC, Al segregated at the grain boundary and came to the surface by rapid grain boundary diffusion.[4,14]

As an additional insight into sintering, Inomata[15] explained why pure SiC cannot be densified without a sintering aid. To do this, he introduced the ratio of surface energy to grain boundary energy into the rate equation for densification. The high ratio obtained (e.g., $\sqrt{3}/2$) means that the powder cannot be intrinsically sintered to a high density.

To use SiC materials extensively, forming techniques such as slip casting, extrusion, or injection molding have been developed in Japan. As a result of the success of these techniques, pressureless sintering will find further applications.

Hot pressing has made it possible to select various sintering aids. Nakamura and Asai[16] studied the effect of the addition of various aids on grain size and strength, as shown in Figure 3.4.2. The aids were

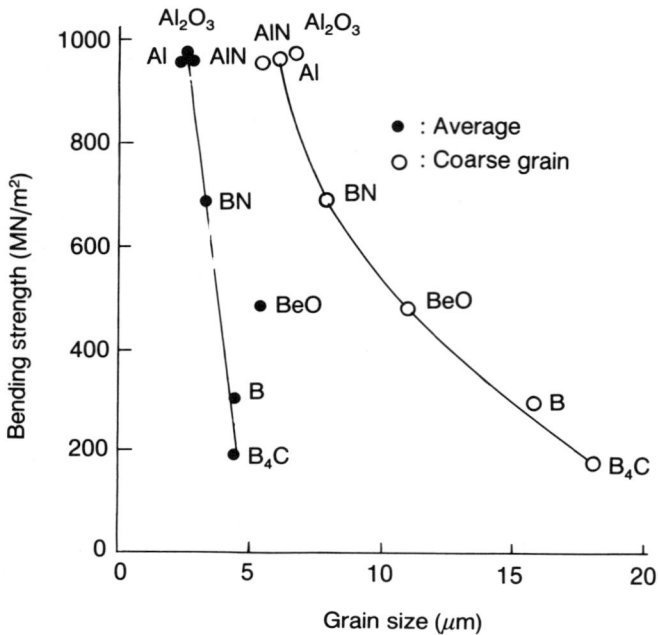

Figure 3.4.2 Effect of sintering aids on the grain size and bending strength of hot-pressed SiC. The amount of each additive was 1–2% [from K. Nakamura and O. Asai, *Kagaku Kogyo (Chem. Eng.)* 33:977 (1982)].

added to α-SiC powder with a grain size of 2 μm and hot pressed at a pressure of 20 MPa at 2040°C for 1 hour in a vacuum. Iseki and co-workers[17] obtained high-density SiC by hot pressing at temperatures as low as 1650°C with a pressure of 50 MPa using Al-B-C addition. This sintering aid allowed hot pressing at lower temperature but decreased its high-temperature strength. This seemed to be due to the formation of low melting compounds such as $Al_8B_4C_7$, whose phase relation was reported by Inomata and co-workers.[18]

Chemically vapor-deposited SiC has been developed for coating particle fuel for high-temperature gas-cooled reactors and is considered to be the most favorable material for the first wall of thermonuclear fusion reactors.

3.4.5 Properties and Applications of SiC Ceramics

A variety of sintered bodies are available from various companies. Several of their specifications are quoted in Table 3.4.2. Along with

Table 3.4.2 Fabrication Methods of SiC Ceramics Used by Five Manufacturers

	Reaction Sintering Shin-etsu Chemical Co., Ltd.	Pressureless Sintering			Hot-pressing Hitachi, Ltd.
		NGK Spark Plug Co., Ltd.	Kyocera Co., Ltd.	Ibiden Co., Ltd.	
Grade	SE-10	EC-422	SC-201	SC-850	SC-101
Density (g/cm³)	3.10	3.13	3.1	3.08-3.15	3.2
Bending strength (MN/m²)	540	540	490	850	440
Young's modulus (GN/m²)	390	440	390	400	
Coefficient of thermal expansion (10⁻⁶/°C)	4	4.8 (RT to 1200°C)	4.2 (RT to 800°C)	4.6 (RT to 1200°C)	3.7 (RT to 400°C)
Thermal conductivity (W/cm·K)	1.7	0.6	0.7	0.8	2.7

the companies included in the table, Asahi Glass Co., Ltd., and NGK Insulators, Ltd., among others, supply various kinds of SiC ceramics.

These ceramics have been used or are proposed for use in numerous components in addition to the uses mentioned earlier — for example, guide rings for fishing rods, golf clubs, mechanical seals, nozzles for sand blasting or burners, tubes for heat exchangers, and skid pads or buttons for steel making.

SiC with high thermal conductivity and low electrical conductivity has been developed by Hitachi, Ltd., by hot pressing with a BeO addition.[16] Its coefficient of thermal expansion is $3.7 \times 10^{-6}/°C$, close to that of Si metal. These characteristics qualify this SiC to be applied in heat sinks and substrates of highly integrated circuits.

A composite of Si_3N_4 reinforced with SiC whiskers was prepared by hot pressing with a Y_2O_3-La_2O_3 addition, and the resulting composite has a 3-point bending strength of about 700 MPa from room temperature to 1300°C.[19] Because the composite has high electrical conductivity, it can be electro-spark machined.

Organosilicon polymer has been applied to make igniters and heating elements.[20] Igniters improve gas ignition and response characteristics. This small-size igniter is excellent for use in home range ovens or for space-heating furnaces.

References

1. Prochazka, S., *Ceramics for High-Performance Applications*, J. J. Burke et al., ed. Chestnut Hill, Mass.: Brook Hill Pub. Co., 1974, p. 239.
2. Yajima, S., Hayashi, J., and Omori, M., *Chem. Letters* 931 (1975).
3. Hase, T., and Suzuki, H., *Yogyo-Kyokai-Shi (J. Ceram. Soc. Jpn.)* 86:541 (1978).
4. Hase, T., Suzuki, H., and Iseki, T., *Yogyo-Kyokai-Shi* 87:576 (1979).
5. Hojo, J., Miyachi, K., Okabe, Y., and Kato, A., *J. Am. Ceram. Soc.* 66:C-114 (1983).
6. Ohkohchi, M., and Ando, Y., *Yogyo-Kyokai-Shi* 90:673 (1982).
7. Yajima, S., *Am. Ceram. Soc. Bull.* 62:893 (1983).
8. Hase, T., and Suzuki, H., *Yogyo-Kyokai-Shi* 88:161 (1980).
9. Böcker, W., and Hausner, H., *Powder Met. Int.* 11:83 (1979).
10. Omori, M., and Takei, H., *J. Am. Ceram. Soc.* 65:C-92 (1982).
11. Suzuki, H., and Hase, T., *J. Am. Ceram. Soc.* 63:349 (1980).
12. Bourdillon, A. J., Jepps, N. W., Stobbs, W. M., and Krivanek, O. L., *J. Microscopy* 124:49 (1981).

13. Ogbuji, L. U., *Surfaces and Interfaces in Ceramic and Ceramic-Metal Systems,* J. Pask and A. Evans, eds. New York: Plenum Press, 1981, p. 713.

14. Tajima, Y., and Kingery, W. D., *J. Mat. Sci.* 17:2289 (1982).

15. Inomata, Y., *Yogyo-Kyokai-Shi* 90:527 (1982).

16. Nakamura, K., and Asai, O., *Kagaku Kogyo (Chem. Eng.)* 33:977 (1982).

17. Iseki, T., Arakawa, K., Matsuzaki, H., and Suzuki, H., *Yogyo-Kyokai-Shi* 91:349 (1983).

18. Inomata, Y., Tanaka, H., Inoue, Z., and Kawabata, H., *Yogyo-Kyokai-Shi* 88:353 (1980).

19. Ueno, K., and Toibana, Y., *Yogyo-Kyokai-Shi* 91:491 (1983).

20. Nakamura, Y., and Yajima, S., *Am. Ceram. Soc. Bull.* 61:572 (1982).

3.5 Fabrication and Properties of Sialon Ceramics

Mamoru Mitomo

3.5.1 Introduction

While investigating the reaction between Si_3N_4 and densification aids, workers observed that Al_2O_3 dissolved into β-Si_3N_4.[1,2] The phase diagram of the Si_3N_4-SiO_2-Al_2O_3-AlN system (Figure 3.5.1) reveals that in β-Si_3N_4, Al and O substitute for Si and N, respectively.[3,4] The solid solution is referred to as β-sialon, and its general formula is $Si_{6-z}Al_zO_zN_{8-z}$. Although there are other sialons, such as X-phase and AlN polytype phases,[4] effort has focused mainly on the fabrication of β-sialon ceramics because of their superior creep and oxidation resistance.

A new type of sialon with an α-Si_3N_4 structure has recently been developed.[5,6] The dissolution of Li, Mg, Ca, Y, or rare earth metals (except La and Ce) into interstitial sites has stabilized the structure. The valency compensation was made by partial substitution of Si with Al and N with O. The general formula for α-sialon is $M_x(Si,Al)_{12}(O,N)_{16}$, where M is a metal as stated above and $0 < x \leq 2$. The metal-to-nonmetal ratio in the network composed of $(Si,Al)(O,N)_4$ tetrahedra is maintained at $3:4$. The region for the formation of β- and α-sialon is represented by a triangle of Si_3N_4-$Al_2O_3 \cdot AlN$-YN $\cdot$ 3AlN in the Y-Si-Al-O-N system (Figure 3.5.2).[7] The Si_3N_4-AlN-Y_2O_3 system has been employed for ease of fabrication.

This section describes fabrication methods for sialons and important factors affecting sintering behavior. Mechanical and thermal properties of sialons are given in relation to the composition and

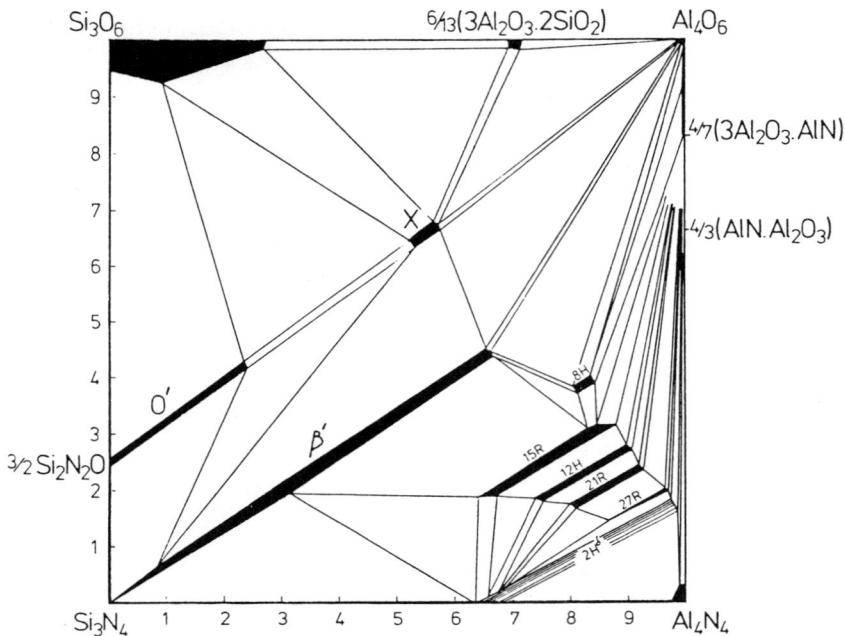

Figure 3.5.1 Phase relations in the Si_3N_4-SiO_2-Al_2O_3-AlN system [from K. H. Jack, *J. Mat. Sci.* 11:1135 (1976); reprinted with permission of Chapman and Hall, Ltd.].

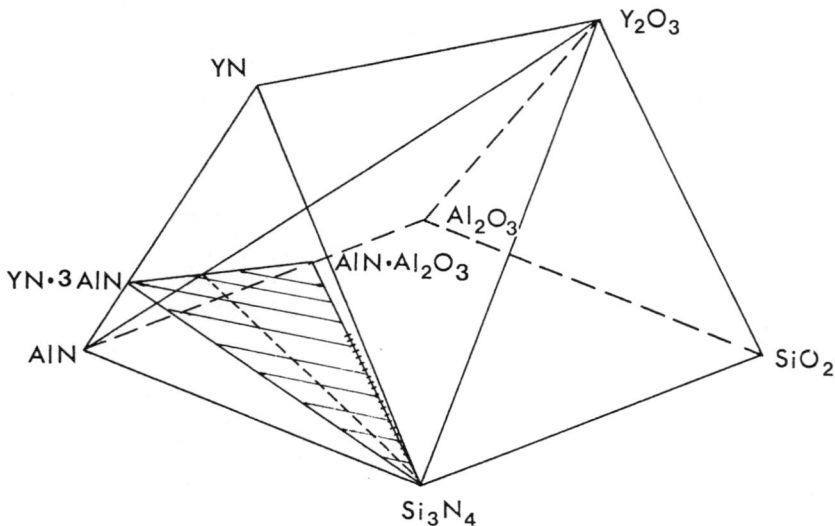

Figure 3.5.2 Representation of the system Y-Si-Al-O-N (from M. Mitomo et al., *Proc. International Symposium on Ceramic Components for Engines*, Hakone, Japan, 1983).

microstructure of sintered materials. The relation between β- and α-sialon is also briefly discussed.

3.5.2 Fabrication and Properties of β-Sialon Ceramics

Powder mixtures in the Si_3N_4-SiO_2-AlN or Si_3N_4-Al_2O_3-AlN systems have been used to fabricate β-sialon ceramics. The mixture forms an oxygen-rich liquid phase at about 1650°C, the composition of which is close to that of the X-phase. The liquid phase reacts with Si_3N_4 and AlN to form β-sialon grains. Sintering and the formation of β-sialon takes place simultaneously at 1600–1800°C, so that the amount of the liquid phase decreases as the reactions progress. The liquid is therefore called a "transient liquid." Good mechanical and thermal properties of sialon materials are related to a smaller residual inter-granular phase than is found in sintered Si_3N_4 materials.

Wills and co-workers[8] prepared $Si_4Al_2O_2N_6$ sialon from a mixture of 50 (mol%) Si_3N_4, 25 Al_2O_3, and 25 AlN. The powder compacts were heated at 1740°C for 1 hour in 1 atm N_2. No information was given on how to prevent thermal decomposition of the compacts, which is the most serious problem in nitrogen ceramics sintering. These workers reported that significant variables affecting sintering were milling time and the type of Si_3N_4 powder used. Bending strength of the materials was 352 MPa from room temperature to 1200°C and decreased at higher temperatures.

Briggs[9] obtained sintered β-sialon by heating the compacts in a Si_3N_4 powder bed and the screw-top closure of the graphite crucible. This yielded high-density material with a z = 4 composition having a maximum bending strength of 420 MPa. Briggs also reported that ease of sintering depends on the composition; sintering was more difficult as the mixture became richer in Si_3N_4.

Gauckler and co-workers[10] fabricated β-sialon ceramics from a powder mixture of Si_3N_4-Al_2O_3-AlN and SiO_2-AlN systems. The compacts were placed in an alumina crucible with loose powder of the same composition. Without the crucible and packing powder, the compacts decomposed thermally, which resulted in the formation of AlN polytype phases and low-density materials. These workers pointed out that it was necessary to shift the overall composition to a higher oxygen content with respect to β-sialon composition by oxidation of the AlN surface in order to fabricate high-density materials.

The relations among sinterability of compacts, overall composition, and thermal decomposition have been investigated.[11] Thermal decomposition of sialon shifts the overall composition toward the AlN corner in the phase diagram of the Si_3N_4-SiO_2-Al_2O_3-AlN system.

Gaseous products were SiO and N_2, and solid products were AlN polytypes.[10,11] When the overall composition became nitrogen-rich with respect to β-sialon composition, the compacts did not densify even under hot pressing. Therefore, one of the most important factors in fabricating high-density materials is to prevent thermal decomposition during sintering to maintain composition in the oxygen-rich region.

Compacts from a powder mixture of the Si_3N_4-Al_2O_3-AlN system were successfully sintered at 1800°C in a loose powder of Si_3N_4 and SiO_2.[11] The mixture of Si_3N_4 and SiO_2 forms Si_2N_2O at high temperatures. The calculated SiO pressure on Si_2N_2O was 4.8×10^{-1} atm at 1800°C and was high enough to prevent thermal decomposition of β-sialon. The effect of composition on the density of sintered materials was also reported (Figure 3.5.3). The minimum amount of excess

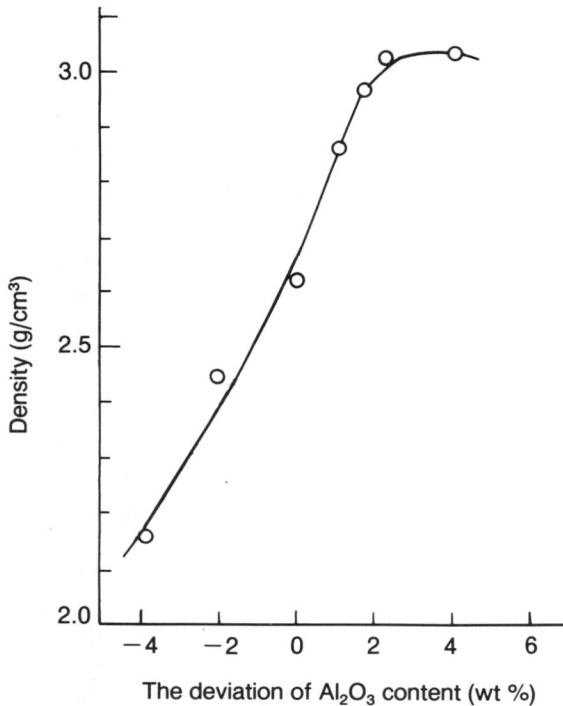

Figure 3.5.3 The effect of the deviation in Al_2O_3 content from β-sialon composition on densification [from M. Mitomo et al., *J. Mat. Sci.* 14:2309 (1979); reprinted with permission of Chapman and Hall, Ltd.].

Al_2O_3 needed for high-density materials, > 2.90 g/cm³ (93% theoretical value), was 1.5 wt%. The amount of excess Al_2O_3 was minimized by preventing thermal decomposition during sintering. The bending strength of materials obtained by this method was 490 MPa at room temperature and 480 MPa at 1200°C. High-temperature strength was improved by minimizing the amount of intergranular glassy phase in sintered materials.

Lumby and co-workers[12] sintered a z = 0.5 composition using Y_2O_3 or Y_2O_3-Al_2O_3 as densification aids. They developed two types of materials. One contained yttrium aluminum garnet (YAG) as an intergranular phase. Bending strength of the materials was 450–500 MPa at room temperature, and strength was retained up to 1300°C. The other materials had a glassy phase at the grain boundaries. The mechanical properties at low temperature were improved when compared with those of materials containing YAG, as shown in Table 3.5.1,[13] but were degraded at temperatures higher than 1000°C.

Creep and oxidation resistance of β-sialon were measured and compared with those of reaction-bonded (RB) and hot-pressed (HP) Si_3N_4 and sintered SiC.[14,15] Creep and oxidation resistance for sialon were equal to that for RB-Si_3N_4 and better than that for HP-Si_3N_4, but worse than that for SiC. The sintered sialon had good corrosion resistance to alkaline metals and molten ferrous alloys.[12,15]

The fabrication of translucent sialon ceramics[16] showed the possibility of optical applications under severe mechanical and thermal stress conditions.

Table 3.5.1 Physical and Mechanical Properties of a β-Sialon Material [from N. E. Cother and P. Hodgson, *Trans. J. Brit. Ceram. Soc.* 81:141 (1982); reprinted with permission].

Mechanical properties at room temperature	
Modulus of rupture (MPa)	828
Weibull modulus	15
Tensile strength (MPa)	400
Hardness (VHN, GPa)	17.6
Fracture toughness (MN/m³/²)	5
Thermal properties	
Thermal expansion coefficient (1/K)	3.2×10^{-6}
Specific heat (J/g·K)	0.71
Thermal conductivity (J/cm·sec·K)	0.2–0.25
Thermal shock resistance (ΔT)	510
Electrical resistivity (Ω·cm)	10^{12}

3.5.3 Fabrication and Properties of α-Sialon Ceramics

There is a miscibility gap between Si_3N_4 and α-sialon because β-Si_3N_4 is stable at high temperatures. The solid solubility of Y in Y-α-sialon was x = 0.3–0.8 in the general formula at 1750°C, as shown in Figure 3.5.4. The dissolution of a minimum amount of metal is required to stabilize the structure.[17] In this region, single-phase materials of α-sialon can be fabricated; whereas in a range x = 0–0.3, materials are composed of α-sialon and β-Si_3N_4. The amount of α-sialon in the materials decreased with decrease in Y content. The materials can be referred to as "partially stabilized" sialon ceramics.

The powder mixture of the Si_3N_4-$Y_2O_3 \cdot 9AlN$ system yielded sintered α-sialon by hot pressing or pressureless sintering at 1700–1750°C.[6] The effect of SiO pressure on α-sialon sintering was lower than that on β-sialon because of the lower oxygen content in α-sialons.[18]

The dissolution of metals into interstitial sites of α-Si_3N_4 was confirmed by analyzing X-ray diffraction patterns. Relative intensities in the patterns depend largely on the amount and kind of dissolved metal.[17]

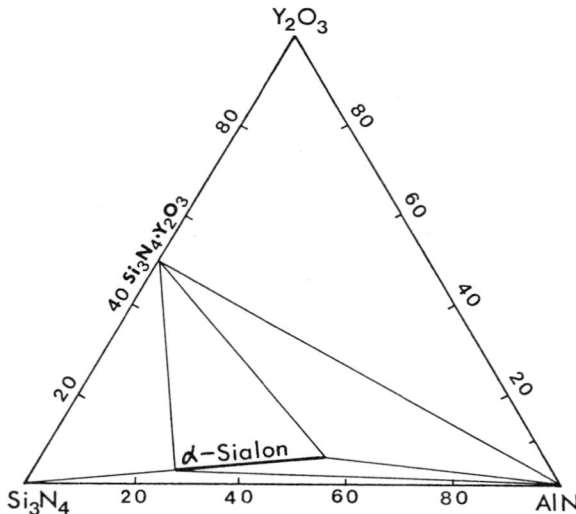

Figure 3.5.4 Solid solubility of Y-α-sialon at 1750°C. (from M. Mitomo et al., *Proc. International Symposium on Ceramic Components for Engines*, Hakone, Japan, 1983).

Preliminary investigations on the mechanical properties of α-sialon ceramics revealed that bending strength and thermal shock resistance were comparable to those of β-sialon ceramics.[6] The bending strength of α-sialon containing various metals was 420–605 MPa at room temperature. The values depend on the kind and the amount of dissolved metal.[19] Strength at 1200°C decreased to 316–372 MPa because of the presence of an intergranular glassy phase. Fracture toughness was 3.6–3.7 MN/m$^{3/2}$ at room temperature and was independent of the kind of dissolved metal.

The thermal expansion coefficient was measured as $3.3–3.5 \times 10^{-6}/°C$ by the X-ray method.[17] A higher expansion value was measured by a dilatometer.[20] The DC electrical conductivity of Y-α-sialon was 1.0×10^{-7} $(\Omega \cdot cm)^{-1}$ at 700°C, which was on the same order as that of β-sialon. However, the value increased to 4.9×10^{-4} $(\Omega \cdot cm)^{-1}$ in Li-Y-α-sialon.[21] Further improvements in mechanical, thermal, and electrical properties could be made by controlling composition and microstructure.

3.5.4 Relation of α- and β-Sialon

The monotropic phase transformation from α to β was observed during heating of Si_3N_4. The results showed that the β-form is stable at high temperatures. There is still a question as to whether the α-form is stable at low temperatures[22] or unstable at all temperatures.[23]

The β-Si_3N_4 structure was stabilized by substituting Al for Si and O for N, respectively. The α-Si_3N_4 structure was stabilized by dissolution of metals into interstitial sites. It was difficult to transform α-sialon to β-sialon without change in composition by heating.[18] The compositions of α- and β-sialon are different, as shown in Figure 3.5.2. The transformation from α- to β-sialon or vice versa took place together with chemical reactions, which resulted in the change in compositions.[5] For example, a reaction of Y-α-sialon and Al_2O_3 forms β-sialon and $Y_2Si_2O_7$, and that of β-sialon and Ca_3N_2 and AlN forms α-sialon at 1750°C.[2] The stability relation of the α- and β-structures are summarized as follows:

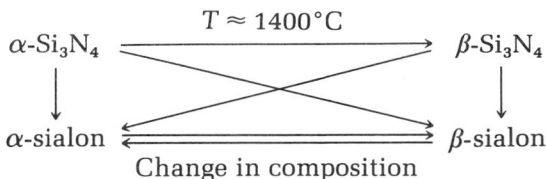

$$
\begin{array}{ccc}
& T \approx 1400°C & \\
\alpha\text{-}Si_3N_4 & \longrightarrow & \beta\text{-}Si_3N_4 \\
\downarrow & \times & \downarrow \\
\alpha\text{-sialon} & \rightleftarrows & \beta\text{-sialon} \\
& \text{Change in composition} &
\end{array}
$$

3.5.5 Conclusion

Solid solutions of Si_3N_4 are called sialons. Heating of a mixture of Si_3N_4 and some sintering aids results in sintered sialon. The sintering is accompanied by sialon formation through a "transient liquid." In β-sialon, Al substitutes for Si in the β-Si_3N_4 structure, whereas metals dissolve into interstitial sites in α-sialon. The sintered materials have high creep, oxidation, or corrosion resistance, and high strength as a result of small amounts of intergranular phases.

References

1. Oyama, Y., and Kamigaito, O., *Jpn. J. Appl. Phys.* 10:1637 (1971).
2. Jack, K. H., and Wilson, W. I., *Nature Phys. Sci.* (London) 238:28 (1972).
3. Gauckler, L. J., Lukas, H. L., and Petzow, G., *J. Am. Ceram. Soc.* 58:346 (1975).
4. Jack, K. H., *J. Mat. Sci.* 11:1135 (1976).
5. Hampshire, S., Park, H. K., Thompson, D. P., and Jack, K. H., *Nature* 274:880 (1978).
6. Mitomo, M., Tanaka, H., Muramatsu, K., Ii, N., and Fujii, Y., *J. Mat. Sci.* 15:2661 (1980).
7. Mitomo, M., Izumi, F., Bando, Y., and Sekikawa, Y., *Proc. International Symposium on Ceramic Components for Engines*, Hakone, Japan, 1983, p. 377.
8. Wills, R. R., Stewart, R. W., and Wimmer, J. M., *J. Am. Ceram. Soc.* 60:64 (1977).
9. Briggs, J., *Mat. Res. Bull.* 12:1047 (1977).
10. Gauckler, L. J., Boskovic, S., Naik, I. K., and Tien, T. Y., *Ceramics for Advanced Heat Engines*, National Technical Information Service, CONF-770110, 1977, p. 321.
11. Mitomo, M., Kuramoto, N., and Inomata, Y., *J. Mat. Sci.* 14:2309 (1979).
12. Lumby, R. J., North, B., and Taylor, A. J., *Ceramics for High Performance Applications*, vol. 2, J. J. Burke et al., eds. Chestnut Hill, Mass.: Brook Hill Pub. Co., 1978, p. 893.
13. Cother, N. E., and Hodgson, P., *Trans. J. Brit. Ceram. Soc.* 81:141 (1982).
14. Birch, J. M., and Wilshire, B., *J. Mat. Sci.* 13:2627 (1978).
15. Schlichting, J., *Nitrogen Ceramics*, F. L. Riley, ed. Amsterdam: Noordhoff, 1977, p. 627.
16. Mitomo, M., Moriyoshi, Y., Sakai, T., Ohsaka, T., and Kobayashi, M., *J. Mat. Sci. Letters* 1:25 (1982).
17. Park, H. K., Thompson, D. P., and Jack, K. H.: *Science of Ceramics*, vol. 10, H. Hausner, ed., Ger. Ceram. Soc., 1980, p. 251.

18. Mitomo, M., and Fukunaga, O., *Yogyo-Kyokai-Shi* 89:631 (1981).
19. Tanaka, H., Mitomo, M., and Tsutsumi, M., *Yogyo-Kyokai-Shi* 90:406, (1982).
20. Demit, J., Torre, J. P., and Cabannes, F., *Science of Ceramics*, vol. 10, H. Hausner, ed., Ger. Ceram. Soc., 1980, p. 51.
21. Mitomo, M., and Uemura, Y., *J. Mat. Sci.* 16:552 (1981).
22. Messier, D. R., Riley, F. L., and Brook, R. J., *J. Mat. Sci.* 13:1199 (1978).
23. Blegan, K., *Special Ceramics No. 6*, P. Popper, ed., Brit. Ceram. Res. Assoc., 1975, p. 223.

3.6 Fabrication and Properties of Carbon/Carbon Composites

Shiushichi Kimura and Eiichi Yasuda

3.6.1 Introduction

Carbon is one of the most versatile of materials; it has high resistance to chemical attack, high refractoriness, and high thermal conductivity in addition to being very light in weight. The covalent nature of the bonding of atoms in carbon makes it most interesting, offering wide scope for the development of a strong material in the form of fiber. Recently, through the use of polyacrylonitril (PAN)-based carbon fiber, a strength of 5500 MPa and a Young's modulus of 450 GPa have been commercially achieved.

Carbon/carbon (C/C) composites have a bright future in space and bio-material engineering because of their unique properties of high specific strength, refractoriness, and bio-compatibility. C/C composites have quite recently found wide application in Concord jet planes for brake shoes,[1] in the space shuttle for leading edges,[2] for endoprosthesis in orthopedic surgery (artificial hip joints),[3] and in the synthetic root of a human tooth.[4,5] This section reviews the current understanding of C/C composite fabrication and properties, and makes some microstructural observations.

3.6.2 Fabrication of C/C Composites

Carbon fiber is used as a filler for C/C composites. It was first developed by Shindo[6] from PAN in 1960. Its strength and modulus are high in the longitudinal direction because of its physical form and special structure, which depend on the raw material and pyrolysis conditions, and low at right angles to the fiber axis.[7]

The properties of the C/C composite depend strongly on the direction of weave. The woven fabric is classified into three types: unidirectional (1D), two-dimensional (2D), and three-dimensional (3D or nD). As 1D and 2D fabrics have strong anisotropic characteristics, they should be used only after the material is designed for specifically desired properties. The characteristics of nD fabrics such as 3D, 4D, and 6D fabric were calculated by Maistre,[8] who concluded that 4D was the best fabric because of its open porosity, isotropy, rigidity, nondelamination, and maximum fiber content. The fiber content of the fabric is controlled mainly by the weaving method and is normally between 40 and 60%. The open pores in the woven fabric should be filled by matrix carbon in the manner shown in Figure 3.6.1. There are three types of matrix carbon: thermo-plastic (TP), thermo-setting (TS) resins derived carbon, and chemically vapor-deposited (CVD) carbon. As shown in Figure 3.6.1, there are several ways of making C/C composites — by carbonization, graphitization, machining, and retreatment.

As the name suggests, the carbonization of TP resin takes place through a liquid phase, and the yield of carbon does not exceed more than 60%. To increase the carbon content, it is necessary to reimpregnate several times; in spite of this, it is difficult to improve on the density beyond 1.8 g/cm³. An autoclave technique can be used for

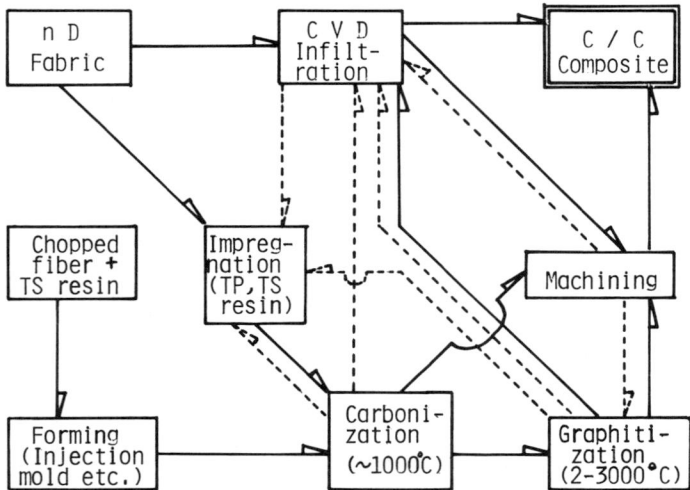

Figure 3.6.1 Fabrication process of C/C composite: solid lines, general process; dotted line, retreatment.

increasing the yield of TP carbon to as high as 85%, and a dense composite of 1.87 g/cm³ can be obtained by reimpregnating once. However, one drawback to this process is the difficulty of suppressing or eliminating pores in the matrix.[9]

For the purpose of economics, petroleum and/or coal tar pitch is used as the resin. Pitch has a wide range of molecular weights and contains carbon black and inorganic substances. Such a type of pitch is very difficult to characterize. Inagaki and co-workers[10] used a solvent fractionation technique for preparing the matrix resin materials, which provided an easier way of characterizing the solubility of mixtures with several ratios of n-hexane, bezene, and pyridine. Depending on the molecular weight, the fractionated pitch is classified according to the microstructure of flow type and mosaic type.

TS resin shows nonplasticity during carbonization and shows high carbon yield (phenolic resin: ~45%; furan resin: ~60%; polyimide and poly-phenylene: ~80%). TS resin causes thermal shrinkage during carbonization and becomes a glasslike carbon that is difficult to graphitize even when heated to above 3000°C. The degree of shrinkage during carbonization affects the microstructure of the matrix. When the shrinkage is great, fiber pullout or microcracking of the matrix occurs; when it is small, the matrix remains a glasslike carbon; when shrinkage is about 40–60 v/o, the graphitization of the matrix occurs at higher heat treatment.[11] TS resin is, however, easier for making high-density material and for maintaining the shape of the fabric.

As it is essential to handle nD fabrics with great care, chopped fiber can be used to fabricate a C/C composite. As shown in the lower part of Figure 3.6.1, many powerful techniques such as injection molding and hand lay-up are used.

Although CVD is an expensive technique, it is the best way to maintain the shape of the fabric without fiber damage. In this method, hydrocarbon gas such as methane or propane is introduced into the fabric and then heated at a high temperature (800–2000°C) and decomposed into carbon. As Kotrensky[12] has discussed, there are three types of CVD techniques: isothermal, temperature gradient, and pressure gradient. The isothermal method calls for simple equipment. The outer surface of the specimen, which is in contact with the hydrocarbon gas first, is preferentially covered by CVD carbon, as a result of which it is difficult to infiltrate the center part of the specimen. The temperature gradient method requires a suscepter inside the specimen to heat it by induction. This produces a low-porosity composite. The carbon depositions of these two methods are con-

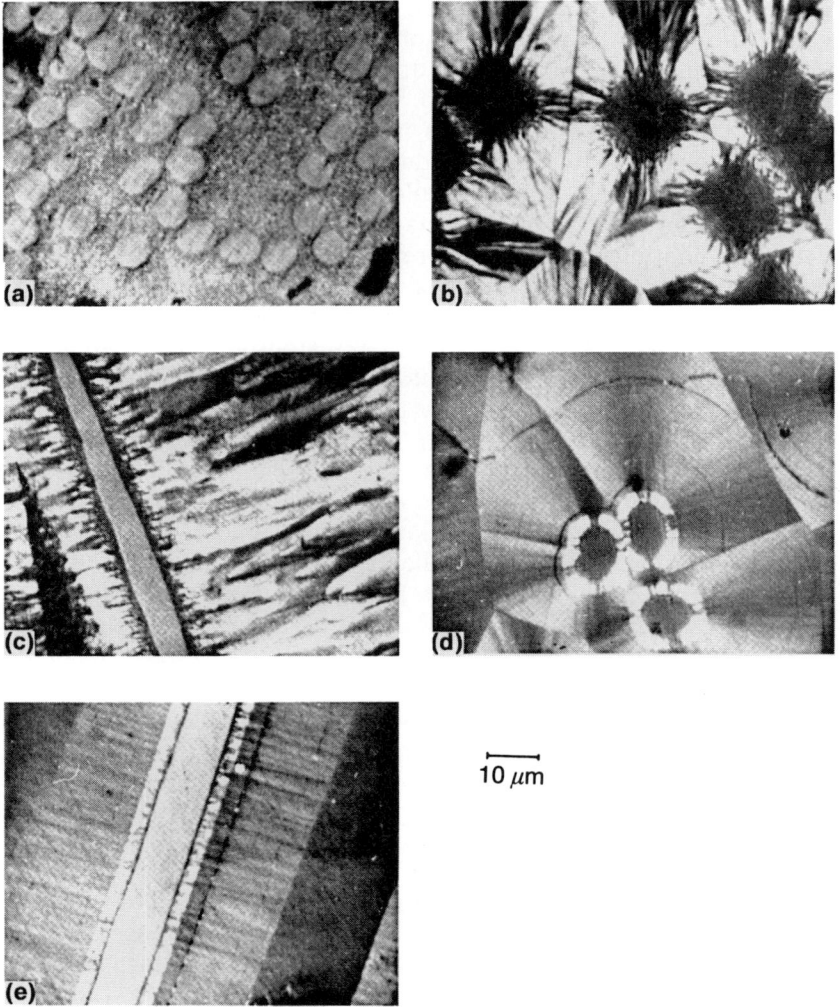

Figure 3.6.2 Microstructure of CVD carbon matrix. (a) ISO carbon; (b) ISO + RC carbon (⊥); (c) ISO + RC carbon (∥); (d) RC + SC carbon (⊥); (e) RC + SC carbon (∥). The symbols ⊥ and ∥ refer to views perpendicular and parallel to the fiber axis, respectively [from S. Kimura et al., *High Temp. High Press.* 13:193 (1981)].

trolled by gas diffusion between the outer surface and the deposition parts; the pressure gradient method requires tight contact between the fabric and the gas container. This is not controlled by long-distance diffusion and so produces a dense composite in a short period.[13]

There are three types of CVD carbon: isotropic (ISO), rough columnar (RC), and smooth columnar (SC) structures, as shown in Figure 3.6.2. The structure is controlled mainly by the deposition temperature and the partial pressure of the hydrocarbon gas.[13] Recently, efforts have been made to lower the deposition temperature. Ootani and co-workers[14] have succeeded in lowering the deposition temperature about 700°C by using dichloroethylene.

3.6.3 Microstructure and Properties of C/C Composites

Properties of the C/C composite are controlled by fiber content, fiber alignment, and the microstructure of the matrix carbon. Here, the properties of C/C composites are limited to 1D composite because of the fundamental basis for the estimation of multidirectional composite.

The tensile or bending strength of the 1D composite changes with the fiber content (V_f) and the angle (θ) between the fiber axis and stress direction, depending on the failure mode as shown in the following equations:

$$\sigma_o = \sigma_f \cdot V_f + \sigma_m(1 - V_f) \tag{3.6.1}$$

$$\sigma_c = \sigma_o/\cos 2\theta \tag{3.6.2}$$

$$\sigma_c = \tau_i/\sin \cos \theta \tag{3.6.3}$$

$$\sigma_c = \tau_m/\sin 2\theta \tag{3.6.4}$$

where σ_f is fiber strength, σ_m is the strength of the matrix, τ_i is the shear strength of the fiber/matrix interface, and τ_m is the shear strength of the matrix.

The TS carbon composite with lower heat treatment temperature (HTT) shows brittle fracture because of the strong adhesion between the fiber and the matrix, and the fracture initiates at the glasslike carbon matrix, as shown in Figure 3.6.3. Above an HTT of 2000°C, the composite fractures pseudo-plastically with many pop-in appearances, and the strength increases with an increase in HTT depending on the development of the graphite structure, as shown in Figure 3.6.4.[11] The fracture behavior of TP-derived carbon matrix composite and CVD carbon composite are the same as that of a TS-de-

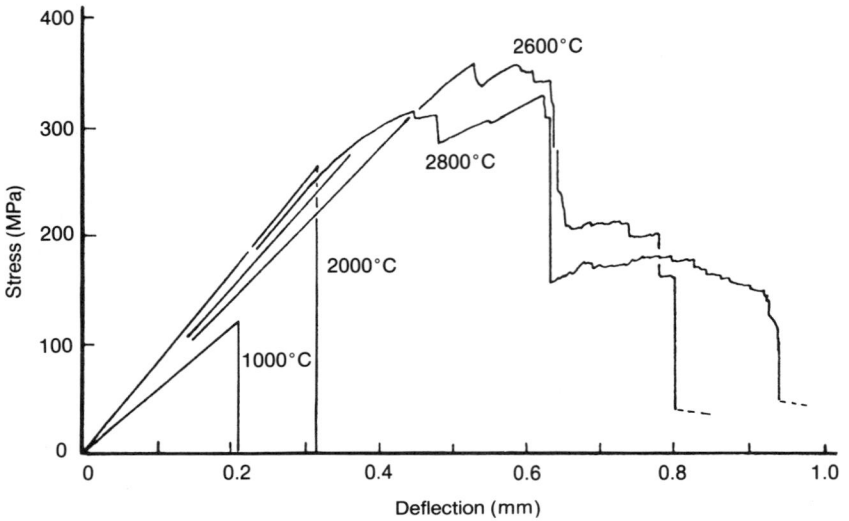

Figure 3.6.3 Fracture behavior in C/C composite of TS resin-derived carbon matrix by 4-point bending test [after H. Tanaka et al., *Jpn. Soc. Comp. Mat.* (trans.) 4:37 (1978)].

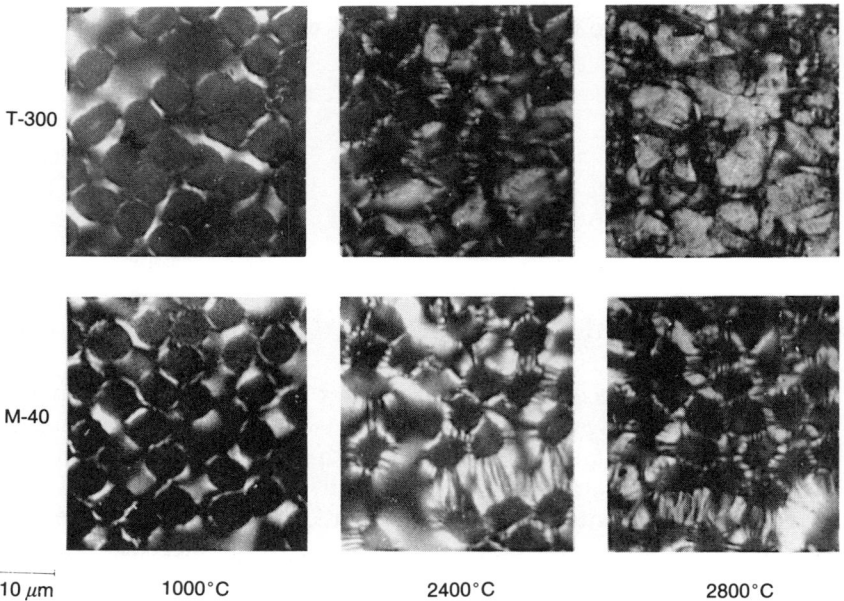

Figure 3.6.4 Microstructure of TS resin-derived carbon matrix. T-300 and M-40 refer to high-strength and high-modulus carbon fiber, respectively.

rived carbon matrix composite with a HTT above 2400°C whose behavior derives from the microstructural orientation of the matrix. The pseudo-plastic fracture manner originates also in the fiber pull-out. The existence of pores decreases the strength exponentially with increasing porosity.[15]

Young's modulus is also controlled by fiber content and the microstructure of the matrix. With an increase of HTT, Young's modulus in the longitudinal direction in TS carbon composite increases from 80 GPa for a HTT of 1000°C to 170 GPa for a HTT of 2800°C; that in the transverse direction decreases from 3 GPa at 1000°C to 1 GPa at 2800°C.[16] These behaviors correspond well with the development and alignment of the graphite layer in the matrix. These mechanical properties are important for designing structural components. In addition to these, the effects of neutron irradiation on mechanical strength should be investigated for possible use in the first wall of fusion reactors.

The thermal properties of C/C composites are also important for high-temperature applications. The thermal conductivity increases by two orders of magnitude in accordance with graphite layer development.[17] Generally speaking, thermal conductivity at ambient temperature is expressed as a product of specific heat, phonon mean free path length, and phonon velocity. Because the specific heat and phonon velocity calculated from Young's modulus are not changed much by the HTT, the thermal conductivity depends mainly on the mean free path length. The crystallite size in the [110] plane, measured by X-ray diffraction, corresponds to the calculated mean free path length.[17] These characteristic phenomena should also be related to the microstructure and given consideration in designing material for brake shoes.

Carbon material is inert to chemical attack except under oxidation and when intercalation compounds are formed. These characteristics are also the same for C/C composites. In a TS carbon composite with a HTT below 2400°C, the matrix is oxidized easily compared with commercial graphite materials. The interface of fiber and matrix and the domain boundary of the matrix, however, are preferentially oxidized in the composite with a HTT above 2400°C.[18]

References

1. *Aircraft Engineering*, September 24–26, 1976.
2. Becker, P. R., *Am. Ceram. Soc. Bull.* 60:1210 (1981).
3. Brueckmann, H., and Huettinger, K. J., *Biomaterials* 1:67 (1981).

4. Ootani, S., and Kojima, A., *Fine Ceramics* 12:151 (1982).
5. Fitzer, E., and Huttner, W., *J. Phys. D. Appl. Phys.* 14:347 (1981).
6. Shindo, A., *Rpt. of Research Inst. of Tech. Oosaka,* 12(2):110, 119 (1960).
7. Mckee, D. W. et al., *Chemistry and Physics of Carbon,* vol. 8. P. L. Walker, et al., eds. New York: Dekker, 1973, p. 151.
8. Maistre, M. A., *Ext. Abst. 14th Biennial Conference on Carbon,* 1979, p. 230.
9. Kawamura, K. et al., *Tanso* 109:46 (1982).
10. Inagaki, M. et al., *Carbon* (in press); Kimura, S. et al., *Rpt. RLEM TIT* (in press).
11. Tanaka, H. et al., *Trans. Jpn. Soc. Comp. Mat.* 4:37 (1978).
12. Kotlensky, W. V., *Chemistry and Physics of Carbon,* vol. 9, P. L. Walker, Jr., et al., eds. New York: Dekker, 1973, pp. 174–262.
13. Kimura, S. et al., *High Temp. High Press.* 13:193 (1981).
14. Ootani, S. et al., *J. Chem. Soc. Jpn.* 4:494 (1979).
15. Kimura, S. et al., *Proc. International Symposium on Factors in Densification and Sintering of Oxide and Non-Oxide Ceramics,* 1977, pp. 229–308.
16. Yasuda, E. et al., *Tanso* 100:3 (1980).
17. Kimura, S., et al., *Proc. International Symposium on Carbon in Japan,* 1982, pp. 410–413.
18. Yasuda, E., et al., *Trans. Jpn. Soc. Comp. Mat.* 6:14 (1980).

3.7 Slow Crack Propagation in Glass and Ceramics

Naohiro Soga

3.7.1 Introduction

A fracture mechanics study on glass, carried out in the 1970s by Wiederhorn and co-workers,[1] has revealed clearly that subcritical crack growth is responsible for the static fatigue of glass. Since then, the determination of crack velocity in the low velocity range has become an important subject in the study of the strength of ceramic materials in both crystalline and glassy states, because such data on subcritical crack growth are useful not only to explain the strength variation of ceramic samples but also to estimate their lifetime on the basis of the relationship of the stress intensity factor (K_I) and crack velocity (v). A number of papers appeared along this line in the 1960s and 1970s, but few by Japanese researchers. Recently, however, many attempts to obtain the K_I-v relationship for structural materials are being made at various laboratories in Japan. Some of these attempts are described here (based on the published reports).

3.7.2 Measuring Method

Usually, the K_I-v relation of a ceramic material is determined by the double-torsion or double-cantilever technique. However, these techniques require larger specimens than those for bending tests. Some attempts have been made to establish a method utilizing smaller specimens. Recently, a simple method for measuring the K_I-v relation of brittle ceramic materials was developed by Nishikawa and Nishida,[2,3] who used the 3-point bending tests on bar specimens with an appropriate chevron notch angle under a constant deflection condition. The accuracy of the method was tested on glass specimens by comparing the results obtained by two different methods: One is the K_I-v relation calculated through the compliance analysis of load relaxation curves obtained under a constant deflection, and the other is by direct observation of crack propagation in the notched area with time by means of a video camera. These two results agreed well with each other and also with the previous literature data. This method (referred to as the chevron notch technique in this section) has been used to determine the K_I-v relations for various ceramic materials not only at room temperature but also at high temperatures.

Another method now being tried involves measuring the crack tip position of a micro-indented crack on the smooth specimen surface as a function of time during constant loading and then calculating K_I and v. This method (referred to as the micro-indentation technique here) was applied not only on transparent glass samples[4] but also on polycrystalline Si_3N_4 samples at high temperatures to obtain the data at very low crack velocities.[5]

3.7.3 Glass

When the K_I-v relation is determined under conditions in which there are various amounts of corroding or attacking species at different temperatures, useful information about the reaction involved in stress corrosion can be obtained, including the order of reaction, activation energy, and activation volume. According to Wiederhorn,[1] the stress-enhanced chemical reaction between water and glass was found to be of the first order at high water-vapor pressures but became a half-order at low pressures. Such a change in the order of reaction is difficult to explain with the stress-corrosion theory of

Hillig and Charles.[6] The recent data on soda-lime silicate glass by Soga and co-workers,[7] taken at room temperature in atmospheres containing only water-vapor of 5.3–1333 Pa by means of the double-torsion technique, show that the crack velocity (or the reaction rate) is linearly proportional to the water-vapor pressure, yielding a first-order reaction even at low pressure in accordance with the theory. These investigators attributed the difference between Wiederhorn's results and their own to be the large mean free path and high diffusion constant of water molecules under reduced pressure.

This linearity was confirmed recently on soda-lime silicate glass by Nishida and Nishikawa,[8] who used the chevron notch technique and obtained the first-order reaction in the water-vapor pressure range of 0.53–2146 Pa under reduced total pressures. Both of these data indicate the disappearance of region II, probably because of the rapid diffusion of water vapor to the crack tip.

The stress dependence of crack velocity is usually expressed as $v = AK_I^n$, A and n being the material constants. The reported value of n for silicate glasses is usually about 25–30. The recent data by Miyata and co-workers[4] using the micro-indentation technique gave the value of n to be 28 in air (50% RH) and 70 in dry nitrogen at room temperature. However, the data on fused silica determined by Sakaguchi and co-workers[9] using the double-cantilever beam technique show that $n = 38$–44 in air (0.08–75% RH) as well as in distilled water (24–70°C). They reported the activation energy for the stress corrosion of fused silica to be 97.6 kcal/mol, which seems quite high when compared with the other reported values of 33 kcal/mol for fused silica[10] and 23 kcal/mol for soda-lime silicate glass.[11]

Stress corrosion by gases other than H_2O has rarely been reported. Recently, Soga and co-workers[12] investigated the stress corrosion of fused silica and soda-lime silicate glass by H_2S gas at 17–64°C. The linear dependence of v on H_2S concentration at constant K_I gave a first-order reaction for the stress corrosion of both glasses by H_2S, but the reaction rate was much slower than that with H_2O. The activation energy of the reaction by H_2S was 38 kcal/mol for fused silica and 27 kcal/mol for soda-lime silicate glass. These values were slightly higher (by several kcal), than those of the reaction by H_2O, and this difference was attributed to the difference in size and polarization of H_2O and H_2S molecules.

3.7.4 Ceramics

Although the K_I-v relation for polycrystalline alumina has been reported in the literature, the dependence of subcritical crack growth on the microstructure of ceramics has not been understood clearly. The recent report by Shiono and co-workers[13] deals with this problem. The chevron notched specimens of α-alumina single crystal and two kinds of polycrystal specimens were fractured by the 4-point bending technique under a crosshead speed of 0.005 mm/min in air (20°C, 67% RH) and in distilled water. Stable fracture was achieved, and the load deflection curves were analyzed by using the compliance method. The curve shifted toward the high K_I side when the magnitude of effective fracture energy of the specimen was high. Three different K_I-v relations were obtained. The values of n for single crystals and large- and small-grain polycrystalline specimens were 65, 50, and 27, respectively. These values were about the same both in air and in water. When the small-grain alumina polycrystalline specimens were tested under various water-vapor concentrations, the K_I-v relations gave a first-order reaction.[14] However, virtually no change in the K_I-v relation was found for single-crystal specimens tested in air and in water. These results are taken to indicate that the stress corrosion of polycrystalline α-alumina occurs mainly at the glassy phase in grain boundaries.

The effect of the addition of ZrO_2 to α-alumina ceramics on the K_I-v relation was examined by Takatsu and co-workers.[15] The K_I of α-alumina ceramics was increased 60% by the addition of 10% ZrO_2, while n was decreased from 90 to 60.

An automatic system of measuring K_I-v relation by the double-torsion technique was recently constructed at the Government Industrial Research Institute, Nagoya.[16] It was used to determine the K_I-v relation of hot-pressed Si_3N_4 in the velocity range of 10^{-2}–10^{-6} m/sec, which gave $n = 109 \pm 13$. For purposes of comparison, the double-cantilever beam technique was also tried on the same sample in the slower crack velocity range of 10^{-6}–10^{-9} m/sec. The value of n was found to be 122, which is close to the value cited above by the double-torsion technique in the high crack velocity range but about 20% higher than the value of 85 predicted in the range of 10^{-6}–10^{-10} m/sec, based on the recent fatigue data of hot-pressed Si_3N_4 cited by Yamauchi and co-workers.[17]

As for the determination of the high temperature K_I-v relation, the chevron notch technique apparently can be employed easily. Nishida and Nishikawa[18] measured the K_I-v relation of hot pressed β-alumina at 1300°C in the velocity range of 10^{-4}–10^{-6} m/sec and determined the value of n to be about 10. They also applied the chevron notch technique to obtain the K_I-v relation for reaction-bonded Si_3N_4 specimens with a notch angle of 120° in N_2, air, and O_2 atmosphere at 1400°C.[19] Although it was expected that the crack velocity in Si_3N_4 might be accelerated in oxidizing conditions as a result of stress corrosion, it was decelerated slightly in air and very much in O_2. The fracture surface in N_2 clearly showed the occurrence of an intergranular-type fracture, whereas the fracture surface in air or O_2 was flat and covered with glassy phase containing some β-cristobalite crystallites. From these observations, the investigators concluded that the stress corrosion in Si_3N_4 may become active in air or O_2 atmospheres, but the chemical reaction of Si_3N_4 and O_2 may also lead to the crack's blunting at the tip, resulting in a slow-down of the crack velocity. However, their data contain some problems that need to be clarified. For example, the value of n calculated for the N_2 condition is quite low (~2) but becomes higher in O_2. Clearly, a certain load-relaxing process is taking place in N_2, but this process is affected by the existence of O_2.

The crack velocity in sintered Si_3N_4 was determined at 1100– 1300°C in air down to 10^{-12} m/sec by Kawai and co-workers using the micro-indentation technique.[5] They observed two different K_I-v relations in low and high crack velocity ranges. The relation in the low velocity range gave $n = 11-12$, which is similar to the value obtained from the tensile rupture tests.

The slow crack growth in ceramics may be followed by acoustic emission (AE).[10] This was recently examined by Iwasaki and co-workers on hot-pressed Si_3N_4 at room temperature in air, using the double-torsion technique.[20] The AE count rate was linearly proportional to the crack growth velocity in the range of 10^{-4} m/sec. However, it was shown that AE characteristics could not be compared directly with K_I or v when the crack propagation proceeded along different paths.

As for the traditional ceramic materials, the K_I-v relation for an electrical porcelain was measured by Matsui and co-workers[21] using the double-torsion method in air, water, and kerosene in the velocity range of $10^{-2}-10^{-9}$ m/sec. Only region I was observed in water in this velocity range, but in kerosene, regions II and III were observed. The values of n and A were found to be 39 and -247 in region I. Theoretically, v should be independent of K_I in region II, but it showed some K_I dependence ($n = 10-15$) because of the heterogeneous microstructure of the porcelain body. These data were successfully applied to predict a failure time of less than 1000 seconds. The effect of pH on crack growth was also examined, but virtually no change was observed between the K_I-v relations in water and NaOH aq (pH = 13) or H_2SO_4 aq (Ph = 1).

The K_I-v relations for hardened gypsums were measured by Takatsu and co-workers using the double-torsion method in air, water, and kerosene.[22] The value of n under dry conditions as well as in kerosene was about 16; it was quite low (3–5) in water. This difference was attributed to the stress corrosion of gypsum by water.

References

1. Wiederhorn, S. M., *Fracture Mechanics of Ceramics*, vol. 2, R. C. Bradt et al., eds. New York: Plenum Press, 1974, p. 613.

2. Nishida, T., Ueda, K., Hayashi, K., and Nishikawa, T., *Yogyo-Kyokai-Shi* 90:14 (1982).

3. Nishida, T., and Nishikawa, T., *Yogyo-Kyokai-Shi* 90:282 (1982).

4. Miyata, N., Taneda, N., and Jinno, H., *Proc. Annual Meeting of Japan Ceramic Society*, Japan, 1983, p. 469.

5. Kawai, M., Abe, H., and Nakayama, J., *Proc. First Symposium on High-Temperature Materials*, Yogyo-Kyokai, Japan, 1981, p. 55.

6. Hillig, W. B., and Charles, R. J., *High Strength Materials*, V. F. Zackay, ed. New York: John Wiley & Sons, 1965, p. 682.

7. Soga, N., Okamoto, T., Hanada, T., and Kunugi, M., *J. Am. Ceram. Soc.* 62:309 (1979).

8. Nishida, T., and Nishikawa, T., *Proc. 26th Japan Congress on Materials Research*, Society of Materials Science, Japan, 1983, p. 282.

9. Sakaguchi, S., Sawaki, Y., Abe, Y., and Kawasaki, T., *J. Mat. Res.* 17:2878 (1982).

10. Evans, A. G., *J. Mat. Sci.* 7:1137 (1972).

11. Wiederhorn, S. M., and Bolz, L. H., *J. Am. Ceram. Soc.* 53:543 (1970).

12. Soga, N., Mori, K., and Hirao, K., *Nihon-Kagaku-Kaishi* 1481 (1981).

13. Shiono, T., Ota, R., and Soga, N., *J. Soc. Mat. Res.* (Japan) 32:1254 (1983).

14. Soga, N., Shiono, T., and Hirao, K., *Proc. 20th Symposium on Basic Science of Ceramics*, Osaka, Japan, 1982, p. 33.

15. Takatsu, M., and Takahashi, I., *Proc. Annual Meeting of Japan Ceramic Society*, Tokyo, Japan, 1983, p. 483.

16. Wakaki, F., Matsuno, Y., and Sakuramoto, H., *Proc. Annual Meeting of Japan Ceramic Society*, Tokyo, Japan, 1983, p. 485.

17. Yamauchi, Y., Sakai, S., Ito, M., and Ito, S., *Proc. Annual Meeting of Japan Ceramic Society*, Tokyo, Japan, 1983, p. 475.

18. Nishida, T., and Nishikawa, T., *Yogyo-Kyokai-Shi* 89:544 (1981).

19. Nishida, T., Takei, Y., and Nishikawa, T., *Yogyo-Kyokai-Shi* 90:254 (1982).

20. Iwasaki, H., and Izumi, M., *J. Soc. Mat. Sci.* (Japan) 30:1044 (1981).

21. Matsui, M., Soma, T., and Oda, I., *Fracture Mechanics of Ceramics*, vol. 4, R. C. Bradt et al., eds. New York, Plenum Press, 1978, p. 711; *J. Am. Ceram. Soc.* 63:166 (1980).
22. Takatsu, M., Shinomura, K., Takahashi, I., and Ono, T., *Gypsum & Lime* 173:149 (1981).

3.8 Evaluation of Some Ceramics: Silicon Nitride, Silicon Carbide, and Zirconia

Shoji Ito and Hiroshi Okuda

3.8.1 Introduction

Silicon nitride, silicon carbide, and zirconia, which are classed as high-performance ceramics, are structural or engineering ceramics. Therefore, their mechanical properties and their reliability as structural parts are of importance, and these properties depend on the process of machining as well as sintering. In either case, an accurate evaluation of these properties is necessary, and there is a pressing need for the establishment of evaluation techniques and standardization.

3.8.2 Flexural Testing Method

Among the testing methods for mechanical properties of high-performance ceramics, only the flexural testing method at room temperature has been standardized. Flexural strength is usually measured because it is very difficult to make a test piece accurately and to grip a brittle material in the tensile test, although tensile strength is the datum required most often for designing parts. The flexural testing method is outlined in JIS(R1601) as "Testing Method for Flexural Strength of High-Performance Ceramics." In this industrial standard, the specimen sizes are 4 mm wide by 3 mm high with a 30-mm span for 3-point bending, and for $\frac{1}{3}$ 4-point bending. The specimen surface should be finished to a roughness of 0.8S to avoid the effect of surface flaws by machining. More than ten specimens should be tested under the same conditions.

3.8.3 Statistical Treatment of Strength

The failure probability of ceramic material is held to obey a Weibull distribution function, and the properties of mechanical strength are expressed by the parameters in the following equation:

$$F = 1 - \exp\left\{-\int_v \left(\frac{\sigma - \sigma_u}{\sigma_o}\right)^m dv\right\} \qquad (3.8.1)$$

In this equation the three parameters m, σ_u, and σ_o are constant values for each material. Where m is the Weibull modulus and σ_u is the maximum value of stress under which the specimen will not fail, σ_u is usually equal to zero. From Equation (3.8.1),

$$F = 1 - \exp\left\{-V_E \left(\frac{\sigma_{max}}{\sigma_o}\right)^m\right\} \qquad (3.8.2)$$

where $V_E = \int_v (\sigma/\sigma_{max})^m dv$ is the effective volume determined from the stress distribution and the specimen size; σ_{max} is the maximum value of the stress σ in a specimen. If logarithms of both sides of Equation (3.8.2) are taken, failure probability and stress are a linear relation as follows:

$$\ln \ln \frac{1}{1 - F} = m \ln \sigma_{max} - \ln \frac{\sigma_o^m}{V_E} \qquad (3.8.3)$$

Therefore, the Weibull modulus m is the slope of the data (the straight line) plotted on this chart; that is, the modulus illustrates the amount of scatter of the strength.

3.8.4 Relation of Sample Size and Reliability of Weibull Modulus

For the evaluation of strength properties of ceramic material, the Weibull distribution function, mean strength σ_m, and Weibull modulus m are the most basic and important statistical values to be applied. As these parameters are obtained from finite sample sizes, the values vary with those of the populations. The amount of scatter differs with that of mean strength and that of the Weibull modulus; furthermore, these depend on the sample size. The relation of the sample size n and the coefficient of variation c (=standard deviation/mean value) obtained by computer simulation is shown in Figure 3.8.1. The coefficient of variation decreases with a larger sample size; however, the value of the Weibull modulus is approximately ten times larger than that of the mean strength. That is, mean strength is obtained with high reliability through a relatively small sample size, whereas a very large sample size is required to obtain the Weibull modulus with the same degree of reliability. When these statistical values are obtained with some test pieces, the above results must be considered.

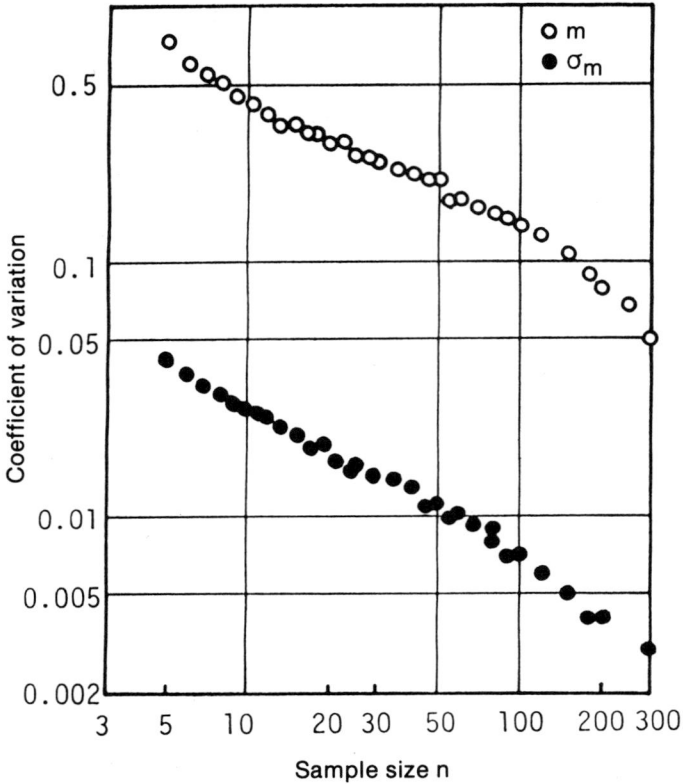

Figure 3.8.1 Relation of coefficient of variation and sample size of Weibull modulus and mean strength.

3.8.5 Factors Influencing Strength

Pores, inclusions, and other inherent internal defects as well as roughness, surface flaws, or other external defects influence the strength of a ceramic material. In the case of failure resulting from the former, the apparent strength of the material is measured. However, for failures caused by the latter, the strength is less than that which is apparent for the material. In the former, m and σ_o are constants, the values of which show the strength property; in the latter, the values differ with the surface character of the specimens. Moreover, when each sampled specimen fails because of various defects, the Weibull plot sometimes is not linear.

The mean strength depends on the effective volume V_E, as shown in Equation (3.8.2). Therefore, the strength of a specimen from a test method with a large specimen size or large effective volume will yield a lower value than that from a test method with a small specimen size or a small effective volume. Deterioration in strength of a large specimen occurs because the probability of the presence of a critical flaw is larger than in a small specimen.

3.8.6 Deterioration of Strength by Surface Machining Flaws

Accurate evaluation of the mechanical properties of ceramic material is very important when using the material for structural parts; otherwise, the strength of ceramics depends on the surface roughness and the machining process of the test piece. Sometimes a specimen with a rough surface fails at a stress far lower than the essential strength of the material. Therefore, in the machining of ceramic parts as well as in the evaluating of strength, the relation of the strength of the part and the machining process is very important.

The effect of surface finishing on the strength of the specimen is often shown by the relation of the bending strength and the roughness. Finely finished specimens give the highest and most constant values in strength tests. But roughly finished specimens, those which have more than several μm of roughness, give lower values compared to the former, and the strength decreases to almost half the original value with a lowering of the roughness. The decrease of strength with lowering of the roughness is due to the occurrence of surface flaws from the machining process. It does not always follow, however, that a decrease in strength depends on the surface roughness. Surface flaws are considered to have directional qualities for the machining direction, and the flaw size is affected by the machining condition.

The relation of the grinding condition and the bending strength in hot-pressed silicon nitride is shown in Figure 3.8.2. The strength properties of bending test pieces, the surfaces of which are finished parallel to length (A) and perpendicular to lengths (B) and (C) by diamond grinding wheels of 400 and 200 mesh, are very different from one another for the same material. In the case of condition (A), the fractures that start from a surface flaw by grinding are 8% of all fractures; in the case of condition (C), the fractures from a surface flaw are 88% of all fractures. The strength properties of the bending test pieces for which the surfaces are ground and removed 5 μm (D) and 10 μm (E) under the same conditions as (A) after grinding under condition (C) are shown in Figure 3.8.3. In contrast, the relation of the

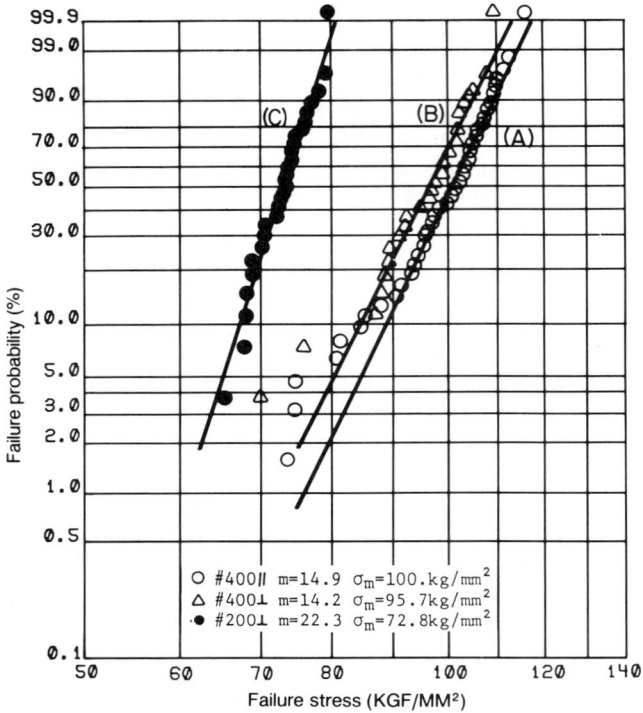

Figure 3.8.2 Relation of strength and grinding direction of hot-pressed silicon nitride.

surface flaw size a and the 3-point bending strength σ_c is expressed as follows:

$$K_{IC} = \sigma_c \sqrt{\pi a}\, F(\xi) \tag{3.8.4}$$

where K_{IC} is the fracture toughness and $F(\xi)$ is a constant, the value of which is determined by the shape of a specimen. The flaw size a is obtained from the following equation:

$$\sigma_0 \sqrt{\pi a}\, F(\xi) = \sigma_1 \sqrt{\pi(a - d_1)}\, F(\xi) \tag{3.8.5}$$

where σ_0 and σ_1 are the strengths before and after grinding parallel to the specimen length, and d_1 is the depth of the grinding. From Equation (3.8.5) and the results shown in Figure 3.8.3, a 27% decrease in strength is obtained from a surface flaw made by grinding with a 200-mesh diamond wheel that causes a flaw about 22 μm in depth. A flaw caused by a 400-mesh wheel is about 10 μm in depth and results

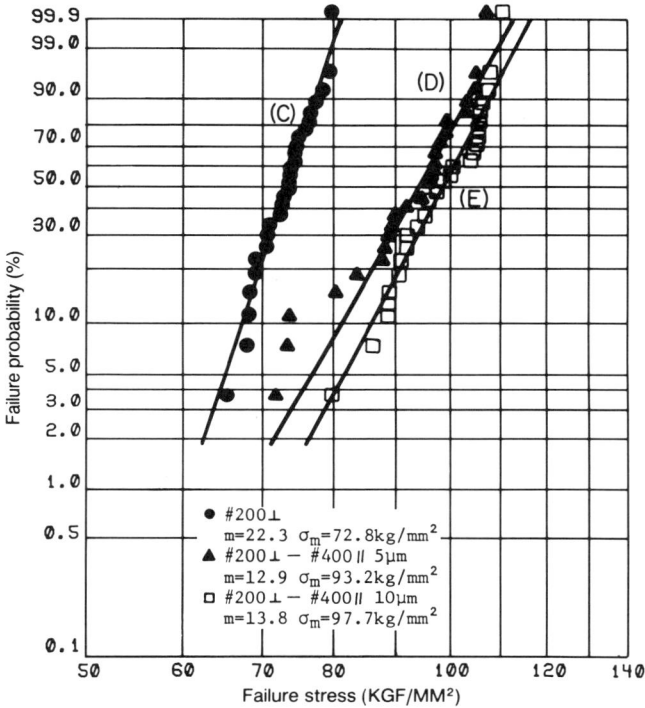

Figure 3.8.3 Increase in strength after removal of the surface finished perpendicular to the length by 400-mesh grinding wheel.

in only a 4% decrease in strength. These amounts of strength decreases resulting from grinding are different for different materials. Silicon carbide is more sensitive to surface flaws than silicon nitride. In the case of hot-pressed silicon carbide, the strengths of the specimens ground by a 400-mesh diamond wheel vary with the grinding direction by some 50%.

3.8.7 Strength Properties at High Temperatures

At temperatures up to 1500°C, the strength properties of these ceramic materials are especially important. There are many difficult problems in measuring high-temperature strength, which is sensitive to temperature, atmosphere, loading rate, structure of jig, and other factors. Several Weibull plots showing the high-temperature strengths of $HP\text{-}Si_3N_4$ and HP-SiC are shown in Figure 3.8.4. In the

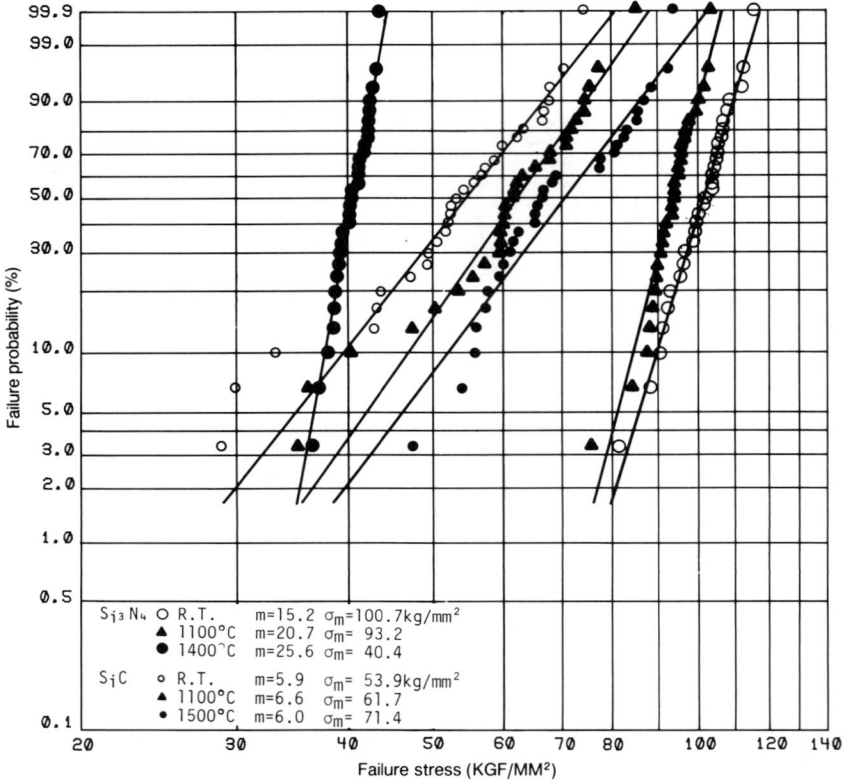

Figure 3.8.4 High-temperature strengths and Weibull moduli of hot-pressed silicon nitride and hot-pressed silicon carbide.

case of HP-Si$_3$N$_4$, the decrease in strength at high temperature is remarkable, and the Weibull modulus improves with higher temperature. In the case of HP-SiC, the strength increases a little at higher temperature, and the Weibull modulus does not vary up to 1500°C.

In evaluating strength properties at high temperatures, the deformation by load cannot be neglected. Some ceramic material is deformed at temperatures above 1100°C, and the amount of deformation depends on the kind of material, the temperature, and other factors. In any case, creep deformation is the main concern, which is why the effect of the loading rate must be taken into account when measuring strength at high temperature.

3.8.8 Tension Test

At present the strength of a ceramic material is measured by flexure tests in most cases. However, in the design of ceramic parts, tensile strength is the primary requirement. Gripping hard and brittle materials and uniformly stretching them are generally difficult. Consequently, many kinds of tension tests have been carried out.

Figure 3.8.5 gives the results of a tension test. In the method employed, a thin plate test piece, of which the gripped ends have rubber sheets, is held by flat gripping devices to prevent fracture of

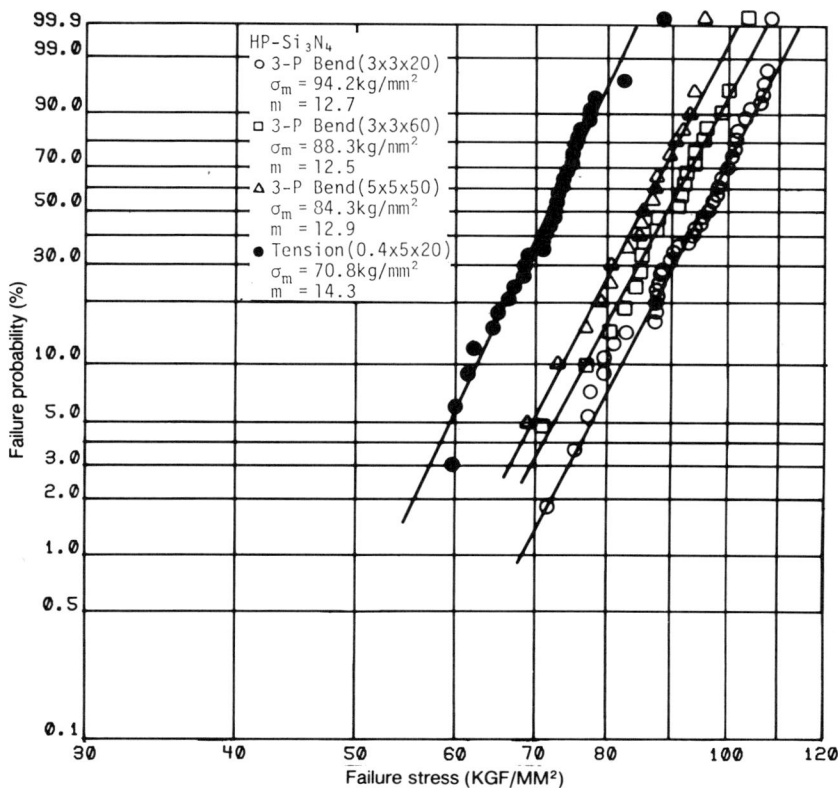

Figure with axes: Failure probability (%) vs Failure stress (KGF/MM²)

Legend:
HP-Si$_3$N$_4$
o 3-P Bend(3x3x20)
σ_m = 94.2kg/mm^2
m = 12.7
□ 3-P Bend(3x3x60)
σ_m = 88.3kg/mm^2
m = 12.5
△ 3-P Bend(5x5x50)
σ_m = 84.3kg/mm^2
m = 12.9
● Tension(0.4x5x20)
σ_m = 70.8kg/mm^2
m = 14.3

Figure 3.8.5 Failure probability of hot-pressed silicon nitride in tension test and 3-point flexure test.

the gripped ends, and at the same time the testing error resulting from the bending moment is decreased by the elastic deformation of the thin test piece. Several Weibull plots of flexure strength for different specimen sizes are given in Figure 3.8.5, and these Weibull moduli have nearly identical values. However, the mean strengths decrease with the effective volume. These differences in mean strength in each size of specimen show the size effect of ceramic materials.

References

1. Weibull, W., *J. Appl. Mech.* 18:293 (1951).
2. Ito, S., Sakai, S., and Ito, M., *Proc. 25th Japanese Congress on Materials Research,* Japan, 1982, p. 218.
3. Kawai, M., Abe, H., and Nakayama, J., *Proc. International Symposium on Factors in Densification and Sintering of Oxide and Non-Oxide Ceramics,* Hakone, Japan, 1978, p. 545.
4. Kirchner, H. P., Gruver, R. M., and Richard, D. M., *The Science of Ceramic Machining and Surface Finishing,* NBS Spec. Pub. No. 562, 1979, p. 23.
5. Rice, R. W., and Mecholsky, J. J., *The Science of Ceramic Machining and Surface Finishing,* NBS Spec. Pub. No. 562, 1979, p. 351.
6. Andersson, C. A., and Bratton, R. J., *The Science of Ceramic Machining and Surface Finishing,* NBS Spec. Pub. No. 562, 1979, p. 563.
7. Katz, R. N., and Lenoe, E. M., *Treatise on Mat. Sci. Tech.* 9:248.

3.9 Fatigue Life Prediction of Glass and Ceramics

Osami Kamigaito

3.9.1 Introduction

Prediction of fatigue life is very important in industrial applications of brittle materials such as glass and ceramics. In the past, predictions have been made by measuring the lifetime or fracture stress of the material under much more severe conditions than those of practical use. This method appears substantially correct when compared with the results of current ceramic fracture mechanics; however, it lacks a scientific basis. Currently, predictions are being made on the basis of the fracture mechanics of ceramics. This consists mainly of two techniques: estimating the lifetime of a ceramic having a crack of a given initial length under a given stress, and determining the distribution function of the initial crack length. The former technique is based on mechanics and the latter on an application of statistical theory.

In this section, theoretical as well as experimental aspects are described.

3.9.2 Prediction of Fatigue Life of Glass and Ceramics

3.9.2.1 *Homogeneous System*

The subcritical crack growth in a brittle material can be expressed as follows:[1]

$$v = \frac{da}{dt} = AK_I^n = AY^n \cdot \sigma^n \cdot a^{n/2} \qquad (3.9.1)$$

$$(n \gtrsim 20)$$

where v, a, t, A, K_I, n, Y, and σ stand, respectively, for the crack propagation velocity, crack length, time, a constant depending on humidity in the environment, the stress intensity factor, a material constant, a geometrical factor, and stress. The solution of Equation (3.9.1) cannot be given in an analytical function in general. Careful consideration of this equation, however, shows that the lifetime can be approximated by solving the equation in some small range of the crack length a.[2] Moreover, it is noteworthy that σ is a periodical function of time (period: ω), because most practical components are used under nearly periodic stress. In such a case, Equation (3.9.1) gives the following:

$$a_i^{-\frac{n-2}{2}} - a_N^{-\frac{n-2}{2}} = NH\sigma_0^n$$

$$G = Y^n A(n-2)/2$$

$$\sigma = \sigma_O f(t) \qquad (3.9.2)$$

$$H = G \int_0^\omega f^n(t)dt$$

where a_N is the crack length at the end of the Nth period, and $f(t)$ is a function of time. Equation (3.9.2) can be applied to mechanical as well as thermal stress.

In an approximation of the first order, thermal stress σ_T is proportional to the temperature change ΔT_O at an arbitary fixed time. Then

σ_T is given as follows:

$$\sigma_T = \Delta T_O\, g(t) \tag{3.9.3}$$

where g(t) is a function of time. The lifetime is given by making a_N equal to the length of the ceramic, which is so much longer than a_i that a_N can be neglected in comparison with a_i. Therefore, the lifetime N is given by the following:

$$N = a_i^{-\frac{n-2}{2}} H^{-1} \sigma_O^{-n} \tag{3.9.4}$$

$$N = a_i^{-\frac{n-2}{2}} H_T^{-1} \Delta T_O^{-n}, \qquad H_T = G\int_0^\omega g^n(t)dt \tag{3.9.5}$$

where N and N_T are life-times under mechanical stress and thermal stress, respectively.

According to Equations (3.9.4) or (3.9.5), the number of ceramics with a lifetime of N is the same as those with an initial crack length of a_i, so the distribution of a_i determines lifetime as well as the fracture stress σ_f. Therefore, the distribution of σ_f can be used instead of that of a_i. The distribution of σ_f is known to be represented by the Weibull distribution:

$$P = \exp\left[-V_O(\sigma_f/\sigma_O)^m\right] \tag{3.9.6}$$

where P, V_O, σ_O, and m stand, respectively, for the cumulative survival probability at the stress of σ_f, the stressed volume, a normalization constant, and the Weibull modulus.

On the basis of fracture mechanics, σ_f is expressed as follows by using a constant, C:

$$\sigma = Ca_i^{1/2} \tag{3.9.7}$$

Equations (3.9.4) through (3.9.7) give the following:

$$\ln(-\ln P) = (m/n)\ln N + m\ln\sigma_O + C_M \tag{3.9.8}$$
(for mechanical stress)

$$\ln(-\ln P) = (m/n)\ln N + m\ln(\Delta T_O) + C_T \tag{3.9.9}$$
(for thermal stress)

where P is the cumulative survival probability at the lifetime of N or N_T, and C_M and C_T are constants. Using Equations (3.9.8) or (3.9.9), the lifetimes can be predicted by testing the ceramics under conditions in which the maximum stress or thermal shock severity is higher than that in practical use, and f(t) as well as g(t) are selected to be the same as in practical use. Actually, σ_O and ΔT_O in the test condition are not much different from those in practical use, as n is very large. For example, an increment of 20% in σ_O or ΔT_O causes a decrease in the lifetime on the order of two. Hence, the condition is very similar to the practical one.

Evaluation of Equations (3.9.8) and (3.9.9) was accomplished by applying mechanical stress and thermal shock to glass and ceramics by water quenching. Figure 3.9.1 shows some typical examples. The results agree well with the formula, with the exception of the result

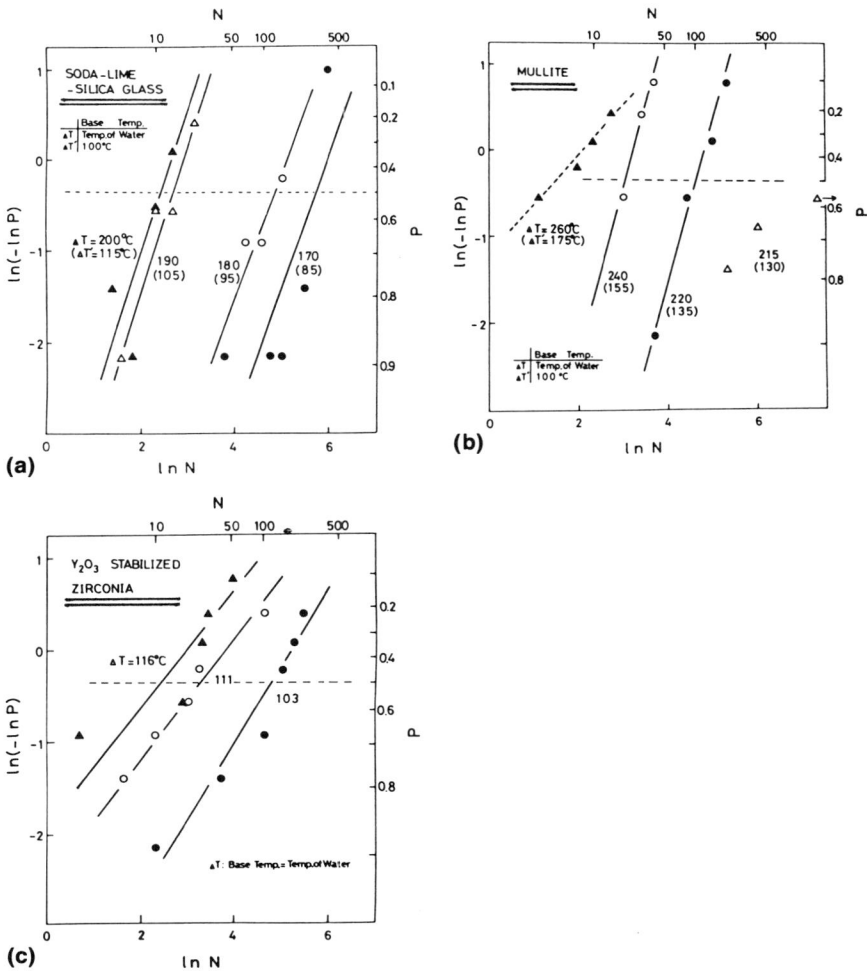

Figure 3.9.1 Survival probability P plotted against fatigue life, N under various thermal shock severities ΔT.

for sintered mullite (Figure 3.9.1b). For mullite the line for $\ln(-\ln P) - \ln N$ has a different inclination for $\Delta T_O = 260°C$. This was not predictable from Equation (3.9.9). This discrepancy is thought to result from heterogeneity in the structure of the sintered mullite and is discussed later. The agreement proves the validity of Equations (3.9.8) and (3.9.9).

In a similar way, thermal fatigue life under mechanical load was studied. The result is expressed as follows:[3]

$$\ln(-\ln P) = \frac{m}{n}\ln N + \frac{m}{n}\sigma_{Mo}$$
$$+ \frac{(n-1)m}{n}\ln(\Delta T) + C \tag{3.9.10}$$

$$1/(n-1) = \sigma_{Mo}/\sigma_{To} \tag{3.9.11}$$

where σ_{Mo}, σ_{To}, and C stand, respectively, for the maximum mechanical stress, the maximum thermal stress, and a constant.

The validity of the formula was proved by quenching glass rods and mullite rods under bending stress. Some examples are given in Figure 3.9.2. Moreover, the maximum thermal stress σ_{To} was estimated from Equations (3.9.10) and (3.9.11). The result agreed with the value calculated on the basis of elastic deformation mechanics com-

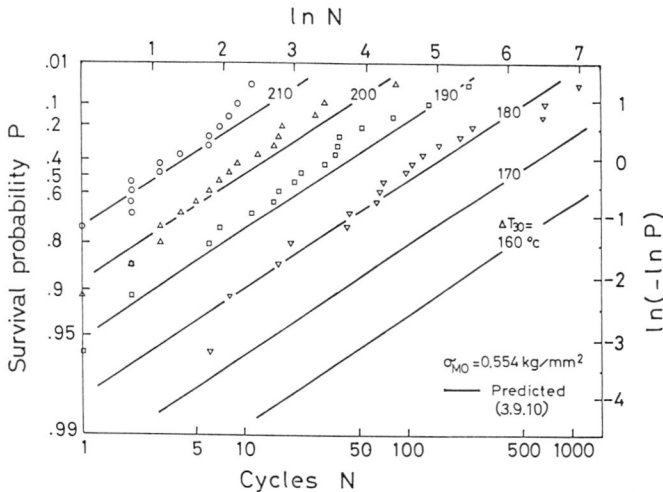

Figure 3.9.2 Survival probability P plotted against fatigue life N under various thermal shock severities ΔT at the stress of $\sigma_{Mo} = 0.554$ Kg/mm².

bined with thermal diffusion theory. The agreement also substantiates the validity of the theory.

3.9.2.2 Heterogeneous System

The theory just mentioned is based on the assumption of homogeneous structure. However, most ceramics are substantially heterogeneous because they contain a boundary phase as well as the matrix. Therefore, some formulation based on a heterogeneous system is needed. This formulation is made using a heterogeneous model composed of two phases of the size of δ_A and δ_B distributed alternatively. As an example, the static fatigue life L_s of a ceramic in which the initial crack length is of the same order as the grain size, and for which condition (3.9.12) is satisfied, is given by Equation (3.9.13):[4]

$$\delta_A / H_A \sigma_0^{nA} \ll \delta_B / H_B \sigma_0^{nB} \qquad (3.9.12)$$

where the subscripts A and B mean that the variable with A or B concerns the phase A or B. And

$$L_s = (\delta_B/\delta_A + \delta_B)(a_i + \delta_B)^{(2-nB)/2}/H_B \sigma_0^{nB} \qquad (3.9.13)$$

Formula (3.9.13) was proven on glass ceramics devitrified at various temperatures. One example is given in Figure 3.9.3. Formula (3.9.12) is substantially the same as Equation (3.9.4) derived for a homogeneous system. Condition (3.9.12) imposed on δ_A, δ_B, and so forth is satisfied in most high-performance ceramics. Hence, prediction of

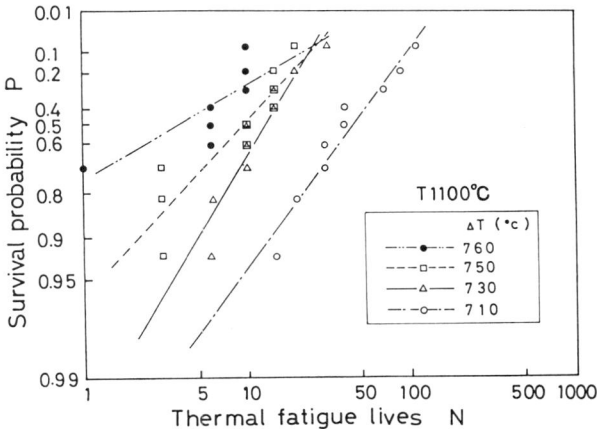

Figure 3.9.3 Survival probability P plotted against fatigue life N under various thermal shock severity ΔT for lithia-glass ceramics devitrified at 1100°C.

lifetime based on Equations (3.9.4) and (3.9.5) is thought to be correct in most cases.

In addition, the analysis of a heterogeneous system reveals that the line $\ln(-\ln P) - \ln N$ changes its slope as the composition or structure changes. This seems to explain the presence of exceptional lines for ceramics composed of glass or crystal, such as sintered mullite and glass ceramics.

3.9.2.3 Flaw Matrix

According to Equations (3.9.4), (3.9.5), and (3.9.13), the following equations hold for homogeneous as well as heterogeneous systems:

$$(N_e/N_n) = (N'_e/N'_n) = (N_{Te}/N_{Tn})$$
$$= (N'_{Te}/N'_{Tn}) = (a_n/a_e)^{(n-2)/2} \quad (3.9.14)$$

where N and N_T stand for fatigue life and thermal fatigue life, subscripts n and e mean that that variable with n or e stands for the life of ceramics with initial crack lengths of a_n or a_e under an arbitrarily given stress, and the prime means that the life is given under another stress. On the basis of fracture mechanics, the flexural strength σ_f as well as short time strength σ_s is related to the initial crack length as follows:

$$(\sigma_{fe}/\sigma_{fn})^{n+1} = (\sigma'_{fe}/\sigma'_{fn})^{n+1}$$
$$= (\sigma_{se}/\sigma_{sn})^{n-2} = (a_n/a_e)^{n-2/2} \quad (3.9.15)$$

where subscripts and primes have the same meaning as in Equation (3.9.14). Then Equations (3.9.14) and (3.9.15) are all equated.

The probability that a ceramic has a lifetime of N_e or N_{Te}, or a

Table 3.9.1 Failure Probability of Ceramics Surviving Proof Test

g \\ k	P_{ug} 0.2	0.3	0.5	0.7	1.0
1.0	5.5E-9	3.2E-7	5.2E-5	1.5E-3	5.3E-2
1.2	3.3E-14	1.9E-12	3.1E-10	9.1E-9	3.2E-7
1.4	9.2E-19	5.3E-17	8.8E-15	2.5E-13	9.0E-12
1.5	8.5E-21	4.9E-19	8.1E-17	2.3E-15	8.3E-14
1.8	3.5E-26	2.0E-24	3.3E-22	9.6E-21	3.4E-19
2.0	2.7E-29	1.6E-27	2.6E-25	7.5E-24	2.6E-22
2.5	6.9E-36	4.0E-34	6.6E-32	1.9E-30	6.8E-29

Note: $EX = 10^x$, $ng = 80$, and $m = 10$.

strength of σ_{fe} and so forth, is identical with the probability that it has a crack of initial crack length a_e, according to Equations (3.9.14) and (3.9.15). Therefore, the following matrix, a "flaw matrix" composed of the variables given in Equations (3.9.14) and (3.9.15) and the probability P_j, with which the crack of a_j occurs, is an invariant against a stressing manner change:[5]

$$
(M) = \begin{pmatrix} P_1 & (\sigma_{f1}/\sigma_{fm})^{n+1} \\ P_2 & (\sigma_{f2}/\sigma_{fm})^{n+1} \\ \cdot & \cdot \\ \cdot & \cdot \\ \cdot & \cdot \\ P_m & 1 \\ \cdot & \cdot \\ \cdot & \cdot \\ \cdot & \cdot \\ P_z & (\sigma_{fz}/\sigma_{fm})^{n+1} \end{pmatrix} = \begin{pmatrix} P_1 & N_1/N_m \\ P_2 & N_2/N_m \\ \cdot & \cdot \\ \cdot & \cdot \\ \cdot & \cdot \\ P_m & 1 \\ \cdot & \cdot \\ \cdot & \cdot \\ \cdot & \cdot \\ P_z & N_z/N_m \end{pmatrix}
$$

$$
= \begin{pmatrix} P_1 & N_{T1}/N_{Tm} \\ P_2 & N_{T2}/N_{Tm} \\ \cdot & \cdot \\ \cdot & \cdot \\ \cdot & \cdot \\ P_m & 1 \\ \cdot & \cdot \\ \cdot & \cdot \\ \cdot & \cdot \\ P_z & N_{Tz}/N_{Tm} \end{pmatrix} = \begin{pmatrix} \cdots \end{pmatrix} \tag{3.9.16}
$$

The matrix depends only on the distribution of the initial crack length. Determination of one of the values of N, σ_f, and so on enables prediction of lifetime under arbitrary stress for an arbitrary probability value by means of the matrix. The merit of the matrix lies in the fact that it does not assume any type of distribution in strength and other properties.

Testing the matrix by placing glass rods and stabilized zirconia under mechanical and thermal stress established its validity.

The matrix proves the validity of the tests made on the basis of experience, as mentioned earlier, as it shows that long-life ceramics have high strength. As an example, the matrixes for stabilized test-tube-type zirconia (O_2-sensor) are given in Figure 3.9.4 for thermal shock severity and survival probability when heating and cooling by air. The two matrixes are nearly the same.

$$
(M)1 = \begin{pmatrix}
0.1 & 0.75 \\
0.2 & 0.82 \\
0.3 & 0.89 \\
0.4 & 0.95 \\
0.5 & 1.00 \\
0.6 & 1.04 \\
0.7 & 1.09 \\
0.8 & 1.12 \\
0.9 & 1.16
\end{pmatrix}
\qquad
(M)2 = \begin{pmatrix}
0.1 & 0.71 \\
0.2 & 0.80 \\
0.3 & 0.89 \\
0.4 & 0.94 \\
0.5 & 1.00 \\
0.6 & 1.06 \\
0.7 & 1.09 \\
0.8 & 1.14 \\
0.9 & 1.17
\end{pmatrix}
$$

Heating   Cooling

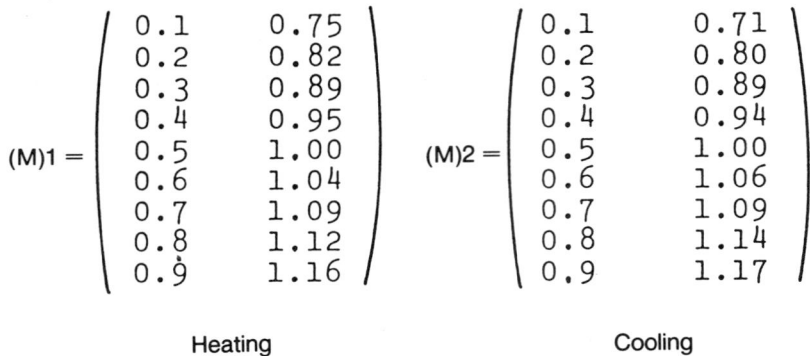

Figure 3.9.4 Flaw matrixes for zirconia O_2-sensor: $(M)_1$ for heating; $(M)_2$ for cooling.

3.9.2.4 Failure Probability After Proof Test

Proof testing is useful for improving the reliability of ceramics and the failure probability after the test was studied by Evans and Fuller.[6-8] However, some aspects of the test are still unknown, especially the failure probability of the ceramics that survived the test in relation to the safety factor for the test. The safety factor is defined as the ratio of the proof stress to the minimum stress required for a ceramic to possess the lifetime required for practical use, σ_g. These have been studied by the present author and co-workers on the assumption of a Weibull distribution for fracture stress.

On the basis of fracture mechanics, the failure probability, P_{ug}, is given as a function of the safety factor k as follows:[9]

$$P_{ug} = -(m/2)[1 - \{1 + k^{2-n_s}\}^{-2/n_s-2}] \ln P_{gk}$$

$$P_{gk} = \exp\left[-\{\Gamma(m + 1/m)kg\}^m\right]$$

(3.9.17)

where n_g, T, and g stand, respectively, for the value of n at the critical stress intensity factor, the gamma function, and the ratio of σ_g to the mean fracture stress, $\sigma(g = \sigma_g/\overline{\sigma})$. As seen from Equation (3.9.17), P_{ug} decreases with k, depending on m, g, and n_g. One example of the calculation of P_{ug} is given in Table 3.9.1 for typical values of n_g, m, and g. The minimum value is less than 1 ppm in the example. Numerical calculation of Equation (3.9.17) shows that the probability is 1 ppm or less for the value of k over a wide range of n, m, and g and that the value ranges from 1.2 to 1.8. Therefore, a safety factor of 1.2 to 1.5 is enough for high reliability in a ceramic. The calculation also shows that $k = 1$ is not enough for achieving a probability of 1 ppm, which is needed for automotive components. The study proves the possibility of achieving highly reliable ceramics with a probability of failure of 1 ppm by proof test.

Okuda and Ito[10] also studied the lifetime of ceramics under cyclic load after proof test. They showed that ceramics have lifetimes longer than a certain value, depending on the peak level of the cyclic load, and that the minimum value decreases with the peak level. This follows the prediction formula made on the basis of fracture mechanics.

Proof testing is applied to many practical components such as zirconia O_2-sensor in Nippon Denso Co., Ltd., and high reliability is achieved.

3.9.3 Distribution of Fracture Stress

Many authors have studied the distribution of ceramic fracture stress. In these studies a Weibull distribution is assumed in most cases, and the distribution has proved to represent the actual distribution rather well; however, the data for lower stress are known to deviate from this distribution. Recently, Kase proposed to study the distribution using a double exponential-type function.[11] He made an analysis of the fracture stress of hot-pressed Si_3N_4 (given by Ito and co-workers[12]) on the basis of the distribution, and showed that the distribution represents the actual data well. Analysis using this distribution is now being conducted in Japan.

Analysis based on multi-modal Weibull distributions,[13] including the bi-model one, is also being studied.[14-16] In addition, the location (surface or volume) of the flaw responsible for failure of some ceramics is being determined.

Kamiya and the present author[17] studied the method to more accurately estimate the statistical parameters of Weibull distribution of fracture stress by a computer simulation in a manner similar to that studied by Trustrum and Jayatilaka.[18] By using random numbers and assumed Weibull parameters, a computer developed 1000 groups of fracture stress. In these data the value of the cumulative probability of failure for a given rank is fixed because the sample size determines the probability for each rank. The value of the stress, however, scatters. Scattering is much more likely for a sample deviating far from the mode than for one near the mode, as sample density is high near the mode. Therefore, a datum deviated far from the mode is less valuable for parameter estimation than one near the mode. Hence, omitting the data of less value is expected to result in more accurate estimation of parameters. According to the study, omitting about 2% of the samples, those which are the smallest or the largest and their neighbors, is the best for accurate estimation. Moreover, the sample size needs to be 40 or more for accurate estimation. Analysis by this method results in an accuracy of about 10–15% for the estimation of the Weibull parameters m and $\bar{\sigma}$.

3.9.4 Conclusion

The studies discussed in this section are thought to be useful for improving the reliability of ceramics. With these results, the application of ceramics is expected to be extended to include more varied engineering parts, such as automobile engine components and machining tools.

References

1. Evans, A. G., *Fracture Mechanics of Ceramics I*. New York: Plenum Press, 1976, p. 17.
2. Kamiya, N., and Kamigaito, O., *J. Mat. Sci.* 14:573 (1979).
3. Kamiya, N., and Kamigaito, O., *J. Mat. Sci.* 17:3149 (1982).
4. Kamiya, N., and Kamigaito, O., *J. Mat. Sci.* (forthcoming).
5. Kamiya, N., and Kamigaito, O., *Internat. J. Fatigue* (forthcoming).
6. Evans, A. G., and Fuller, E. R., *Mat. Trans.* 5:27 (1974).
7. Ritter, J. E., Jr., Oates, P. B., Fuller, E. R., Jr., and Wiederhorn, S. M., *J. Mat. Sci.* 15:2275 (1980).
8. Fuller Jr., E. R., Wiederhorn, S. M., Ritter Jr., J. E., and Oates, P. B., *J. Mat. Sci.* 15:2282 (1980).
9. Kamigaito, O., and Kamiya, N., *J. Ceram. Soc. Jpn.* (forthcoming).
10. Okuda, H., and Ito, M., *News from Government Industrial Research Institute, Nagoya* 372 (1983).
11. Kase, S., *Ceramics Japan* 17:545 (1982).
12. Ito, S., Sakai, S., and Ito, M., *J. Soc. Mat. Sci. Jpn.* 30:1019 (1981).
13. Bolotin, V. V., *Statistical Methods in Structural Mechanics*. New York: Holden-Day, 1969, p. 64.

14. Matsuo, Y., and Sato, H., *Trans. Jpn. Soc. Mech. Eng.* 45-390A:171 (1979).

15. Matsuo, Y., *Trans. Jpn. Soc. Mech. Eng.* 46-406A:605 (1980).

16. Matsuo, Y., Paper presented at the Symposium of the Japanese Society of Mechanical Engineers, Japan, 1982, p. 51.

17. Kamiya, N., and Kamigaito, O., *J. Mat. Sci.* (forthcoming).

18. Trustrum, K., and Jayatilaka, A. D., *J. Mat. Sci.* 14:1080 (1979).

CHAPTER

4

ELECTRONIC CERAMICS

4.1 Overview

Hiroaki Yanagida

The development of fine ceramics is encouraged by latent but potential needs for functional materials to be used in information-communication media, high-temperature machines, precision machinery, and bio-implants. All four fields are now experiencing very rapid growth; the first is the most prominent in Japan. Although recent attention has been focused on the other fields, this field's share in fine ceramics and its average growth rate is around 25% per year.

There are three reasons for the remarkable development of electronic ceramics in Japan. First, the rapid growth of the electronics industry has created an intense requirement for better electronics materials. Second, the Japanese have shown an impressive aptitude for technology and are skilled in the fine arts. Third, education and training have made it possible for people to respond quickly to rapidly changing requirements.

In the development of electronic ceramics technology, ultra-high purity of starting materials and precise mixing technologies were first achieved. Then precise shaping and machining technologies were developed, and the ability to accurately reproduce quality and shape even in the case of very tiny specimens was acquired. Finally, various methods for producing the desired components were introduced.

239

Table 4.1.1 Classification of Electronic Ceramics

Functions	Material and Its State[a]	Applications
Insulation	Al_2O_3 (st, sc) SiC(+BeO, st) C (diamond, sc, fl)	IC substrate
Dielectricity	$BaTiO_3$(st)	Capacitor
Piezoelectricity	$Pb(Zr_xTi_{1-x})O3$ (st, pl) ZnO (fl, or) SiO_2 (sc) PZT (pd, embedded in PVDF)	Piezolighter, piezofilter, Surface wave transducer, Piezo-vibrator Flexible piezodetector
Pyroelectricity	PZT (sc, pl)	IR detector
Ferroelectricity	PLZT (sc, pl)	Optical shutter, Optical memory
Semiconducting	SiC (st), $LaCrO_3$ (st) SnO_2 (st, po) Transient metal oxides (st) $ZnO(+Bi_2O_3$, st) $BaTiO_3(+La_2O_3$, st)	Heater, electrode Gas defector Thermistor Varistor PTC-thermistor
Ionic conduction	β-Al_2O_3 (st) $ZrO_2(+Y_2O_3$, st)	Na-S battery O_2-sensor

Electron emitting	LaB_6 (sc)	Electron beam cathode
Luminescence	Y_2O_2S:Eu (pd) ThO_2:Nd (st) Al_2O_3:Cr (sc)	Cathode luminescence IR laser VL laser
Translusence	Al_2O_3(+MgO, st) SnO_2 (fl)	Na-lamp tube Translucent electrode
Polarization	PLZT (st, pl)	Optical shutter
Unharmonic oscillation	$Ba_2Na\ Nb_5O_{15}$ (sc)	IR detector
Reflection	SnO_2 (fl) TiO_2 (fl) Ferrite (fl)	Energy-saving plate glass
Light guide	SiO_2 (fb) SiO_2-GeO_2 (fb)	Optical communication fiber
Soft magnetism	$Zn_{1-x}Mn_xFe_2O_4$ (st, sc) γ-FE_2O_3 (pd)	Magnet cove, magnet head Magnetic tape
Hard magnetism	$SrO\cdot6Fe_2O_3$ (st) $SrO\cdot6Fe_2O_3$ (pd, embedded in gum)	Magnet Magnet seal

[a] fb: fiber, fl: film, po: preferred orientation, pd: powder, pl: polarized, po: porous, sc: single crystal, st: sintered body

These efforts were supported by application and trials of the various materials made, and by well-established control technologies for crystal structure, grain boundary, vacancy, and surface structures.

The properties of ceramics thus obtained are of a wide variety and are very precise. This great variety is indicated in Table 4.1.1. As detailed explanations of the various kinds of materials appear in the following sections of this chapter, only a few major points will be discussed here.

Insulation requirements are being met with sintered bodies of alumina, an area well developed in Japan. Very precise shaping and quick response to the needs of the electronics industry have been the keys to the development of these integrated circuit (IC) substrates. Recently, however, requirements have arisen for better heat-conducting substrates than those of alumina. Single-crystal alumina (sapphire) is sometimes used as silicon on sapphire (SOS) substrates, and paths for enforced heat elimination are sometimes provided.

There are two promising candidates to fill the need for better heat-conducting materials than alumina. One is hot-pressed silicon carbide with a small amount of beryllia as a sintering aid. The sintered body is electrically an insulator but thermally an excellent heat conductor. The other is diamond film obtained through a chemical vapor dispersion (CVD) method, with a film shape sufficient for a substrate. Diamond is the best heat conductor if it is very pure.

Capacitors with multilayer structures have been developed recently that require a high and sophisticated level of technology in the fabrication process. In another area, piezoelectric ceramics are now the key components of electronic apparatus for television, FM radio, and the like.

Pyroelectric ceramics are used as infrared (IR) detectors of obstacles in guard systems. Various other kinds of semiconducting ceramics have also been developed. Examples are lanthanum chromite heating elements, semiconductor-type gas sensors, and zinc oxide varistors. Research has also been done and progress made on working mechanisms for semiconductor-type gas sensors.

Progress has been made in still other areas. A number of ionic conductors have recently been developed. Advances have been made in color television through development of high-quality phosphors such as $Y_2O_2S:Eu$. Sodium lamps with translucent alumina tubes are now being commercially produced and used on highways. Light guides made of very pure silica are being tested for practical use. Optical communication systems using optical fibers have now been designed and constructed, and there has been substantial growth in magnetic tapes for home video use. These developments reflect how keen ceramic scientists in Japan are to find and develop new functional materials for use in future electronic devices.

The Japanese Ministry of Education, Science, and Culture helped promote this drive by sponsoring a three-year (1982–1984) research project entitled "Functional Ceramics" to stimulate research in universities. The sections in this chapter, most of which deal with electronics ceramics, represent the fruits of this effort.

References

1. *Reports for Development in Technologies and Applications of Fine Ceramics,* Japan Society for Fine Ceramics, April, 1983.
2. Yanagida, H., ed., *Fine Ceramics.* Ohm-Co. Ltd., 1982, pp. 5–6.
3. Development by Hitachi Lab. of Hitachi Co., Ltd. News appeared in *Bull. Ceram. Soc. Jpn.* 16(4):273 (1981), ref. 2., p. 213.
4. Developed by National Institute for Researchers in Inorganic Materials (Tsukuba). Oral presentation at the Annual Meeting of the Ceramic Society of Japan, Kyoto, 1982.
5. Yanagida, H., and Koizumi, M., *Am. Ceram. Soc. Bull.* 61(9):929 (1982).

4.2 Ceramic Substrates

Mitsuru Ura

4.2.1 Introduction

Ceramic substrates have been used often for hybrid integrated circuits (HICs) and for the packaging of semiconductor IC chips. The market for these ceramic substrates has enlarged in recent years with the development of the electronics industry.

The following characteristics are required of ceramic substrates: good electrical insulation, high thermal conductivity, mechanical strength, chemical stability, and a thermal expansion coefficient near that of semiconductor silicon. At present, alumina (Al_2O_3) has been the principal ceramic substrate because it satisfies most of these requirements and its cost is relatively low.

The need to reduce the size and weight of HICs has resulted in improved packing density, and the integration density of semiconductor ICs (LSIs, VLSIs) has also been improved. These factors have resulted in an increase in the density and amount of circuit heat generation. Consequently, the thermal conductivity and thermal expansion coefficient of alumina are no longer suitable. In package systems using conventional alumina ceramics, damage and failures have become significant problems. To solve these problems, considerable effort has been devoted to the development of new ceramics superior to alumina.

Beryllium oxide (BeO, beryllia) is well known as a ceramic having high thermal conductivity, about eight times as high as that of alumina (99%) ceramics. The thermal expansion of BeO ceramics, however, is nearly twice as large as that of semiconductor silicon. Therefore, mounting an LSI of large chip size on a BeO substrate induces a large strain on soldered parts. This causes significant problems such as chip cracks and fatigue ruptures. Aluminum nitride (AlN) ceramics have also been examined for purposes similar to those just discussed, as their thermal conductivity is considerably lower than that of BeO ceramics. In addition, a diamond film prepared by CVD has been studied.[1] There are several remaining problems with this film, however, such as film quality, affinity with substrate material, and thermal conduction of the substrate. Because the thermal expansion coefficient of diamond is about half that of silicon, the problem of strain induced by mismatching with LSI chips is significant in the same manner as with BeO ceramics.

Against this background, a new silicon carbide (SiC) ceramic has been developed recently which has higher thermal conductivity than aluminum metal, a thermal expansion coefficient nearly equal to that of semiconductor silicon, and good electrical insulation.[2-4] It has been thought difficult to obtain both high thermal conductivity and electrical insulation properties in the same material. This new ceramic, named "Hitaceram SC-101," is being sold by Hitachi, Ltd.

In the sections that follow, the production method, characteristics, mechanism causing high thermal conductivity and high electrical insulation, and some sample applications of new SiC ceramics are introduced.

4.2.2 Highly Thermally Conductive and Electrically Insulating SiC Ceramics

4.2.2.1 Fabrication Process

New SiC ceramics were fabricated from α-SiC powder and a small amount of beryllia (BeO) powder. The α-SiC powder used was a commercially available abrasive powder that had an average grain size of 2 μm. After pure BeO fine powder as a sintering aid was added to the SiC powder, the composite was mixed and prepressed. The green body was set in graphite dies of the hot-pressing furnace and pressed at a load of 30 MPa. Then the furnace was evacuated to a pressure of 1–10 MPa. Hot pressing was carried out at 2050°C for 1 hour. After hot pressing, the sintered body was taken out of the graphite dies, and the surface was ground with a diamond tool. The relative density of the sintered body was usually above 99% of the theoretical density of SiC.

4.2.2.2 Characteristics

The new SiC ceramics consist of pyramidal grains whose sizes are uniformly distributed around the mean value of 5 μm. An observation with a high-resolution transmission electron microscope (HRTEM) indicated that no grain boundary phase exists at most of the boundaries, even at the resolution range where a 0.25-nm lattice image of β-SiC is observed. The sintered material consists mostly of 6H-SiC grains with small amounts of polytypes 4H and 15R.

Table 4.2.1 summarizes thermal conductivity, the thermal expansion coefficient, electrical resistivity, and the dielectric constant of the new SiC ceramics, together with the properties of other substances for comparison. Thermal conductivity at room temperature is 270 W/mK, higher than that of aluminum and about 16 times higher than that of alumina (92%) ceramics. The mean thermal expansion coefficient in a temperature range from 0 to 400°C is 3.7×10^{-6}/K, nearly equal to that of silicon single crystals used in semiconductor devices.

4.2.2.3 Mechanism of High Thermal Conductivity

Single-crystal SiC of high purity is well known to have the highest thermal conductivity of all ceramic materials except diamond.[5] The conventional SiC sintered body for use as a structural material has a large porosity, many impurities, and lattice defects. These scatter phonons of the heat carrier and inhibit heat conduction. In the new SiC ceramics, the sintered material with a small amount of BeO additive produces high density and few impurities or lattice defects to act as a phonon-scattering center.

Figure 4.2.1 is a transmission electron microphotograph of a region near the small-angle grain boundary where two basal planes of 6H-SiC encounter each other. In this specimen, both basal planes are parallel to the incident electron beam. At the boundary, the lattice images of the grains are observed to be connected continuously, dis-

Table 4.2.1 Properties of New SiC Ceramics and Various Materials

Material	Thermal Conductivity (W/m·K)	Thermal Expansion Coefficient[a] ($\times 10^{-6}$/K)	Electrical Resistivity ($\Omega \cdot$ cm)	Dielectric Constant at 1 MHz
New SiC	270	3.7	$>10^{13}$	45, 15[b]
Structural SiC	60–80	4.2	$<10^{3}$	—
BeO (99.5%)	240	7.5	$>10^{14}$	6.7
Al$_2$O$_3$ (92%)	17	6.5	$>10^{14}$	8.5
AlN	100	4.5	$>10^{14}$	8.8
Al	239	26.5	2.7×10^{-6}	—
Si	125	3.5	10^{-3}–10^{3}	12

[a] 0–400°C
[b] 1 GHz

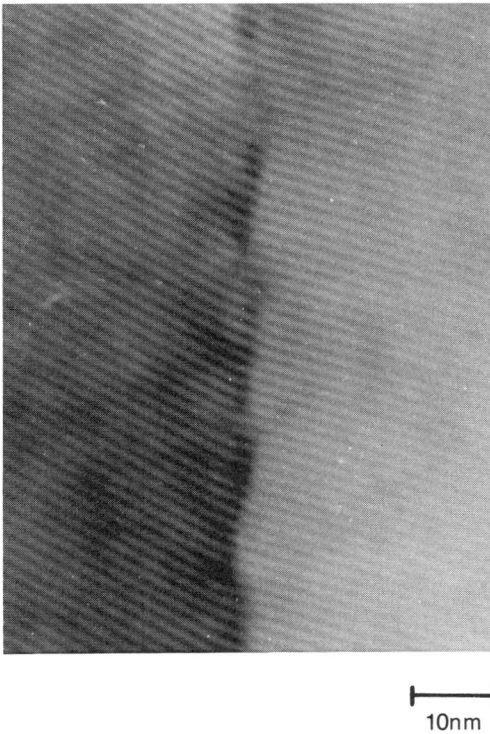

Figure 4.2.1 TEM micrograph of a grain boundary where two basal planes of 6H-SiC meet at a small angle. The lattice images of the 6H-SiC grains are observed.

tributing edge dislocations in some places. This means that an epitaxial growth occurs at the grain boundary to reject the existence of the second phase. The regular pattern of the lattice image in the grain indicates that few lattice defects exist in this material.

On the basis of this description, the mechanism for the high thermal conductivity of the new SiC ceramics is interpreted as follows. The sintered body has few phonon-scattering centers such as impurities and defects (pore, vacancy, dislocation, and inclusion). Thus, the sintered material has an intrinsic thermal conductivity like that of a single crystal.

4.2.2.4 Electrical Properties of the Intra- and Inter-Grain[3]

One of the features of the new SiC ceramics is high electrical insulation; their resistivity is higher than $10^{13}\Omega \cdot cm$. Electrical insulation of

a sintered material should be caused either by the high insulation of the grain of the sintered body, as with cases of alumina and beryllia, or by the high resistive barrier in the vicinity of a grain boundary. To ascertain the high resistance property, it is necessary to measure electrical resistance at the grain boundary and within the grain. Figure 4.2.2 is a schematic of the geometry of the micro-electrodes on the surface of the new SiC ceramics. The micro-electrodes were prepared by photolithography of an evaporated aluminum film. Figure 4.2.3 shows the measured results of current characteristics versus voltage (I-V) between each pair of electrodes; (a) corresponds to the case when two electrodes (1) and (4) located within the same grain exhibit ohmic characteristics and have a low resistivity. In this case, resistivity is assumed to be about $20\Omega \cdot$ cm, assuming that the grain shape is a cube of about 5 μm. Figure 4.2.3b, the case in which a grain boundary is located between the two electrodes (2) and (3), shows varistor characteristics with a breakdown voltage of about 5 V. These experimental results suggest that the electrical insulation in the new SiC ceramics is induced mainly by the existence of the potential barrier in the vicinity of the grain boundaries.

Two possible cases are considered in the interpretation of high electrical resistivity at the grain boundaries. One is that barriers may be formed by thin insulating layers located at the grain boundaries, and the other is that depletion layers are formed on both sides of the

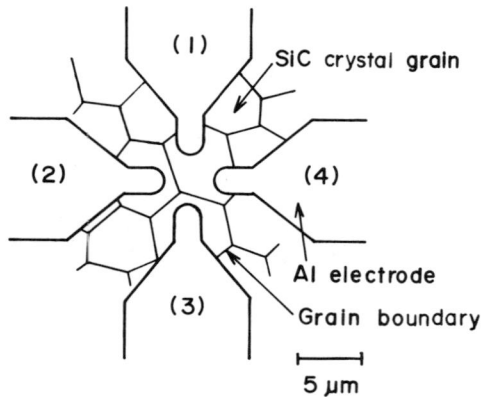

Figure 4.2.2 Schematic of the aluminum micropattern electrodes on the surface of the new SiC ceramics. Electrodes (1) and (4) are located within the same grain; electrodes (2) and (3) have a grain boundary.

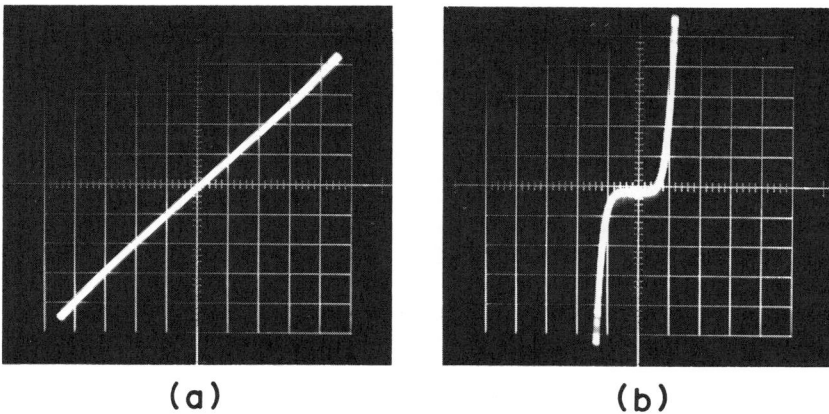

(a)　　　　　　　　　　(b)

Figure 4.2.3 I-V characteristics measured with microelectrodes shown in Figure 4.2.2. (a) The case without any grain boundary between electrodes (1) and (4) (X: 2 V/div.; Y: 50 μA/div.); (b) the case with a grain boundary between electrodes (2) and (3) (X: 5 V/div.; Y: 1 μA/div.).

grain boundaries by carriers trapped at the grain boundaries. With regard to the former model, as previously described, the second phase has not been observed. This suggests that the latter model is adequate. In this case, the width of the depletion layer varies with the applied voltage, and the capacitance of a specimen usually decreases with applied voltage. The relationship of the capacitance and the applied voltage is expressed by the following equation:[6]

$$(1/C - 1/2C_0)^2 = 2/\epsilon e^2 nd^2 \, (\phi + edV) \qquad (4.2.1)$$

where C is the capacitance per unit area and unit thickness of a specimen, ϵ is the permittivity of SiC (9.8 ϵ_0), e is the electron charge, n is the free carrier density, ϕ is the barrier height, d is the grain size, and V is the applied voltage per unit thickness. C_0 is the value of C when V = 0. The left side of Equation (4.2.1), $(1/C - 1/2C_0)^2$, versus the electric field is plotted in Figure 4.2.4. The result shows a linear relation. This indicates that the relation of Equation (4.2.1) holds very well. From these results, it is reasonable to conclude that the depletion layers created near grain boundaries may be the cause of the barriers, as with zinc oxide varistors.

Both the free carrier density n in grains and the grain size d are calculated from slope a of the straight line and value b of the inter-

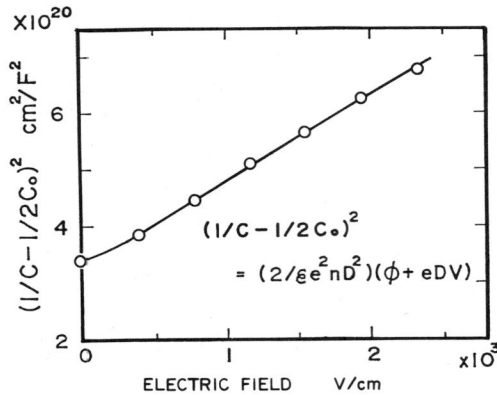

Figure 4.2.4 The electric field dependence of the capacitance plotted as $(1/C - 1/2C_0)^2$ versus the applied field.

secting point on the ordinate in Figure 4.2.4:

$$d = \phi a/eb \qquad (4.2.2)$$

$$n = 2b/\epsilon\phi a \qquad (4.2.3)$$

Assuming ϕ equals the activation energy of 0.8 eV, the grain size d is estimated from Equation (4.2.2) to be 4 μm, which is consistent with the mean grain size obtained from the microstructure observation. The carrier concentration n is estimated to be about $4 \times 10^{17} \mathrm{cm}^{-3}$ from Equation (4.2.3). This value is in agreement with the solubility of Be atoms in SiC around 2050°C, $10^{17} - 10^{18} \mathrm{cm}^{-3}$.[7] This value is 2–4 orders smaller than the solubility of boron (B) or aluminum (Al), which is used as an additive for SiC ceramics for structural material. It is known that in zinc oxide varistors the barrier height ϕ is increased as the carrier concentration in the grain is decreased.[8] The new SiC ceramics are also considered to behave similarly.

4.2.2.5 Applications

The new SiC ceramics are highly suitable materials as packing substrates for semiconductor devices — for example, as a packaging substrate for the high heat generation of the super high-speed logic LSIs used in large-scale computers,[9] a heat sink substrate for the high-reliability semiconductor laser diodes applied in optical communcation,[10] the microwave power transistors used in moving vehicle telecommunication instruments such as car telephones, and for IMPATT diodes. These ceramics are also suitable as a substrate in HIC and power modules used in control and power circuits, and as a core material for the precise resistors used in measurement instruments. As discussed earlier, these ceramics are expected to contribute to extended design flexibility and to improved reliability in the package system of semiconductor devices that will lead to higher overall performance.

References

1. Spitsyn, B. V., Bouilov, L. L., and Derjaguin, B. V., *J. Cryst. Growth* 52:219 (1981).
2. Ura, M., *Ceramic Data Book '82*, Kogyoseihin Gijutsu Kyokai, Tokyo, 1982, p. 90.
3. Maeda, K., Miyoshi, T., Takeda, Y., Nakamura, K., Ogihara, S., and Ura, M., *Proc. International Symposium on Grain Boundaries and Interfaces in Ceramics, Annual Meeting, American Ceramics Society*, Cincinnati, 1982.
4. Ogihara, S., Maeda, K., Takeda, Y., Nakamura, K., and Ura, M., *High Thermal Conductivity and High Electrical Resistivity in SiC Ceramics Containing BeO as Additives, 85th Annual Meeting, American Ceramics Society*, Chicago, 1983.
5. Slack, G. A., *J. Phys. Chem. Sol.* 34:321 (1973).
6. Mukae, K., Tuda, K., and Nagasawa, I., *J. Appl. Phys.* 50:4475 (1979).
7. Vodakov, Y. A., and Mokhov, E. N., *Proc. 3rd SiC Conference*, 1973, p. 508.
8. Miyoshi, T., Maeda, K., Takahashi, K. and Yamazaki, T., *Advances in Ceramics*, vol. 1. American Ceramics Society, 1981, p. 309.
9. Usami, M., Hosokawa, S., Anzai, A., Otsuka, K., Masaki, A., Murata, S., Ura, M., and Nakagawa, M., *Proc. 1983 IEEE International Conference on Computer Design*, New York, 1983, p. 275.
10. Tuji, S., Mizuishi, K., Nakayama, Y., Shimaoka, M., and Hirao, M., *Jpn. J. Appl. Phys.* 22:239 (1982).

4.3 Piezoelectric and Pyroelectric Ceramics

Kikuo Wakino

4.3.1 Introduction

After the fundamental studies on lead zirconate titanate $Pb(Zr, Ti)O_3$ by Shirane and co-workers[1-2] and by Sawaguchi,[3] its high potentialities as an electromechanical transducer were discovered by Jaffe and co-workers.[4] Since then, various modifications of Pb(Zr, Ti)O$_3$ have been extensively investigated to improve the properties for various practical applications, including vibrators, filters, pick-up elements, buzzers, speakers, piezoelectric sparkplugs, resonators, ultrasonic delaying devices, and ultrasonic testing systems. These applications have been for the most part successful.

Pyroelectric or ferroelectric crystal gives rise to a pyroelectric signal, depending on the rate of change in its temperature. Both piezoelectric and pyroelectric ceramics are discussed in detail in the sections that follow.

4.3.2 Piezoelectric Ceramics

Although the high-performance character of lead zirconate titanate ceramics has provided many useful applications, more and more special requirements must be met, including higher mechanical quality, more stable temperature characteristics, better performance up to higher frequency, and larger anisotropy in electromechanical coupling. To meet these requirements, widely ranging developmental work, from raw material and processing to product design, has occurred in the following areas:

1. Improvement of Pb(Zr, Ti)O$_3$ ceramics by modification with additives and new processing methods.
2. Development of anisotropic materials such as PbTiO$_3$, PbNb$_2$O$_6$, Bi layer structure-type compounds and SbSI, all of which have sintering problems.
3. Development of piezoelectric thin films such as ZnO, AlN, and PbTiO$_3$ and their high-frequency applications.
4. Development of composites with plastic material for flexible, high-compliance transducers.
5. Multilayer structures for more highly sensitive electromechanical transducers.

4.3.2.1 Pb(Zr, Ti)O$_3$

Complex perovskite compounds — for instance, Pb(Mg$_{1/3}$Nb$_{2/3}$)O$_3$ — were first reported by Smolenskii and Agranovskaya,[5] and multiple systems such as Pb(Mg$_{1/3}$Nb$_{2/3}$)O$_3$-PbZrO$_3$-PbTiO$_3$ were developed thereafter.[6] These works extended the variety of compositions with useful piezoelectric properties.

The properties of PbZrO$_3$-PbTiO$_3$ in solid solution are widely

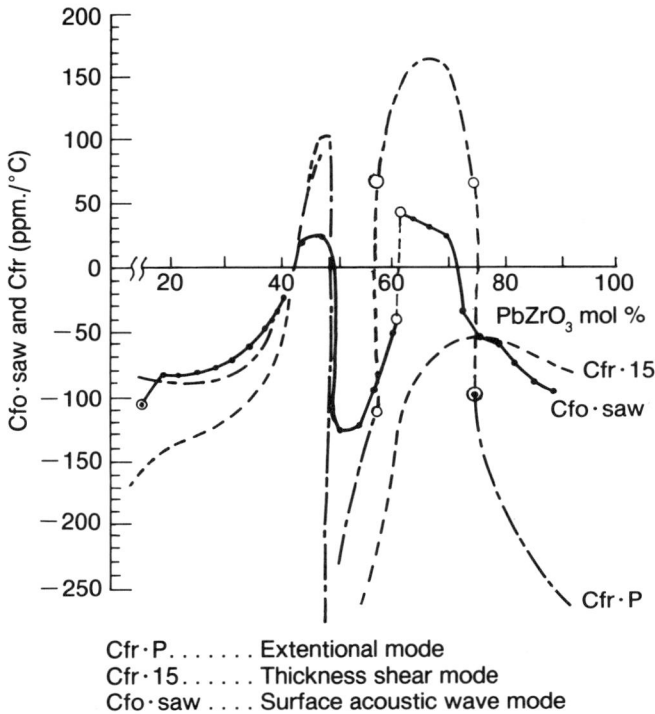

Cfr·P . . . . Extentional mode
Cfr·15 . . . . . . Thickness shear mode
Cfo·saw . . . . Surface acoustic wave mode

Figure 4.3.1 Dependency of temperature coefficient of resonant frequency on the molar ratio $PbZrO_3/PbTiO_3$ in $Pb(Zr, Ti)O_3$.

varied by changing the molar ratio, additives, manufacturing procedures, and so on. The resonance frequency-temperature coefficient can be controlled by adjusting the $PbZrO_3/PbTiO_3$ molar ratio in a $PbZrO_3$-$PbTiO_3$ binary system, as shown in Figure 4.3.1.[7]

In the case of high-frequency applications, such as resonators and surface acoustic wave (SAW) devices, piezoelectric ceramics must be particularly voidless and uniform. In voidless fine ceramics, extra attention is given to such points as (1) adjusted composition, fine particle size, and complete dispersion throughout the material; (2) uniform dense packing of the green body, and (3) atmospheric composition and its pressure control in the sintering process.

4.3.2.2 PbTiO₃

Because $PbTiO_3$ material has useful features such as a low dielectric constant (~ 190), high thickness mode coupling factor, high mechanical quality factor, high stability, and high Curie temperature ($\sim 490°C$), it is a desirable stable piezoelectric material for high-frequency and high-temperature applications. Initially, ceramics of high $PbTiO_3$ content were very porous and fragile because of the strong spontaneous strain occurring at their cubic-tetragonal transition. Moreover, their resistivity was insufficient for polling treatment against the high coercive field.

The creations of cation vacancies in $PbTiO_3$ resulting from a small substitution of Nb^{5+} or Ta^{5+} for Ti^{4+} are effective in producing strong, relatively dense ($\sim 90\%$ theoretical) $PbTiO_3$ ceramics.[8]

Modified $PbTiO_3$ ceramics incorporated with 2.5 mol% La_2O_3 and 1.0 mol% MnO_2 having a dielectric permittivity of $\epsilon_{33}^T/\epsilon_0$ 170, a coupling factor K_{33} of 0.46, and Q_m of 1100 were investigated.[9] This resulted in the successful development of ceramic very-high-frequency (VHF) resonators.[10]

Because of their small Poisson's ratio, $PbTiO_3$ ceramics are capable of trapping vibrational energy at the third harmonic mode and suppressing undesirable modes, such as spurious modes. They are thus suitable for high-frequency resonators.[11]

The near-zero temperature resonance coefficient frequency, as low as that of AT-cut quartz, is produced by adjusting the La content by substituting it for Pb. Furthermore, these modified ceramics are dense and easily sintered because of a decrease in crystal deformation.[12]

Properties such as velocities and electromechanical coupling factors for bulk waves and SAWs of the ceramic system (Pb, Ln)(Ti, Mn, In)O_3 vary monotonically with the ionic size of the rare earth element Ln. Very small temperature coefficients of SAW delay time, less than $1 \times 10^{-6}/°C$, occur over the wide temperature range of -10 to $60°C$ in the composition of $(Pb_{1-(3/2)x+(1/2)z}Nd_x)$ $(Ti_{1-y-z}Mn_yIn_z)O_3$.[13]

In contrast, the lowest temperature coefficient of radial mode resonance frequencies, less than $1 \times 10^{-6}/°C$, occurs over the temperature range of -10 to $+50°C$ in the composition $(Pb_{0.91}La_{0.04}Nd_{0.04})(Ti_{0.92}Mn_{0.02}In_{0.06})$, as shown in Figure 4.3.2.[14] These stable piezoelectric ceramics are potential materials for resonator and filter applications.

The system (Pb, Ca)[Ti, $(Co_{1/2}W_{1/2})$]O_3 + MnO, NiO, which has a large electromechanical coupling factor ratio (K_t/K_p larger than 10), was especially investigated for application as an array-type ultrasonic transducer in ultrasonic testing medical systems such as the ultrasonic reflectoscope.[15]

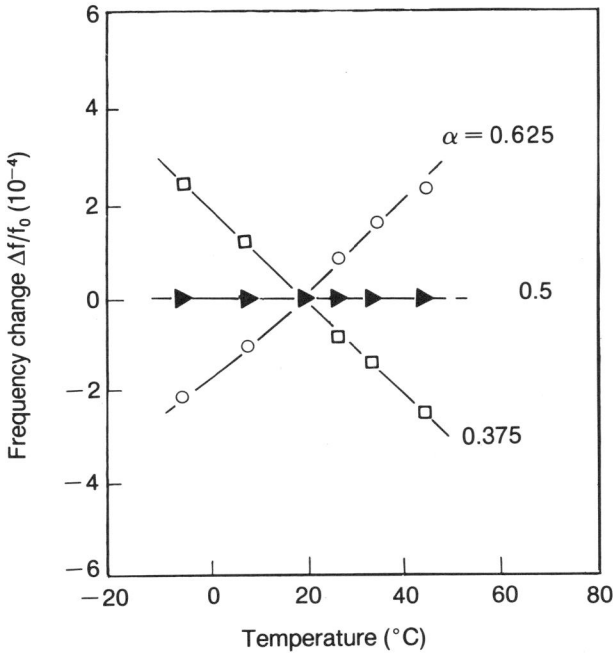

Figure 4.3.2 Temperature dependence of radial resonance frequency of $(Pb_{0.91}(La_{1-x}Nd_x)_{0.08})(Ti_{0.92}Mn_{0.02}In_{0.06})O_3$ [from Y. Ito et al., *Appl. Phys. Lett.* 35:595 (1979)].

4.3.2.3 Grain-Oriented Ceramics

Antimony sulfur iodide (SbSI), a ferroelectric material in which the c-axis is the ferroelectric axis, is known as the material with the largest piezoelectric effect. Some substances, such as SbSI crystal, tend to grow in the form of thin needles along the c-axis and are arranged parallel to the doctor-blade casting direction and perpendicular to the hot-press direction under hot-press forging. These grain-oriented ceramics exhibit strong anisotropic piezoelectric properties similar to single crystals and are very useful as electromechanical transducers. Grain-oriented ceramics have been fabricated by Bi layer-type ferroelectric materials $(PbBi_2Nb_2O_9)$[16] and tungsten-bronze structure-type oxides (Sr, Ba)Nb_2O_6.[17]

Glass ceramics such as lithium disilicate, barium germanium titanate, and barium silicate titanate are prepared as polar piezoelectric materials by crystallizing the glass of the same stoichiometry in a temperature gradient. Lithium borosilicate glass ceramic prepared by the foregoing method exhibits a resonance temperature coefficient of $60 \times 10^{-6}/°C$ and an electromechanical coupling factor of 0.14 at Li_2O-1.8 SiO_2-0.2B_2O_3.[18]

4.3.2.4 Piezoelectric Thin Film

Varius piezoelectric films such as CdS, ZnO, $PbTiO_3$, AlN, PLZT, $LiNbO_3$, $Bi_{12}PbO_{19}$, and $K_3Li_2Nb_5O_{15}$ have been developed. ZnO and AlN must be grown as a single-crystal or c-axis-oriented piezoelectric film to achieve cooperative properties. Consequently, chemical vapor deposition (CVD), RF sputtering, reactive ion plating, and reactive molecular beam epitaxy have been studied. Through them, higher quality and deposition rates have been attained.

Highly oriented ZnO films have been synthesized successfully on glass, fused quartz, silicon, sapphire, and metal substrates by DC, RF, magnetron sputtering, ion plating, and CVD techniques. The c-axis orientation of ZnO films formed by RF planar magnetron sputtering techniques on glass is perpendicular within 2° to the substrate surface, as shown in Figure 4.3.3. These piezoelectric films are used in large quantities for SAW devices such as TV (PIF) filters. The important factors for fabricating c-axis-oriented ZnO film by the sputtering method are the deposition rate, the substrate temperature, and the composition of carrier gas.[19]

AlN is one of the promising thin-film piezoelectric materials for high-frequency application as a SAW device as a result of its high SAW velocity of 5650 m/sec (as fast as silicon or sapphire substrate) and fairly large piezoelectric coupling factor. Highly oriented AlN films can be prepared by the CVD method or by growing epitaxially from $(CH_3)_3Al$ and NH_3 on sapphire substrates heated at about 1200°C.[20] Single-crystal or c-axis-oriented AlN film grown at low substrate temperatures of 50 to 500°C on a sapphire basal plane or a glass substrate by RF reactive planar magnetron sputtering has been reported.[21] As a result of its low temperature producibility, an aluminum or fine gold film electrode can be placed on top of AlN film as well as at the interface of the film and the substrate, which is very convenient in fabricating such items as SAW devices.

4.3.2.5 Polymer Ceramic Composites

Solid materials such as $Pb(Zr, Ti)O_3$ have high piezoelectric constants compared with plastic piezoelectric films such as polyvinylidene fluoride (PVDF). They are, however, very hard and brittle. The composite systems with a polymer medium, such as PVDF and $Pb(Zr, Ti)O_3$ dispersoid, are very useful because of their plasticity

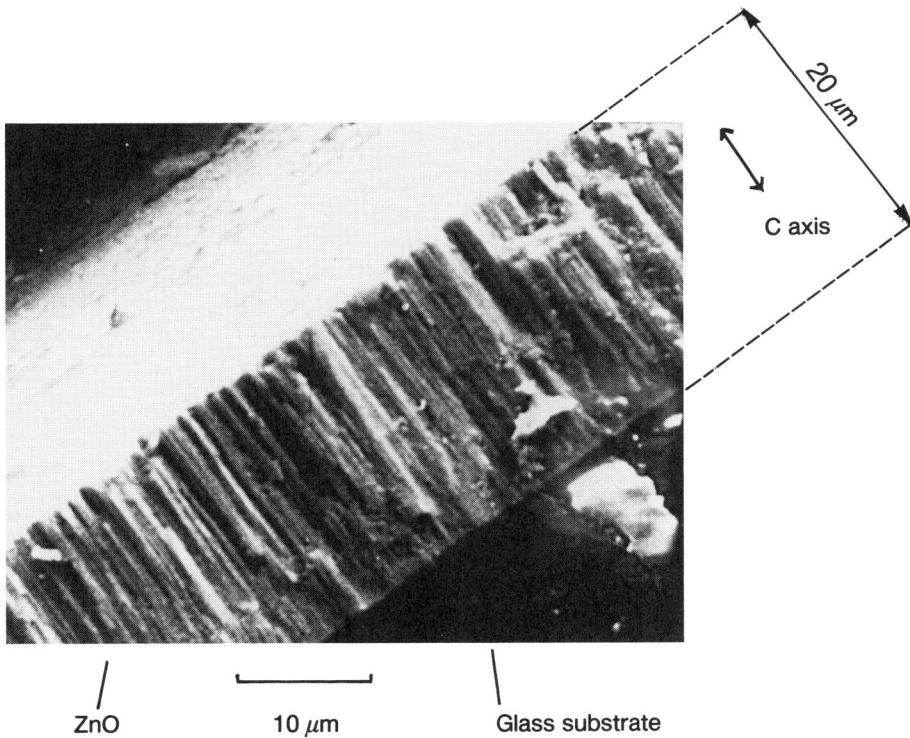

Figure 4.3.3 SEM micrograph of the fractured section of ZnO film deposited by sputtering.

and are easy to mold into various shapes such as thin film. A binary system consisting of PVDF and Pb(Zr, Ti)O_3 ceramic powder having a piezoelectric coefficient of d_{31} over 50×10^{-12}C/N was developed and has already been used to make keyboards.[22]

System Pb(Zr, Ti)O_3 ceramics have been limited to transducers used under hydrostatic conditions because of their low hydrostatic piezoelectric coefficient (d_h) and voltage coefficient (g_h). This results from the coupling of d_{33} and d_{31} coefficients, shown as $d_h = d_{33} + 2d_{31}$, and the reduction of $g_h = d_h/\epsilon_{33}$ by their high dielectric permittivity ϵ_{33}. It is possible that a properly designed composite material of Pb(Zr, Ti)O_3-polymer phase might decouple d_{33} and d_{31} and lower the dielectric permittivity, resulting in improved value of d_h and g_h. A Pb(Zr, Ti)O_3 composite made by embedding extruded Pb(Zr, Ti)O_3 rods into an epoxy matrix, investigated by Klicker and co-workers,[23] showed a high g_h, 25 times that of solid Pb(Zr, Ti)O_3 ceramics.

4.3.2.6 Stacked-Type Structure

Multiple stacked piezoelectric transducers have been fabricated by stacking, as with the mica capacitor. One hundred sheets of Pb(Zr, Ti)O$_3$ ceramic disks 1 mm thick and 32 mm in diameter showed a large displacement of 90 μm at 1500 V and quick response within 1 ms and generated a large mechanical power of over 3 tons.[24]

Recently, by the tape casting process developed for multilayer ceramic capacitors, highly compact and highly sensitive micro-displacement transducers were developed. These operate under low applied voltage (below 200 V) and are useful for mirror control devices[25] or small-size piezoelectric ceramic actuators with the strain of 8.7 × 10^{-4} at 230 V.[26]

4.3.3 Pyroelectric Ceramics

Current practical pyroelectric materials are shown in Table 4.3.1. As noted earlier, pyroelectric or ferroelectric crystal provides a pyroelectric signal, depending on the rate of change in its temperature.

4.3.3.1 Triglycin Sulfate (TGS)

TGS crystal is excellent in the important properties (pyroelectric coefficient, dielectric constant, dielectric loss) that affect its figure of merit as a pyroelectric sensor. TGS crystal applications, however, are limited to high-grade devices such as infrared ray visicon targets because of its water solubility and low Curie temperature of 49°C.

4.3.3.2 LiTaO$_3$

LiTaO$_3$ single crystal has high stability, relatively high figure of merit, and stability over a wide temperature range (-20°C to $+100$°C). It is used in infrared sensor[27] for cooking and intruder alarms.

4.3.3.3 Pb(Zr, Ti)O$_3$

Pb(Zr, Ti)O$_3$ ceramics, after polling, exhibit good pyroelectric properties. These materials are not water soluble; they are highly mass producible and operate at higher temperatures because of their high Curie temperatures.

The pyroelectric coefficient depends on the composition of the system Pb(Zr, Ti)O$_3$, and the optimum value can be obtained in 50 PbZrO$_3$-40 PbTiO$_3$-10 Pb(Sn$_{1/2}$Sb$_{1/2}$)O$_3$.[28] Pb(Zr, Ti)O$_3$ ceramics have already been put to practical use as intruder alarms and in automatic door systems.

Table 4.3.1 Properties of Representative Practical Pyroelectric Materials

	TGS	LiTaO$_3$	LiNbO$_3$	SBN^a	PZT^b	PbTiO$_3$	PVDF
Curie temperature T_c (°C)	49	618	1210	115	220	470	~120
Pyroelectric coefficient λ $(10^{-8} \cdot cm^{-2} \cdot k^{-1})$	4.0	2.3	30	6.5	18	6.0	0.24
Dielectric constant	35	43	0.4	380	380	200	11
Volume specific heat C_v $(J \cdot cm^{-3} \cdot k^{-1})$	2.5	3.2	2.8	2.1	2.4	3.2	2.4
Figure of merit $\lambda/(\epsilon \cdot C_v)$ $(10^{-10} C_v \cdot cm \cdot J^{-1})$	4.6	1.3	0.48	0.8	2.0	0.94	0.9

^{a} Sr$_{0.48}$ Ba$_{0.52}$ Nb$_2$O$_6$
^{b} Pb(Zr, Ti)O$_3$–Pb(Sn$_{1/2}$ Sb$_{1/2}$)O$_3$

4.3.3.4 PbTiO₃

System $PbTiO_3$, because of its high Curie temperature, large spontaneous polarization, and low dielectric constant, is suitable for infrared sensors. Modified ceramics, such as $PbTiO_3$-$La_{2/3}TiO_3$-MnO_2, are also being put to practical use.[29] Highly oriented pyroelectric thin film has been investigated by sputtering techniques.[30]

4.3.4 Conclusion

Although many kinds of piezoelectric and pyroelectric materials have been investigated and developed, the useful materials are limited to $Pb(Zr, Ti)O_3$, $PbTiO_3$, and $LiTaO_3$ because of their excellent and stable characteristics.

Piezoelectrics are mainly used in the area of sensors (pick-ups, microphones, keyboards, etc.,), electromechanical transducers (vibrators, actuators, etc.) or signal devices (filters, traps, resonators, etc.). Pyroelectricity is widely used for infrared sensors (intrusion alarms, cooking sensors, etc.).

Currently, piezoelectric and pyroelectric material designs, and the relationship of microstructure control and its characterization, are being extensively investigated. This highly accurate control by technology will ensure a bright future for new electronic ceramics.

References

1. Shirane, G., Suzuki, K., and Takeda, A., *J. Phys. Soc. Jpn.* 7:12 (1952).
2. Shirane, G., and Suzuki, K., *J. Phys. Soc. Jpn.* 7:333 (1952).
3. Sawaguchi, E., *J. Phys. Soc. Jpn.* 8:615 (1953).
4. Jaffe, B., Roth, R. S., and Marzullo, S., *J. Appl. Phys.* 25:809 (1954).
5. Smolenskii, G. A., and Agranovskaya, A. I., *Soviet Phys, Solid State* 1(10):1429 (1960) (in English).
6. Ouchi, H., Nagano, K., and Hayakawa, S., *J. Am. Cer. Soc.* 48(12):630 (1965).
7. Ogawa, T., and Wakino, K., *J. Jpn. Soc. Powder Powder Metall.* 24:123 (1977) (in Japanese).
8. Subbarao, E. C., *J. Am. Cer. Soc.* 43(3):119 (1960).
9. Ikegami, S., Ueda, I., and Nagata, T., *J. Acoust. Soc. Am.* 50(4):1060 (1971).
10. Sasaki, R., Nagata, T., and Matsushita, S., IEEE Trans. BTR 17:195 (1971).
11. Tanaka, H., and Shimizu, H., IECE of Japan US71-3 (1971) (in Japanese).
12. Ueda, I., Nishida, M., Kawashima, I., and Ouchi, H., IECE of Japan US80-25 (1980) (in Japanese).

13. Ito, Y., Takeuchi, H., Jyomura, S., Nagatsuma, K., and Ashida, S., *Appl. Phys. Lett.* 35:595 (1979).
14. Takeuchi, H., Ito, Y., Nagatsuma, K., Jyomura, S., and Ashida, S., *Jpn. J. Appl. Phys.* 19:L487 (1980).
15. Honda, H., Yamashita, Y., and Uchida, K., IECE of Japan US81-20 (1981) (in Japanese).
16. Igarashi, H., Matsunaga, K., Taniai, T., and Okazaki, K., *Am. Ceram. Soc. Bull.* 57:815 (1978).
17. Nagata, K., Kawatani, Y., and Okazaki, K., *Jpn. J. Appl. Phys.* 22:1353 (1983).
18. Halliyal, A., Bhalla, A. S., Newnham, R. E., and Cross, L. E., *J. Appl. Phys.* 53:2871 (1982).
19. Mitsuyu, T., Ohji, K., Yamazaki, O., and Wasa, K., IECE of Japan US80-60 (1980) (in Japanese).
20. Morita, M., Uesugi, N., Isogai, S., Tsubouchi, K., and Mikoshiba, N., *Jpn. J. Appl. Phys.* 20:17 (1981).
21. Shiosaki, T., Yamamoto, T., Oda, T., Harada, K., and Kawabata, A., *Jpn. J. Appl. Phys.* 20(Suppl. 20-3):149 (1981).
22. Kitayama, T., *Ceramics* 14(3):209 (1979) (in Japanese).
23. Klicker, K. A., Biggers, J. V., and Newnham, R. E., *J. Am. Ceram. Soc.* 64(1):5 (1981).
24. Yamashita, S., IECE of Japan US79-46 (1979) (in Japanese).
25. Uchino, K., Nomura, S., Cross, L. E., and Newnham, R. E., *Electronic Ceramics* 11:67 (autumn 1980) (in Japanese).
26. Takahashi, S., Ochi, A., Yonezawa, M., Yano, T., Fukui, I., and Hamatsuki, T., IECE of Japan CPM83-8 (1983).
27. Kuwano, Y., Nakano, S., Yokoo, T., and Kishi, Y., IECE of Japan, ED80-27 (1980) (in Japanese).
28. Iida, Y., Ogawa, T., and Toyoda, M., Trans. IEE of Japan, 52-A70 (1977) 547 (in Japanese).
29. Ishigaki, T., and Ueda, I., *Electronic Ceramics* 12:31 (1981) (in Japanese).
30. Okuyama, M., Matsui, Y., Nakano, H., Nakagawa, T., and Hamakawa, Y., *Jpn. J. Appl. Phys.* 18:1633 (1979).

4.4 Ferroelectric and Electrooptic Materials

Yoshio Furuhata and Gyozo Toda

4.4.1 Introduction

Since the discovery of $BaTiO_3$ in Japan, Japanese workers have been making significant contributions to the field of fundamental and applied research on ferroelectrics. Although most fundamental studies on ferroelectrics have been carried out on large single crystals, the majority of applied studies have been made on ceramics because of the ease of preparation and cost, and the variety of compositions and properties.

Ferroelectrics are materials with hysteresis loops in the polarization-electric field relation. They show strong anomalies in many of their physical properties such as dielectric constants, pyroelectric coefficients, piezoelectric constants, electrooptic constants, and others. Some of these properties have actually been used in the design of devices.

Various developments in ferroelectric ceramic materials and their applications over the last decade in Japan are described in subsection 4.4.2. Subsection 4.4.3 gives a brief review of electrooptic ceramics and their applications.

4.4.2 Physical Properties and Applications of Ferroelectric Ceramics

4.4.2.1 Dielectric-Related Properties

The high dielectric constants of ferroelectric ceramics have been exploited in ceramic capacitors. Multilayer ceramic capacitors featuring large capacitance with small size have been in practical use since 1970. Materials for such multilayer capacitors must have both a high dielectric constant and a low sintering temperature. These requirements are met by the $Bi_4Ti_3O_{12}$-$PbTiO_3$ binary system developed by Takahashi and co-workers[1] and the $Pb(Zr_{1/3}Nb_{2/3})O_3$-$Pb(Fe_{1/2}Nb_{1/2})O_3$-$Pb(Fe_{2/3}W_{1/3})O_3$ ternary system reported by Yonezawa and co-workers.[2] The binary system has a dielectric constant of 18,000 and can be sintered at less than 1050°C. The ternay system has a dielectric constant of 14,000 and a sintering temperature of less than 900°C. Materials for high-voltage (HV) ceramic capacitors must have a high dielectric constant and a low dielectric loss. The $(Sr, Mg)TiO_2$-$Bi_2O_3 \cdot nTiO_2$ system developed by Yamamoto and co-workers[3] and the $(Sr, Pr, Ca)TiO_2$-$Bi_2O_3 \cdot nTiO_2$ system investigated by Nishigaki[4] seem suitable for use in HV capacitors. The former has a dielectric constant of 1000 and a dielectric loss of 0.02%; the latter has a dielectric constant that increases to 3000 with an applied bias field and a dielectric loss of 0.9%.

Thin films having high dielectric constants should be used as the insulating layer in order to realize thin-film EL devices that can be operated at low voltage with high brightness. Okamoto and co-workers[5] have employed ferroelectric $PbTiO_3$ thin film having a dielectric constant of 100 – 200 and have obtained a brightness of 300 fL at a driving voltage of only 60 volts. Fujita and co-workers[6] have employed $SrTiO_3$ thin film having a dielectric constant of 200 and have achieved a brightness of 30 fL at 100 volts.

Although the most unique property of ferroelectrics is the reversibility of its spontaneous polarization, few applications have utilized this polarization reversal. Ferroelectric recording is one such application. Tanaka, Niitsuma and co-workers[7-10] devised a reproducing method using the pyroelectric effect of PZT ceramics and showed the possibility of realizing ferroelectric recording. Kumada[11] constructed an FE/PC device consisting of a transparent PLZT ceramic plate and a photoconductive film to prove that a black-and-white image could be xerographically developed by immersing the plate in a liquid toner developer.

With a ferroelectric-semiconductor combination, one can build a field effect device that has a memory and allows continuous, nondestructive readout of data. Sugibuchi, Kurogi, and co-workers[12,13] investigated a field-effect transistor (FET) that consisted of a ferroelectric $Bi_4Ti_3O_{12}$ film deposited on a Si substrate. Higuma, Matsui, and Okuyama[14-16] have developed field-effect transistors (MOSFETs) with thin ferroelectric gate insulators of SbSI, PZBFN, PLZT, or $PbTiO_3$. These devices are electrically rewritable and programmable at lower driving energies and with shorter write-and-erase times than those presently used.

By using the dramatic change in the dielectric constant of ferroelectrics during polarization reversal, a pulse voltage can be generated in a circuit combining a choke coil with a ferroelectric capacitor. Akamatsu[17] used the voltage caused by polarization reversal in $BaTiO_3$-family ceramics as the starting voltage for a fluorescent lamp. Matsuyama and co-workers[18] applied the pulse voltage generated in(Pb, Ba)(Zr, Ti)O_3 ceramics to the glow starter of Na-or metal-halide-type high-pressure discharge lamps. These starters have been put to practical use.

4.4.2.2 *Mechanical-Related Properties*

Piezoelectric ceramics and devices utilizing their electromechanical properties are described in section 4.4.

Ceramics for *surface acoustic wave* (SAW) devices are required to have a low dielectric constant. They must also be nonporous and have suitable low-frequency temperature characteristics. A number of efforts to develop ceramic materials to meet these requirements have been made. Ogawa and co-workers[19] found a null temperature coefficient for SAW velocity in certain compositions of Pb(Sn, Sb, Ti, Zr)O$_3$ ceramics. Takeuchi, and co-workers[20,21] investigated (Pb, Nd)(Ti, Mn, In)O$_3$ ceramics that have very small TCD over a wide temperature range, depending on their composition.

Electrostriction is a phenomenon in which strain is proportional to the square of the applied electric field. Because electrostrictive strain is usually very small, little attention has been given to it so far. However, Nomura, Uchino, and others[22-26] conducted intensive investigations on electrostriction in ferroelectric perovskite materials. They found that the strain induced by a field in relaxor ferroelectrics with diffuse phase transitions, such as those in the PMN family, is comparable to that in such normal piezoelectric ceramics as PZT or BaTiO$_3$. They also found that the hysteresis of strain or the aging effect associated with variations of the field is negligibly small. Using these materials, they fabricated a displacement transducer, a deformable bimorph mirror, a bistable optical device of the Fabry-Perot type, a pressure gauge, and other devices.

The fully ferroelectric/partially ferroelastic materials such as PZT or BaTiO$_3$ exhibit a *shape memory effect* that can be manipulated not only by applying mechanical stress but also by an electric field.

Uchino and co-workers[27] found this shape memory effect in the electrically induced ferroelectric phase of (Pb, Nb)(Zr, Sn, Ti)O$_3$ ceramics, which are antiferroelectric at room temperature. Kumada[28] has manufactured a transparent piezoelectric speaker that uses a PLZT ceramic plate that is concavely deformed by the application of shape memory effect. He has also constructed[29] a display device, similar to the Fericon, in which the image is stored by means of surface deformation in the electrically induced ferroelectric phase of antiferroelectric PLZT.

4.4.2.3 Thermal-Related Properties

The development of bulk pyroelectric ceramics and their applications is described in section 4.3. The following deals with pyroelectric devices that have thin-film structures.

Hamakawa and co-workers have asserted that thin film is a good structure for solving the problems of bulk-type devices such as low mass productivity and low sensitivity. They have fabricated IR-OFETs by depositing a PbTiO$_3$ thin film on the gate of a Si metal oxide semiconductor field-effect transistor (MOSFET). This device shows relatively high sensitivity and fast response. Moreover, they developed a new type of pyroelectric infrared sensor made with a PbTiO$_3$ thin film and a bipolar transistor constructed on a silicon wafer. Device performance was greatly improved in the high-frequency region.

4.4.2.4 Electrical- and Optical-Related Properties

The development of *semiconducting BaTiO$_3$-family ceramics* and their practical applications is detailed in sections 4.5 through 4.8, and *electrooptic ceramics* and their applications are dealt with in subsection 4.4.3.

An increase in transparency with irradiation by light has been observed by Endo and co-workers[32] under a longitudinal electric field in PLZT ceramics. This phenomenon seems to be a sidelight of the *photorefractive effect*, which is an optically induced change in refractive index. They proposed new types of optical information storage and display devices using this phenomenon.

Photochromism, or optically induced color change, has been observed by Yamaji and co-workers[33] and Ohno and co-workers[34] in some impurity-doped opaque PZT ceramics. Additionally, Tanaka and co-workers[35] investigated the photochromic effect in Fe-doped transparent PLZT ceramics and reported that the ceramics are darkened by irradiation with blue light and returned to their original transparent state by heat treatment at 200°C.

Finally, Uchino[36] investigated the *bulk photovoltaic effect* due to asymmetry in the ionization cross section for polarized inpurities in PbTiO$_3$-family and PLZT-family ceramics. They found that on average, the photocurrent is larger in the PbTiO$_3$ family than in the PLZT family, but that the photovoltage is higher in the PLZT family than in the PbTiO$_3$ family. They constructed a light intensity sensor and a light spot position using this effect.

4.4.3 Electrooptic Ceramics

There have been a number of studies of sintering processes, thin film technologies, microstructures, characteristic properties, and new devices in lanthanum-modified lead zirconate-titanate ceramics (PLZT)[37] with high optical transparency and good electrooptic characteristics. Many new electrooptic ceramics have been developed.

4.4.3.1 Materials and Processings

To obtain a high degree of optical quality in polycrystalline ceramics, it has been necessary to remove the impurities and residual pores in the sintered bodies[38,39] and to reduce the anisotropy of the crystal

266

Table 4.4.1 Composition and Properties of New Electrooptic Ceramics

Materials	Composition	T(%) (t, mm)	γ_c (10^{-10} m/V)	R (10^{-16} m²/V²)	Ref.
PLNZT[a] (Pb, La)(Nb, Zr, Ti)O₃	8/65/35	10–20 (0.2)	4.21	—	41
	13/65/35		7.08	—	
	15/65/35		—	5.77	
(Pb, Ba)(Zr, Ti)O₃	3/70/30	55–60 (0.2)	—	—	42
(Pb, Sr)(Zr, Ti)O₃	2/72/28		—	—	
PBLN[b] (Pb$_{1-y}$, Ba$_y$)$_{1-x}$(La$_x$, Nb$_{2-x/5}$)O₆	4/60/40	40–60 (0.2)	6.66	—	43
	8/60/40		—	2.09	44
PLMNZT Pb$_{1-}$La (Mg$_{1/3}$Nb$_{2/3}$) Zr$_y$, Ti$_{z1-/4}$O₃	/x/y/z	~70 (1.0)	—	—	45
(Sr$_{1-x}$La$_x$)(Li$_{1/4}$, Nb$_{3/4}$)$_{1-y}$Ti$_y$O₃		55 (0.4)	—	—	46
(Pb, La)(Zn, Nb, Zr, Ti)O₃		40–60 (0.3)	—	—	47
PLLZT	10/65/35	50–60 (0.13)	—	—	48
Pb(La$_{1/2}$Li$_{1/2}$)(Zr, Ti)O₃	5/53/47		2.4	—	49
	10/53/47		5.8	—	

Material	Composition	T (t)	R	χ_c	Ref.
BPN[c]	18/45/55		—	—	
BCN	13/45/55	60 (0.2)	2.27	—	
BSN	18/50/50		6.60	1.10	50
	12/50/50		—	—	
SCN	15/50/50		4.02	5.11	
	12/50/50		6.65	—	
SZN	17.5/60/40		—	4.62	51
	17.5/65/35		6.62	—	
BZN	20/60/40		—	0.38	
CZN	20/65/35		—	—	
PBN[d]	16.8/46/54	~70	—	—	
	15/52/48		8.0	—	52
	15/53/47		10.5	—	
PSN	15/50/50	~70	—	—	
NaNbO$_3$-BaTiO$_3$	70/30	75 (0.35)	—	—	53
(Sr, Ba)Nb$_2$O$_3$	Sr: 0.5	45 (0.2)	—	—	54
PBLN	Pb/La: 55/8	60 (0.2)	—	—	55
	60/8		—	2.78	
(Pb, Ba, La)Nb$_2$O$_6$	70/2		3.04	—	

T: transmittance; t: thickness; χ_c: linear electrooptic coefficient; R: quadratic electrooptic coefficient.

a $xPb(La, Nb)O_3 - (100 - x)(yPbZrO_3 - zPbTiO_3)$ is simplified as x/y/z.

b La/Pb/Ba

c $xBa(Pb_{1/3}, Nb_{2/3})O_3 - (1 - x)\,Pb(Zr_y, Ti_{1-y})O_3$ is simplified as BPN, where x = 100x, y = 100y, and z = 100(1 − y), respectively (C: Ca, S: Sr, Z: Zn).

d $Ba_4Nb_{2(3-x)/5}O_3 - Pb(Zr, Ti)O_3$ is simplified as PBN and PSN (S = Sr).

lattices.[40] On the basis of these concepts, many electrooptic ceramics with perovskite and tungsten-bronze structures have been studied.

The new materials with the ABO_3 perovskite structures are classified as $Pb(Zr, Ti)O_3$ systems both with and without La and with the A or B site of the ABO_3 partly substituted by various elements. The materials having the tungsten-bronze structure are $(Pb, Ba, La)Nb_2O_6$ and $(Sr, Ba)Nb_2O_6$. The composition and some properties of these materials are shown in Table 4.4.1.[41-55]

Most of the studies on the sintering process of electrooptic ceramics concern improvement on the sintering atmosphere in order to fabricate the highly optical transparent PLZT. Okazaki and co-workers[56] and Nagata and co-workers[57] reported that highly transparent PLZT was obtained by controlling the amount of excess PbO in the PLZT using a two-stage sintering process that combined vacuum hot pressing and atmosphere sintering. Horibe and co-workers[58] developed a modified sintering method for PLZT consisting of sintering in O_2 (1100°C, 40 hours) followed by hot isostatic pressing in Ar (1100°C, 2 hours, 18 kg/cm²). A low-cost method of fabricating PLZT is attained by using a three-step sintering atmosphere $(O_2-N_2-O_2)$ during sintering without pressure.[59]

Attempts have also been made to obtain electrooptic ceramics, such as relatively low-temperature sintering of $(Pb, Bi)(Zr, Ti)O_3$[60] with ultra-high pressure (2000 atm, 800°C) and fabricating transparent $70NaNbO_3-30BaTi]_3$ by the unidirectionally solidifying method.[61]

Ferroelectric devices for optoelectronics demand good transparency as well as low driving voltage, miniaturization, and cost reduction. To meet these requirements, investigators have made a considerable number of attempts to prepare a translucent PZT thin film,[62,63] a transparent PLZT thin film,[64-73] and thin film optical guides using $LiNbO_3$,[74-86] KLN,[87] $Sr_2Nb_2O_7$,[88,89] and BGO.[90]

Polycrystalline thin films of PZT or PLZT have been fabricated on a platinum or fused quartz substrate by RF sputtering or by using electron beam evaporation. Thin films with perovskite structure were obtained at substrate temperatures above 550°C and at substrate temperatures lower than 400°C with subsequent heat treatment at 750°C for 3 hours.

The following PLZT thin films with good crystalline and optical properties were epitaxially grown on various single crystal substrates; (111) PLZT//(0001) sapphire at 700°C, (100) PLZT//(100) $SrTiO_3$ at 700°C, and (100) PLZT//(100) MgO at 500°C. The PLZT thin films on (111) GaP and (100) GaAs were also single crystals with a (100) plane.

Single-crystal thin films of $LiNbO_3$ with small optical propagation losses have been epitaxially grown by various methods, such as EGM,[74,75] CVD,[78] LPE,[79-81] and CLE,[82] on T-cut $LiTaO_3$ substrates. Optical guide layers of $LiNbO_3$ with excellent properties have been fabricated by in-diffusion.[83-86] Thin films deposited on fused quartz or Y-cut sapphire substrates by RF sputtering[76,77] at a substrate temperature of 400°C were found to be polycrystalline.

Single-crystal films of (001) KLN and (110) KLN were grown on (001), KBN and (100) KBN substrates, respectively, by RF sputtering and use of an EGM technique. Single-crystal films of (001) KLN were epitaxially grown on a (01 – 2) sapphire substrate at substrate temperatures above 600°C by RF sputtering. The optical propagation losses in these films were relatively small.

4.4.3.2 Microstructures and Properties

The electrical and optical properties of ceramics depend on microstructure, especially grain size. Jyomura and co-workers[93] investigated the isothermal grain growth of PLZT with various La concentrations ranging from 0 to 10 at% and showed that the constants n and k greatly depend on the La content, as shown in Figure 4.4.1, when the sintering time (t) dependence of grain size (D) was expressed in the normal grain growth formula $D^n = kt$.

This section reports on various items requiring attention in the design of PLZT devices, including uniform or nonuniform polarization of PLZT,[97] the effect of heat treatment on local polarization of PLZT,[98] the relation of the poling direction and internal stress induced by dc field application and the anisotropic fracture toughness K_{IC} of PLZT,[99] the optical and ferroelectrical homogeneity of large-scale PLZT,[100] and the existence of a lapped surface layer of (Pb, Ba, Sr)(Zr, Ti)O_3 having a 0.1- to 0.2-μ, thick nonferroelectric layer of small dielectric constant with two-dimensional tensile stress.[101]

The electrooptic light deflection phenomenon of PLZT (that is, 100% deflection efficiency and a large deflection angle are produced at a low driving voltage, either AC or DC[102]) and the anisotropies of transmittance and birefringence of grain-oriented (Pb, Ba, La)Nb_2O_6 ceramics[103] were also investigated.

4.4.3.3 Applications

Several types of devices using PLZT are reported, including a memory-display device with an antiferroelectric phase of PLZT,[104] a real-time graphic display,[105] a matrix display,[106] and an analog space modulator.[107] However, the largest application of electrooptic ceramics is

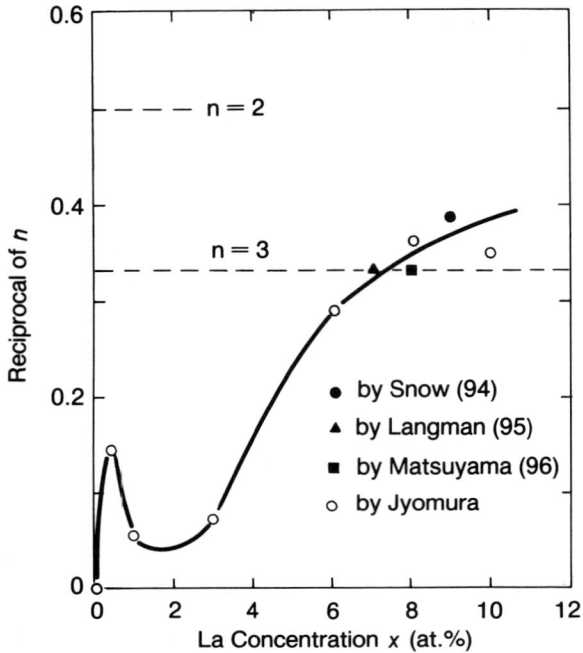

Figure 4.4.1 Dependence of constant *n* or La concentration [from S. Jyomura et al., *J. Am. Ceram. Soc.* 64:C-55 (1981)].

in the PLZT optical shutter. A very light eyeglass-type stereoscopic viewer that operates at low voltage[108] and an instrument for stereoscopic observation and three-dimensional measurement of SEM images[109] have been developed. Also reported are an improvement in the wavelength dependence of PLZT shutter transmittance by using a modified electrode structure,[110] a battery-operated PLZT shutter for color veiwfinders,[111] and a PLZT 100-bit linear array shutter that presents a diffraction-limited Fourier transform pattern suitable for a high-density, one-dimensional hologram.[112]

Other attractive applications of PLZT as optical shutters are an electrooptical gate array for an optical printer (gate number: 200; response: 10 μs, transmittance: max. 45%),[113] and a linear-sequence color viewfinder for monochromatic television consisting of a PLZT shutter, an RGB color filter, and a crossed polarizer, as illustrated in Figure 4.4.2.[114]

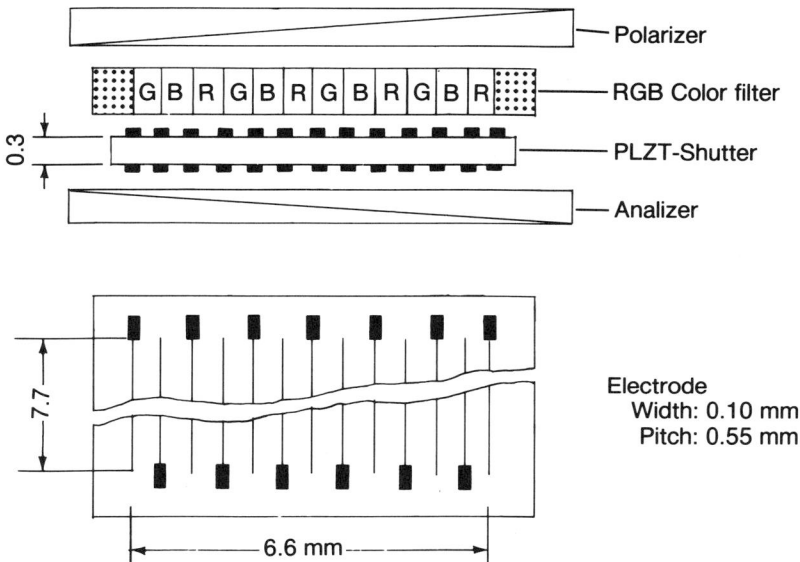

Figure 4.4.2 Construction of PLZT shutter with RGB color filter for monochromatic TV (from M. Himuro et al., *Proc. FMA-4*, 1983, p. 68).

References

1. Takahashi, H. et al., *Nikkei Electronics* 132:84 (1979) (in Japanese).
2. Yonezawa, M. et al., *Proc. FMA-1*, 1977, p. 297; *Proc. FMA-2*, 1979, p. 215.
3. Yamamoto, K. et al., *Electro-ceramics* 6:9 (1975); 9:35 (1978).
4. Nishigaki, S., *Proc. FMA-4*, 1983.
5. Okamoto, K. et al., *Jpn. J. Appl. Phys. Suppl.* 20-1:215 (1981).
6. Fujita, Y. et al., *Proc. 3rd International Display Research Conference*, 1983.
7. Tanaka, H., and Sato, R., *Trans. IECEJ* 52A:436 (1969); 53A:343 (1970).
8. Niitsuma, H., and Sato, R., *Tech. Rept. Tohoku Univ.* 39:199 (1974).
9. Niitsuma, H. et al., *Trans. IEEJ* 94A:69 (1974); 95A:87 (1975); 97A:133 (1977).
10. Niitsuma, H. et al., *Proc. FMA-1*, p. 91.
11. Kumada, A., *Jpn. J. Appl. Phys. Suppl.* 16-1:325 (1977).
12. Sugibuchi, K. et al., *J. Appl. Phys.* 40:2871 (1975).
13. Kurogi, Y. et al., *Jpn. J. Appl. Phys. Suppl.* 44:197 (1975).

14. Higuma, Y. et al., *Proc. 9th CSSD*, 1977, p. 1111.
15. Matsui, Y. et al., *Proc. FMA-1*, 1977, p. 37; *Proc. FMA-2*, 1979, p. 239.
16. Okuyama, M. et al., *Jpn. J. Appl. Phys.* 18:1111 (1979).
17. Akamatsu, M. Jpn. Patent S48-28726 (1973).
18. Matsuyama, I. et al., *Jpn. J. Appl. Phys.* 16:1871 (1977).
19. Ogawa, T. et al., *Spring Meeting Powder & Powder Metallurgy of Japan*, 1976, p. 128.
20. Ito, Y. et al., *Appl. Phys. Lett.* 35:593 (1979); *J. Appl. Phys.* 52:3223 (1981).
21. Takeuchi, H. et al., *Jpn. J. Appl. Phys.* 19:L487 (1980); *Proc. IEEE US*:400 (1980).
22. Nomura, S. et al., *Mat. Res. Bull.* 14:769 (1979); *Proc. FMA-2*, 1979, p. 133; *Phys. Stat. Sol.* a57:317 (1980); *Ferroelectrics* 41:251 (1981).
23. Uchino, K. et al., *J. Appl. Phys.* 51:1142 (1980); 52:1455 (1981); *Jpn. J. Appl. Phys.* 20:L367 (1981); 21:596 (1982); Suppl. 20-4:171 (1981); Suppl. 20-4:225 (1981); *J. Phys. Soc. Jpn. Suppl.* B47:45 (1980); *J. Mat. Sci.* 16:569 (1981); *Appl. Opt.* 20:3077 (1981); *Phase Transition* 1:333 (1980).
24. Kuwata, J. et al., *Jpn. J. Appl. Phys.* 19:2099 (1980).
25. Gomi, M. et al., *Jpn. J. Appl. Phys.* 20:L375 (1981).; *Appl. Opt.* 21:2616 (1982).
26. Sato, T. et al., *Appl. Opt.* 21:3669 (1982).
27. Uchino, K. et al., *Annual Meeting Jpn. Phys. Soc.*, 1983, p. 112; *Fall Meeting Jpn. Phys. Soc.*, 1983, p. 74.
28. Kumada, A., *Nikkei Electronics* 70 (1981) (in Japanese).
29. Kumada, A., *Hitachi Rev.* 56:79 (1974) (in Japanese).
30. Okuyama, M. et al., *Jpn. J. Appl. Phys. Suppl.* 20-1:315 (1981).
31. Okuyama, M. et al., *Jpn. J. Appl. Phys. Suppl.* 21-1:225 (1982).
32. Endo, W. et al., *Fujitsu Sci. Tech. J.* 125 (1975); *J. Appl. Phys. Suppl.* 44:93 (1975).
33. Yamaji, A. et al., *Annual Meeting Jpn. Soc. Appl. Phys.*, 1972, p. 29a-D10.
34. Ohno, O. et al., *Jpn. J. Appl. Phys.* 12:317 (1973).
35. Tanaka, K. et al., *Electron Lett.* 10:350 (1974); *J. Am. Cer. Soc.* 59:465 (1975); *Jpn. J. Appl. Phys.* 16:1327 (1977).
36. Uchino, K. et al., *Annual Meeting Jpn. Phys. Soc.*, 1983, p. 113; *Proc. FMA-4*, 1983, p. 53.
37. Heartling, G. H., and Land, C. E., *J. Am. Ceram. Soc.* 54:1 (1971).
38. Coble R. L., *J. Appl. Phys.* 32:787 (1961).
39. Jorgensen, P. J., and Westbrook, J. H. *J. Am. Ceram. Soc.* 47:332 1964).
40. Miyauchi, K., and Toda, G., *J. Am. Ceram. Soc.* 58:361 (1975).
41. Okazaki, J., Nagata, K., Saeki, H., and Kiuchi, O., *Memories of the Defense Academy Japan*, vol. 8, 1973, p. 131.

42. Miyauchi, K., and Toda, G., *J. Am. Ceram. Soc.* 58:157 (1975).

43. Yokosuka, M., *Jpn. J. Appl. Phys.* 16:379 (1977).

44. Yokosuka, M., and Marutake, M., *Proc. FMA-1,* 1977, p. 187.

45. Kawashima, S., Nishida, M., Matsuo, Y., and Ouchi, H., *J. Jpn. Soc. Powder Powder Metall.* 172 (1977).

46. Ichinose, N., Mizutani, T., Hiraki, H., and Takahashi, T., *Proc. FMA-1,* 1977, p. 169.

47. Nagata, K., Schmitt, H., Stathakis, K., and Muser, H. E., *Proc. FMA-1,* 1977, p. 181.

48. Masuda, Y., Jumonji, M., and Wada, M., *Proc. FMA-1,* 1977, p. 195.

49. Masuda, Y., Baba, A., and Wada, M., *Proc. FMA-2,* 1979, p. 179.

50. Yokosuka, M., Miura, S., Ochiai, T., and Marutake, M., *Proc. FMA-3,* 1981, p. 75.

51. Ochiai, T., Yokosuka, M., Miura, S., and Marutake, M., *Proc. FMA-3,* 1981, p. 79.

52. Miura, S., Yokosuka, M., Ochiai, T., and Marutake, M., *Proc. FMA-3,* 1981, p. 83.

53. Ito, S., Kokubo, T., and Tashiro, M., *Am. Ceram. Soc. Bull.* 58:591 (1979).

54. Nagata, K., Yamamoto, Y., Igarashi, H., and K. Okazaki, K., *Ferroelectrics* 38:853 (1981).

55. Nagata, K., Kawatani, Y., and Okazaki, K., *Jpn. J. Appl. Phys.* 22:1353 (1983).

56. Okazaki, K., Ohtsubo, I., and Toda, K., *Ferroelectrics* 10:195 (1976).

57. Nagata, K., Schmitt, H., Stathakis, K., and Muser, H. E., *Proc. 3rd CIMTEC,* 1976, p. 27.

58. Horibe, Y., Eda, K., and Okinaka, H., *National Tech. Rept.* 28:1098 (1982) (in Japanese).

59. Wakino, K., Nani, K., and Ozawa, K., Jpn. Patent 56-23946 (1981).

60. Koizumi, M., Shimada, M., and Ishitobi, H., Jpn. Patent 56-23945 (1981).

61. Ito, S., Kokubo, T., and Tashiro, M., *Am. Ceram. Soc. Bull.* 58:591 (1979).

62. Oikawa, M. et al., *Appl. Phys. Lett.* 29:491 (1976).

63. Okada, A., *J. Appl. Phys.* 48:2905 (1977); 49:4495 (1978).

64. Matsunami, H. et al., *Jpn. J. Appl. Phys.* 15:1163 (1976); *J. Electron Mat.* 7:229 (1978).

65. Tanaka, K. et al., *Jpn. J. Appl. Phys.* 15:1381 (1976).

66. Ishida, M. et al., *Appl. Phys. Lett.* 31:433 (1977); *J. Appl. Phys.* 48:951 (1977); *Proc. FMA-1,* 1977, p. 31.

67. Nakagawa, T. et al., *Jpn. J. Appl. Phys.* 18:897 (1979).

68. Higuma, H. et al., *Jpn. J. Appl. Phys.* 16:1707 (1977).

69. Ishida, M. et al., *J. Cryst. Growth* 45:393 (1978).

70. Matsunami, H. et al., *Proc. FMA-2*, 1979, p. 161.
71. Usuki, T. et al., *Proc. FMA-2*, 1979, p. 167.
72. Okuyama, M. et al., *Appl. Phys.* 21:339 (1980).
73. Adachi, H. et al., *Proc. FMA-4*, 1983, p. 1.
74. Miyazawa, S. et al., *Appl. Phys. Lett.* 23:198 (1973); *J. Appl. Phys.* 46:2223 (1975).
75. Fukunishi, S. et al., *Appl. Phys. Lett.* 24:424 (1974).
76. Takada, S. et al., *Appl. Phys. Lett.* 24:490 (1974).
77. Minakata, M. et al., *Appl. Phys. Lett.* 26:395 (1975).
78. Fushimi, S. et al., *Jpn. J. Appl. Phys.* 13:1895 (1974).
79. Muto, K. et al., *Annual Meeting Jpn. Soc. of Appl. Phys.*, 1974, p. 99.
80. Miyagawa, S. et al., *Appl. Phys. Lett.* 26:8 (1975).
81. Kondo, S. et al., *Appl. Phys. Lett.* 26:489 (1975); *J. Cryst. Growth* 46:314 (1979).
82. Fukuda, T., and Hirano, H., *Appl. Phys. Lett.* 28:575 (1976); *J. Cryst. Growth* 50:291 (1980).
83. Noda, J. et al., *Appl. Phys. Lett.* 27:15 (1975); *J. Appl. Phys.* 49:3150 (1978).
84. Naitoh, H. et al., *Appl. Opt.* 16:2546 (1977).
85. Fukuma, M. et al., *J. Appl. Phys.* 49:3693 (1978).
86. Sugii, K. et al., *J. Mat. Sci.* 13:523 (1978).
87. Adachi, M. et al., *Jpn. J. Appl. Phys.* 17:2053 (1978); 18:193 (1979); 18:1637 (1979); *Ferroelectrics Proc. FMA-2*, 1979, p. 173; *Jpn. J. Appl. Phys. Suppl.* 20-4:17 (1981).
88. Ishitani, A., and Kimura, M., *Appl. Phys. Lett.* 29:289 (1976).
89. Ohi, T. et al., *Proc. 3rd Symposium on Optical Guide Electronics*, 1979, p. 132.
90. Mitsuya, T. et al., *J. Electrochem. Soc.* 123:94 (1976).
91. Okazaki, K., and Nagata, K., *J. Am. Ceram. Soc.* 56:82 (1973).
92. Jyomura, S., Matsuyama, I., and Kumada, A., *Ferroelectrics* 15:51 (1977).
93. Jyomura, S., Matsuyama, I., and Toda, G., *J. Am. Ceram. Soc.* 64:C-55 (1981).
94. Snow, G. S., *J. Am. Ceram. Soc.* 56:91 (1973).
95. Langman, R. A., Runk, R. B., and Butler, S. R., *J. Am. Ceram. Soc.* 56:486 (1973).
96. Matsuyama, I., Noro, T., and Jyomura, S., *J. Jpn. Soc. Powder Powder Metall.* 22:198 (1975) (in Japanese).
97. Niitsuma, H., Owada, J., and Sato, R., *Proc. FMA-1*, 1977, p. 97.
98. Niitsuma, H., Owada, J., and Sato, R., *Proc. FMA-2*, 1979, p. 209.

99. Sato, H., Yamamoto, T., Igarashi, S., and Okazaki, K., *Proc. FMA-4*, 1983, p. 82.

100. Yamashita, K., Miyauchi, K., Watanabe, S., and Toda, G., *J. Jpn. Soc. Powder Powder Metall.* 24:152 (1977) (in Japanese).

101. Jyomura, S., Matsuyama, I., and Toda, G., *J. Appl. Phys.* 51:5838 (1980).

102. Watanabe, T., *Proc. FMA-3*, 1981, p. 87.

103. Nagata, K., Kawatani, Y., and Okazaki, K., *Jpn. J. Appl. Phys.* 22:1353 (1983).

104. Kumada, A., Toda, G., and Otomo, Y., *Suppl. Jpn. J. Appl. Phys.* 43:150 (1974).

105. Sakuma, H., and Matsumura, M., *NEC Research and Development* 42:32 (1976).

106. Suzuki, K., Kitta, K., Toda, G., and Kumada, A., *Suppl. Jpn. J. Appl. Phys.* 45:131 (1976).

107. Kumada, A., Suzuki, K., and Kitta, K., *Suppl. Jpn. J. Appl. Phys.* 44:85 (1975).

108. Kumada, A., Kitta, K., Kato, Y., and Komoda, T., *Proc. FMA-1*, 1977, p. 205.

109. Kato, Y., Fukuhara, S., and Komoda, T., *Scanning Electron Microscopy* 1:41 (1977).

110. Tanaka, K., Tamaguchi, M., Seto, H., Murata, M., and Wakino, K., *Proc. FMA-4*, 1983, p. 64 (in Japanese).

111. Murano, K., Himuro, M., Watanabe, Y., Matsumoto, S., and Nishigaki, S., *Proc. FMA-4*, 1983, p. 66 (in Japanese).

112. Hayashi, S., Ueno, K., Saku, T., and Iwamura, H., *Proc. FMA-1*, 1977, p. 199.

113. Iwaoka, H., and Sugiyama, T., *Tech. Rept. Yokogawa Electric* 26:3 (1982) (in Japanese).

114. Himuro, M., Murano, K., Nishigaki, S., Masatoki, T., and Ohno, K., *Proc. FMA-4*, 1983, p. 68 (in Japanese).

4.5 Ceramic Semiconductors: ZnO Nonlinear Resistors

Masaru Miyayama and Hiroaki Yanagida

4.5.1 Introduction

Zinc oxide nonlinear resistors (varistors) are multiphase ceramic devices exhibiting highly nonlinear current-voltage (I-V) characteristics useful in electrical circuits as protection against transients.

Breakdown, which occurs over a voltage range corresponding to 2.5 – 4 V per grain boundary, can be described by an empirical equation: $I = (V/C)^\alpha$ where I is current, α has values greater than 30 for commercial varistors, and C corresponds to applied voltage V at a 1-mA current.

A typical varistor composition contains about 97 mol% ZnO; the balance consists of oxides of Bi, Sb, Co, Mn, and Cr. Recent microstructure studies have shown that the electrical barriers at the grain boundary responsible for nonlinear properties are associated with a narrow ($\leqq 10$ nm) segregated layer of these additives, typically Bi, rather than being the result of a continuous second phase between the ZnO grains, as was first supposed.[1,2]

Recent studies on varistors are almost all limited to the following three aspects: lowering of the breakdown voltage, the mechanism of electrical degradation, and model studies using metal oxide heterojunctions or single crystals with an intermediate layer. All three are briefly reviewed below.

4.5.2 Lowering of the Breakdown Voltage

Lower voltage applications, such as integrated circuit protection, require breakdown voltages in the 5 – 15 V range. Because breakdown voltage V_B is proportional to the number of grain boundaries, low-voltage varistor devices can be obtained by reducing the number of grain boundaries within a sample.

Several approaches to lower V_B have been attempted. Selim and co-workers reported varistors made by diffusing Bi, Pb, and Si from the surface into a pure polycrystalline ZnO substrate.[3] Such devices exhibited nonlinear properties with a V_B of less than 20 V and an α of 15. Multilayer ZnO varistors[4] and thin-film varistors made through RF sputtering[5] have also been reported. In both varistors, a V_B of around 10 V was obtained. However, surface layer devices have a nonvariable V_B, and thin-film devices have too small a volume to permit high surge energy absorption.

Recently, Eda and co-workers reported a low-voltage ZnO varistor with extraordinarily large grain size.[6] This varistor was made by sintering a mixture of ZnO fine powder, additives, and ZnO seed grains with grain sizes of 63 – 105 μm. The seed grains were obtained by sintering ZnO containing 0.5 mol% BaO and removing the BaO by washing the sintered body in boiling water. The device has a grain size of around 500 μm and a low V_B of 6 V/mm, as seen in Figure 4.5.1.

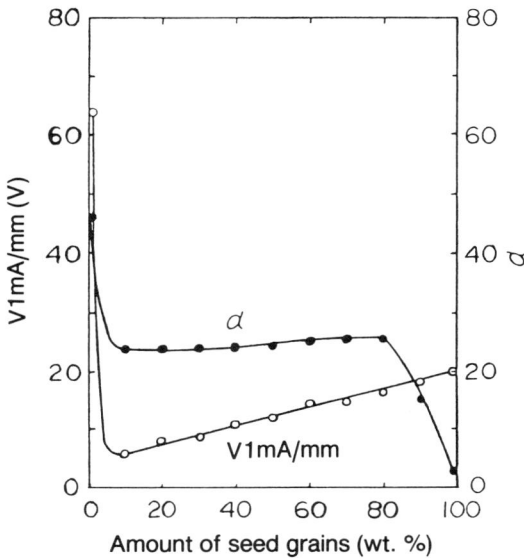

Figure 4.5.1 Effect of seed grains on breakdown voltage (V_{1mA}/mm) and nonohmic exponent α in the system; ZnO, $Bi_2O_3(1.0)$, $Co_2O_3(0.5)$, $MnO_2(0.5)$, $TiO_2(0.5)$, $SnO_2(0.5$ mol%) [from K. Eda et al., *Jpn. J. Appl. Phys.* 54:1095 (1983)].

4.5.3 Degradation Mechanism

When ZnO varistors are used as surge absorbers, the line voltage is continuously applied to the varistors, resulting in the flowing through of a small leakage current. The leakage current gradually increases and eventually leads to thermal runaway, a critical problem in surge absorbers.

On the basis of measurements of I-V, dielectric characteristics, and thermally stimulated current (TSC), Eda and co-workers postulated that the degradation caused by dc biasing is attributable to the asymmetrical deformation of Schottky barriers resulting from ion migrations in Bi_2O_3-rich intergranular layers and in the depletion layers of the Schottky barriers.[7] Gupta and co-workers have also proposed that this degradation is associated with the diffusion of interstitial Zn in the depletion layer.[8,9] Sato and co-workers explained the degradation on the basis of TSC data,[10] holding that trapping centers in a forward-biased depletion layer tend to capture

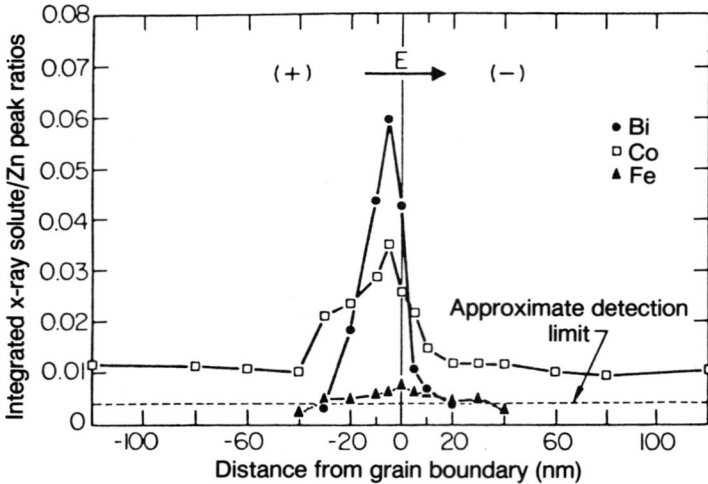

Figure 4.5.2 Solute profiles across grain boundary oriented at high angle to the degrading electric field [from Y. M. Chiang and W. D. Kingery, *J. Appl. Phys.* 53:1765 (1982)].

electrons flowing in a conduction band, whereas upon reversal of the applied field, the charges trapped within this layer begin to be freed.

However, a marked asymmetry in the distribution of Bi and Co with respect to the physical location of the boundary has been directly observed with STEM in heavily degradated ZnO varistors[11] (Figure 4.5.2). These results are consistent with the migration of positive ions to the boundary under DC bias. The amount of Co accumulated in the region adjacent to the boundary is consistent in sign and mobility with the presence of a small fraction of interstitial solute cations.

Hayashi and co-workers reported that the increase in leakage current during dc biasing is primarily attributable to a decrease in the width of Schottky barriers.[12] The decrease in the width of these barriers and an asymmetrical change in forward- and reverse-biased barriers can be explained by surplus positive charges formed in the reverse-biased depletion layer resulting from the migration of donor ions.

4.5.4 Model Study

Electrical properties of $ZnO-Bi_2O_3$ heterojunctions have an important influence on varistor properties. Low has made thin-film ZnO-

Bi_2O_3 junctions using sputtering techniques and measured their I-V characteristics.[13] The junction breakdown voltage ranged from 2.3 to 3.0 V when the ZnO was positively biased.

Eda has also studied the electrical properties of the junction made by sputtering Bi_2O_3 containing oxides of Co, Mn, Zn, and the like onto a polycrystalline ZnO substrate.[14] He postulated an equivalent circuit taking three types of grain boundaries into account: one with a thick and one a thin Bi_2O_3-rich intergranular layer, and one with no intergranular layer, as shown in Figure 4.5.3. From the measured and calculated I-V and dielectric characteristics, it was assumed that the grain boundary with no intergranular layer is related to the breakdown region with a high α value, and the grain boundary

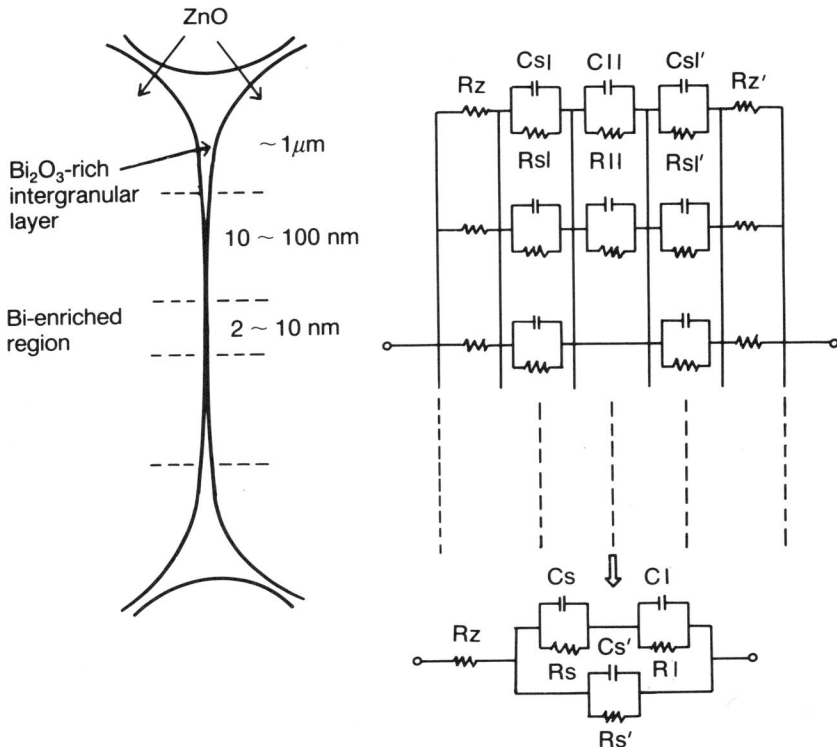

Figure 4.5.3 Microstructure of grain boundary and equivalent circuit of ZnO varistors (from K. Eda, *Grain Boundaries in Semiconductors*, H. J. Leamy and G. E. Pike, eds. New York: North-Holland, 1982).

with a thin intergranular layer is related to the pre-breakdown region of the I-V curve and degradation.

Crystalline ZnO plates with an intermediate layer (40 μm thick) consisting of a mixture of Bi_2O_3, MnO_2, and Co_3O_4 have been reported to show nonlinear I-V characteristics with a V_B of 3.5 V and an α of 8 – 11.[15] When a sandwich of two ZnO pellets and a powder mixture of Bi_2O_3 and $Zn_7Sb_2O_{12}$ spinel was heated at 1000°C, an epitaxial layer of ZnO, which is less conductive than the bulk grains, was observed to form on the pellet surfaces.[16]

References

1. Clarke, D. R., *J. Appl. Phys.* 49:2407 (1978).
2. Kingery, W. D., Vander Sande, J. B., and Mitamura, T., *J. Am. Ceram. Soc.* 62:221 (1979).
3. Selim, F. A., Gupta, T. K., Hower, P. L., and Carlson, W. G., *J. Appl. Phys.* 51:765 (1980).
4. Shohata, N., Matsumura, T., Utsumi, K., and Ohno, T., *Advances in Ceramics*, vol. 1, Levinson, L. ed. Columbus, Ohio: American Ceramics Society, 1981, p. 349.
5. Eda, K., Eguchi, H., Okinaka, H., and Matsuoka, M., *Jpn. J. Appl. Phys.* 22:202 (1983).
6. Eda, K., Inada, M., and Matsuoka, M., *J. Appl. Phys.* 54:1095 (1983).
7. Eda, K., Iga, A., and Matsuoka, M., *J. Appl. Phys.* 51:2678 (1980).
8. Gupta, T. K., Carlson, W. G., and Hower, P. L., *J. Appl. Phys.* 52:4104 (1981).
9. Gupta, T. K., and Carlson, W. G., *J. Appl. Phys.* 53:7401 (1982).
10. Sato, K., and Takada Y., *J. Appl. Phys.* 53:8819 (1982).
11. Chiang, Y. M., and Kingery, W. D, *J. Appl. Phys.* 53:1765 (1982).
12. Hayashi, M., Haba, M., Hirano, S., Okamoto, M., and Watanabe, M., *J. Appl. Phys.* 53:5754 (1982).
13. Lou, L. F., *J. Appl. Phys.* 50:555 (1979).
14. Eda, K., *Grain Boundaries in Semiconductors*, H. J. Leamy and G. E. Pike, eds. New York: North-Holland, 1982, pp. 381–392.
15. Schwing, U., and Hoffman, B., *J. Appl. Phys.* 51:4558 (1980).
16. Baumgartner, I., and Einzinger, R., *Material Science Monographs*, vol. 14, D. Kolar et al., eds. Amsterdam: Elsevier 1982, pp. 367–371.

4.6 Ceramic Semiconductors: Negative Temperature Coefficient (NTC) Thermistors

Kunihito Koumoto and Hiroaki Yanagida

4.6.1 Introduction

Precise temperature measurement is increasingly required in such industries as automobiles, computers, home electronics, and office automation. Temperature control is also important for furnaces, reaction vessels, and many other processes in industries. Ceramic NTC thermistors have been developed and used to fulfill these requirements. Temperatures to be detected range from below 0 to above 1000°C, depending on the area in which a thermistor is utilized. Although no one device capable of covering the entire temperature range has been developed, low-, medium-, and high-temperature thermistors are now available. In this section, fundamental characteristics common to most NTC thermistors will be discussed to provide a basic understanding of these thermistors.

4.6.2 Fundamental Characteristics

4.6.2.1 Resistance-Temperature Characteristics

The temperature dependence of resistance in a thermistor is generally expressed as:

$$R = R' \exp(Q/kT) \tag{4.6.1}$$

where Q is the apparent activation energy, k the Boltzmann constant, T the absolute temperature, and R' a preexponential term (Figure 4.6.1a). Choosing a standard temperature T_0 (such as room temperature) at which resistance is R_0, resistance at temperature T can be expressed as

$$R = R_0 \exp[B(1/T - 1/T_0)] \tag{4.6.2}$$

where $B\ (=Q/k)$ is the so-called B constant. Temperature coefficient of resistance α is written as follows and expresses the sensitivity of a thermistor to temperature variation:

$$\alpha = (1/R)(dR/dT) = -B/T^2 \quad [\%/K] \tag{4.6.3}$$

A typical NTC thermistor has about 5 to 10 times as large an α value compared with those utilizing such metals as Pt and Ni.[1]

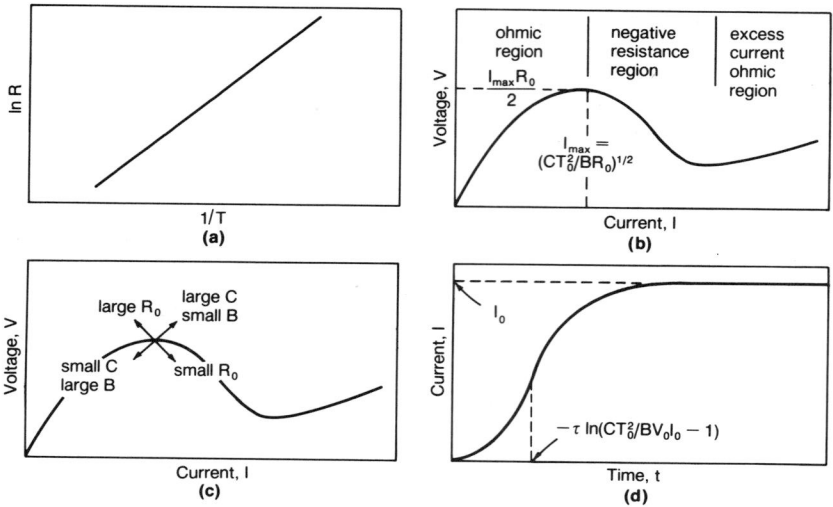

Figure 4.6.1 Fundamental characteristics of a NTC thermistor: (a) resistance-temperature; (b) and (c) current-voltage; and (d) current-time.

4.6.2.2 Current-Voltage Characteristics

When electric power P ($=V \cdot I$) is applied, the temperature of a thermistor increases from self-heating (Joule heat). If the temperature of a thermistor increased from T_0 to T, the following equation could be obtained:

$$P = V \cdot I = C(T - T_0) \qquad [\text{mW/K}] \qquad (4.6.4)$$

where C is the thermal dissipation constant, which depends on the shape and size of the thermistor and the surrounding atmosphere.

When direct current is applied and increased, the output voltage changes, as shown in Figure 4.6.1b. When the current is small, the voltage increases linearly (ohmic region). As the current becomes large, the resistance decreases from self-heating, and the output voltage decreases with increasing current (negative resistance region). As the current is further increased, ohmic behavior caused by excess current is observed (excess current ohmic region). The current and voltage at the turning point from an ohmic to a negative resistance region can be obtained from Equations (4.6.2) and (4.6.4) as follows:

$$I_{max} = (CT_0^2/BR_0)^{1/2}, \quad V_{max} = (R_0/2)(CT_0^2/BR_0)^{1/2} \qquad (4.6.5)$$

How I_{max} and V_{max} change with the changes in B, C, and R_0 is illustrated in Figure 4.6.1c. In cases where a thermistor is used for temperature sensing, the resistance change with the temperature in the ohmic region in which I is much smaller than I_{max} is utilized. However, a thermistor can also be employed as a vacuum gauge, hypsometer, liquid surface sensor, and the like, by utilizing the voltage change with the change in the surrounding atmosphere (a change in C) in the negative resistance region under a fixed current.[2]

4.6.2.3 Time-Current Characteristics

The response time of a thermistor with temperature variation is an important factor in actual application. When the surrounding temperature varies from T_0 to T_1, the temperature of the thermistor varies exponentially with time to reach T_1. This can be expressed as follows:

$$T = T_0 + (T_1 - T_0)[1 - \exp(-t/\tau)] \qquad (4.6.6)$$

where τ is the thermal time constant and is equal to H/C where H is the heat capacity of the thermistor. The smaller τ is, the faster the thermistor can follow the variation in the surrounding temperature and the more suitable it is for thermo-sensing.

How the current varies with time when a constant DC voltage V_0 is applied at T_0 is demonstrated in the following example. Assuming that a thermistor self-heats to T_1 and the current increases to I_0 after a steady state is reached, the resistance variation with time would be calculated from Equations (4.6.2), (4.6.4), and (4.6.6) as follows:

$$R = R_0[1 - BV_0I_0\{1 - \exp(-t/\tau)\}/CT_0^2] \qquad (4.6.7)$$

The time variation of the current is inversely proportional to that of the resistance. The current-time curve has a spinode as shown in Figure 4.6.1d, from which it can be seen that the time to reach a steady state decreases with a smaller τ.

4.6.3 Some Features of NTC Thermistors

NTC thermistors should have the following fundamental properties: a large B constant, a large thermal dissipation constant, and a small thermal time constant. The resistance of the device should lie in a reasonable range for ordinary electric circuits to give rise to rather high output voltages under constant direct current.

From the viewpoint of the dominating charge carrier, NTC thermistors can be classified into three groups: p-type semiconductors (holes), n-type semiconductors (electrons), and ionic conductors (ions). The resistivity ρ of a thermistor is inversely proportional to the

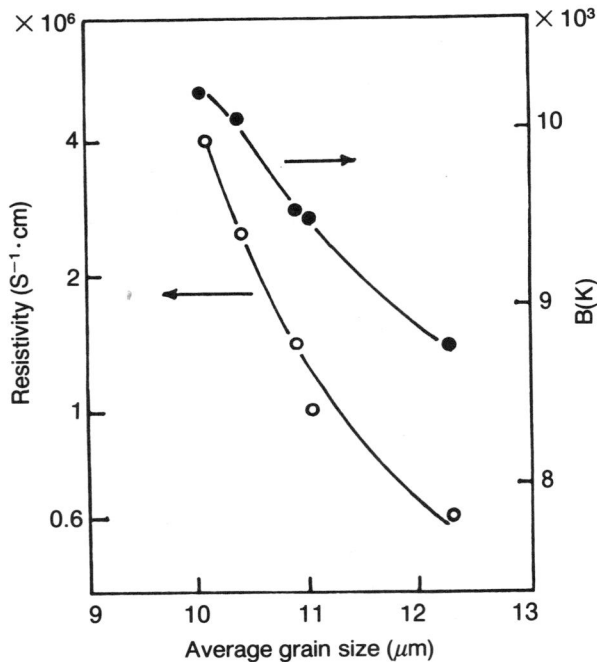

Figure 4.6.2 Grain size dependencies of resistivity and B constant for $(NiO)_{0.9}(TiO_2)_{0.1}$ ceramics fired at $1300°C$.

product of the concentration and the mobility of dominating charge carriers. The B constant is determined by the temperature dependence of the resistivity. Both ρ and B are approximately intrinsic to the chosen composition of a material. In semiconductors ρ and B of the chosen material could be modified either by doping an insulating material of similar composition (dilution principle) or by doping a small amount of additives with different valences (valency control). Base materials for ionic conductors usually have rather high resistivity and low phase stability, making it essential that the doping method introduce ionic defects and stabilize the structure.

Because most NTC thermistors are in a polycrystalline form, both ρ and B are affected by the microstructure (grain size, grain boundaries, pores, etc.). The potential barriers formed at the grain boundaries from segregation or precipitation of the impurities and additives have an especially large influence on the total resistivity and the B constant. Both ρ and B of sintered NiO doped with TiO_2

decreases as the average grain size increases,[3] as shown in Figure 4.6.2. Thus, microstructure control in the processing stage is quite important in obtaining reproducible devices. The B constant of commercially available NTC thermistors ranges from ~1000 K to ~20,000 K. The resistance-temperature characteristics of various NTC thermistors are shown in Figure 4.6.3.[1-7]

To increase the thermal dissipation constant of a thermistor, the surface area should be increased. To decrease the thermal time constant, the heat capacity (volume) should be decreased. Hence, a small thermistor with large surface area would be a good device. Currently available thermistors come in several configurations, including bead,

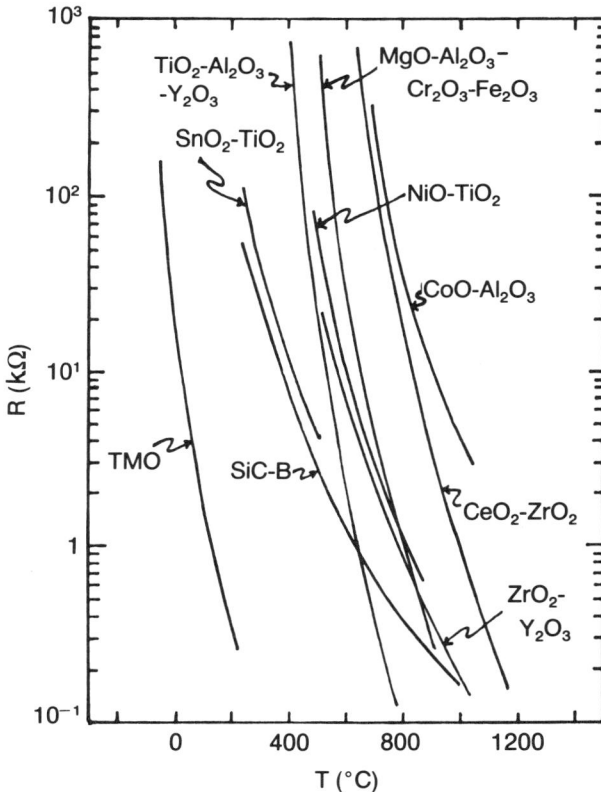

Figure 4.6.3 Resistance-temperature characteristics of various NTC thermistors (TMO = transition metal oxides).

disc, rod, thick film, and pellet types.[8] Microbead and thin-film techniques are becoming of greater importance.[9]

References

1. Nakamura, Y., *Electronic Ceramics*, Spring 1975, p. 63.
2. Yanagida, H., and Takata, M., *Electronic Ceramic Materials*, Tokyo: Gihodo, 1983, p. 96.
3. Kato, T., and Yanagida, H., *Proc. Annual Meeting of the Ceramic Society of Japan*, Tokyo, 1981, p. 219.
4. Matsuo, Y., and Hayakawa, S., U.S. Pat. No. 3962145 (June 1976).
5. Plaschinsky, N. T., U.S. Pat. No. 3598764 (August 1971).
6. Yamada, T., and Ushida, Y., *Electronic Ceramics*, Autumn 1978, p. 59.
7. Futaki, H., *Thermistor and Its Application*, Tokyo: Nikkan Kogyo Shinbun, 1969, p. 4.
8. Kamohara, N., *Sensor Tech.* 1:62 (1981).
9. Shimura, Y., *Sensor Tech.* 1:47 (1981).

4.7 Ceramic Semiconductors: Positive Temperature Coefficient (PTC) Materials

Makoto Kuwabara and Hiroaki Yanagida

4.7.1 Introduction

A great number of studies have been made on the PTC of electrical resistivity in doped semiconducting barium titanate ceramics since the discovery of the PTC effect was first reported.[1] These studies have emphasized both the application of the effect and the mechanism itself. The PTC property has been used for many applications, including constant temperature heating elements, degaussing components for color television, and starters for motors. Several models[2-4] have been proposed to interpret the mechanism of the effect. Of these, the barrier layer model proposed by Heywang[3] and further developed by Jonker[5] and Daniels and co-workers[6] has been accepted as one of the most successful. These achievements in both practical application and understanding of the PTC property have brought about the development of other electronic ceramics with nonlinear grain boundary properties, such as varistors,[7] barrier layer (BL) capacitors,[8] and high-Q ferrites with insulating grain boundaries.[9] Although the development of PTC material technology and the theory of the PTC effect have been reviewed in detail by Kulwicki[10] and Jonker[11] individually, this section provides another review focusing on progress made in understanding the PTC effect on the basis of recently observed experimental evidence.

4.7.2 Some Features of the PTC Effect

The PTC effect has been confirmed to originate from the grain boundary property and to be associated with the ferroelectric-to-paraelectric phase transition in semiconducting barium titanate ceramics. The following experimental observations serve to review its features.

1. Only barium titanate ceramics made semiconducting through doping with small amounts (≤ 0.3 at%) of donor elements such as Ln, Sb, Bi, and Nb have been found to exhibit a pronounced PTC effect. The addition of donor elements beyond 0.4 at% made the materials insulating with a normal negative temperature coefficient (NTC) of resistivity rather than a PTC property.
2. The PTC curves for the resistivity-temperature characteristic have been observed in various shapes and found to be very sensitive to the procedure and conditions employed in preparing the ceramics.
3. The magnitude of the PTC effect has been found to be significantly influenced by the partial pressure of oyxgen in the sintering atmosphere and to be enhanced by the addition of acceptor-like transition elements such as Mn and Cr.[12]

These features of the PTC characteristic have been observed mostly in large-grained, high-density barium titanate ceramics produced through conventional methods. They have been broadly derived through use of the Heywang model with the aid of barium titanate defect chemistry.[13,14] However, there has never been any definite experimental proof of the validity of the Heywang model in conjunction with a successful interpretation of all the shapes of the PTC curves reported in the literature.

4.7.3 The PTC Effect in Porous BaTiO₃ Ceramics

A series of studies[15-23] of PTC characteristics has been made on porous barium titanate ceramics to clarify the following ambiguities

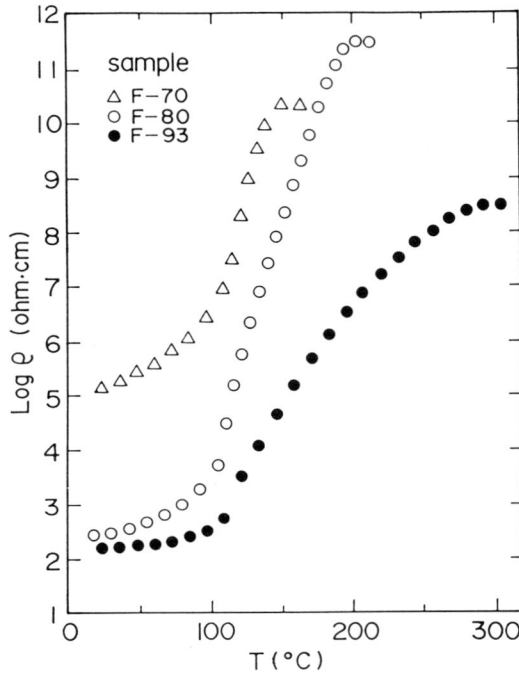

Figure 4.7.1 Resistivity-temperature characteristics for porous PTC materials with three different relative sintered densities. Figures that appear in the sample numbers indicate the relative sintered densities of the bodies.

in the Heywang model:

1. Which type of current generates the PTC property, diffusion-type or space-charge-limited current (SCLC) type?
2. What is the exact nature of surface acceptor states assumed in the model?
3. Why have so many different shapes of PTC curves been observed in samples produced under different sintering conditions but with the same composition?
4. Is the high-field dielectric constant really necessary in explaining the lowering of the grain boundary potential barrier height below the Curie point?

Typical PTC characteristics observed in porous semiconducting barium titanate ceramics with three different porosities are shown in Figure 4.7.1.[18] The nature of the characteristics occurring when there has been no addition of acceptor elements such as Mn or Cr has been found to be closely connected with the ceramic microstructure.[15,16] Furthermore, the magnitude of the effect appears to depend on the relative sintered density and the average grain size of the ceramics and to be independent of the heating schedules employed for sintering.[17] These features of the PTC effect are quite surprising and lead to an important conclusion: in small-grained, porous barium titanate ceramics, well-developed potential barriers can be formed at the grain boundaries simply by sintering the materials in air, where slow cooling after sintering for oxidation of the grain boundaries is not required for enhancing the PTC effect.

The influence of stoichiometry on the magnitude of the PTC effect has also been investigated, as shown in Figure 4.7.2. Different features of the nonstoichiometry dependence of the PTC effect have been observed for two groups of samples, one with BaO-rich compositions and the other with TiO_2-rich compositions. The differences can be interpreted in terms of their grain structures.[16] It was found that the addition of excess BaO ($\lesssim 3$ mol%) yields small-grain, distinguishable grain structures producing large PTC effects, whereas the addition of excess TiO_2 ($\gtrsim 2$ mol%) causes exaggerated grain growth

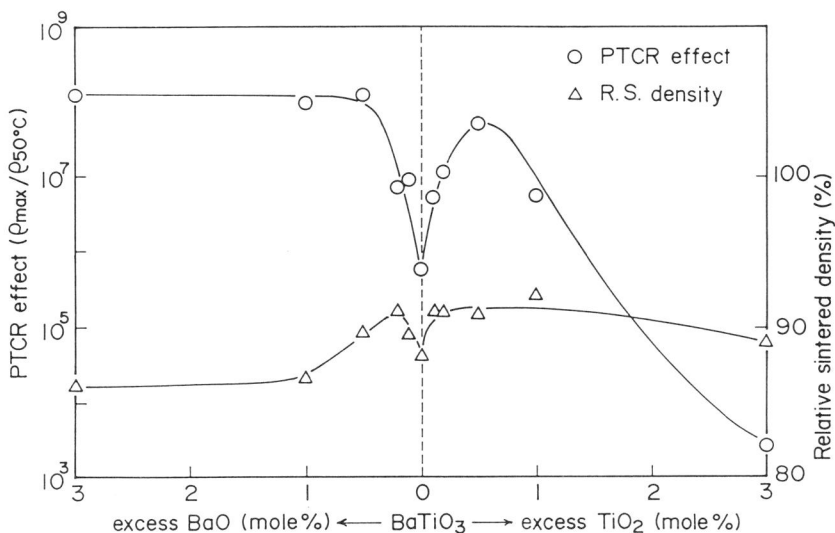

Figure 4.7.2 PTC effect and relative sintered densities as a function of excess BaO or TiO_2 added to samples.

leading to large-grain structures. Grain boundaries without well-developed potential barriers have been confirmed to exist in large-grain barium titanate ceramics. These provide little PTC effect.[24]

Studies on the ambient gas dependence of the PTC characteristic have, however, revealed that oxygen atoms adsorbed on the grain surfaces act as surface acceptors.[22] Figure 4.7.3 shows the typical ambient gas dependence of the PTC characteristic obtained for a porous barium titanate ceramic. The degradation in the PTC characteristic observed in a CO atmosphere was completely recovered by reheating the material in oxygen to 350°C, confirming that the adsorption of oxygen is required for the appearance of large PTC effects.

4.7.4 Conclusion

From the overall experimental results obtained for porous semiconducting barium titanate ceramics, answers to the foregoing questions with respect to the Heywang model were conclusively given. First, a diffusion-type current dominates at the grain boundaries in materials generating a PTC effect.[19] Second the nature of surface acceptor states

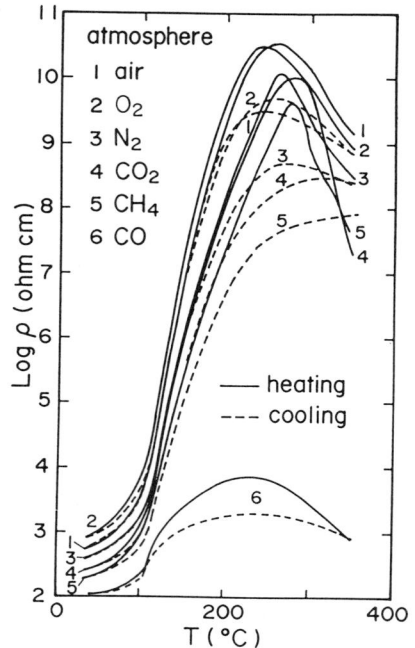

Figure 4.7.3 Influence of ambient gas on the resistivity-temperature characteristic of a porous PTC material.

is adsorbed oxygen atoms or molecules.[22] Third, many different shapes of PTC curves, observed especially in large-grain PTC materials, can be attributed to the distribution morphology of grain boundaries with low potential barriers. And last, the existence of a zero-bias current, obtained by extrapolation of the log I versus V plot to V = 0, proves that the high-field dielectric constant assumed in the Heywang model is not necessary for explaining the low room-temperature resistivity of the PTC materials. The low-field dielectric constant of the material can explain the entire PTC phenomenon in conjunction with the influence of spontaneous polarization on the lowering of room-temperature resistivity.[5]

References

1. Haaijman, P. W., Dam, R. W., and Klasens, H. A., German Pat. 929350 (June 1955).
2. Saburi, O., *J. Phys. Soc. Jpn.* 14:1159 (1959).
3. Heywang, W., *J. Am. Ceram. Soc.* 47:484 (1964).
4. Peria, W. T., Bratshun, W. R., and Fenity, R. D., *J. Am. Ceram. Soc.* 44:249 (1961).
5. Jonker, G. H., *Solid State Electron.* 7:895 (1964).
6. Daniels, J., Hardtl, K. H., and Wernicke, R., *Philips Tech. Rev.* 38:73 (1978–79).
7. Matsuoka, M., *Jpn. J. Appl. Phys.* 10:736 (1971).
8. Waku, S., *ARSG on Appl. Ferroelectrics in Jpn.* 12:12-65-392 (1963).
9. Akashi, T., *Jpn. J. Appl. Phys.* 30:928 (1961).
10. Kulwicki, B. M., *Grain Boundary Phenomena in Electronic Ceramics*, L. M. Levinson, ed., Columbus, Ohio: American Ceramics Society, 1981, p. 138.
11. Jonker, G. H., *Grain Boundary Phenomena in Electronic Ceramics*, L. M. Levinson, ed. Columbus, Ohio: American Ceramics Society, 1981, p. 155.
12. Matsuoka, T., Matsuo, Y., Sasaki, H., and Hayakawa, S., *J. Am. Ceram. Soc.* 55:108 (1972).
13. Wernicke, R., *Philips Res. Rep.* 31:487 (1976).
14. Seuter, A. M. J. H., *Philips Res. Rep. Suppl.* 3 (1974).
15. Kuwabara, M., *J. Am. Ceram. Soc.* 64:639 (1981).
16. Kuwabara, M., *J. Am. Ceram. Soc.* 64:C-170 (1981).
17. Kuwabara, M., *Jpn. J. Appl. Phys. Suppl.* 20-4:131 (1981).
18. Kuwabara, M., *Additives and Interfaces in Electronic Ceramics*, M. F. Yan and A. H. Heuer, eds. Columbus, Ohio: American Ceramic Society, 1983, p. 137.

19. Kuwabara, M., *Additives and Interfaces in Electronic Ceramics*, M. F. Yan and A. H. Heuer, eds. Columbus, Ohio: American Ceramic Society, 1983, p. 128.
20. Kuwabara, M., *J. Mat. Sci. Lett.* 2:403 (1983).
21. Kuwabara, M., and Kumamoto, K., *J. Am. Ceram. Soc.* 66:C-214 (1983).
22. Kuwabara, M., and Inoue, H., *Proc. International Meeting on Chemical Sensors*, Fukuoka, 1983, p. 182.
23. Kuwabara, M., *Solid State Electron.* 27:929 (1984).
24. Nemoto, H., and Oda, I. *J. Am. Ceram. Soc.* 63:398 (1980).

4.8 Ceramic Semiconductors: Gas Sensors

Masaru Miyayama and Hiroaki Yanagida

4.8.1 Introduction

Semiconductor gas sensors utilize the change in resistivity occurring when detectable gases are adsorbed on the sensor surface. Since the proposal made in 1962 by Seiyama and co-workers on gas sensors,[1] a number of studies have been undertaken. Some of the gas sensors subsequently developed are now commercially available as detectors or alarms for combustible gases or humidity. In 1983 the first international meeting on chemical sensors was held in Fukuoka, Japan, where many types of gas sensors were presented.

4.8.2 Combustible Gas Sensors

In gas sensors utilizing SnO_2- or ZnO-based ceramics, the resistivity of the sensors when exposed to combustible gases decreases because of the electron transfer caused by a chemical reaction of the gases with chemisorbed oxygen on the sensor surface. It is known that the sensitivity and selectivity of SnO_2 or ZnO sensors are greatly enhanced by adding small amounts of activators such as Pd and Pt. In recent years many kinds of activators have been studied in addition to noble metals. These include Ag added to SnO_2 for H_2 gas,[2] PdCl to ZnO for H_2 gas,[3] $V-Mo-Al_2O_3$ to ZnO for halogenated hydrocarbon gases,[4] and $NiO-SiO_2-Al_2O_3$ to ZnO for C_2H_5OH gas.[5] The suppressing effect of some additives on the sensitivity of certain gases has also been examined, including the addition of Pt-P and Rh-P to ZnO for C_2H_5OH gas[6] and SiO_2 film coating on SnO_2 for all but H_2 gas.[7]

Applications of these sensors in thin film devices have been studied extensively. One example is an ultrafine particle SnO_2 film (with a median particle size of several nm) produced through the evaporation of Sn metal in a low-oxygen-pressure atmosphere.[8] This film can be made selectively sensitive to combustible gases and humidity by choosing the film depositing conditions and operating temperature, as shown in Figure 4.8.1. A thin film SnO_2 sensor made through vapor deposition of Pd-doped SnO_2 has also been reported. This sensor consists of an SnO_2 film (0.3–0.35 μm thick), an SiO precoated ferrite substrate and an RuO_2 thick film as a heater, and has preferential sensitivity for CO and C_2H_5OH gases.[9] A hybrid sensor capable of detecting C_2H_5OH gas and humidity separately has been developed through unification of a screen-printed ZnO thick film with hydroxyapatite porous ceramics and RuO_2 electrodes.[10]

Studies on the sensing mechanism are also proceeding. Yamazoe and co-workers reported that the addition of a small amount of Ag to an SnO_2 sensor greatly enhances the sensitivity to H_2 gas from RT to 250°C.[2] Measuring with XPS the redox properties of the SnO_2 surface

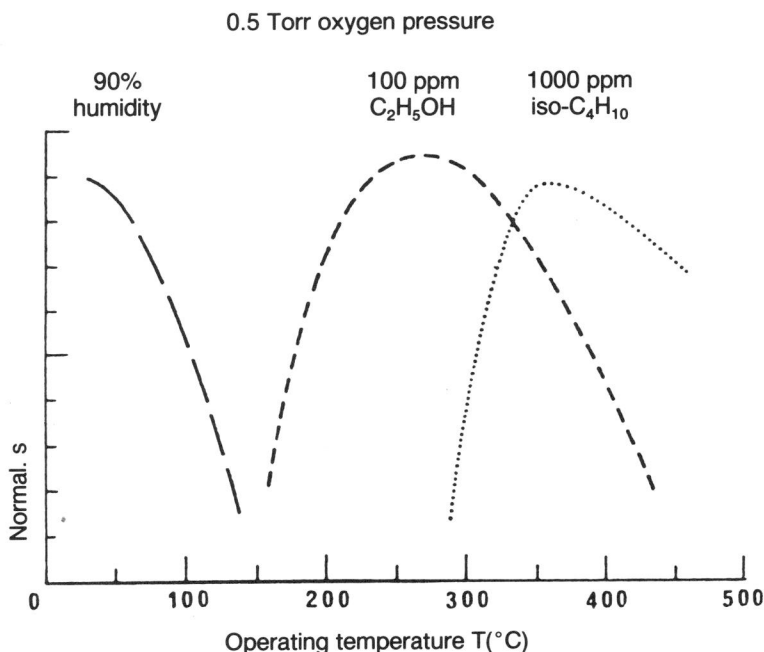

Figure 4.8.1 The sensitivity of the tin oxide ultrafine particle film made under 0.5 Torr oxygen pressure as a function of the sensor operating temperature [from H. Ogawa et al., *J. Electrochem. Soc.* 128:2020 (1981)].

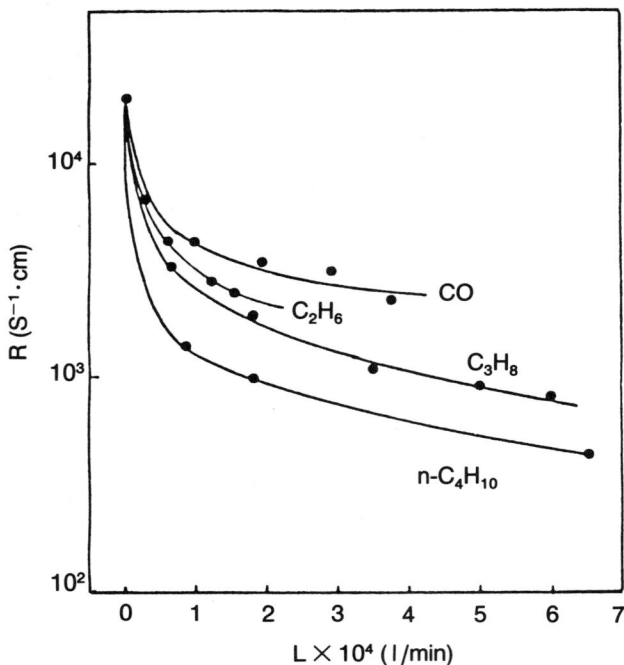

Figure 4.8.2 Resistivity plotted against the rate of consumption of adsorbed oxygen in various detective gases for ZnO at 400°C (after H. Yanagida et al., *Chemical Sensors*, T. Seiyama et al., eds. Tokyo: Kodansha, 1983).

and binding energies of $O_{1s}1/2$ and $Sn_{3d}5/2$ indicated that the marked sensitivity of Ag-SnO$_2$ is associated with the change of electrical interaction between Ag and SnO$_2$, whereas the spillover effects of H$_2$ and O$_2$ seem to be instrumental in Pd-SnO$_2$. Yanagida and co-workers measured the changes of resistivity in ZnO and the extent of conversion of combustible gases to CO$_2$ simultaneously.[11] The amount of oxygen consumed to cause the same resistivity was different for each gas and was smaller for a larger concentration of carbon atoms per unit volume, as shown in Figure 4.8.2. These results suggest that transiently oxidized intermediates on the sensor surface have some role in determining the resistivity of a ZnO sensor.

Perovskite oxides LnMO$_3$ (Ln = La − Gd, M = Cr, Mn, Fe, Co) mixed with rare earth transition metal are known to exhibit alcohol-sensing characteristics. The sensing mechanism is ascribed to a chemical reaction of alcohols with oxygen in the lattice. Arakawa and co-workers estimated the binding energy (ΔH) of oxygen coordinating to the metal ions and the energy (ΔE) needed to promote a change in conductivity after injection of CH_3OH.[12] It was found that the decrease in ΔH corresponded closely to the decrease in ΔE, with $LnCoO_3$ exhibiting minimum values of ΔH and ΔE. Changes in resistivity of γ- and α-Fe_2O_3 for combustible gases are also thought to be due to the partial reduction of Fe_2O_3 to Fe_3O_4.[13]

4.8.3 Humidity Sensors

Humidity sensors can be classified into two types according to whether conduction is electronic or ionic. Humidity sensors of the ionic conduction type have already been developed in Japan using porous ceramics such as $MgCr_2O_4$-TiO_2,[14] TiO_2-V_2O_5,[15] $ZnCr_2O_4$-

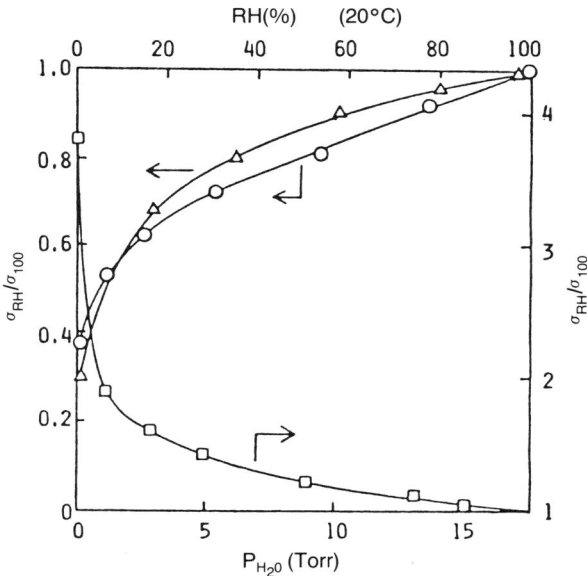

Figure 4.8.3 Conductivity ratio-humidity characteristics at 400°C.

　　　　　　○ $SrSnO_3$　　　　(n-type)

　　　　　　△ $Sr_{0.9}La_{0.1}TiO_3$ (n-type)

　　　　　　□ $SrTiO_3$　　　　 (p-type)

σ_{100}: conductivity at 100% relative humidity (after H. Arai et al., *Chemical Sensors*, T. Seiyama et al., eds. Tokyo: Kodansha, 1983).

$LiZnVO_4$,[16] and $(MO)_{1-x}(AO_{0.5})_x(Fe_2O_3)$[17] ($M = Mg, Zn; A = Li, Na, K$). In this type, the conductivity is usually enhanced by physisorption or capillary condensation of water at room temperature. The protons dissociated from water molecules are probably the dominant carriers. The ceramic body of the $ZnCr_2O_4$-$LiZnVO_4$ sensor consists of $ZnCr_2O_4$ spinel grains and a glassy vanadium compound ($LiZnVO_4$) situated on the surface of the spinel grains. The glassy vanadium compound is a reversibly hygroscopic material.

In electronic conduction-type sensors such as perovskite-type oxides[18] and ZrO_2-MgO,[19] electrons transferred from chemisorbed water molecules to oxides are the dominant carriers. Arai and co-workers have found that perovskite-type oxides ABO_3 ($A = Ca, Sr$; $B = Sn, Ti$) containing La ions at site A exhibit humidity-sensing characteristics[18] (Figure 4.8.3). They also examined the semiconducting properties (n- or p-type), microstructure, and water-vapor pressure dependence of conductivity of the oxides, and proposed the dissociative adsorption of water vapor on ionized oxygen vacancies as the humidity-sensing mechanism.

References

1. Seiyama, T., Kato, A., and Fujiishi, K., *Anal. Chem.* 34:1502 (1962).
2. Yamazoe, N., Kurokawa, Y., and Seiyama, T., *Chemical Sensors*, T. Seiyama et al., eds. Tokyo: Kodansha, 1983, pp. 35–40.
3. Yoneyama, H., Li, W. B., and Tamura, H., *Chemical Sensors*, T. Seiyama et al., eds. Tokyo: Kodansha, 1983, pp. 113–118.
4. Shiratori, M., Katsura, M., and Tsuchiya, T., *Chemical Sensors*, T. Seiyama et al., eds. Tokyo: Kodansha, 1983, pp. 119–124.
5. Matsuzawa, T., Sugai, T., and Okuda, A., *Chemical Sensors*, T. Seiyama et al., eds. Tokyo: Kodansha, 1983, pp. 108–112.
6. Katsura, M., Shiratori, M., Takahashi, T., Yokomizo, Y., and Ichinose, N., *Chemical Sensors*, T. Seiyama et al., eds. Tokyo: Kodansha, 1983, pp. 101–106.
7. Fukui, K., and Komatsu, K., *Chemical Sensors*, T. Seiyama et al., eds. Tokyo: Kodansha, 1983, pp. 52–56.
8. Ogawa, H., Abe, A., Nishikawa, M., and Hayakawa, S., *J. Electrochem. Soc.* 128:2020 (1981).
9. Oyabu, T., *J. Appl. Phys.* 53:2785 (1982).
10. Komine, Y., Sawada, T., and Sato, K., *Proc. 2nd Sensor Symposium, Institute of Electrical Engineers of Japan*, 1982, pp. 199–203.
11. Yanagida, H., Koumoto, K., Miyayama, M., and Saito, S., *Chemical Sensors*, T. Seiyama et al., eds. Tokyo: Kodansha, 1983, pp. 95–100.

12. Arakawa, T., Ohara, N., Kurachi, H., and Shiokawa, J., *Chemical Sensors*, T. Seiyama et al., eds. Tokyo: Kodansha, 1983, pp. 159–164.
13. Nakatani, Y., Sakai, M., and Matsuoka, M., *Jpn. J. Appl. Phys.* 22:912 (1983).
14. Nitta, T., Terada, Z., and Hayakawa, S., *J. Am. Ceram. Soc.* 63:295 (1980).
15. Katayama, K., and Akiba, T., *Chemical Sensors*, T. Seiyama et al., eds. Tokyo: Kodansha, 1983, pp. 433–438.
16. Uno, S., Harata, M., Hiraki, H., and Yokomizo, Y., *Proc. 2nd Sensor Symposium, Institute of Electrical Engineers of Japan*, 1982, pp. 85–88.
17. Suzuki, T., and Matsui, N., *Chemical Sensors*, T. Seiyama et al., eds. Tokyo: Kodansha, 1983, pp. 381–386.
18. Arai, H., Ezaki, S., Shimizu, Y., Shippo, O., and Seiyama, T., *Chemical Sensors*, T. Seiyama et al., eds. Tokyo: Kodansha, 1983, pp. 393–398.
19. Nitta, T., Fukushima, F., and Matsuo, Y., *Chemical Sensors*, T. Seiyama et al., eds. Tokyo: Kodansha, 1983, pp. 387–392.

4.9 Ionic Conductors

Masayuki Nagai

4.9.1 Introduction

Ionic conductors are solids that have a high electrical conductivity well below their melting points as a result of ionic motion. Recent extensive work in this field has markedly increased the number of new cation and anion conductors. Cation conductors consist of alkali, copper, silver, proton, and other ion conductors; anion conductors are almost exclusively composed of fluorine and oxygen ion conductors. There has been considerable interest in sodium and oxygen ion conductors, and more recently in lithium and proton conductors, mainly because of their promising applications.

This section reviews recent progress in ionic conductors with special emphasis on lithium, proton, and anion conductors.

4.9.2 Lithium Ion Conductors

Lithium ion conductors are of importance for their application as solid electrolyte membranes in high-energy-density batteries. Besides ordinary Li^+ conductors involving Li_4ZrO_4, Li_2O, and Li_5AlO_4, several materials have been reported to exhibit a high ionic conductivity.

The temperature dependence of the conductivity for prominent Li^+ conductors known to date is shown in Figure 4.9.1. The highest

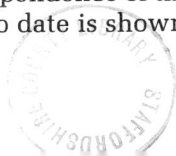

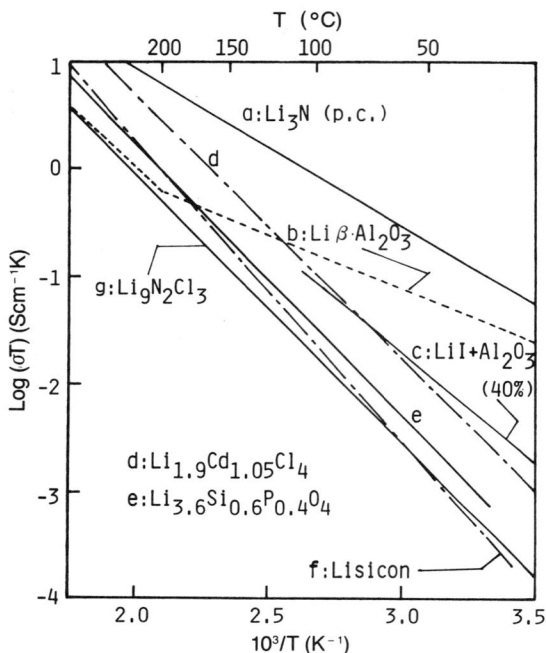

Figure 4.9.1 Temperature dependence of ionic conductivity for prominent Li$^+$ conductors: Li$_3$N (Ref. 1); Li β-Al$_2$O$_3$ (Ref. 2); LiI + 40%Al$_2$O$_3$ (Ref. 3); Li$_{3.6}$Si$_{0.6}$P$_{0.4}$O$_4$ (Ref. 4); Lisicon (Ref. 5); Li$_9$N$_2$Cl$_3$ (Ref. 6); Li$_{1.9}$Cd$_{1.05}$Cl$_4$ (Ref. 7).

conductivity of ~3 × 10^{-4} (Ω·cm)$^{-1}$ at ambient temperature was reported for the layer structured Li$_3$N,[1] where Li$^+$ moves predominently in the hexagonally packed Li$_2$N$^-$ layer. However, there are major disadvantages concerning practical use, including its low decomposition voltage (as low as 0.445 V at 298°K) and the formation of electrically short-circuiting dentrites.

To overcome these problems, ternary compounds based on Li$_3$N have been developed. The conducting phase Li$_9$N$_2$Cl$_3$ in the system Li$_3$N-LiCl has a conductivity of 3 × 10^{-5} (Ω·cm)$^{-1}$ and a decomposition voltage of 2.52 V at 373°K.[6] This compound has an antifluorite structure with 10% of the Li$^+$ site being vacant. The presence of hydrogen in this structure was reported to affect the vacancy concentration as well as the activation energy for conduction.[7] Recently, other types of chlorides such as Li$_{1.9}$Cd$_{1.05}$Cl$_4$ with the spinel structure were found to exhibit a high ionic conductivity.[8]

Another class of Li$^+$ conductors are the solid solutions based on either Li_4SiO_4 or $\gamma_{II}Li_3PO_4$. Those based on Li_4SiO_4 include the partial solid solutions with Li_4GeO_4, Li_5AlO_4, and Li_3PO_4, whereas the $\gamma_{II}Li_3PO_4$ type consists of Lisicon $Li_{14}Zn(GeO_4)^5$ and Li_3VO_4-Li_4GeO_4 solid solutions,[10] which contain a high concentration of interstitial Li^+. One of the problems regarding practical use is that most of these conductors are thermodynamically unstable with Li and/or cathode active materials. The possible candidates are considered to be $Li_{3.6}Si_{0.6}P_{0.4}O_4$, $Li_{3.4}Si_{0.4}$-$V_{0.6}O_4$, and amorphous compounds in the system Li_2O-SiO_2-ZrO_2 because they react very slowly with Li.[11]

The search for new Li^+ conductors has resulted in the general validity of the enhancement of ionic conductivity by orders of magnitude in dispersed two-phase mixtures of LiI and Al_2O_3 or SiO_2,[3] which may not be attributed to the formation of defects by a classical doping process. Structural properties of the electrically insulating second phase were found to be of minor influence, whereas the amount and particle size of the second phase have shown a drastic effect.[12,13] Although the mechanism has not been clarified, the effect of moisture and the formation of a conducting layer at the phase boundary would be responsible for this enhancement.

4.9.3 Sodium Ion Conductors

Sodium ion conductors have the potential for use in several electrochemical devices, including sodium-sulfur storage cells, electrochemical sensors, and electrochromic displays. The most extensively studied compounds are β and β''-Al_2O_3. However, degradation and economical problems prevent these devices from general utilization. Therefore, searches for other Na^+ conductors have been continued, leading to a new type of conductor, $Na_3Zr_2PSi_2O_{12}$ (Nasicon),[14] with a three-dimensional framework structure.

The transport properties of Nasicon are clearly equivalent to those of β''-Al_2O_3 (~ 0.4 $(\Omega \cdot cm)^{-1}$ at 573°K. Since then, a number of studies on substitution of tetragonal and/or octahedral sites of the Nasicon-type structure have been reported in order to synthesize new Na^+ conductors. The compound $Na_{3.1}Zr_{1.55}Si_{2.3}$-$P_{0.7}O_{11}$ was reported to have an ionic conductivity of 2.3×10^{-3} $(\Omega \cdot cm)^{-1}$, which exceeds that of Nasicon by half an order of magnitude at room temperature.[15] Other conductive phases were found in the system $Na_{1+x}Y_xZr_{2-x}(PO_4)_3$[16] and $Na_{1+x}(Cr, In, Yb)_xZr_{2-x}(PO_4)_3$.[17] As a large number of compounds have been reported to be stabilized with the Nasicon-type structure, it is likely that other highly conductive phases will be developed in the future.

In spite of the high conductivity and low sintering temperature, there is a difficulty associated with the fabrication of Nasicon. This difficulty is related to thermodynamic stability, especially the problem of free zirconia and the phase transition. Recently, it was suggested that the Nasicon-type compounds would generally exhibit two-phase transition in the temperature range of 298 to $573°K$.[18] Static corrosion tests have demonstrated that the electrochemical cells composed of Nasicon have not reached an acceptable level for application.[19]

4.9.4 Proton Conductors

The feature of proton conductors is unique as a result of the absence of an electron cloud. Basically, three conduction mechanisms have been proposed. One is the jump of single protons as in H_xWO_3, H_xMoO_3, and $HTaWO_6$.[20] The second is the proton transport resulting from complex ions diffusing as a whole, such as H_3O^+ in partially dehydrated $H_3O^+\beta$- and $\beta''-Al_2O_3$.[21] The third possibility is to have a Grotthus-type mechanism, which is possible in compounds with a network of hydrogen bonding connecting proton donor molecules with proton acceptor ones. The third mechanism is proposed in fully hydrated $H_3O^+\beta$ and $\beta''-Al_2O_3$[21] and $H_2Sb_4O_{11} \cdot nH_2O$.[20]

A compilation of representative proton conductors that were recently developed is shown in Figure 4.9.2. In general, fast proton conductors contain structural water and high valent cations and possess an acidic character. H_3O^+, NH_4^+, and $H_3O^+/NH_4^+\beta''-Al_2O_3$[24] are regarded as some of the most promising materials for use in solid electrolyte cells because of their thermal stability. However, their conductivity is not sufficient for practical applications at the moment.

Recently, proton conductors at elevated temperatures have been developed. Some compounds based on the composition of $SrCeO_3$ were found to exhibit a high proton conductivity on exposure to a flow of steam or hydrogen.[26] They can be utilized as a solid electrolyte for galvanic cell-type gas sensors and steam concentration cells.

4.9.5 Other Cation Conductors

Two new types of cation conductors with the $\beta''-Al_2O_3$ structure were recently developed. One is polycrystalline $K\beta''-Al_2O_3$ fabri-

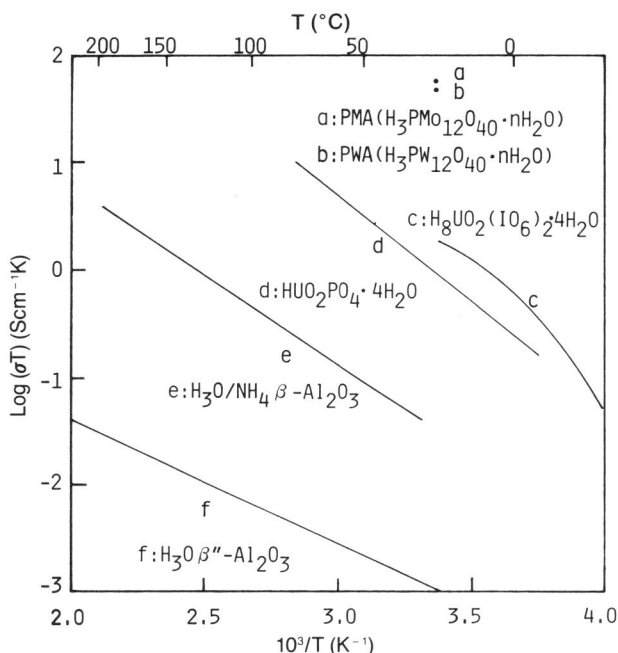

Figure 4.9.2 Conductivity characteristics of representative proton conductors: H_3O^+ β''-Al_2O_3 (Ref. 21); PMA and PWA (Ref. 22); $HUO_2PO_4 4H_2O$ (Ref. 23); $H_8UO_2(IO_6)_2 4H_2O$ (Ref. 24); H_3O^+/NH_4^+ β''-Al_2O_3 (Ref. 25).

cated by vapor phase ion exchange, which was reported to have a high conductivity comparable to $Na\beta''$-Al_2O_3.[27] The other is $Pb\beta''$-Al_2O_3 fabricated by liquid-phase ion exchange. Although high ionic conductors of divalent cations are rare, it showed an exceptionally high conductivity of 4.6×10^{-3} $(\Omega \cdot cm)^{-1}$ at $313°K$.[28]

From the viewpoint of theoretical consideration, much work has been devoted to the understanding of the dynamic behavior and the local structure of mobile ions. In relation to this, the mixed alkali effect in mixed monovalent cation conductors has attracted considerable interest for the past several years. This effect has been observed in β-Al_2O_3[29] and β-gallate.[30] Although none of the models proposed to date win universal acceptance, weak electrolyte models, site preference energy, and cooperative vibration of mobile ions are possible explanations.[31]

4.9.6 Fluorine Ion Conductors

Relatively high ionic conductivities have been reported for fluorides because of certain features of fluorine ions, such as their monovalence, small size, and strong ionic character. These properties make F^- conductors useful for electrochemical devices, including batteries, infrared detectors, and gas sensors. The conductivity and activation energy for prominent conductors are summarized in Table 4.9.1. A comparison of these conductivities with those for other types of ion conductors leads to the conclusion that F^- in fluorides with the fluorite structure have a greater mobility than O^{2-} in isostructural doped ZrO_2, CeO_2, and Bi_2O_3. Additionally, the ionic conductivity at ambient temperature for β-$PbSnF_4$[32] or $NH_4Sn_2F_5$[35] is nearly the same order of magnitude as that of fast cation conductors such as $RbAg_4I_5$ and $Rb_4Cu_{16}Cl_{13}I_7$.

However, two common disadvantages of fluorides should be noted: they have low melting points ($PbSnF_4$: $T_m = 663°K$, $TlSn_2F_5$: $T_m = 475°K$) and tend to be decomposed by moisture in air.

Another feature of the fluorides shown in Table 4.9.1 is that the best conductivity is obtained with stoichiometric compounds such as $PbSnF_4$ and $NH_4Sn_2F_5$. Generally, it is possible to improve the conductivity by doping to produce vacancies and/or interstitial ions. However, in contrast to oxides with the fluorite structure, it is difficult to approach the performance of the best ion conductors in the

Table 4.9.1 Comparison of Conductivity and Activation Energy for the Major F^- Ion Conductors

Formula	Structure	Conductivity $(\Omega \cdot cm)^{-1}$	Activation Energy (eV)	Reference
β-PbF_2	Fluorite	10^{-6} (20°C)	0.45	32
β-$PbSnF_4$	Fluorite	8×10^{-2} (150°C)	0.14	32
$KBiF_4$	Fluorite	10^{-4} (20°C)	0.38	32
CaF_2	Fluorite	10^{-11} (150°C)	1.04	33
LaF_3	Tysonite	10^{-2} (200°C)	0.40	34
$NH_4Sn_2F_5$	KSn_2F_5-type	10^{-1} (80°C)	0.35	35

fluorides, as the introduced defects do not contribute to the conductivity because of strong interaction.[36]

4.9.7 Oxygen Ion Conductors

Oxygen ion conductors such as ZrO_2, CeO_2, ThO_2, and Bi_2O_3 with a fluorite structure have been studied in great detail because of their use in oxygen sensors, fuel cells, and other electrochemical devices. Conductivity as a function of temperature for major O^{2-} conductors is shown in Figure 4.9.3. The most commonly utilized material is stabilized zirconia in the system CaO-ZrO_2 and Y_2O_3-ZrO_2, whereas the highest conductivity for O^{2-} conductors was reported to be ~1 $(\Omega \cdot cm)^{-1}$ at 1073°K in the system Y_2O_3-Bi_2O_3.[37] The fluorite-structured solid solutions based on ThO_2 have the advantage that they can be employed as a solid electrolyte in a highly reducing atmosphere.[42]

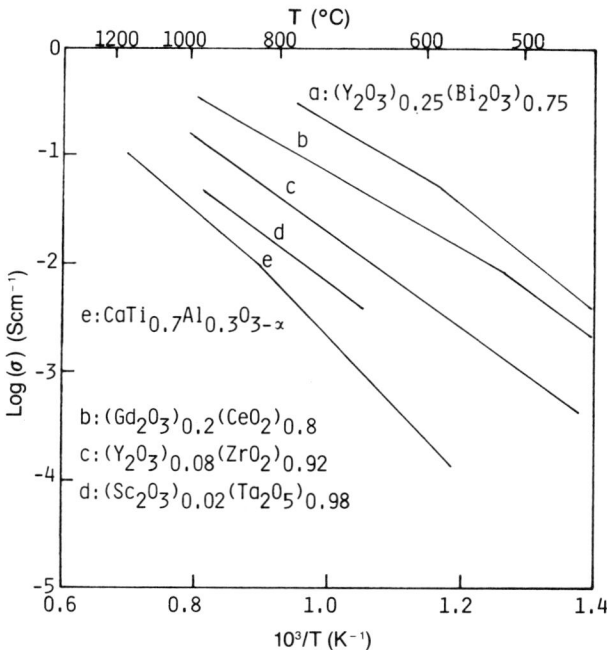

Figure 4.9.3 Conductivity as a function of temperature for major O^{2-} conductors: Y_2O_3-Bi_2O_3 (Ref. 37); Gd_2O_3-CeO_2 (Ref. 38); Y_2O_3-ZrO_2 (Ref. 39); Sc_2O_3-Ta_2O_5 (Ref. 40); Al_2O_3-$CaTiO_3$ (Ref. 41).

Although much work has been done on these conductors, their thermodynamic behavior has not been entirely clarified. For example, new ordered phases were recently found in the system CaO-ZrO_2[43] and Y_2O_3-ZrO_2.[44] The temperature dependence of the diffusion coefficient for O^{2-} in the system CaO-ZrO_2 suggests that there could be a phase transition in the cubic zirconia region.[45]

It is well known that conductivity as a function of the total dopant concentration goes through a maximum, indicating a strong interaction effect involving oxygen vacancies. Attempts to explain this unusual behavior have been made by several investigators,[46] and such explanations as the cluster model, the variation of activation energy, the vacancy near neighbor interaction, and the free vacancy model have been offered, but none of them succeeded in explaining the observed properties entirely.

With regard to new types of O^{2-} conductors, α-Ta_2O_5 doped with Sc_2O_3 was recently found to exhibit a high conductivity.[40]

4.9.8 Conclusion

This section has summarized recent progress in ionic conductors. As general guiding principles to develop new ionic conductors are not yet established, fundamental studies on fabrication, structure, and properties are of importance. Cooperation of material scientists with theoreticians seems to be essential for further progress in this field.

References

1. Boukamp, B. A., and Huggins, R. A., *Phys. Lett.* 58A:231 (1976).
2. Whittingham, M. S., and Huggins, R. A., *NBS Spec. Publ.* 364, R. S. Roth and S. J. Schneider, eds. Washington, DC: National Bureau of Standards, 1972, p. 139.
3. Liang, C. C., *J. Electrochem. Soc.* 120:1289 (1973).
4. Hu, Y-W., Raistrick, T. D., and Huggins, R. S., *Mat. Res. Bull.* 11:1227 (1976).
5. Hong, H. Y-P., *Mat. Res. Bull.* 13:117 (1978).
6. Hartwig, P., Weppner, W., and Wichelhaus, W., *Mat. Res. Bull.* 14:493 (1979).
7. Asai, T., Kawai, S., Nagai, R., and Mochizuki, S., *J. Phys. Chem. Solids* (forthcoming).
8. Kanno, R., Takeda, Y., and Yamamoto, O., *Mat. Res. Bull.* 16:999 (1981).

9. Kuwano, J., and West, A. R., *Mat. Res. Bull*, 15:1661 (1980).

10. Khorassani, A., and West, A. R., *Solid State Ionics* 7:1 (1982).

11. Miyauchi, K., Matsumoto, K., Kanehori, K., and Kudo, T., *Solid State Ionics* 9/10:1469 (1983).

12. Wagner Jr., J. B., *Mat. Res. Bull.* 15:1691 (1980).

13. Fujitsu, S., Miyayama, M., Koumoto, K., and Yanagida, H., *Abstracts of the 21st Meeting on Basic Science of Ceramics*, 1983, p. 11 (in Japanese).

14. Hong, H. Y.-P., *Mat. Res. Bull.* 11:173 (1976).

15. Alpen, U. V., Bell, M. F., and Höfer, H. H., *Solid State Ionics* 3/4:215 (1981).

16. Nagai, M., Fujitsu, S., and Kanazawa, T., *J. Am. Ceram. Soc.* 63:476 (1980).

17. Delmas, C., Viala, J. C, Olazcuaga, R., Flem, G. L., and Hagenmuller, P., *Solid State Ionics* 3/4:209 (1981).

18. Boilot, J. P., Collin, G., and Comes, R., *Solid State Comm.* (forthcoming).

19. Gordon, R. S., Miller, G. R., McEntire, B. J., Beck, E. D., and Rasmussen, J. R., *Solid State Ionics* 3/4:243 (1981).

20. Arribart, H., Piffard, Y., and Doremieux-Morin, C., *Solid State Ionics* 7:91 (1982).

21. Baffier, N., Badot, J. C., and Colomban, P., *Solid State Ionics* 2:107 (1980).

22. Nakamura, O., Kodama, T., Ogino, I., and Miyake, Y., *Chem. Lett.* 17 (1979).

23. Shilton, M. G., and Howe, A. T., *Mat. Res. Bull.* 12:701 (1977).

24. Shilton, M. G., and Howe, A. T., *Fast Ion Transport in Solids*, P. Vashishta, J. N. Mundy, and G. K. Shenoy, eds. New York: Elsevier North-Holland, 1979, p. 727.

25. Farrington, G. C., and Briant, J. L., *Fast Ion Transport in Solids*, P. Vashishta, J. N. Mundy, and G. K. Shenoy, eds. New York: Elsevier North-Holland, 1979, p. 395.

26. Iwahara, H., Esaka, T., Uchida, H., and Maeda, N., *Solid State Ionics* 3/4:359 (1981).

27. Crosbie, G. M., and Tennenhouse, G. J., *J. Am. Ceram. Soc.* 65:187 (1982).

28. Farrington, G. C., and Dunn, B., *Solid State Ionics* 7:267 (1982).

29. Chandrashekhar, G. V., and Foster, L. M., *Solid State Comm.* 27:269 (1978).

30. Foster, L. M., Anderson, M. P., Chandrashekhar, G. V., Burns, G., and Bradford, R. B., *J. Chem. Phys.* 75:2412 (1981).

31. Hunter, C. C., Ingram, M. D., and West, A. R., *Solid State Ionics* 8:55 (1983).

32. Tiller, C. O., Lilly, A. C., and Laroy, B. C., *Phys. Rev.* B8:4787 (1973).

33. Reau, J. M., Lucat, C., Portier, J., and Hagenmuller, P., *Mat. Res. Bull.* 13:877 (1978).

34. Reau, J. M., and Portier, J., *Solid Electrolytes*, P. Hagenmuller and W. V. Gool, eds. New York: Academic Press, 1978, p. 313.
35. Uraibi, Z. A., Ph.D. thesis, University of Montpellier (1981).
36. Portier, J., Reau, J. M., Matai, S., Soubeyroux, J. L., and Hagenmuller, P., *Solid State Ionics* 11:83 (1983).
37. Takahashi, T., Iwahara, H., and Arao, T., *J. Appl. Electrochem.* 5:187 (1975).
38. Kudo, T., and Obayashi, H., *J. Electrochem. Soc.* 122:142 (1975).
39. Bauerler, J. E., *J. Phys. Chem. Solids* 30:2651 (1969).
40. McHale, A. E., and Tuller, H. L., *Solid State Ionics* 5:515 (1981).
41. Takahashi, T., and Iwahara, H., *Energy Conversion* 11:105 (1971).
42. Worrell, W. L., *Solid Electrolytes*, S. Geller, ed. New York: Springer-Verlag, 1977, p. 143.
43. Pascual, C., and Duran, P., *J. Am. Ceram. Soc.* 66:23 (1983).
44. Hellmann, J. R., and Stubican, V. S., *J. Am. Ceram. Soc.* 66:260 (1983).
45. Ando, K., and Oishi, Y., *Proc. International Conference on Sensors*, Fukuoka, 1983, p. 251.
46. Subbarao, E. C., and Ramakrishnan, T. V., *Fast Ion Transport in Solids*, P. Vashishta, J. N. Mundy, and G. K. Shenoy, eds. New York: Elsevier North-Holland, 1979, p. 653.

4.10 New Solid-Solution Ceramics with Temperature-Stable High Dielectric Constant and Low Microwave Loss

Noboru Ichinose

4.10.1 Introduction

It is well known that materials with a high dielectric constant and a low dielectric loss at microwave frequency can function as electric resonators. They are called dielectric resonators and are utilized for filters and stabilization of oscillation in microwave integrated circuits.

Materials applicable to such microwave devices are expected to have high dielectric permittivity, a small temperature coefficient, and low dielectric loss. It is highly preferable for the temperature coefficient to be controllable according to the device specifications.

In the 1960s, TiO_2 (rutile) with a relative dielectric constant of $\kappa = 100$ and a dielectric quality factor of $Q \cong 10,000$ at microwave frequency was most often used as a dielectric resonator. However, the value of the resonant frequency coefficient τ_f is $+400$ ppm/°C, which is too high for practical applications. Since then, a number of ceramics with temperature-stable high dielectric constants containing TiO_2, such as $BaO\text{-}TiO_2$,[1] $ZrO_2\text{-}SnO_2\text{-}TiO_2$,[2] $MgO\text{-}TiO_2$,[3] and others, have been explored.

The dielectric properties of the $(Sr_{1-x}Ca_x)\{(Li_{1/4}Nb_{3/4})_{1-y}Ti_y\}O_3$ system with and without a doping material such as V_2O_5 have been investigated, and successful results have been obtained. The $Sr(Li_{1/4}Nb_{3/4})O_3$ compound was reported to have a perovskite-type structure and high dielectric constant, $\kappa = 40$.[4] However, the temperature coefficient of the dielectric constant was not reported. This value has been measured and determined to be -6 ppm/°C. Moreover, it was found that the substitution of Ca for Sr in the above-mentioned system changed the sign of this coefficient from negative to positive.[5]

Ceramic bodies of this compound of more than 99% theoretical density were obtained by minimizing the stoichiometric shift from the ideal chemical formula, adding some doping material such as V_2O_5, and sintering in an oxygen atmosphere.[6] These ceramics have high optical transmittance over the wide wavelength region of 0.35 to 10 μm.

The next sections report the dielectric and optical properties of the $(Sr_{1-x}Ca_x)\{(Li_{1/4}Nb_{3/4})_{1-y}Ti_y\}O_3$ system.

4.10.2 Experimental Procedure

4.10.2.1 Sample Preparation

High-purity $SrCO_3$, $CaCO_3$, Li_2CO_3, Nb_2O_5, TiO_2, and V_2O_5 raw materials were used. Table 4.10.1 gives impurities of these main mate-

Table 4.10.1 Impurities in the Raw Materials (Emission Spectrographic Analysis)

	Impurities (ppm)			
	Al	Si	Pb	Fe
$SrCO_3$	—	3–10	—	3–10
$CaCO_3$	—	—	—	3–10
Li_2CO_3	10–30	30–100	—	3–10
Nb_2O_5	—	3–10	—	—
TiO_2	30–100	100–300	10–30	3–10

rials without V_2O_5. They were weighed accurately, according to the chemical formula $(Sr_{1-x}Ca_x)\{(Li_{1/4}Nb_{3/4})_{1-y}Ti_y\}O_3$, and mixed well with distilled water in an alumina pot mill. More Li_2CO_3 was weighed than in the formula to adjust for vaporization loss during the fabrication processes. Dried batches were calcined at 1000–1200°C for 2–8 hours. Thermogravimetric analysis (TGA) was performed to choose the calcining temperature. During calcining it is necessary to complete the solid-state reaction of the raw materials. If this is not done, the reaction inhomogeneity hinders the densification of this system. The prefired materials were then reground in the alumina pot mill. They were pressed and sintered at 1250–1400°C in air or an oxygen atmosphere for 2–12 hours.

In order to characterize the compounds formed, all samples were analyzed by X-ray and microstructural methods. Densities were measured by water immersion. The microstructure of the sintered bodies was observed by etching the polished surface with HF (10%) at room temperature for several minutes.

4.10.2.2 Measurements

Dielectric constants were measured by the dielectric resonator method[7,8] on samples with dimensions $7^{\varnothing} \times 10–19$ mm. Figure 4.10.1 shows the modified experimental set-up for the measurements of dielectric permittivities and their temperature coefficients in the microwave frequency region as reported elsewhere. Dielectric properties were routinely measured as a function of temperature at the X-band. Resonant frequency (f) and half-width (Δf) were determined by measurements on ceramics machined into a rectangular dielectric resonator $(5 \times 5 \times 3 - 5 \times 5 \times 4$ mm$)$ and positioned in a waveguide. The measurements were performed in the temperature range of 30 to 210°C.

The unloaded Q of the dielectric resonator is set equal to two times the loaded Q, which is calculated using f and Δf. The relation of the temperature coefficients $(1/\kappa \cdot d\kappa/dT)$ of the dielectric constant and those of the resonant frequency is

$$\frac{1}{\kappa}\frac{d\kappa}{dT} = -2\left(\frac{1}{f}\frac{df}{dT} + \frac{1}{L}\frac{dL}{dT}\right) \qquad (4.10.1)$$

where $1/L \cdot dL/dT$ is the thermal expansion coefficient. In the composition range investigated, the thermal expansion coefficient appeared to be almost a constant $11 \times 10^{-6}/°C$ value.

Optical measurements were accomplished using a spectrometer (Hitachi, EPI-G3-type) on polished samples with parallel surfaces.

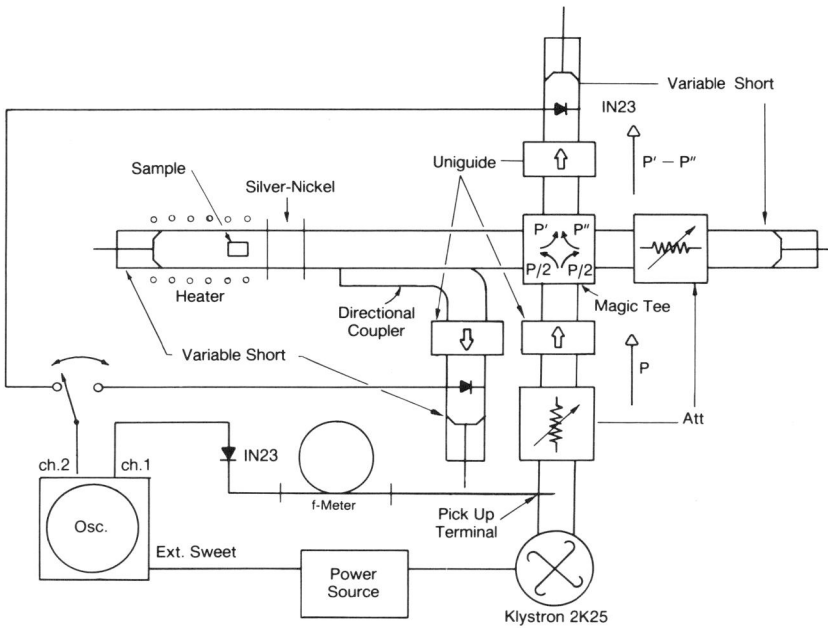

Figure 4.10.1 Modified experimental set-up for unloaded Q and measurements of dielectric permittivities and their temperature coefficients in the microwave frequency region.

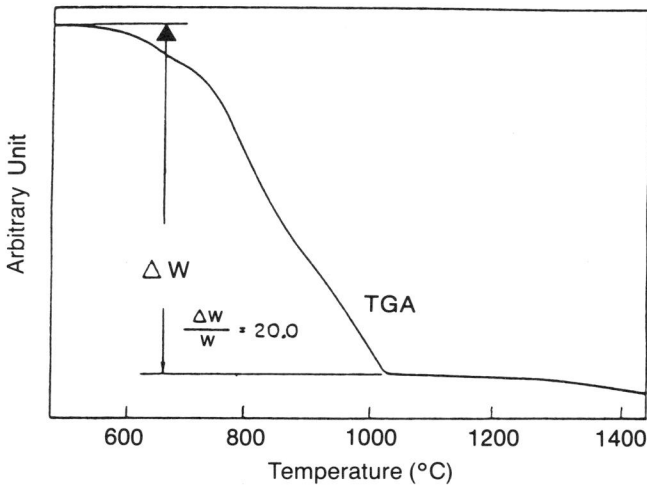

Figure 4.10.2 Thermogravimetric analysis data of the composition $Sr(Li_{1/4}Nb_{3/4})O_3$.

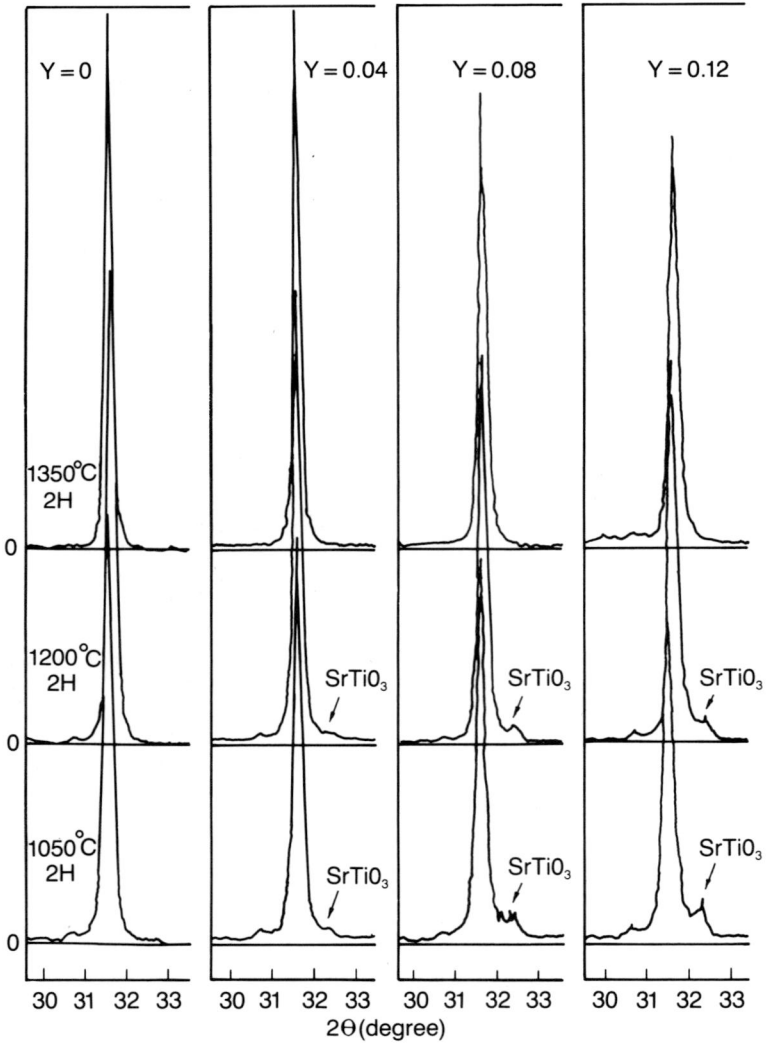

Figure 4.10.3 X-ray diffraction [110] peak profile in the system $Sr\{(Li_{1/4}Nb_{3/4})_{1-y}Ti_y\}O_3$ as a function of y and the sintering conditions.

4.10.3 Results

4.10.3.1 Reactions and Crystal Structure

The TGA curve is shown in Figure 4.10.2. From this measurement it was concluded that thermal decomposition of the carbonates is completed at 1000°C. This is confirmed by the weight loss, ΔW, as shown in this figure. Therefore, a calcining temperature above 1000°C was used.

The X-ray diffraction and microstructural analyses of samples heated for 2 hours at 1350°C in air show that they are single-phase perovskite-type compounds. Reaction at lower temperatures often results in compounds that disappear when the reaction proceeds to completion. From Figure 4.10.3 it can be seen that samples other than $y = 0$ have extra peaks corresponding to the phase $SrTiO_3$ both at 1200 and 1050°C. In the samples in the system $(Sr_{1-x}Ca_x)\{(Li_{1/4}Nb_{3/4})_{1-y}Ti_y\}O_3$, solid-state reactions were completed at a sintering temperature above 1300°C in air. In the case of oxygen atmosphere, the sintering temperature is lower.

The lattice constants of the single-phase compounds are shown in Table 4.10.2. The value for the compound $Sr(Li_{1/4}Nb_{3/4})O_3$ is slightly larger than the reported one ($a = 3.996$ Å).[4] This difference has not yet been fully evaluated. As shown in Table 4.10.2, the lattice constants in the system $(Sr_{1-x}Ca_x)\{(Li_{1/4}Nb_{3/4})_{1-y}Ti_y\}O_3$ decrease steadily with an increase of both x and y.

4.10.3.2 Sinterability

Ceramic bodies of this compound of more than 99% theoretical density were obtained by minimizing the stoichiometric shift from the ideal chemical formula, adding some doping material such as V_2O_5, and sintering in an oxygen atmosphere. As Figure 4.10.4 indicates,

Table 4.10.2 Composition Dependence of the Lattice Constant in the System $(Sr_{1-x}Ca_x)\{(Li_{1/4}Nb_{3/4})_{1-y}Ti_y\}O_3$

X \ Y	0	0.04	0.08	0.12
0	4.006	4.004	4.000	3.996
0.04	4.003	3.994	3.994	3.991
0.08	4.001	3.994	3.993	3.989
0.12	3.998	3.995	3.989	3.985

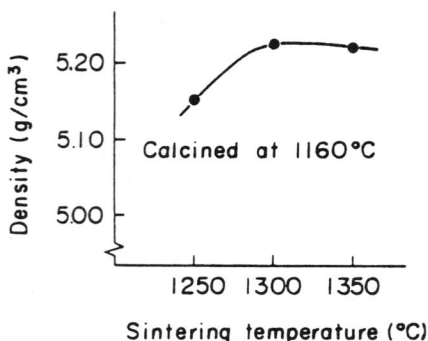

Figure 4.10.4 Sintering temperature dependence of density of $(Sr_{0.92}Ca_{0.08})\cdot\{(Li_{1/4}Nb_{3/4})_{0.92}Ti_{0.08}\}O_3$.

the density reaches a 5.23 g/cm³ maximum when samples are calcined at 1160°C for 8 hours and sintered at 1300°C. This value is more than 99% of the theoretical density (5.263 g/cm³). Density as a function of the amount of doped V_2O_5 is shown in Figure 4.10.5. It can be seen from this figure that the doping materials are effective for densification at the lower sintering temperature.

If they are fabricated without additional Li_2O or sintered in an air atmosphere, Li vaporization induces a stoichiometric shift from the ideal formula and hinders densification. Only 98% of the theoretical density has been achieved. These ceramics do not have good optical transmittance at frequencies in the visible part of the spectrum. The

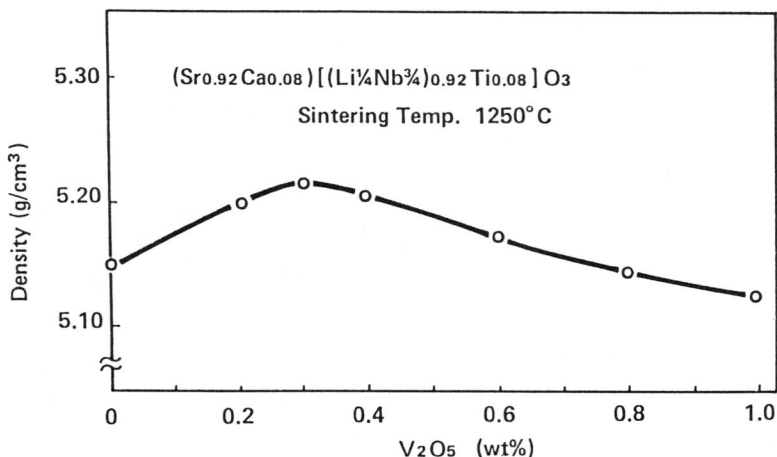

Figure 4.10.5 Density as a function of doped V_2O_5 amount.

oxygen atmosphere prevents Li vaporization[9] and promotes diffusion of ions in the ceramic body. These effects are the cause of the densification in this this system.

The grain size distribution of the typical ceramics sintered at 1350°C for $x = y = 0.08$ is from 10 to 30 μm.

4.10.3.3 Dielectric and Physical Properties

Table 4.10.3 gives the dielectric constants and their temperature coefficients of the $(Sr_{1-x}Ca_x)\{(Li_{1/4}Nb_{3/4})_{1-y}Ti_y\}O_3$ system at 9 GHz. The dielectric constant was almost independent of the Ca substitution but was more affected and increased by the introduction of Ti into the octahedral sites of the perovskite structure. The temperature coefficient was controllable between $+30$ and $-70 \times 10^{-6}/°C$, depending on the chemical composition. The unloaded Q for the compounds in this system was larger than 3000. The dielectric constant increased with density according to the equation $\kappa = 17\rho - 44$ in the narrow density range, $5.15 < \rho < 5.26$ for $x = y = 0.08$ compound.

Table 4.10.3 (a) Composition Dependence of the Dielectric Constant in the System $(Sr_{1-x}Ca_x)\{(Li_{1/4}Nb_{3/4})_{1-y}Ti_y\}O_3$

X \ Y	0	0.04	0.08	0.12
0	38.2	40.0	41.8	43.2
0.04	38.4	40.3	42.3	44.6
0.08	38.3	39.7	42.5	45.2
0.12	38.3	38.7	41.4	45.8

Table 4.10.3 (b) Composition Dependence of the Temperature Coefficient in the System $(Sr_{1-x}Ca_x)\{(Li_{1/4}Nb_{3/4})_{1-y}Ti_y\}O_3$

X \ Y	0	0.04	0.08	0.12
0	-6	-17	-66	-70
0.04	-0	-10	-44	-60
0.08	$+8$	-2	-30	-65
0.12	$+30$	$+22$	$+8$	-58

$(\times 10^{-6}/°C)$

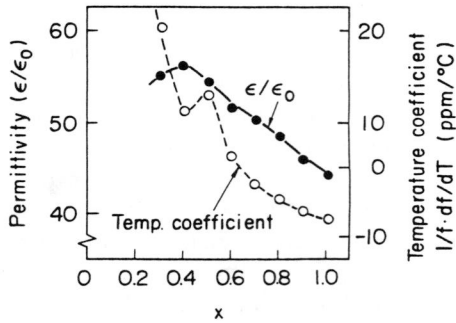

Figure 4.10.6 Dielectric properties in the $(Sr_{1-x}Ca_x)\{(Li_{1/4}Nb_{3/4})_{0.70}Ti_{0.30}\}O_3$ system.

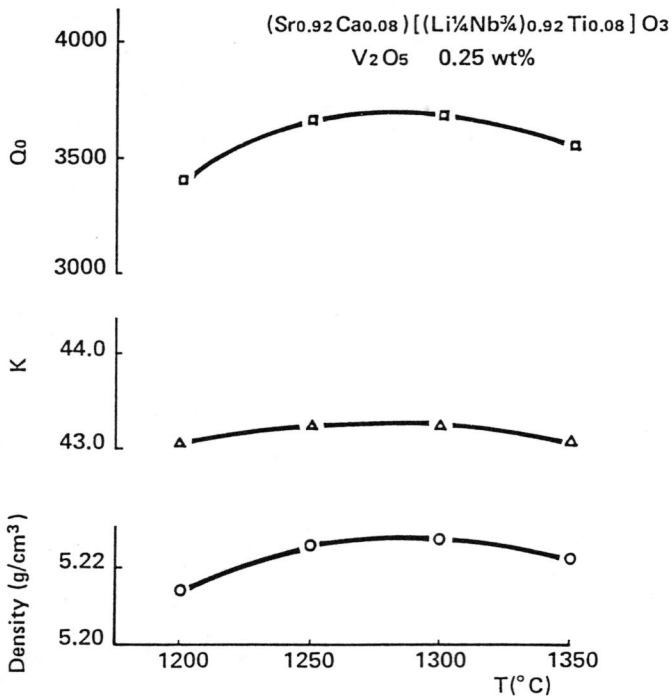

Figure 4.10.7 Sintering temperature dependence of density, dielectric permittivity, and Q_0.

Dielectric constant dependence on the Ca amount is shown in Figure 4.10.6, when the Ti amount is 30 at%. The dielectric constant exhibited the maximum value near the $x = 0.40$ composition. Also, tan δ showed a maximum value near this compound. X-ray diffraction revealed that the morphotropic phase boundary existed near $x = 0.40$. The deformation from the cubic structure of the $x > 0.40$ compound has not yet been clarified. Figure 4.10.7 shows the influence of the doping materials as a function of the sintering temperature. The remarkable change resulting from doping V_2O_5 is not exhibited in this figure.

The dielectric and physical properties of a typical $x = y = 0.08$ compound for this system without V_2O_5 are shown in Table 4.10.4 with the data of Al_2O_3 (98%) ceramics. It can be seen from this table that the thermal conductivity is smaller than that of Al_2O_3. The polished surface roughness of the ceramics was 0.05 μmR_{max}, as shown in Figure 4.10.8. These ceramics are comparatively easy to polish.

As the data in Table 4.10.4 indicate, these materials are considered suitable for substrates used in the microwave region.

4.10.3.4 Optical Properties

Good optical transmission was observed for dense ceramics with a theoretical density of more than 99%. Figure 4.10.9 shows transmittance plotted as a function of wavelength (sample thickness: 0.4 mm).

Table 4.10.4 Dielectric and Physical Properties of the Compound $(Sr_{0.92}Ca_{0.08})\{(Li_{1/4}Nb_{3/4})_{0.92}Ti_{0.08}\}O_3$

	Compound	Alumina (98%)
Permittivity (9 GHz)	43.2	9.5
Temperature coefficient (ppm/°C)	−30	+120
tan δ	3×10^{-4}	2.8×10^{-4}
Density (g/cm³)	5.21	3.8
Flexure strength (kg/mm²)	15	35
Coefficient of thermal expansion (°C⁻¹)	11.2	7.3
Thermal conductivity (Cal/cm·s·°C)	0.003	0.06
Resistivity (Ω·cm)	4×10^{17}	$>10^{14}$
Crystal system	Cubic	Tetragonal

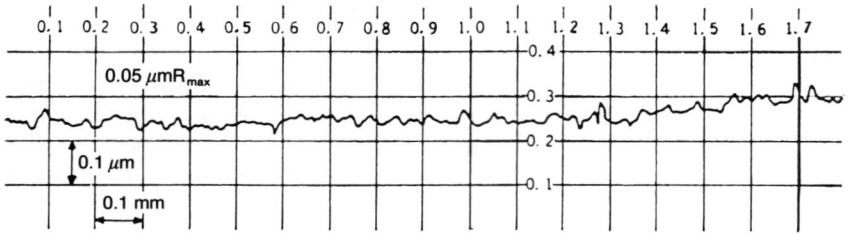

Figure 4.10.8 Polished surface roughness.

There is high optical transmittance between $\lambda = 0.35$ to $10\,\mu$m. Curve
(a) shows the fundamental absorption edge of the $x = y = 0.08$ composition to be at $\lambda = 0.35\,\mu$m. The edge shifts to the longer wavelength
side and the transmittance in the visible part of the spectrum becomes lower with decreasing density. The transmittance thickness
dependence is represented as follows:

$$I/I_o = (1 - k)^2 e^{-kt} \tag{4.10.2}$$

where t is the thickness and k is a constant that depends on wavelength.

The fabrication process, especially calcining, affected the optical
properties. When the calcining temperature was lower than $1160°$C,
the maximum density value became somewhat lower than that calcined at $1160°$C, but better optical transmission was obtained. The
cause of this phenomenon was not ascertained; However, it is

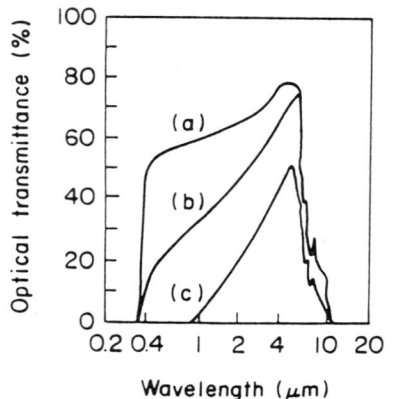

Figure 4.10.9 Optical transmittance as a
function of wavelength: (a) 99.8%, (b)
99.4%, and (c) 99.0% of theoretical density.

thought that the optical properties depend not only on density but also on grain size and other unknown scattering factors.

4.10.4 Microwave Applications

Ceramics in the system $(Sr_{1-x}Ca_x)\{(Li_{1/4}Nb_{3/4})_{1/y}Ti_y\}O_3$ are suitable for tapped delay lines and microwave circulators because they have high dielectric permittivity compared with that of Al_2O_3.[10] Compact circuits are obtained using these materials. Figure 4.10.10 shows the power propagation property of new-type circulators. $MgTiO_3$ ($\kappa = 16$) is used for conventional-type circulators. The volume of new-type circuits is half of that of conventional-type circuits.

4.10.5 Conclusions

The $(Sr_{1-x}Ca_x)\{(Li_{1/4}Nb_{3/4})_{1-y}Ti_y\}O_3$ system has good dielectric properties at 9 GHz. A typical composition has the following properties: $\kappa = 42.3$, $1/\kappa \cdot d\kappa/dT = 0 \times 10^{-6}/°C$, and $Q_0 = 3500$.

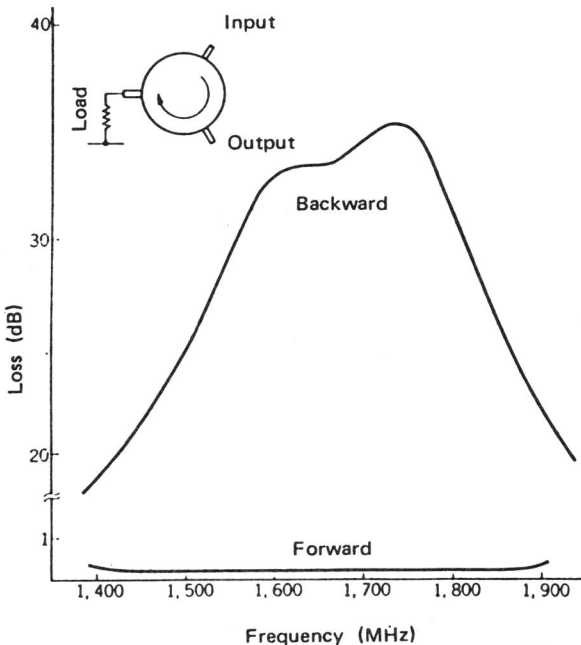

Figure 4.10.10 Power propagation property of circulator.

Dense ceramics of this system with more than 99% of theoretical density were obtained by minimizing the amount of stoichiometric shift from the ideal chemical formula and sintering in an oxygen atmosphere. These ceramics have high optical transmittance over the wide wavelength region from 0.35 to 10 μm.

References

1. O'Bryan, H. M., Thomson, J., and Plourde, J. K., *J. Am. Ceram. Soc.* 57:450 (1974).
2. Wakino, K., Nishikata, T., Tamura, S., and Ishikawa, Y., *1975 IEEE MTT-S International Microwave Symposium Digest.* New York: IEEE, 1975, p. 63.
3. Sato, T., Miyamoto, R., and Fukazawa, A., *Proc. 3rd Meeting Ferroelectric Materials and Their Applications*, Kyoto, 1981; in *Jpn. J. Appl. Phys.* 20: Suppl. 151 (1981).
4. Ch'ang, W., Bader, V. I., Krainik, N. N., Mylnikova, I. E., and Tutov, A. G., *Izv. Akad, Nauk, SSSR, Neorgan; Mat.* 8:1631 (1971).
5. Ichinose, N., Mizutani, T., Hiraki, H., Okuma, H., *Ceramurgia International* 3:100 (1977).
6. Ichinose, N., and Mizutani, T., *Ceram. Bull.* 62:407 (1983).
7. Cohn, S. B., and Kelly, K. C., IEEE Trans. *Microwave Theory Tech.* 14:406 (1966).
8. Hakki, B. W., and Coleman, P. D., IRE Trans. *Microwave Theory Tech.* 8:402 (1960).
9. Amemiya, M., *J. Inorg. Nucl. Chem.* 34:3405 (1972).
10. Mizutani, T., Okuma, H., and Ichinose, N., *Toshiba Rev.* 32:88 (1977) (in Japanese).

4.11 Magnetic Recording Media

Yoshiyasu Koike

4.11.1 Introduction

Since the magnetic audio-recorder was invented by Poulsen in 1898, applications for magnetic recording technologies have been expanding, spreading to almost every household. Magnetic recording media have made remarkable progress, changing form and substance to meet the challenges for high recording density as well as for durable products. The appearance of video recorders, first introduced in 1955 for use by broadcasters and then for consumer use, accelerated the demand for recording tapes of increasingly high density. As a result, the development of better magnetic materials was pursued. First, chromium dioxide particles were available commercially. Second, existing ferric oxide $(\gamma - Fe_2O_3)$ was improved by successfully impregnating the surface with cobalt.

Further demands for higher-density recording media are imminent. New 8-mm portable video cameras have appeared on the market recently, and twice as much recording density is required for these. Metal particles and metal thin films are possible candidates. Recent developments in perpendicular magnetic recording, demonstrated by Iwasaki and others, offer attractive improvements in the ability to record and read back information at high densities.[1] Most of the techniques that have been published to date involve the deposition of a Co-Cr layer onto a suitable substrate by sputtering techniques. Although the sputter techniques produce films with excellent uniformity and magnetic properties, the deposition rate is rather slow, and the ability to deposit the layers on continuous webs while retaining those excellent properties has yet to be demonstrated.

Attempts have been made to fabricate perpendicular recording media employing particulate coating techniques.[2] One of the most promising of these is the use of fine barium-ferrite particles.

This section is concerned with the recent advances that have been made in magnetic recording materials, and particularly with barium ferrite particles. Particle fabrication methods for barium ferrite are briefly reviewed. A glass crystallization method has been found suitable for producing very fine particles with narrow size distribution and excellent dispersibility. The magnetic properties of the particles and the tapes are described.

4.11.2 Developments in Magnetic Recording Media

The first major event in the development of magnetic recording media took place when magnetic particles coated on a strip of paper or plastic appeared in 1935. Iron particles and iron oxide particles were tried during the early stages of development. Soon, acicular γ-Fe$_2$O$_3$ took over because of its better recording performance and chemical stability, along with its lower production cost. The following subsections briefly review recent developments in magnetic recording particles.

4.11.2.1 *γ-Fe₂O₃ Particles*

Since iron oxide particles were first used in magnetic recording in the 1930s, these particles have played a major role in magnetic recording material production, accounting for 90% of all recording materials. The standard method of making $\gamma\text{-Fe}_2\text{O}_3$ particles is to use small acicular goethite particles ($\alpha\text{-FeOH}$) as seeds. Through dehydration of goethite to hematite ($\alpha\text{-Fe}_2\text{O}_3$) and reduction of hematite to magnetite (Fe_3O_4), the $\gamma\text{-Fe}_2\text{O}_3$ is obtained by oxidizing Fe_3O_4.[3] In attempts to make particles of greater acicularity and better uniformity, the basic method has been modified at every step. For easier dispersibility of particles in magnetic paints, the goethite particles are coated with organic or inorganic compounds to isolate individual particles and prevent sintering during the dehydration and reduction steps.

To improve recording performance or, more specifically, to increase recording density, attempts have been made to reduce particle size to lower the recording noise level and to increase coercivity for use at a shorter wavelength. The improvements in coercivity are relatively modest, from 290 to 390 Oe, and short of high-density recording, which requires more than 500 Oe coercivity. These requirements are met by two different kinds of particles.

4.11.2.2 *Chromium Dioxide Particles*

Chromium dioxide particles were developed by the DuPont Company in the 1960s.[4] They were the first ones with high coercivity (more than 450 Oe) available commercially. Chromium dioxide is not a naturally occurring compound. It is usually made by thermal decomposition of CrO_3 under high pressure in the presence of water. Many elements, as additives to the starting materials, have been tested to improve the properties or to modify the processing conditions. High coercivity particles of more than 550 Oe were introduced in 1978.[5] These second-generation CrO_2 particles have an average particle length of 0.6 μm, an average aspect ratio of 20:1, and a specific surface area of 20–30 m²/g. These data are listed in Table 4.11.1 along with other properties and those of other materials. The CrO_2 particles had a recording performance superior to that for cobalt-doped $\gamma\text{-Fe}_2\text{O}_3$, particularly for use at short wavelengths, and could have become mainstream in the recording media, had efforts to increase the Co-modified $\gamma\text{-Fe}_2\text{O}_3$ coercivity not been made.

4.11.2.3 *Cobalt-Modified γ-Fe₂O₃ Particles*

Attempts to increase the coercivity of $\gamma\text{-Fe}_2\text{O}_3$ particles by adding small amounts of cobalt began in the mid-1950s. Although the coerci-

Table 4.11.1 Physical and Magnetic Properties of Magnetic Particles

Magnetic Particle	Particle Length (μm)	Aspect Ratio	Specific Surface Area (m²/g)	Coercivity H_c (θ_c)	Saturation Magnetization σ_s (emu/g)
γ-Fe_2O_3	0.3–0.6	10	20–30	250–450	70–75
Co-γ-Fe_2O_3	0.3–0.4	10	20–30	500–800	70–75
CrO_2	0.2–0.7	10–20	24–40	430–750	70–90
Fe (metal)	0.2–0.4	~6	40–50	900–1600	~160

vity was controlled in a wide range with the amount of cobalt addition, instability in the magnetic properties with changes in temperature was a major problem to solve. The remanence was found to decrease after storage at 40–100°C.[6] This effect was attributed to the cation vacancies in γ-Fe_2O_3, which allow cobalt ions to diffuse more easily. The problem has been solved by confining the cobalt ions to the surface of the particles. For example, γ-Fe_2O_3 particles are coated with cobalt salt and heat treated at a relatively low temperature (250°C) in a nitrogen atmosphere, allowing cobalt to diffuse into the surface of the particles.[7] The Co-impregnated γ-Fe_2O_3 particles have several advantages over CrO_2 particles, one of which is their low production cost.

Much effort has been expended to improve the recording performance of these particles. A common practice is to reduce the particle size, making the distribution as sharp as possible. Recent Co-modified γ-Fe_2O_3 particles, for example, have a length of 0.3–0.4 μm, achieving excellent playback performance on video recorders.

4.11.2.4 Metal Particles

Metal particles have naturally superior magnetic properties. Their saturation magnetization is more than twice that of γ-Fe_2O_3, and coercivities of up to 1500 Oe are now common. The idea of using metal particles is old. In 1928 a patent was filed for coating iron particles on a strip of paper; however, protecting them from oxidation by the atmosphere has been a challenging task, and it is one reason why these particles have become available only recently.

There are several methods of making metal particles. One is the reduction in hydrogen of iron oxides and oxyhydroxides.[8] The protective surface is obtained by exposing freshly prepared particles to a mixture of nitrogen and oxygen. Although complete passivation of such highly reactive materials will probably be difficult to attain, it can be expected to slow the corrosion sufficiently to provide enough longevity for actual use.

4.11.2.5 Metal Thin Films

Magnetic materials mentioned so far are all particulate; recording media are made with them by using a resinous binder. Continuous metal films, currently available commercially, are made by vacuum deposition of cobalt alloys having 0.1 μm thickness and about 700-Oe coercivity. The films are homogeneously made of closely packed fine metal grains. The saturation magnetization is much higher than for the particulate, ensuring higher output voltage. The films show excellent high-frequency recording performance. Their shortcomings are poor durability and a propensity to corrode. Improvements in these shortcomings are now under way, to take advantage of the potential advantages of metal thin films.

The recording wavelength currently used by most video recorders is $1.5 - 1.7\,\mu$m, and that of the next generation will be $0.7 - 0.8$ μm. A recording density about twice as high will be required to make reductions in the size and weight of an 8-mm video camera feasible and to ensure high-quality pictures and long recording time. In meeting this requirement, metal oxide particles such as γ-Fe_2O_3, Co-modified γ-Fe_2O_3, and CrO_2 cannot be used. Metal particles and thin films are considered to be potential candidates for such a use. Metal particulate tapes are an extension from the present production technology and can be easily mass produced. Because these tapes have 1500-Oe coercivity, the mass production of sendust or amorphous metal heads with the capacity to generate a higher magnetic flux density is a prerequisite. Although improvements in durability and corrosion resistance are now being realized, the thin films have an advantage in that they can be used with conventional ferrite heads. It is clear that the recording performance of thin films is superior to that of metal particulate tape, but a final decision on the selection should be made in light of the overall properties of the media and their cost.

4.11.3 Perpendicular Magnetic Recording

A conventional magnetic tape is made of numerous acicular particles such as γ-Fe_2O_3. Information is stored by magnets composed of a group of particles whose magnetization is oriented in the left or right direction along the tape's longitudinal direction. This is called longitudinal recording (Figure 4.11.1). The length of the magnets corresponds to a half-wavelength of the recording. In general, when a bit of magnetic material is placed into a magnetic field, magnetic poles (N and S) appear on both ends, making it magnetized. Inside the material, a field opposing the magnetization reduces the overall field strength. This is called the demagnetization field. The magnitude of the demagnetization field is determined by a demagnetization factor that depends on the shape of the sample. For instance, for a long pole with a small cross section, the factor approaches zero, and the demagnetization field can be neglected. When the cross section becomes larger and the length shorter, the demagnetization factor approaches 1 and cannot be neglected. In longitudinal recording, the increase in the recording density corresponds to reducing the length

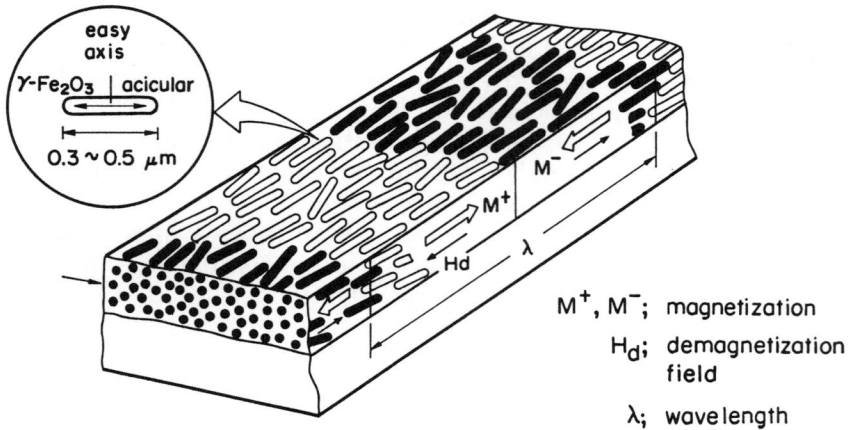

Figure 4.11.1 Schematic of longitudinal recording medium.

of the magnets or the wavelength. The shorter the wavelength becomes, the larger the demagnetization factor becomes, resulting in reduced magnetization.

In perpendicular magnetic recording, magnets whose length is limited by the tape thickness, with width corresponding to a half recording wavelength, are aligned perpendicularly with reference to

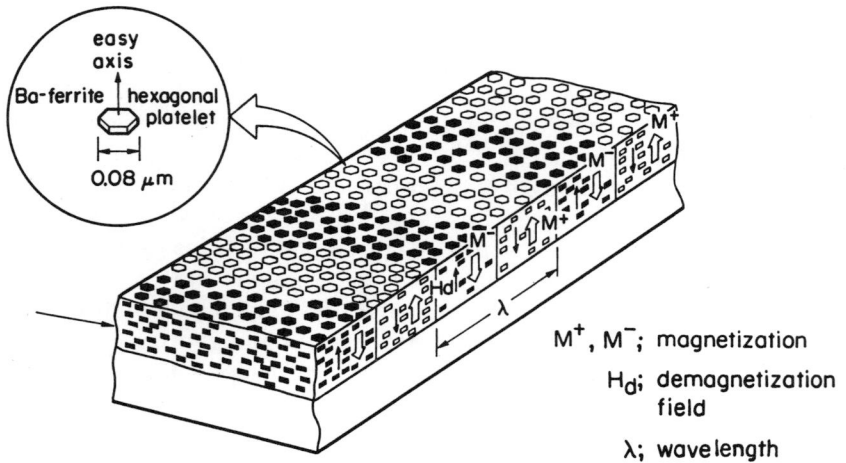

Figure 4.11.2 Schematic of perpendicular recording medium.

the tape surface (Figure 4.11.2). Hence, achieving a higher density does not require shortening the magnet length. Instead, the width is reduced, which results in a smaller demagnetization factor. Furthermore, as the recording density becomes higher, the field generated by the neighboring magnets in longitudinal recording enhances the demagnetization field, which results in further weakening of magnetization. However, in perpendicular recording the field caused by neighboring magnets reduces the demagnetizing field and enhances magnetization.

In 1978 Iwasaki, with a solid theoretical background in the superiority of perpendicular recording over conventional longitudinal recording for high-density recording, demonstrated that sputtered Co-Cr films had the highest recording density thus far obtained.[1] The sputtered Co-Cr columnar grains, about 0.05 μm in diameter, grow perpendicular to the base to form a polycrystalline structure. The easy axis for magnetization coincides with the c-axis of the columnar grains. The high saturation magnetization, inherent in metal thin films, together with a high squareness ratio (more than 0.95), make the Co-Cr sputtered films an almost ideal medium for perpendicular recording. Sputtering techniques produce films with excellent uniformity and magnetic properties, but the deposition rate is rather slow. High sputtering productivity on continuous webs has not yet been realized.

A few attempts have been made to realize perpendicular recording with conventional particulate constructions. One such attempt involves orienting acicular γ-Fe_2O_3 particles perpendicular to the coating surface. Appropriate techniques are necessary to align and stand the needlelike particles on the base films.[2]

Platelet particles, whose easy axis is perpendicular to the platelet surface, are more suitable for perpendicular magnetization. A hexagonal platelet made from barium ferrite particles is a promising candidate. One of the requirements for high-density recording is that particle size be sufficiently smaller than a half-wavelength. The barium ferrite particles currently available are microns in size. For submicron wavelength recording, it is imperative to limit the particle size to less than 0.1 μm with as sharp a distribution as possible. The higher the recording density, the smoother the required surface. The surface smoothness depends on the dispersibility of particles in resinous binders.

For magnetic properties, coercivity should be controlled to between 500 and 1500 Oe for recording and playback with magnetic heads. The following subsections review magnetic properties for barium ferrite particles and several fabrication methods

4.11.4 Magnetic Properties of Barium Ferrite Particles

Barium ferrite has high magnetic anisotropy because of its high anisotropic crystal structure. Once it is magnetized along the hexagonal axis, a large amount of energy is necessary to reduce the magnetization. Because it possesses the property, barium ferrite has been used to make a permanent magnet.

For use in magnetic recording, the particles should have irreversible magnetization at a relatively high field. Otherwise, a recorded signal would be erased when the external field is removed.

The particle should have uniform magnetization throughout its grain, or a single magnetic domain. The particle size should be small enough to be a single domain, about 0.5 μm for the barium ferrite.[9] Saturation magnetization σ_s for particles with 0.15-μm average diameter is 68 emu/g, and coercivity H_c is 5000 Oe. Coercivity varies from 4900 to 5500 Oe as temperature changes from -200 to 150°C.[10] The Curie temperature is 450°C, which would cause no problems under normal recording conditions. The coercivity is too large to use unless measures are taken to reduce it.

There are several methods to reduce the coercivity. One is to use large particles, several microns in diameter. Such large particles inevitably consist of several domains, where the previously stated drawbacks are apparent. Another method is the substitution of Co^{2+} into barium ferrite ($BaFe_{12}O_{19}$ or $BaO \cdot 6Fe_2O_3$). The coercivity decreases with the addition of Co^{2+}. However, at the same time the easy axis changes from the hexagonal c-axis to a direction parallel to the hexagonal plane. Therefore, the c-axis is no longer an easy axis.[11] The third method is to reduce the crystal anisotropy by substituting divalent and tetra-valent metal ions such as Co^{2+} and Ti^{4+} for tri-valent iron Fe^{3+}. As a chemical formula, this can be expressed as $BaCo_x^{2+}Ti_x^{4+}Fe_{12-2x}^{3+}O_{19}$. For example, the substitution amount $x = 0.5$ can reduce the coercivity by 53%, and at the same time the saturation magnetization is reduced by 17%.[12] The 53% reduction in the coercivity is not sufficient for magnetic recording, for a large amount of energy is required to drive the magnetic head.

Recent developments in fabrication techniques have made it possible to reduce the coercivity of barium ferrite particles suitably for perpendicular recording. The following section reviews fabrication methods.

4.11.5 Barium Ferrite Particle Fabrication

4.11.5.1 Ceramic Process

Barium ferrite, used for plastic magnets, is usually processed by the ceramic method. Here, $BaCO_3$ and Fe_2O_3 are mixed and heated at high temperature ($\sim 1300°C$) in a rotary kiln. The sintered agglomerates obtained are broken into small particles less than 1 μm in diameter with a single domain. In this process, crystal defects, introduced during the breaking-up process, reduce the coercivity. Tempering at relatively low temperature regains part of the lost coercivity by annealing out the crystal defects. However, the process results in a large particle diameter and broad size distribution, which are hazardous for high-density recording.

4.11.5.2 Co-Precipitate Tempering[13]

Aqueous solution of $BaCl_2$ and $FeCl_3$ are mixed with supersaturated NaOH under strong stirring action. A co-precipitate containing Fe^{3+} is then obtained. It is tempered at around 900°C after being filtered and rinsed thoroughly with water. The resulting barium ferrite particles are about 0.1 μm in diameter with a relatively sharp size distribution. However, partially sintered agglomerates are inevitable during tempering, where the co-precipitates react with each other and grow. As a result, a breaking-up process, although not as heavy as in the ceramic process, is necessary.

4.11.5.3 Hydrothermal Process[14,15]

A high-alkali aqueous solution of Fe^{3+} and Ba^{2+} with pH > 11 is heated between the boiling temperature (100°C) and the critical temperature of water (370°C) in an autoclave. Because in this method the reaction takes place in an aqueous solution, particles do not form agglomerates and are easily dispersible for coating. Very fine particles can be obtained by controlling the autoclave temperature and the alkali concentration, but the saturation magnetization and the coercivity tend to decrease rather rapidly as the particle diameter is reduced. When the autoclave temperature is relatively low ($< 180°C$), very fine particles of $BaO \cdot 4.5\ Fe_2O_3$ are formed. At high temperature (250–300°C), antiferromagnetic $BaFe_4O_7$ is formed that has no spontaneous magnetization. In the hydrothermal process, there are several phases to form, depending on the processing conditions, so that it is a little complicated to control the magnetic properties.

4.11.5.4 Flux Method

Alkali metal and alkaline earth metal chlorides have a high iron oxide dissolving capacity at high temperatures. Alkali metal salts, $BaCO_3$, and FeOOH, are melted at about 1000°C, and then the melt is cooled to precipitate barium ferrite particles out of the matrix. Because the particle size is rather large (1–1.5 μm) with this method, some improvements have been accomplished to take advantage of the flux and the co-precipitate method. The Ba^{2+} and Fe^{3+} co-precipitates, obtained from the process, are heated with NaCl to cause barium ferrite particles to nucleate and grow in the NaCl matrix.[16] After the NaCl is cooled and dissolved with water, well-separated individual particles are obtained with sharp size distribution.

4.11.5.5 Glass Crystallization

As with the flux method, in this process $BaCO_3$ and Fe_2O_3 are mixed with glass-forming material such as B_2O_3 and heated to form a homogeneous glass melt.[17] To control the coercivity, a small amount of CoO and TiO_2 is added to $BaCO_3$, Fe_2O_3, and B_2O_3. The melting is carried out in a crucible with a high-frequency induction furnace. The melt is dropped between two high-velocity rotating rollers to secure a glassy state by rapid quenching. The molten droplets are formed into glass flakes, which are subsequently heated to crystallize barium ferrite particles within the glassy matrix. With a heated ascetic acid dilute solution, the glassy matrix is dissolved to extract the particles. Because in this method spontaneous nucleation takes place homogeneously within the amorphous flakes on heating, very fine particles with a diameter of less than 0.1 μm are easily obtained. The particles are crystallized virtually without any contact with one another, as they are separated by the matrix, so that they are easily dispersed within the resin binder.

4.11.6 Characteristics of Barium Ferrite Particles Produced by Glass Crystallization Method

Some properties of the barium ferrite produced by the glass crystallization method are listed in Table 4.11.2.[18] Figure 4.11.3 is a transmission electron micrograph of the particles. The particles are seen as a hexagonal platelet with about 0.08-μm average diameter and 0.03-μm thickness. The specific surface area for the particles is 22 m^2/g, which coincides with the 24 m^2/g value computed from the average diameter (0.08 μm) and thickness (0.03 μm). Considering the

Table 4.11.2 Some Typical Properties of
Barium Ferrite Particles
Prepared by the Glass
Crystallization Method [from O.
Kubo et al., *IEEE Trans. Magn.*
MAG-18:1122 (1982)]

Diameter	0.08 μm
Thickness	0.03 μm
Specific weight	5.25 g/ml
Specific surface area	22 m^2/g
Coercivity	900 Oe
Saturation magnetization	58 emu/g
Curie temperature	350°C

error in measuring the thickness, the difference has no significance. Rather, it indicates that the particles have few defects, such as voids found in γ-Fe$_2$O$_3$.

As mentioned before, coercivity is controlled by substituting Co^{2+} and Ti^{4+} for part of the Fe^{3+}. In Figure 4.11.4, coercivity and

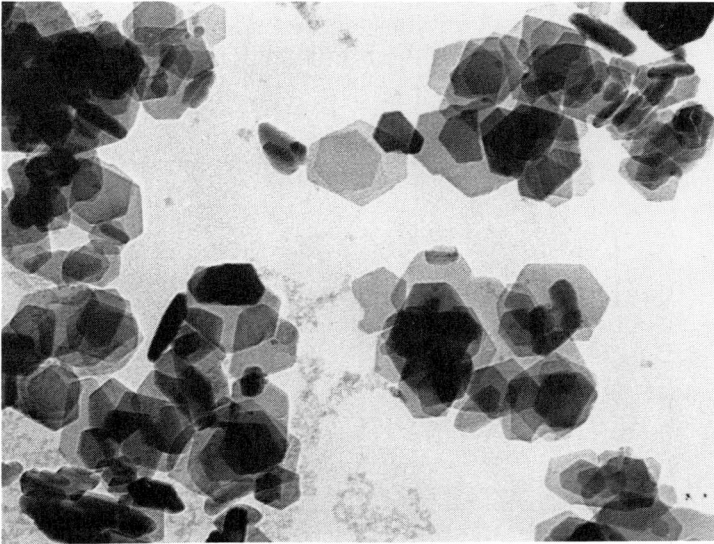

X 120,000

Figure 4.11.3 Transmission electron micrograph of barium ferrite particles.

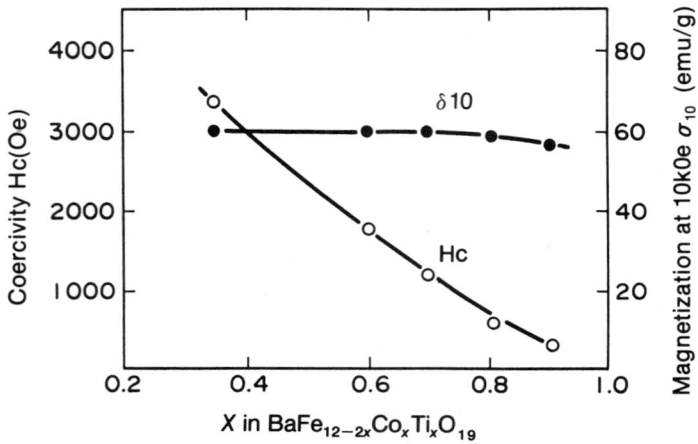

Figure 4.11.4 Effects of Co and Ti substitution on magnetic properties.

magnetization at 10 kOe are plotted against the amount of substitution, x, in a molar fraction ($BaFe^{3+}_{12-2x}Co^{2+}_{x}T^{4+}_{ix}O_{19}$). The magnetization at 10 kOe is almost constant (58–60 emu/g) within experimental error, whereas the coercivity decreases substantially with the amount of substitution x, without changing the particle shape and size.

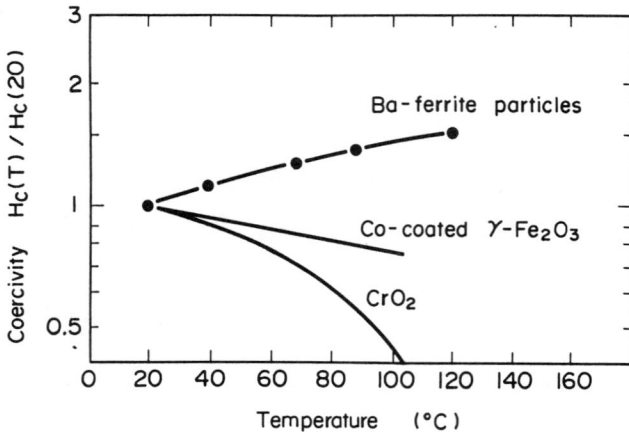

Figure 4.11.5 Coercivity temperature dependence for Co-γ-Fe$_2$O$_3$, CrO$_2$, and Ba-ferrite particles [from O. Kubo et al., *IEEE Trans. Magn.* MAG-18:1122 (1982)].

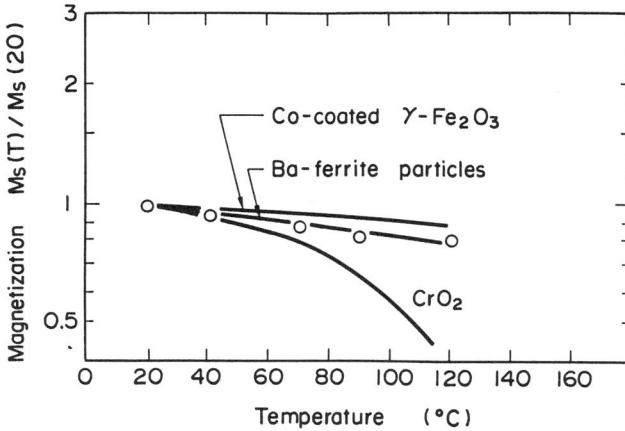

Figure 4.11.6 Magnetization temperature dependence for Co-γ-Fe$_2$O$_3$, CrO$_2$, and Ba-ferrite particles [from O. Kubo et al., *IEEE Trans. Magn.* MAG-18:1122 (1982)].

The temperature dependences of the coercivity and saturation magnetization for barium ferrite are shown in Figures 4.11.5 and 4.11.6, respectively, with those for Co-coated γ-Fe$_2$O$_3$ and CrO$_2$,[18] where the coercivity and saturation magnetization are normalized with the values at 20°C, $H_c(20)$ and $\sigma_s(20)$. The barium ferrite coercivity increases with temperature, whereas that for Co-doped γ-Fe$_2$O$_3$ and CrO$_2$ has an adverse tendency. The saturation magnetization for barium ferrite particles decreases as temperature increases, but not as rapidly as that for CrO$_2$.

Figure 4.11.7 shows typical hysteresis curves for the perpendicular ($\perp$) and parallel ($//$) directions of a barium ferrite tape. The residual magnetization ($M_{r//}$) and coercivity ($H_{c//}$) values for the parallel direction are substantially smaller than those for perpendicular ($M_{r\perp}$ and $H_{c\perp}$). The squareness ratio is above 0.9, indicating a high orientation degree.[19]

Wavelength response curves for the perpendicular media of sputtered Co-Cr film and barium ferrite particulate coating tape, as well those for conventional longitudinal Co-γ-Fe$_2$O$_3$ and Fe metal tapes, are shown in Figure 4.11.8. Although the barium ferrite tape has lower output than the Co-Cr film, it surpasses Fe particulate tape at short wavelengths in spite of the fact that its coercivity ($H_c = 1250$ Oe) and saturation magnetization ($M_s = 125$ emu/cm^3) values are smaller than those for the metal tape ($H_c = 1470$ Oe, $M_s = 356$ emu/cm^3). This demonstrates favorable characteristics of the perpendicu-

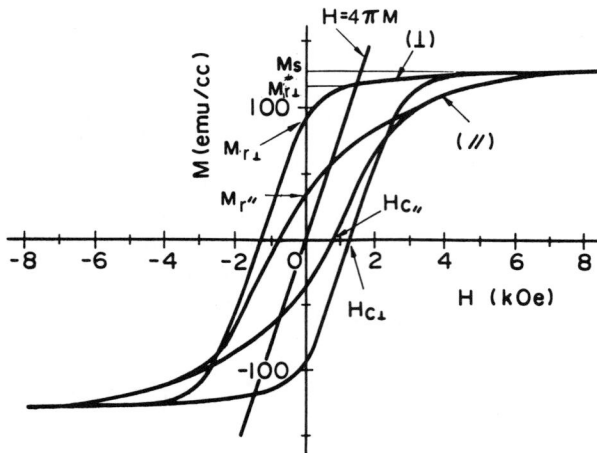

Figure 4.11.7 Typical barium ferrite tape hysteresis curves for perpendicular ($\perp$) and parallel ($//$) direction [from T. Fujiwara et al., *IEEE Trans. Magn.* MAG-18:1200 (1982)].

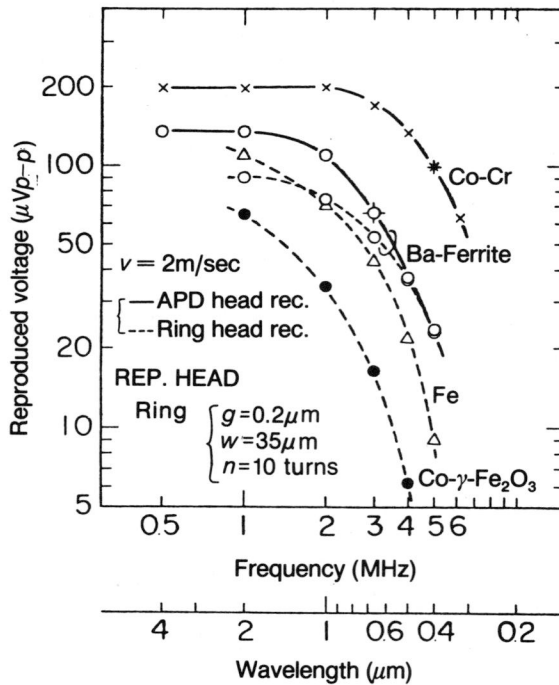

Figure 4.11.8 Wavelength response curves for perpendicular and longitudinal media [from T. Fujiwara et al., *IEEE Trans. Magn.* MAG-18:1200 (1982)].

332

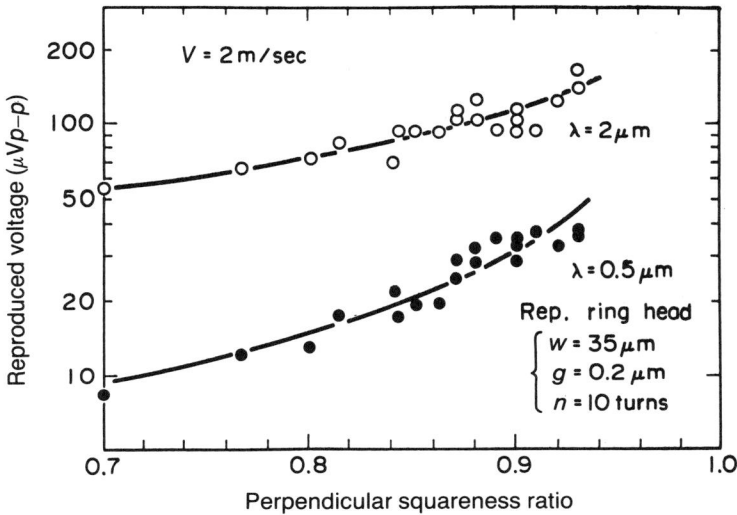

Figure 4.11.9 Perpendicular squareness effect on reproduced output [from T. Fujiwara et al., *IEEE Trans. Magn.* MAG-18:1200 (1982)].

lar recording for high-density recording. Furthermore, the reproduced output is increased with the perpendicular squareness ratio (Figure 4.11.9). The effect is more conspicuous for use at a short wavelength.

4.11.7 Conclusion

Recent advances in the development of magnetic recording technology call for high-density recording media, for which small, uniform, and highly dispersable and orientable particles with appropriate coercivity and high saturation magnetization—or, alternatively, thin films having similar properties—are essential. In the last few years the properties and the fabrication process of particles of all kinds have been greatly improved, particularly those of metal and barium ferrite particles.

   Hitherto it has been difficult to fabricate submicron-size barium ferrite particles, whose magnetic properties are sufficiently adjusted for magnetic recording. Recent studies on the fabrication method have made it possible to make very fine particles (less than 0.1 μm) in diameter) with well-defined diameters and narrow size distribution. The coercivity can be controlled in a wide range of values without substantially reducing the saturation magnetization. The glass crystallization method has a high potential for producing particles suitable for perpendicular magnetic recording. The first step has been a study on particulate perpendicular magnetic recording media. Particulate media have an advantage over thin-film media with their superior durability, reliability, and high productivity. In addition, long experience has been gained in their manufacture.

There are several applications of the perpendicular recording media apart from video tapes. Among these are, for example, audio pulse code modulation (PCM) tapes and flexible disk memories. Further development is expected in the near future.

References

1. Iwasaki, S., and Ouchi, K., *IEEE Trans. Magn.* MAG-14:849 (1978).
2. Speliotis, D. E., and Luek, L. B., *Symposium on Magnetic Media Manufacturing Methods* SM-4:MMS-C-3 (1984).
3. Osmond, W. P., *Proc. Physical Society* B66:265 (1953).
4. Ingraham, D. N., and Swoboda, T. J., U.S. Pat. 2, 923, 683 (1960).
5. Hiller, D. M., *J. Appl. Phys.* 49:1821 (1978).
6. Köster, E., *IEEE Trans. Magn.* MAG-8:430 (1972).
7. Imaoka, Y., Umeki, S., Kubota, Y., and Tokuoka, Y., *IEEE Trans. Magn.* MAG-14:649 (1978).
8. van der Giessen, A. A., and Klomp, C. J., *IEEE Trans. Magn.* MAG-5:317 (1969).
9. Shirk, B. T., and Buessem, W. R. *J. Am. Ceram. Soc.* 53:192 (1970).
10. Craik, D. J., and Tebble, R. S., *Rep. Progr. Phys.* 24:116 (1961).
11. Stuijts, A. L., and Wijn, H. P. J., *Philips Tech. Rev.* 19:209 (1958).
12. Casimir, H. B. G. et al. *J. Phys. Radium* 20:360 (1959).
13. Haneda, K., Miyakawa, C., and Kojima, H., *J. Am. Ceram. Soc.* 57:354 (1974).
14. Kiyama, H., *Bull. Chem. Soc. Japan* 49:1855 (1976).
15. Takada, T., and Kiyama, M., *FERRITES: Proc. International Conference,* Kyoto, 1970, p. 69.
16. Hilbst, H., *Angew. Chem. Inst. Ed. Engl.* 21:270 (1982).
17. Tanigawa, H., and Tanaka, H., *Osaka Kogyo Gijutsu Shikensho Koho* 15:285 (1964).

18. Kubo, O., Ido, T., and Yokoyama, H., *IEEE Trans. Magn.* MAG-18:1122 (1982).
19. Fujiwara, T., Isshiki, M., Koike, Y., and Oguchi, T., *IEEE Trans. Magn.* MAG-18:1200 (1982).

4.12 Amorphous Ceramics

Itaru Yasui

4.12.1 Introduction

The term "amorphous ceramics" was initially used to denote a group of ceramic materials, in contrast to "amorphous metals." The term applied to a group of amorphous ceramic materials synthesized by a type of quenching method from materials that ordinarily have a crystalline form. The history of amorphous ceramics was initiated in 1967 by Sarjeant and co-workers,[1] but after amorphous $LiNbO_3$ was reported by Glass and co-workers[2] in 1977, many tests were made with the aim of obtaining special properties that were observed only in amorphous states.

The definition of amorphous ceramics has expanded somewhat and is still not clear today. It seems that the term has two slightly different meanings. On the one hand, it refers to a group of amorphous solids whose compositions are different from ordinary silicate glasses; in addition, the term refers to a group of amorphous solids, mainly oxides and halides, made under high quenching conditions. "Amorphous ceramics" is thus broadly defined as a new class of materials that includes amorphous materials synthesized with highly quenching conditions and exotic materials other than normal glass-forming compositions such as silicates.

This section reviews some amorphous solids with exotic compositions and some thin ceramic films made by rapid quenching techniques.

4.12.2 Compositions and Method of Synthesis

Table 4.12.1 is a list of compositions and methods of synthesis found in recent reports. The objects of these studies can tentatively be divided into four groups: (1) solid electrolytes, (2) magnetic materials, (3) ferroelectric materials, and (4) others, including optical fibers, electrochromism, and so on.

Table 4.12.1 Compositions and Synthesis Methods of Amorphous Ceramics Found in Recent Literature

Compositions	Synthesis Methods
Solid Electrolytes	
Ag ion	
$AgX-Ag_2O-M_xO_y$ type	Melt
$AgX-Ag_2S-M_xS_y$ type	Melt
$AgX-Ag_2Se-M_xSe_y$ type	Melt
Li ion	
$Li_2O-LiX-B_2O_3$ type	Melt
Li_2O-LiX-oxysault type	Melt
$Li_2O-M_xO_y$ type	Quench
Li_2S-GeS_2 type	Melt
$LiF-AlF_3$ type	Gas
$Li_2S-P_2O_5-LiI$ type	Melt
$Li_2O-SiO_2-Al_2O_3$ type	Melt · gas
$Li_2O-P_2O_5-SiO_2$ type	Gas
Na ion	
Same as above; replaced with Na	—
F ion	
ZrF_4 system	Melt
Magnetic Materials	
Spinel ferrite-P_2O_5	Quench
Spinel ferrite-Bi_2O_3	Quench
Ferroelectric Materials	
$PbTiO_3-B_2O_3$	Quench
Electrochromism	
Li_2WO_3	Quench
Optical fibers	
$ZrF_4-BaF_2-MF_3$	Melt
ThF_4-BaF_2-X	Melt

Amorphous ceramics can be formed by several methods as follows:

1. Roller quenching method: a twin-roller is common for ceramic materials because of their insufficient affinity with metal rollers.
2. Production from gas phases: sputtering, evaporation, chemical vapor deposition, and so on.
3. Normal processes for the production of silicate glasses: melting mixtures with specified compositions followed by cooling.

4.12.3 Solid Electrolytes

4.12.3.1 Amorphous Lithium Niobates

The first report on amorphous $LiNbO_3$ made by roller quenching showed an extraordinarily high dielectric constant,[2] but later the observed values were interpreted in terms of the high mobility of the Li^+ ions. The ionic conductivity of roller-quenched $LiNbO_3$ amorphous film was found to be 10^{20} times higher than that of a single crystal when compared at room temperature.[3] The ionic conductivity data obtained by Glass and co-workers is shown in Figure 4.12.1. The activation energy was also much lower than that of a single crystal. These findings stimulated related studies in which tests were conducted to attempt to find a new class of amorphous solid electrolytes by roller-quenching methods.

The mechanism of the increase in conductivity and the decrease in activation energy did not seem easy to interpret. It was expected that the difference in the properties can be ascribed to the differences between crystal and amorphous structures. An attempt to elucidate the structure of the amorphous $LiNbO_3$ film by X-ray diffraction analysis was made. According to the results,[4] shown in Figure 4.12.2, the structure units of the amorphous phase were the same as those for the crystalline form, that is, NbO_6 octahedra. These units are connected differently. $LiNbO_3$ crystal has an illmenite structure in which these octahedra are joined by their corners, forming a three-dimensional network. The amorphous form also has a corner-joined network structure, but some parts of the network are similar to the crystal structure of pyrochlore type, which is known as one of the most favorable structures for good ionic conduction.

These results suggest that amorphous materials could have extraordinary properties as a result of the different structures attained by high quenching conditions. The structures of ordinary silicate glasses, however, were found to be very similar to those of corre-

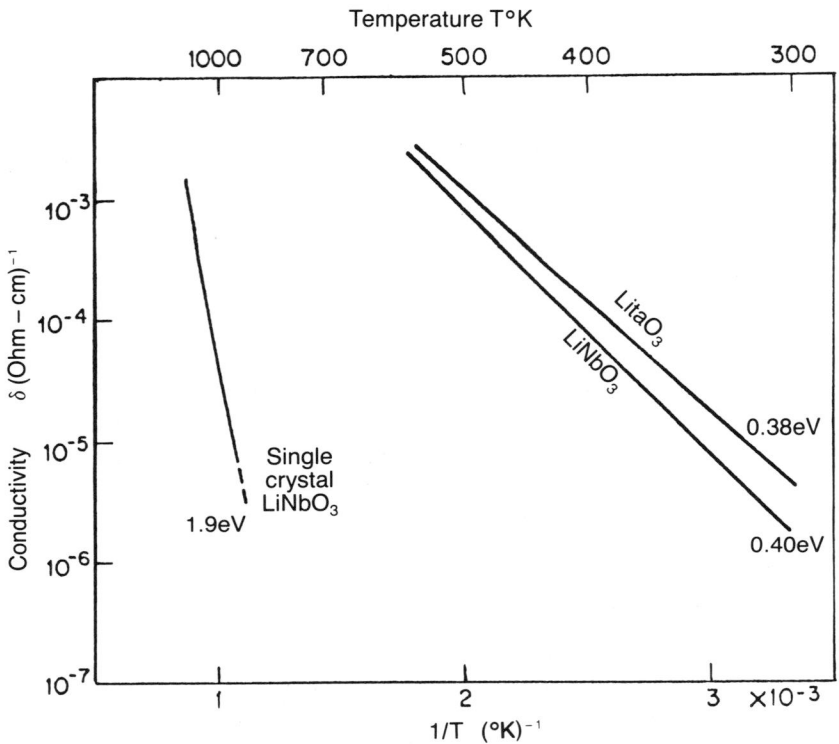

Figure 4.12.1 Ionic conductivity of [*J. Appl. Phys.* 49:4808 (1978)] amorphous LiNbO$_3$ by A. M. Glass and co-workers with that of crystal for comparison.

sponding crystals,[5,6] and they do not depend very much of the rate of cooling from melts. This means that there appear to be two kinds of materials, one that easily takes an amorphous form and one that has very high preference for the crystalline form. Only the amorphous phase made from the materials belonging to the latter kind could have different properties from that of a crystal with the same composition if produced by rapid quenching.

4.12.3.2 *Silver Ion Conducting Glasses*

Kunze[7] first reported on the formation of glasses in the system of AgI-Ag$_2$SeO$_4$. Kuwano and co-workers[8] and Minami and co-workers[9] found new glass-forming systems with a high content of silver halides. These glasses had very high conductivity of silver ions, which was comparable with that of α-AgI. Minami studied the formation and properties of these kinds of glasses very extensively.[11]

4.12.3.3 *Borate Glasses with Lithium Halides*

Levasseur and co-workers first reported a series of glasses in the system of $LiX-Li_2O-B_2O_3$ (X = Cl, Br, I, SO_4, etc.) as new solid electrolytes of lithium ions.[11] The addition of halide ions to oxide glasses increases the conductivity of alkaline ions markedly. The true composition of this system should be determined very carefully, because it changes during the preparation procedure as a result of evaporation and oxidation of LiX.

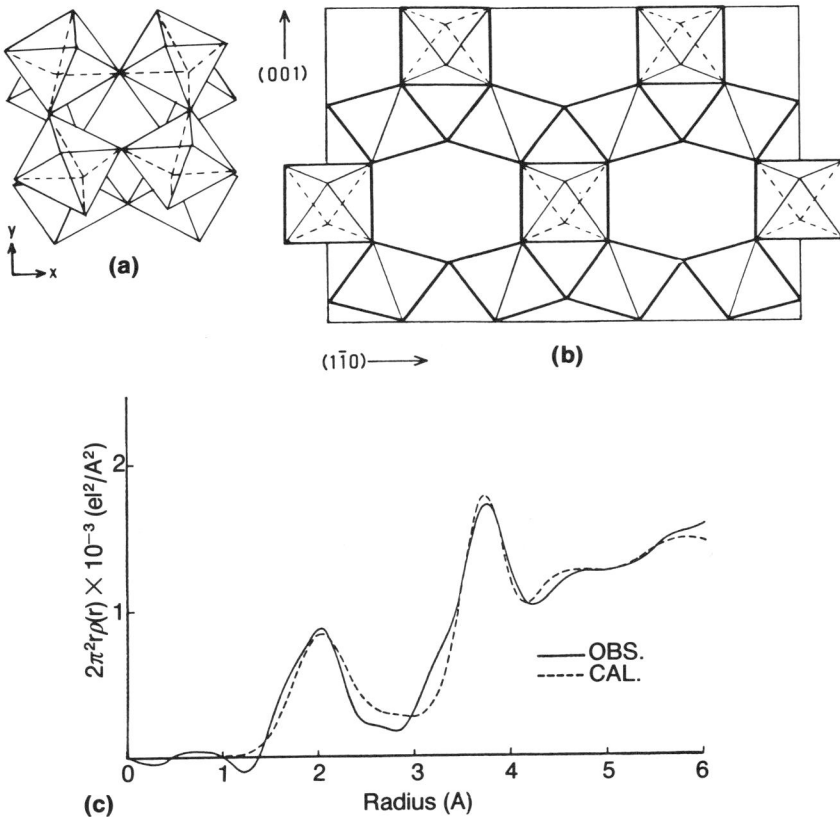

Figure 4.12.2 Structure of amorphous $LiNbO_3$ obtained by X-ray diffraction analysis. Structure model based on illmenite type (a) did not satisfy the observed radial distribution curve (RDF). The mixed model with illmenite type (a) and pyrochlore type (b) produced a good agreement with the observed RDF.

4.12.3.4 *Other Ionic Conductors*

Glass and co-workers studied the system $Li_2O-M_2O_3$ (M = Al, Ga, Bi) with the roller-quenching method.[12] The ionic conductivity of this system was such that the logarithm was proportional to the concentration of Li^+ ions in these specimens regardless of the type of material. Glass and co-workers proposed two hypotheses to interpret this relation: the weak electrolytes model and the random site model. The true mechanism is still unknown.

The system of Li_2O-WO_3, Li_2O-MoO_3, and the three-component system $Li_2O-WO_3-MoO_3$ were also studied.[13-15] In some specimens with higher molybdenum content, mixed conduction was observed.

4.12.3.5 *Evaporated $Li_2O-SiO_2-P_2O_5$ Film*

Miyauchi and co-workes studied the formation and properties of sputtered thin films of this system in order to use it in very thin solid-state batteries.[16] The relation between the Li^+ ion concentration and conductivity, which is similar to those found in the system of $Li_2O-M_2O_3$ by Glass and co-workers,[12] is shown in Figure 4.12.3. This kind of application of solid electrolytes will be expanded in the near future.

4.12.3.6 *Crystalline Ceramic Film Made by the Roller-Quenching Method*

Crystalline ceramic film can be formed by a roller-quenching instrument made for amorphous materials. Bismuth oxide with a small amount of additives was quenched by a twin-roller apparatus, and a

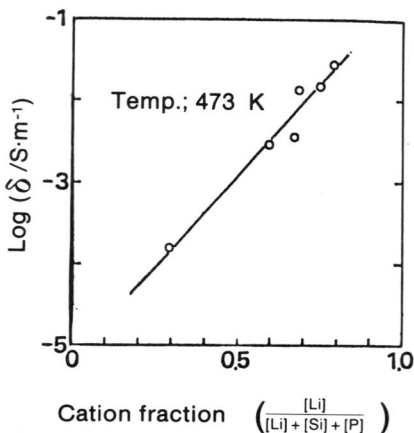

Figure 4.12.3 Relation of concentration of Li^+ ions and ionic conductivity in Li_2O-SiO_2-P_2O_5 system obtained by K. Miyauchi and T. Kudo (*Abstr. 161st ECS Meeting*, 1982, p. 1138).

thin film composed of amorphous and highly orientated δ-Bi$_2$O$_3$ crystal phase was first obtained by Yasui and co-workers.[17] Suzuki and co-workers also made ribbons of the Bi$_2$O$_3$-MoO$_3$ system with several kinds of apparatus, including a single roller, a twin roller, and so on.[18] These materials are interesting in their possible use as oxygen ion conductors for low-temperature applications, because δ-Bi$_2$O$_3$ is known to have higher conductivity of oxygen ions than stabilized ZrO$_2$.

4.12.4 Electrochromism

4.12.4.1 WO$_3$ Thin Film Made by Evaporation

Electrochromism is expected to be used as a new device for watch displays, calculators, and other applications. WO$_3$ thin film is commonly used for this purpose. Recently, several attempts have been made to make an all-solid-state electrochromic display using solid electrolytes.[19]

4.12.4.2 Li$_2$O-WO$_3$ Film Made by the Roller-Quenching Method

Tatsumisago and co-workers found that roller-quenched film in the system of Li$_2$O-WO$_3$ showed the electrochromic effect.[20] When subjected to an electric field, it turned blue, as is the case for evaporated WO$_3$ film. This material appears useful for studying the mechanism of electrochromism, because evaporated film is usually too thin to reveal the structure by the spectroscopic method or diffraction method.

4.12.5 Optical Fibers of ZrF$_4$-Based Glasses

The glass-forming region in ZrF$_4$-BaF$_2$ was first found by Poulain and co-workers.[21] Glass fibers of this system can transmit light with a wavelength up to 8 μm and are a candidate for next-generation optical fibers with ultra-low loss coefficients. Theoretically, a loss less than 0.01 dB/km is expected.

4.12.6 Ferromagnetic Materials

Sugimoto and co-workers reported the formation of amorphous ferrites made by the roller-quenching method.[22] For example, the melts in the system of Mn-Zn ferrite and P$_2$O$_5$ were quenched and ribbons of amorphous phase were obtained. The saturation magnetization was about half that for the crystalline counterpart, so the advantage of amorphous form is still doubtful.

4.12.7 Ferroelectric Materials

The first findings of high dielectric constant in amorphous $LiNbO_3$[2] are now being interpreted in terms of the high ionic conductivity of Li^+ ions. Dielectric constants of sputtered $LiNbO_3$ film were also measured by Wasa.[23] The increase in the real term of the dielectric constants accompanied the increase in the imaginary term; that is, the loss was too high to be used practically.

As for the other system, the properties of roller-quenched $PbTiO_3$ were studied by Tsuya and co-workers.[24] The dielectric constant of the amorphous phase is only half that of crystalline phase, and the advantage of these kinds of materials is not clear thus far.

4.12.8 Conclusion

Amorphous ceramics have been studied extensively only during the last five years. Although there is a wide range of compositions and production methods, applications seem to be narrowing gradually to such areas as solid electrolytes. Because of this short history, there will be a great number of developments in the near future, and amorphous ceramics will become a full-fledged new class of materials.

References

1. Sarjeant, P. T., and Roy, R., *J. Am. Ceram. Soc.* 50:500 (1967).
2. Glass, A. M., Lines, M. E., Nassau, K., and Shiever, J. W., *Appl. Phys. Lett.* 31:249 (1977).
3. Glass, A. M., Nassau, K., and Nergen, T. J., *J. Appl. Phys.* 49:4808 (1978).
4. Yasui, I., Ohta, E., Hasegawa, H., and Imaoka, M., *J. Non-Cryst. Sol.* 52:283 (1982).
5. Yasui, I., Hasegawa, H., and Imaoka, M., *Phys. Chem. Glasses* 24:65 (1983).
6. Imaoka, M., Hasegawa, H., and Yasui, I. *Phys. Chem. Glasses* 24:72 (1983).
7. Kunze, D., *Fast Ion Transport in Solids*, W. van Gool, ed. Amsterdam: North-Holland, 1973, p. 405.
8. Kuwano, J., and Kato, M., *Denki Kagaku Oyobi Kogyo Butsuri Kagaku*, 43:734 (1975).

9. Minami, T., Nambu, H., and Tanaka, M., *J. Am. Ceram. Soc.* 60:467 (1977).

10. Minami, T., *J. Non-Cryst. Sol.* 56:15 (1983).

11. Levasseur, M. A., Cales, B., Reau, J-M., and Hagenmuller, P., *Mat. Res. Bull.* 13:205 (1978).

12. Glass, A. M., and Nassau, K., *J. Appl. Phys.* 51:3756 (1980).

13. Nassau, K., Glass, A. M., Grasso, M., and Olson, D. H. *J. Electrochem. Soc.* 127:2743 (1980).

14. Paik, C-H., Hasegawa, H., and Yasui, I., *Yogyo-Kyokai-Shi.* 91:511 (1983).

15. Tatsumisago, M., Sakono, I., Minami, T., and Tanaka, M., *J. Non-Cryst. Sol.* 46:119 (1981).

16. Miyauchi, K., and Kudo, T., *Abstr. 161th ECS Meeting,* Boston, 1982, p. 1138.

17. Yasui, I., Ohta, E., and Tada, E., *Proc. Annual Meeting of Ceramics Society of Japan,* Tokyo, 1981, p. A-40.

18. Suzuki, T., and Ukawa, S., *J. Mat. Sci.* 18:1845 (1983).

19. Green, M., and Kang, K., *Solid State Ionics* 3/4:141 (1981).

20. Tatsumisago, M., Sakono, I., Minami, T., and Tanaka, M., *J. Mat. Sci.* 17:3593 (1982).

21. Poulain, M., Poulain, M., Lucas, J., and Brun, P., *Mat. Res. Bull.* 10:243 (1975).

22. Sugimoto, M., and Hiratsuka, N., *J. Mag. Mag. Materials* 31–34:1533 (1983).

23. Wasa, K., *Seramikkusu* 17:253 (1982).

24. Tsuya, N., and Arai, K. I., *Jpn. J. Appl. Phys.* 18:461 (1979).

INDEX

G

Gas sensors, 292–296
  combustible, 292–295
  humidity, 295–296
Glass
  alkaline durability of, 109–110
  composition of, 106
  elastic modulus of, 107–108
  fatigue life prediction of, 226–236
    failure probability after proof test, 235
    flaw matrix for, 232–235
    fracture stress distribution, 235–236
    heterogenous system for, 231–232
    homogenous system for, 227–231
  metal alkoxides in synthesis of, 35–38
  optical fibers of, 142–149
    applicability of, 142
    defect size in, 144–146
    drawing of, 143, 147
    interface structure of, 147–149
    mechanical properties of, 143
    plastic coating of, 143, 146, 147–148
    production of, 143
    strength distribution of, 144
    surface flaws of, 143
    surface treatment of, effect of, 146
    tensile strength of, 144
  as piezoelectric materials, 255–256
  rare earth oxides in synthesis of, 105–106
  refractive index of, 108–109
  slow crack propagation in, 212–214
  Vickers hardness of, 108–109
Grafting of clay minerals, 91
Grain boundaries, 82
  of dislocation structures, 120–121
  electrical degradation and, 278
  of magnesium zinc ferrite, 122–130
    electrical properties and, 129–130
    liquid phase sintering and, 128–129
    phase diagram of, 123–124
    wettability and, 125–128
  of positive temperature coefficient material, 287, 289
  of silicon carbide, 247–250
  of silicon nitride, 183
  of zinc oxide varistors, 276–280
Graphite
  diamond synthesis from, 3–7
  in hot pressing, 54
Griffith flaws, 143

H

High-pressure synthesis
  of cubic silicon nitride, 2–3, 9–13
  of diamonds, 3–9
  of layered chalcogenides, 84–86
High-resolution transmission electron microscopy
  of beta-alumina, 99
  of electrically conductive materials, 96–99
  of fine structures in organic materials, 93–104
  of incomplete stage of sintering, 96
  of interface between crystalline and amorphous phases, 100
  interpretation of images of, 94–95
  of rhenium trioxide, 102
Hitaceram SC-101, 244
Hot pressing
  additives for sintering and, 54–58
  application of, 53–61
  atmospheric effects on, 60–61
  of complicated shape ceramics, 58–60
  isostatic, 44–53
    coating method of, 47
    definition of, 44–45
    densification by, 48–49
    equipment for, 50–53
    glass bath method of, 47
    glass capsule method of, 46
    metal capsule method of, 45–46
    sintering plus, 47–48
  of silicon carbide, 192, 193
Humidity gas sensors, 295–296
Hydrothermal reactions, 15–29
Hydrothermal sintering, 25–29
Hydrothermal synthesis, 16
  of berlinite, 17–19
  of ferrites, 19, 21
  growth conditions for, 19–23
  historical perspectives of, 15
  of ilmenite, 24
  of laser emission crystals, 19, 22
  pressure vessel for, 16–17
  representative reactions, 17–25
  of semiconductor crystals, 19, 23
  of tobermorite, 19
  of xonotlite, 19
  of zeolites, 19

I

Ilmenite, 24
Impurities
  dislocation-related phenomenon and, 113